POLITICAL RUSSIAN

NATASHA SIMES AND RICHARD M. ROBIN

An Intermediate Course in Russian Language
for International Relations, National Security and Socio-Economics

A Publication of the American Council of Teachers of Russian
in conjunction with the Paul H. Nitze School of Advanced
International Studies of the Johns Hopkins University

 KENDALL/HUNT PUBLISHING COMPANY
2460 Kerper Boulevard   P.O. Box 539   Dubuque, Iowa 52004-0539

ACKNOWLEDGEMENTS

The authors of Political Russian are pleased to acknowledge important institutional and financial support from the American Council of Teachers of Russian (Research and Development Division) and the Paul H. Nitze School for Advanced International Studies of the Johns Hopkins University in Washington, D. C. In particular, we are grateful to Dr. George R. Packard (Dean, the Paul H. Nitze School) and Dr. Dan E. Davidson (ACTR and Bryn Mawr) for their on-going professional assistance in bringing this project to fruition, and to Dr. Richard D. Brecht (Maryland and ACTR) for his numerous suggestions for sharpening the focus of this text.

The authors also hereby acknowledge a debt of gratitude to our colleagues in the profession and their students who have kindly participated in the test-teaching of these materials: Dr. Frank Miller and Nadezhda Kivenko (Columbia University), Emily Urevich (Foreign Service Institute, U.S. Department of State), Linda S. Tapp (Georgetown University), and to Steven D. Jones, Elizabeth Sandstrom, and Natalia Yudzon (Paul Nitze School, Johns Hopkins University). We want to thank as well Anna M. Connolly for her able and tireless assistance in editing the final drafts of this text and for her useful suggestions concerning their formating. Naturally, the authors have not been able to include every suggestion which we have received in the preparation of this complex project and assume full and exclusive responsibility for the text and any errors it might contain.

We welcome the comments and suggestions of all who use these materials, as we make preparations for its regular revision and updating in the years ahead.

Washington, D. C.
March 1990
N.S. and R.M.R.

PREFACE

HOW TO USE POLITICAL RUSSIAN

It is fast becoming apparent that the United States and the Soviet Union are likely to develop an unprecedented intensive relationship. To deal with the Soviet Union intelligently, the United States needs a growing pool of people capable of communicating with the Russians in their own language. The current situation where, with the exception of professional students of Soviet affairs, almost no American can conduct business in Russian is increasingly unacceptable. It is an obstacle to meaningful U.S.–Soviet interaction, and it puts Americans who are engaged in various activities with the USSR in a disadvantageous position in comparison with their Soviet counterparts.

POLITICAL RUSSIAN is written especially for generalists and practitioners engaged in international relations, foreign trade or people-to-people exchanges with the Soviet Union. The book is aimed at the development of three basic types of skills: **reading, speaking,** and **listening.** We assume that students starting the book have acquired a "first-year" knowledge of Russian and, therefore, have been exposed to a skeletal grammar and lexicon, although we make no assumption about the level of control and expect little more than a *novice*[1] level of proficiency.

The structure of *POLITICAL RUSSIAN* is based on the goal of **functional proficiency** in the three skills, rather than on "covering the grammar", with an added dose of political vocabulary. Each chapter, therefore, is based on directly applicable topics: official visits, international negotiations, economics and trade, national security and arms control and so on.

A direct corollary to proficiency-based language learning is the principle of spiraling or concentric circles. This book is structured around two such concentric circles. In both circles students are presented with *authentic* texts, i.e. unadapted Russian which exposes a student to all elements of authentic language: audiotape excerpts of real radio, actual newspaper articles and realistic speaking situations.

Circle One is aimed at students who have already completed an introductory course and are familiar with but may not have actively mastered the case system and some elements of verb conjugation. The number and scope of the tasks that students can accomplish are limited, because their world of language mastery is still quite small.

----

[1] *The terms NOVICE, INTERMEDIATE, ADVANCED, and SUPERIOR are taken from the proficiency guidelines of the American Council for the Teaching of Foreign Languages, 6 Executive Boulevard, Upper Level, Yonkers, NY 10701.*

Within **Circle One** students expand the scope of their usable language. Speaking and reading vocabulary is widened with the injection of carefully measured doses of political terminology.

A complete coverage of *Circle One* requires about 60 hours of instruction plus homework. A student who has successfully mastered *Circle One* should have attained the following proficiency levels:

Speaking – *intermediate high* with politics, national security, and economics as areas of particular strength ("hot-house specials" in ACTFL terms[2]).

Reading – *advanced plus* with political hot-house special.

Listening – *intermediate high* with political hot-house special.

Reading and listening. Students are taught **strategies** to get the facts from short newspaper and radio reports, using context to help build their vocabulary. Students learn to **skim** and **scan** for as much useful information as can be found in longer and more complicated reports which may be just beyond their immediate level. In addition, emphasis is placed on the use of focusing attention on what *can* be understood, rather than what *cannot* be understood.

Speaking tasks are centered around role-play situations in which students are taught to respond in coherent sentence-length utterances on political topics. Work on speaking in short paragraphs also begins at this level.

Writing is used as a support tool to develop the three primary skills.

Grammatical support for these activities comes in the way of short explanations and exercises designed to give students total control over basic items necessary for sentence structuring and partial control over more complicated items, which are reviewed and expanded in *Circle Two* with an eye for total control. Because the grammatical competence of incoming students cannot be predicted, we have included in **Circle One** a comprehensive review of basic grammar fundamental to communication on the themes introduced, including a systematic review of case distribution. Grammatical structures which play a significant role in political reportage of facts, such as those governing dates and quantities, receive particular emphasis.

---

[2] *A HOT-HOUSE SPECIAL is an area of special interest in which a foreign language speaker shows uncharacteristic fluency and accuracy. In the classic example a former navy pilot is unable to order a cup of coffee in the target language, but he has no difficulty describing how to land a fighter plane.*

In **Circle Two** the students' world of language mastery becomes larger as all of its elements expand.   Active and passive vocabulary is enriched. Reading and listening texts become longer as students learn to understand not only the facts, but also to read "between the lines."   In speaking the emphasis is on connected, paragraphed speech with enough grammatical facility as to be understood in political discussions by Russians not used to dealing with foreigners.   To that end, grammatical concepts originally introduced for partial control are reinforced.   More complicated grammar is introduced first for partial control and then for complete control.

Reading materials include feature-length texts on politics, national security, and economics.   Students are taught not only to skim and scan for immediate access to information, but also to identify supported opinion, as well as to read between the lines for unstated opinion.

Listening materials also go beyond short reports to cover four – five minute newscasts, as well as political speeches.   Students practice Russian-to-English consecutive interpretation in which the main goal is to convey the central facts and opinions of the text.

Speaking exercises are designed to widen the student's control of topics introduced in *Circle One*.   Specific exercises will be created to improve fluency (rate of speech), paragraph structuring, and to widen vocabulary. Conversation management strategies will be heavily emphasized as consistent practice in supporting opinion is introduced.

Grammatical support will come in the way of drills for concepts already introduced leading to full control in all areas of morphology and beyond partial control in syntax and verbal aspect.   Attention will be given to those items which allow for the creation of structured paragraphs in speech. Particular areas of work will include prefixed and unprefixed verbs of motion as lexical items in non-motion contexts, quantities in oblique cases, dependent clauses, tense in complex sentences, and word order.

A complete coverage of *Circle Two* requires about 120 hours of classroom instruction plus homework.   A student who has successfully mastered *Circle Two* should have attained the following proficiency levels:

Speaking – *advanced or advanced plus* for politics, national security, and economics.

Reading – *superior* for politics, national security, and economics.   Students will also be expected to translate texts accurately into standard "politically equivalent" English.

Listening – *advanced plus* for the same areas plus the ability to provide informal (giving the gist) but accurate consecutive interpretation of live speech.

Each lesson of *POLITICAL RUSSIAN* includes:

a) A pre-reading taped audio-comprehension exercise aimed at developing listening comprehension skills. We suggest that students prepare for each new lesson by listening to the audio comprehension exercise and completing the accompanying exercises. The listening text prepares the student for the topic and structures of the lesson.

b) A main text, which is an excerpt of an article or a full article from Soviet periodicals. There are a number of activities that can accompany the main text. Instructors interested in teaching close reading or translation can assign written translations into English or grammatical analysis of the text. Those interested in further work on basic phonetics and intonation can assign phonetic reading based on the accompanying recordings.

c) A pattern-oriented glossary and vocabulary exercises. (In each lesson of Circle One the glossary and the last vocabulary exercise are taped.) Glossaries become the core of the student's vocabulary. Building on these basic linguistic patterns the student will be able to actively operate with a wide range of political, military, and socio-economic concepts.

d) Grammar explanations and exercises, some of which are on tape and are indicated as such. Grammar is presented in each lesson functionally, as needed, and where possible, through charts, tables, and examples without prolonged explanations. Thus, grammar is viewed as a support to communication, and not as an end in itself.

e) Speaking exercises and situations. Students make short reports and recreate situations connected with the theme of the lesson.

f) Comprehensive translation exercises covering all salient lexicon and structures.

g) Global reading skills exercises. Because reading of original texts is the most important source of information, the book sets a goal of teaching students to read quickly, skimming and scanning for specific facts or opinions.

h) Rendering exercises. Students learn to "gist" into simple but serviceable Russian ideas expressed in complicated English. In short, students learn to run (successfully) "on empty."

It should be noted that all the materials intended for oral exercises have stress marks. That is, stresses are marked in the following sections: audio-comprehension exercises, texts, vocabulary lists, vocabulary exercises, speaking exercises, grammar explanations, charts and tables, and, finally, in selected grammar exercises marked accordingly.

With the exception of *rendering* practice *Circle Two* contains two sets of exercises for each chapter.

POLITICAL RUSSIAN features a wealth of integrated texts and exercises. Nevertheless, this is a modular textbook. Instructors are free to pick and choose from the materials without fear that the structure of the book will topple. Exercises in listening, vocabulary development, and speaking are very closely integrated. However, those teachers who choose a greater emphasis on reading or grammatical structure are free to pursue those goals. Cutbacks in the amount of listening-speaking activities covered should not adversely affect work in reading or grammar.

We believe that students completing both *Circle One* and *Circle Two* of *POLITICAL RUSSIAN* will find themselves linguistically well equipped for work in all endeavors concerning issues of Soviet politics, history, government, trade, and national security.

SUGGESTIONS TO THE TEACHER: USE AT HOME AND IN CLASS

The suggestions for managing assignments given below are just suggestions. Different instructors emphasize different skills. *POLITICAL RUSSIAN* has enough built-in modularity so that a teacher who chooses to emphasize reading at the expense of listening or grammatical accuracy is free to do so without fear that the structure of the textbook will fall apart.

We should underscore one point on reading. The contemporary texts for reading are representative of the Soviet media towards the end of the 1980s. However, as *POLITICAL RUSSIAN* went to press, the Soviet political realities were changing so rapidly that some of the texts began to look as if they came from another era. Nevertheless, the texts, all authentic, are an accurate reflection of expository prose on public issues. We highly recommend using the texts for Reading exercises included in each unit as a starting point. They introduce the main vocabulary and structures used for the topic at hand. We encourage instructors to supplement texts for Reading exercises in *POLITICAL RUSSIAN* with their own materials from the Soviet media if they so desire.

Finally, each chapter ends with a "rendering" exercise, which challenges students to say as much as they can, drawing on a relatively small vocabulary and relaying on circumlocution. Many view these exercises as far beyond the students' capabilities and choose not to assign them. However, many teachers will want to see if their students can stretch their language to meet the challenge.

OUTLINE FOR THE PRESENTATION OF ONE LESSON OF *POLITICAL RUSSIAN*

STAGE I

At home

1. Audio comprehension exercise
2. Text:
   - phonetic reading (with the tape)
   - translation
3. Words and expressions:
   - reading with the tape
   - writing English equivalents for each expression (in the book)
4. Grammar:
   - one section should be read, giving special attention to examples

In class

1. Phonetic reading and translation of the text.
2. Audio comprehension exercise:
   - corrected by the instructor outside of class.
3. Checking English equivalents for *Words and Expressions* list.
4. Introduction, if necessary, of grammar and analysis of examples.
5. Grammatical analysis of text (time permitting).
6. Introduction of Reading rule 1. (see Reading ex. 1)

STAGE II

At home

1. Vocabulary exercises:
   - all exercises up to and including *Give Russian equivalents for the following expressions* exercise.
   - words and expressions review.
   - working with the tape.
2. Grammar exercises:
   - as many as the instructor considers appropriate except for the exercise requiring translation into Russian
3. Speaking exercise A.
4. Reading exercise 1.

In class

1. Vocabulary exercises.
2. Speaking exercises.
3. Grammar exercises.
4. Introduction of new grammar (time permitting)
5. Reading exercise:
   - Post-text. (a Pre-text-exercise is to be corrected by the instructor outside of class)

STAGE III

At home

1. Vocabulary exercises:
   - *Fill in the blanks* exercice.
   - listening to the tape.
2. Grammar exercises:
   - translation from English into Russian.
3. New grammar:
   - reading of the explanation of new grammar and analysis of the examples.
4. Speaking exercise B
5. Reading exercise 2.

In class

1. Vocabulary exercises.
2. Speaking exercise.
3. Grammar exercise:
   - checking in class
4. New grammar:
   - analysis of examples and uses of it in the text.
5. Reading exercise 2:
   - Post-text

STAGE IV

At home

1. Vocabulary exercise:
   - *Questions* exercise.
   - tape
2. Grammar exercises:
   - exercises except for a translation exercise.
3. New grammar:
   - read the explanation and analyze the examples.
4. Speaking exercises C, D.
5. Reading exercise 3.

In class

1.   Vocabulary exercise.
2.   Speaking exercises.
3.   Grammar exercises.
4.   New grammar:
      – analysis of examples and uses of it in the text.
5.   Reading exercise 3:
      – Post–text.

STAGE V

At home

1.   Vocabulary review.
2.   Tape.
3.   Rendering.
4.   Speaking exercises D,E,F.
5.   Grammar exercise(s):
      – translation from English into Russian.
6.   Reading exercise 4 (except for lesson one)

In class

1.   Rendering:
      – by paragraphs comparing different ways of expressing the same idea.
2.   Speaking exercise:
      – role–play situations.
3.   Grammar exercise:
      – checking in class.
4.   Reading exercise:
      – Post–text
5.   Quiz:
      1) a role–playing situation
      2) a new reading exercise: Pre–text

New lesson. (same pattern)

An overlap of Stage V of the previous lesson with Stage I of a new lesson is suggested.

The pattern of how to cover a lesson in Circle Two is the same except for:

Vocabulary exercises: from A. up to and including
Give Russian equivalents   - stage II
Fill in the blanks   - stages III, IV

Speaking exercises: A. –   stage II
B. –   stage III
C. –   stage IV
D.   stage V and Quiz

Reading exercise   – Pre-text   stage II
– Post-text   stages III,IV,V.

An overlap of Stage V with Stage I of a new lesson is suggested in Circle Two as well.

TABLE OF CONTENTS

Acknowledgements . . . . . *ii*
Preface
   How to use POLITICAL RUSSIAN . . . . . *iii*
   Suggestions to the teacher . . . . . *vii*

CIRCLE ONE

Lesson One: Визит французского президента

Audio-comprehension exercise 1
Words and expressions 1
Text: Визит французского президента 3
Vocabulary exercises 4
Grammar:
   Prepositional case 6
   Prepositional case: exercises 7
   beginning and *ending* in Russian 11
   beginning and *ending* in Russian: exercises 12
   Verbal aspect 14
   Verbal aspect: exercises 18
Rendering 20
Quoting sources 21
Speaking Exercises 21
Reading Exercises 23

Lesson Two: Американо-британские переговоры

Audio-comprehension exercise 37
Words and expressions 37
Text: Американо-британские переговоры 39
Vocabulary exercises 40
Grammar:
   Accusative case 43
   Accusative case: exercises 44
   Prepositional/accusative case: exercises 48
   Reflexive verbs 49
   Reflexive verbs: exercises 52
   Verbal aspect: exercises (Continued) 56
   ли not *если* 58
   ли not *если*: exercises 58
Rendering 59
Speaking exercises 60
Reading exercises 61

Lesson Three: Соглашение об экономическом сотрудничестве между СССР и ФРГ

Audio-comprehension exercise 81
Words and expressions 81
Text: Соглашение об экономическом сотрудничестве между СССР и ФРГ 84
Vocabulary exercises 84
Grammar:
    Dative case 88
    Dative case: exercises 90
    Russian participles 94
    Present and past active participles 94
    Present and past active participles: exercises 98
Rendering 101
Quoting Sources 102
Speaking exercises 102
Reading exercises 104

Lesson Four: Встреча в Токио

Audio-comprehension exercise 119
Words and expressions 120
Text: Встреча в Токио 122
Vocabulary exercises 123
Grammar:
    Dative case (Continued) 127
    asking and **asking**:   questions versus requests 130
    Dative case: exercises (Continued) 130
    Past and present passive participles 134
    Past and present passive participles: exercises 139
Rendering 142
Speaking exercises 143
Reading exercises 144

Lesson Five: Готовность Москвы

Audio-comprehension exercise 159
Words and expressions 159
Text: Готовность Москвы 161
Vocabulary exercises 162
Grammar:
    Genitive case 166
    –то and *–нибудь* and *ни–...не* constructions 168
    Genitive case: exercises 171
    –то and *–нибудь* and *ни–...не* constructions: exercise 176

Verbal adverbs 177
Verbal adverbs: exercises 182
Rendering 185
Quoting sources 187
Speaking exercises 187
Reading exercises 189

Lesson Six: Призыв Совета мира

Audio–comprehension exercise 205
Words and expressions 206
Text: Призыв Совета мира 207
Vocabulary exercises 208
Grammar:
Comparitive and superlative adjectives 212
Genitive case: (Continued) 214
Comparitive and superlative adjectives: exercises 216
Genitive case: exercises (Continued) 217
Subjunctive and conditional 221
Subjunctive and conditional: exercises 224
Rendering 229
Speaking exercises 230
Reading exercises 231

Lesson Seven: Предстоящие в США выборы

Audio–comprehension exercise 239
Words and expressions 240
Text: Предстоящие в США выборы 242
Vocabulary exercises 243
Grammar:
Instrumental case 246
Instrumental case: exercises 247
Subordinate clauses 252
Subordinate clauses: exercises 255
Rendering 258
Quoting sources 259
Speaking exercises 259
Reading exercises 261

CIRCLE TWO

Lesson One: Правительственный кризис в Италии

PART ONE

Audio-comprehension exercise 273
Text: Правительственный кризис в Италии (part one) 273
Words and expressions 274
Vocabulary exercises 277
Grammar:
     Time expressions 280
     Time expressions: exercise 283
     Verbal aspect 285
     Verbal aspect: exercises 286
Speaking exercises 290

PART TWO

Audio-comprehension exercise 291
Text: Правительственный кризис в Италии (part two) 291
Words and expressions 292
Vocabulary exercises 294
Quoting sources: review 296
Quoting sources: exercises 298
Grammar: Verbal aspect: exercises (Continued) 298
Rendering 301
Speaking exercises 303

Reading exercise 304

Lesson Two: Кто вооружает убийц?

PART ONE

Audio-comprehension exercise 309
Text: Кто вооружает убийц? (part one) 309
Words and expressions 310
Vocabulary exercises 312
Grammar:
     Review of cases: exercises 315
     Review of active participles: exercises 316
     Singular and plural of cognates 317
     Singular and plural of cognates: exercises 320
Speaking exercises 322

PART TWO

Audio-comprehension exercise 323
Text: Кто вооружает убийц? (part two) 323
Words and expressions 324
Vocabulary exercises 326
Grammar:
    "The Measured" 328
    "The Measured": exercises 329
    Review of active participles: exercises (Continued) 329
    Word order in Russian 331
    Word order in Russian: exercises 332
Rendering 335
Speaking exercises 337

Reading exercise 338

Lesson Three: Чрезвычайное положение

PART ONE

Audio-comprehension exercise 343
Text: Чрезвычайное положение (part one) 344
Words and expressions 344
Vocabulary exercises 347
Grammar:
    Review of cases: exercises 350
    Review of passive participles and passive reflexives: exercises . . . 351
Speaking exercises 354

PART TWO

Audio-comprehension exercise 355
Text: Чрезвычайное положение (part two) 355
Words and expressions 356
Vocabulary exercises 358
Grammar:
    Review of passive participles: exercises (Continued) 361
    some, any, and *no* constructions 363
    some, any, and *no* constructions: exercises 364
Rendering 368
Speaking exercises 369

Reading exercise 370

Lesson Four: Демократизация нашей жизни

PART ONE

Audio-comprehension exercise 375
Text: Демократизация нашей жизни (part one) 376
Words and expressions 377
Vocabulary exercises 379
Grammar:
    Review of cases: exercises 381
    Review of imperfective verbal adverbs: exercises 382
Speaking exercises 384

PART TWO

Audio-comprehension exercise 385
Text: Демократизация нашей жизни (part two) 385
Words and expressions 386
Vocabulary exercises 387
Grammar:
    Review of perfective verbal adverbs: exercises 389
    Review of subjunctive: exercises 390
    Aspects in imperatives 393
    Aspects in imperatives: exercises 394
Rendering 395
Speaking exercises 398

Reading exercise 399

Lesson Five: Франция после выборов

PART ONE

Audio-comprehension exercise 405
Text: Франция после выборов (part one) 406
Words and expressions 406
Vocabulary exercises 409
Grammar:
    Review of cases: exercises 412
    Review of conditional clauses: exercise 413
Speaking exercises 415

PART TWO

Audio-comprehension exercise 416
Text: Франция после выборов (part two) 416

Words and expressions 417
Vocabulary exercises 419
Grammar:
    Sequence of tense 422
    Sequence of tense: exercises 422
Rendering 427
Speaking exercises 428

Reading exercise 429

Lesson Six: Экономика на перевале

PART ONE

Audio-comprehension exercise 435
Text: Экономика на перевале (part one) 436
Words and expressions 436
Vocabulary exercises 438
Grammar: Review of cases: exercise 441
Speaking exercises 442

PART TWO

Audio-comprehension exercise 443
Text: Экономика на перевале (part two) 444
Words and expressions 445
Vocabulary exercises 448
Grammar:
    More uses of subjunctive 451
    More uses of subjunctive: exercises 451
    Verbal aspect of modals 452
    Verbal aspect of modals: exercises 454
Rendering 456
Speaking exercises 458

Reading exercise 459

Lesson Seven: Пойдут ли русские к Ла-Маншу?

PART ONE

Audio-comprehension exercise 465
Text: Пойдут ли русские к Ла-Маншу? (part one) 466
Words and expressions 468
Vocabulary exercises 470

Grammar:
    Review of cases: exercises 472
    Quantities in oblique cases 473
    Quantities in oblique cases: exercises 474
Speaking exercises 476

PART TWO

Audio-comprehension exercise 477
Text: Пойдут ли русские к Ла-Маншу? (part two) 478
Words and expressions 479
Vocabulary exercises 480
Grammar:
    Review of cases: exercise 483
    Verbs of motion, carrying and leading in idiomatic usage 484
    Verbs of motion, carrying and leading in idiomatic usage: exercise   486
Rendering 488
Speaking exercises 490

Reading exercise 491

APPENDIX 497

GLOSSARY 509

CHARTS

Prepositional case 32–33
Accusative case 74–75
Dative case 116–117
Genitive case 200–201
Instrumental case 270–271

TABLES

Table 1:	"Some words which require the preposition HA in the prepositional and accusative case" 7
Table 2:	"Some nouns ending in –ý after prepositions B and HA" 7
Table 3:	Verbal aspect 34–35
Table 4:	"The Measured" 76–77
Table 5:	Reflexive verbs 78–79
Table 6:	Active participles 97
Table 7:	Passive participles 137
Table 8:	Passive constructions – summary 138
Table 9:	Tenses in impersonal constructions 156–157
Table 10:	Possession and presence 169
Table 11:	Куда? Где? Откуда? 170
Table 12:	Verbal adverbs 181
Table 13:	Construction of possession 202–203

CIRCLE
ONE

CIRCLE ONE

LESSON ONE

AUDIO-COMPREHENSION EXERCISE

You are about to hear a text about the visit of a French delegation to Moscow. You will probably easily recognize the cognates given below. Look through the words and expressions listed below. Then listen to the text with the following questions in mind. Afterwards, listen to the text again, and write down the answers so as to be able to give the information to a non-Russian speaker.

1. Who visited Moscow?
2. What body invited him?
3. Was the visit official or unofficial?
4. Where were talks held?
5. A number of points were discussed. Name one.
6. How were Franco-Soviet relations characterized?

Cognates

презйдиум
совéт, совéтский
официáльный визйт
прсэидéнт
респýблика
минйстр

WORDS AND EXPRESSIONS   (on the tape)

по приглашéнию – by invitation

председáтель   Совéта Минйстров
                       Президиума Верхóвного Совéта СССР
президéнт
Генерáльный секретáрь ЦК КПСС
премьéр-минйстр
государственный секретáрь   государственный департáмент
госсекретáрь   госдепартáмент

мини́стр иностра́нных дел   министе́рство иностра́нных дел
(Note in US: госсекрета́рь   госдепарта́мент)
мини́стр оборо́ны   министе́рство оборо́ны
        энерге́тики   энерге́тики
        культу́ры   культу́ры
        торго́вли   торго́вли
        фина́нсов   фина́нсов
Note in US: Secretary of Treasury   – The Treasury

                                         (куда́?)
прибыва́ть/прибы́ть   с официа́льным визи́том   в Москву́
     -ют   -бу́дут   – to arrive on an official visit to Moscow

                              (где?)
находи́ться   с неофициа́льным визи́том   в Пари́же
нахо́дятся   – to be in Paris on an unofficial visit
(imperfective only)

                    (отку́да?)
отбыва́ть/отбы́ть   из Москвы́/из Пари́жа

обсужда́ть/обсуди́ть вопро́сы   двусторо́нних свя́зей
(обсужда́ют/обсу́дят)   двусторо́нних отноше́ний
                                         сотру́дничества
                                         взаимопо́мощи
                                         экономи́ческого кри́зиса
                                         энергети́ческого кри́зиса
обсужде́ние

констати́ровать, что... – to state the fact that...
         -уют
(imperfective only)

между́ (кем?)   состоя́лись бесе́ды – there were talks
                                         (о чём?)
мини́страми   о сотру́дничестве
президе́нтами   о двусторо́нних отноше́ниях
                                         о междунаро́дной напряжённости
                                         об эконо́мике
                                         о торго́вле

состоя́ться – (Perfective only)
   -я́тся

стро́иться на осно́ве взаимопонима́ния
   -ятся   равнопра́вия
                      дру́жбы
                      (не)дове́рия
                      взаи́мной по́мощи

отношéния мéжду Фрáнцией и СССР (как?)   развивáются

                                                 успéшно

                                               постоя́нно

                                               бы́стро

                                               мéдленно

развивáться/развúться

     -ются   -овью́тся

СССР, Сою́з Совéтских Социалистúческих Респу́блик, совéтский, совéтские
     грáждане, Москвá
Фрáнция, францу́зский, францу́зы, Парúж, говорúть по-францу́зски
Еврóпа, европéйский, европéйцы
Зáпадная Еврóпа, западноевропéйский
Востóчная Еврóпа, восточноевропéйский
Центрáльная Еврóпа, центральноевропéйский

TEXT: Read the following text; be able to translate it into English in written form.

Визúт францу́зского президéнта

По приглашéнию Президиума Верхóвного Совéта СССР и Совéтского правúтельства в Москвé с неофициáльным визúтом находúлся президéнт Францу́зской Респу́блики. Мéжду председáтелем Президиума Верхóвного Совéта СССР, председáтелем Совéта Минúстров СССР и президéнтом Францу́зской Респу́блики состоя́лись бесéды о бу́дущем совéтско-францу́зском сотру́дничестве. Стóроны обсудúли вопрóсы двусторóнних свя́зей и с удовлетворéнием констатúровали, что отношéния мéжду СССР и Фрáнцией стрóятся на оснóве взаимопонимáния и равнопрáвия. Эти отношéния успéшно развивáются.

VOCABULARY EXERCISES

**Look through the vocabulary to the text «*Францу́зский президе́нт*»; then do the
following exercises.**

A.   Paraphrase the italicized words.

Госуда́рственный секрета́рь
двусторо́нние *свя́зи*
сказа́ть, что...

B.   Give the opposite for the italicized words.

бы́стро развива́ться
односторо́нние отноше́ния
прибыва́ть в Москву́
с *неофициа́льным* визи́том

C.   Fill in the blanks with the appropriate prepositions.

1.   Генера́льный секрета́рь при́был _____ приглаше́нию ЦК КПСС.
2.   Отноше́ния _____ Фра́нцией и СССР постоя́нно развива́ются.
3.   Состоя́лись бесе́ды _____ торго́вле.
4.   Премье́р-мини́стр при́был _____ неофициа́льным визи́том.
5.   Москва́ нахо́дится _____ Восто́чной Евро́пе.
6.   _____ СССР о́тбыл госуда́рственный секрета́рь США.

D.   Give Russian equivalents for the following English phrases.

- by invitation
- to be in Paris on an official visit
- to discuss issues of bilateral relations
- talks on cooperation have taken place
- to be built on the basis of mutual understanding

E.   Fill in the blanks with appropriate words.

               (чем? кем?)   (как?)

1.   отноше́ния ме́жду _____________ развива́ются _____________

                   _____________   _____________

                  (о чём?)

2.   состоя́лись бесе́ды о _____________

                   ____

                    (чего?)   (куда?)
3.   председа́тель ____________ при́был в ____________
                    ____________   ____________

                                        (чего?)
4.   отноше́ния стро́ятся на осно́ве ____________
                                    ____

F.   Make sentences with the appropriate words from the list in the right hand column.

1.   Мини́стр культу́ры   обсужда́л вопро́сы   (чего?)
                    оборо́ны   взаимопо́мощь
                    энерге́тики   вое́нная по́мощь
                    иностра́нных дел   экономи́ческий кри́зис
                    фина́нсов   энергети́ческий кри́зис
                    торго́вли   иностра́нные дела́
                                                 культу́рные свя́зи
                                                 двусторо́нние свя́зи

2.   Госсекрета́рь нахо́дится с официа́льным визи́том   (где?)
                                                 столи́ца СССР
                                                 Центра́льная Евро́па
                                                 Фра́нция, Пари́ж
                                                 Ку́ба

G.   Answer the following questions.   (on the tape)

1.   Как называ́ется глава́ Сове́та Мини́стров?
2.   Как называ́ется глава́ КПСС?
3.   Каки́е вы зна́ете министе́рства?
4.   Кто стои́т во главе́ ка́ждого из них?
5.   Как мо́гут развива́ться отноше́ния ме́жду стра́нами?
6.   На како́й осно́ве отноше́ния мо́гут стро́иться?
7.   Каки́е вопро́сы обсужда́ют гла́вы госуда́рств?
8.   Где живу́т францу́зы?
9.   Англия нахо́дится в Центра́льной Евро́пе?
10.   Где нахо́дится Украи́на?
11.   Где нахо́дится Чехослова́кия?
12.   По́льша - западноевропе́йская страна́?
13.   Кака́я э́то страна́?
14.   На како́м языке́ говоря́т во Фра́нции?

GRAMMAR: PREPOSITIONAL CASE

The prepositional case has three uses:

1.   **After the preposition** *o* **"about" to answer the questions** *о ком, о чём*:

бесе́ды *о* сотру́дничестве	*talks on cooperation*
вопро́с *о* равнопра́вии	*the issue of equality*

Before vowels *a, э, и, о,* and *у*   *o* becomes *об*:

Говоря́т *об* оборо́не.	*Defense is being discussed.*

O becomes *обо* in the following set expressions:

обо всех "about all," *обо всём* "about everything," and *обо мне*

2.   **After the prepositions** *в* **and** *на* **to answer the question** *где* **"where** *at*"
(location):

в Восто́чной Евро́пе	*in Eastern Europe*
в Ю́жной Аме́рике	*in South America*
на америка́нском контине́нте	*on the American continent*
на Ку́бе	*in Cuba*
на перегово́рах	*at the negotiations*

Note that **в** usually means in and is used with buildings, cities, and
countries. **На** usually means on and is used with *events*: *на перегово́рах at
the negotiations*. *На* is also used with compass directions: *на ю́ге in the
south*, and in set phrases such as: *на ро́дине, на о́строве, на контине́нте,
на Аля́ске, на Украйне, на по́чте, на заво́де, на вокза́ле, на стадио́не, на
ры́нке, на би́рже, на фро́нте.* See Table 1.

In addition, **на** and **в** plus prepositional are used in certain set time
expressions having to do with weeks, months, years, and centuries: *на э́той
неде́ле, в про́шлом ме́сяце, в бу́дущем году́, в 1988-ом году́, в про́шлом ве́ке.*

Note a small group of masculine nouns which (in the prepostional case) end
in *ý* after the prepositions **в** and **на**. See Table 2.

3.   **After the preposition** *при* **"under" or "during" (a regime or government):**

при Ста́лине	*under Stalin*
при администра́ции Рейгана	*during the Reagan term*
при Петре́ I (пе́рвом)	*under the reign of Peter the Great*

TABLE 1:   Some words which require the preposition HA in prepositional case:

на	по́чте	на	ро́дине
	заво́де		ю́ге
	фа́брике		се́вере
	стадио́не		ю́го-восто́ке
	вокза́ле		се́веро-за́паде
	ста́нции		би́рже
	контине́нте		ры́нке
	Аля́ске		фро́нте
	Украи́не		
	о́строве		
	(including names of islands: на Ку́бе, на Тайва́не)		

TABLE 2:   Some nouns ending in ý after prepositions B, HA:

на	берегу́	в	(како́м) году́?
	Дону́		кото́ром часу́?
	мосту́		Крыму́
	краю́ (on the edge)		лесу́
	борту́		плену́
	шкафу́		порту́
	льду́		ряду́ (among)
	посту́		краю́ (in the region)
			тылу́
			шкафу́
			строю́

GRAMMAR EXERCISES: PREPOSITIONAL CASE

Read all the grammar related to prepositional case; look through the reference chart at the end of the lesson and the appendix.

A. Find prepositional case in the text; explain its use.

B. Use the proper preposition, O (ОБ,ОБО), В, or HA in the sentences below. Note the exceptions in Table 1 above.

    1.   Что вы зна́ете ____ положе́нии в сове́тской эконо́мике?

2. ___ совещании стороны обсуждали вопросы советско-французского сотрудничества.
3. ___ Восточной Европе почти все страны - члены советского блока.
4. Во время своего визита на прошлой неделе президент хотел говорить ___ обороне.
5. Что СССР хочет увидеть ___ столе переговоров в Женеве?
6. ___ заводах и фабриках прошли митинги протеста.
7. Сколько американцев все еще находится ___ вьетнамском плену?
8. Отношения между США и Канадой строятся ___ основе равноправия.
9. Советский Союз находится ___ двух континентах.
10. Министр иностранных дел дал пресс-конференцию ___ борту авиалайнера.
11. Первая экономическая депрессия произошла ___ 20-х годах.
12. Какое население живет ___ этом маленьком острове в Индийском океане?
13. Город Одесса находится ___ юге европейской части СССР.

C. 1) **Form phrases using the words below according to the pattern–**

> **ПРИ + _(adj) noun_**
> **Prep. case**

Example: При Президенте Картере...
           ⟶ *Under President Carter...*

республиканская администрация
Михаил Горбачёв
лейбористское правительство
президент Никсон
социалисты

2) **Be able to translate the phrases above into English.**

D. 1) **Form phrases using the words below according to the pattern–**

> **В + _(adj) noun_ ГОВОРИТСЯ О + _(adj) noun_**
> **Prep.case**   **Prep.case**

Example: В этой статье говорится о реформах...
           ⟶ *This article deals with reforms...*

газета
документ
конституция

2) **Be able to translate the phrases above into English.**

E.   Answer the following questions using the words in the right-hand column. Watch out for -ý nouns in prepositional case in Table 2. (Find the exercise on the tape)

1.   О чём состоя́лись бесе́ды?

   - сотру́дничество
   - двусторо́нние отноше́ния
   - торго́вля
   - Аля́ска
   - междунаро́дная напряжённость

2.   Где находи́лся Госуда́рственный секрета́рь?

   - За́падная Евро́па
   - ва́жное совеща́ние
   - Фра́нция
   - борт самолёта
   - министе́рство иностра́нных дел

3.   Где они живу́т?

   - Украйна
   - Крым
   - социалисти́ческая страна́
   - белору́сский лес

4.   На чём стро́ятся э́ти отноше́ния?

   - дру́жеская осно́ва
   - равнопра́вная торго́вля
   - взаи́мное дове́рие

5.   О ком писа́ла «Пра́вда?»

   - сове́тский мини́стр
   - Генера́льный секрета́рь
   - америка́нский президе́нт

6.   Где стро́ятся но́вые фа́брики?

   - Дон
   - Ку́ба
   - далёкий се́вер
   - европе́йский контине́нт

7.   При ком э́ти отноше́ния успе́шно развива́лись?

   - Хрущёв
   - социалисти́ческое прави́тельство
   - демократи́ческая администра́ция

8.   О чём говори́тся в э́той статье́?

   - госуда́рственный департа́мент
   - Краснода́рский край
   - фаши́стский плен

9.   Где говорится о мировом рынке?

- французская газета
- длинная статья
- секретный документ

10.   Где работают эти молодые французы?

- нью-йоркская биржа
- морской порт
- остров Сахалин

F.   Write questions for the italicized words in the sentences below using one of the following interrogatives: *о ком? о чём? где? когда? на чём? в чём? при ком? при чём?*

1.   Председатель Президиума Верховного Совета находился с визитом *в Париже.*
2.   В 80-х годах нашего века мир стоял *на краю ядерной катастрофы.*
3.   *В конституции* говорится о свободе слова.
4.   Министры торговли разговоривали *о будущем сотрудничестве между двумя странами.*
5.   *При администрации президента Картера* мы в первый раз услышали об энергетическом кризисе.
6.   *На прошлой неделе* в Москву прибыл министр культуры Болгарии.
7.   Советская пресса писала *о новом Генеральном секретаре.*
8.   *При Сталине* миллионы советских людей находились в лагерях.
9.   *В 1979* году Египет и Израиль подписали соглашение в Кэмп-Дэвиде.
10.   Некоторые американские солдаты все ещё были *во вьетнамском плену.*

G.   Review cardinal numerals in prepositional case.   Consult the appendix. Form phrases with the words below according to the model.   Write out the numerals.

Example: на/ 3/ советская фабрика
        ⟶ Кто работает на *трёх советских фабриках?*

1)   на/ 2/ важная встреча
2)   при/ 5/ последняя администрация
3)   в/ 41/ советское министерство
4)   о/ 4/ государственный секретарь

H.   Review ordinal numerals in prepositional case.   Consult the appendix. Spell out the numerals in the following phrases.

a)	в 1787 году	b)	в 80-х годах	c)	в 19-м веке
	1990		60		20-м
	2000		40		21-м

I.   **Give Russian equivalents for the phrases below. Consult idiomatic use of prepositional case in the chart at the end of the lesson.**

- with the support of
- in the twentieth century
- next week
- in the spirit of cooperation
- in January
- under no circumstances
- first of all

J.   **Write ten sentences to illustrate different uses of prepositional case.**

K.   **Translate the following sentences into Russian:**

1.   Last month the Soviet Foreign Minister was on an unofficial visit to Cuba.
2.   Under what conditions will new factories be built in Eastern Europe?
3.   The newspaper says that in 1976, talks were held on the future of Central Europe.
4.   The French Treasury Minister is confident of his economic reforms program.
5.   There were millions of Soviet soldiers in German captivity in 1942.
6.   International tension existed on the European continent under the Socialist government.
7.   The press accused him of secret negotiations.
8.   Both sides stated that relations between the USSR and France are built on the basis of mutual trust.
9.   Economic crisis began in 1929 on the New York stock exchange.
10. US-Soviet relations have not been developing successfully during the last two administrations.
11. In the course of talks our delegation inquired about three new ports in the North of the USSR.
12. The minister was on board the American plane.

GRAMMAR: *BEGINNING* AND *ENDING* IN RUSSIAN

The sentence "The announcer begins *the broadcast*" has a direct object, whereas the sentence "The broadcast begins at three o'clock" does not. But ask yourself, *what* does the broadcast begin. It begins *itself*. In English the "itself" is understood and deleted. In Russian the "itself" must be expressed by means of *-ся:* Переда́ча начина́ется в три часа́.

Now look at the following examples of verbs for "beginning" and "ending."
Note which have -*ся* and which do not:

Совещáние начинáется сегóдня.	The conference begins (*what? - itself*) today.
Переговóры кончáются зáвтра.	The negotiations end (*what? -themselves*) tomorrow.
Минúстр начинáет своё выступлéние.	The minister is beginning (*what? -not himself, but something else*) his speech.
Минúстр кончáет своё выступлéние.	The minister is finishing (*what? -not himself, but something else*) his speech.

Note that *начинáть/начáть* and *кончáть/кóнчить* are never reflexive before
an infinitive. (If you begin *to do* something, you are beginning *something
else,* not yourself.)

GRAMMAR EXERCISES: *BEGINNING* AND *ENDING* IN RUSSIAN

**A. Add -ся (or -сь) where necessary. Some of the verbs below have various
prefixes, but their meanings remain the same. Be prepared to translate
the sentences.**

1. Новая сессия канадского парламента должна ____________ 8 сентября.
    (начать, начаться)

2. Вскоре после Великой Отечественной Войны 1941-1945 гг. в возрасте 15
    лет Михаил Сергеевич Горбачёв ________________ свою трудовую
    деятельность. (нáчал, нáчался)

3. В 1933 году Константин Устинович Черненко ____________ службу в
    армии. (окóнчил, окóнчился)

4. ____________ передача «За круглым столом». (начинает, начинается)

5. До президентских выборов еще два с лишним года, но кампания уже
    ________________. (началá, началáсь)

6. Сегодня ________________ официальный визит президента Французской
    республики. (закáнчивает, закáнчивается)

7. Обе стороны готовятся к переговорам, но, когда именно они
    ______________, ещё неизвестно. (начну́т, начну́тся)

8. Великая Отечественная война ___________________ 9 мая 1945 года.
    (ко́нчила, ко́нчилась)

9. Я _____________ писать свой первый роман ещё в Союзе, но я отчётливо
    сознавал, что он не может быть опубликован там, и поэтому
    _______________ искать пути, как уехать. (на́чал, на́чался)

B. Now supply the verb under the blank.

1. Вчера в Юрмале __________ строительство нового курортного комплекса.
    began

2. Мы уже _________________ обсуждать этот вопрос.
    have finished

3. В Демократической Республике Афганистан ________________ пе́репись
    is beginning
    населения. (Определяется, сколько человек живёт в этой стране.)

4. Заседание _______________ 17-го мая, но ещё неизвестно, когда оно
    began
    _________________.
    will end

5. Социологи __________________ собирать необходимые данные о разводе,
    will finish
    а потом ___ ____________ общая дискуссия о положении разбитых семей
    will begin
    в обществе.

C. Write five sentences to illustrate the uses of -ся verbs.

GRAMMAR: VERBAL ASPECT

Every Russian verb comes in pairs. This division into pairs is called *verbal aspect*. One category of the pair is called *imperfective aspect,* the other *perfective aspect.*

Imperfective verbs place no time limit on the verb in question. *Perfective* verbs, on the other hand, name specific, limited actions and indicate completion as in the following example.

Министр *встречался* с генералом.
The minister *met (was meeting, used to meet)* with the general.

Министр *встретился* с генералом.
The minister *met* with the general. (There was one completed meeting.)

The aspect distinction between limited and non-limited action has dozens of semantic ramifications. For the time being, however, we will limit ourselves to the basics:

Present tense: Use *imperfective only.* There *is no perfective* in present tense.

Дипломаты встречаются. ——————⟶ *The diplomats meet.*
⟶ *The diplomats are meeting.* OR

Note that it is the *imperfective present* that expresses the present perfect progressive ("has been doing"):

С конца Великой Отечественной войны уровень жизни советского народа неуклонно растёт.
The Soviet people's standard of living *has been growing* constantly since the end of World War II.

Past tense:

USE *IMPERFECTIVE* FOR...

USE *PERFECTIVE* FOR...

<u>Repeated action</u>

<u>Specific action</u> (with a result)

Советский Союз *всегда оказывал* ангольскому народу необходимую помощь.

Советский Союз, конечно, *оказал* ангольцам необходимую помощь

The Soviet Union *always* rendered the support necessary for the Angolan

The Soviet Union naturally offered the Angolans the support necessary.

Note that in this context the *imperfective* **often corresponds to "used to."**

Нау́чно-техни́ческое сотру́дни-чество когда́-то *охва́тывало* но́вые о́бласти произво́дства.

Scientific and technical co-operation *used to* once encompass new areas of industry.

Note that *perfective,* **on the other hand, sometimes corresponds to "have done something."**

Нау́чно-техни́ческое сотру́дни-чество *охвати́ло* но́вые о́бласти произво́дства.

Scientific and technical co-operation *have encompassed* new areas of industry.

<u>Long-term action</u>

Обе стороны́ *до́лго* гото́вились к предстоя́щей встре́че.

Both sides spent *a long while* preparing for the meeting.

<u>Limited-term, specific action</u>

Обе стороны́ подгото́вились к встре́че *за одну́ неде́лю.*

Both sides prepared for the meeting *within a week.* (or)
It took both sides a week to prepare for the meeting.

In this context the *imperfective* often gives the idea of "was doing" or "spent time doing": *Совеща́ние конча́лось.*   (Imp. The conference *was ending.*) Compare with *Совеща́ние ко́нчилось.*   (perf. The conference *ended.*)

Imperfective also conveys <u>"state of being"</u> action.

В соста́в делега́ции входи́ли депута́ты Верхо́вного Сове́та.
The Deputies of the Supreme Soviet *made up* the delegation (i.e., they "were" the delegation.)

В це́нтре внима́ния ра́дио и телеви́дения *находи́лись* вопро́сы пропага́нды.
Issues of propaganda were the center of attention for radio and television.

Переговоры *проходи́ли* в тёплой и дру́жеской обстано́вке.
The negotiations took place in a warm and friendly atmosphere.

Future tense: The rules for present tense above also operate for the future tense.   Look at the following examples:

Long-term action

Limited-term, specific action

Сове́тский Сою́з *всегда́ бу́дет ока́зывать* анго́льскому наро́ду необходи́мую по́мощь.

Сове́тский Сою́з, коне́чно, *ока́жет* анго́льцам необходи́мую по́мощь.

The Soviet Union *always* will render the support necessary for the Angolan people.

The Soviet Union naturally will offer the Angolans the support necessary.

Производи́тельность труда́ *бу́дет расти́* и да́льше.

К 1990-ому го́ду производи́тельность труда́ *возрастёт* на 20 проце́нтов.

Labor productivity will rise further. (*No time limit placed.*)

By 1990 labor productivity will have risen by 20%.

Hard and fast rules

1. Verbs of *beginning* and *ending* начина́ть(ся)/начать(ся), конча́ть(ся)/ко́нчить(ся) always take *imperfective* infinitives: Мы на́чали *гото́виться* ко встре́че.   The verb *продолжа́ть* "to continue" also takes an imperfective infinitive: Они́ продолжа́ют *встреча́ться.*

2. Time expressions with *за* "within a certain time period" and *к* "by a certain time" always use *perfective* verbs (except, of course for the present tense, where there is no perfective):

    Строи́тели *сдаду́т (сда́ли)* пе́рвую о́чередь Ка́мской ГЭС *к нача́лу* сле́дующего фина́нсового го́да.
    The builders will have completed (completed) the first section of the Kamskaya power station by the beginning of the next fiscal year.

    На́ше предприя́тие *вы́полнило (вы́полнит)* пятиле́тку *за четы́ре го́да.*
    Our enterprise fulfilled (will fulfill) the five-year plan in four years.

3. *Нельзя́* takes an *imperfective* infinitive when it means "forbidden" or "must not."   It takes a *perfective* infinitive when it means "impossible."

    Нельзя́ называ́ть всех чле́нов.

    Нельзя́ назва́ть всех чле́нов.

    Not all members may be named.

    It's impossible to name all the members.

4. Some verbs have only one aspect. *Состояться* "to be held" is perfective only: Вчера́ *состоя́лось* заседа́ние комите́та вое́нного плани́рования НАТО. *Nato's Military Planning Committee met yesterday.* Some verbs have only one form for both aspects, e.g. *испо́льзовать* "to use." Many *-овать* verbs of foreign origin have imperfective forms only: *констати́ровать, организова́ть.*

GRAMMAR EXERCISES: VERBAL ASPECT

Read all the grammar related to verbal aspect; look through the Table 3 at the end of the lesson.

A.   Analyze different uses of verbal aspects in the text.

B.   Review all verbs in the vocabulary list, as well as in both sections of Grammar. Conjugate the following verbs.

прибывать/прибыть
находиться
обсуждать/обсудить
констатировать
развиваться/развиться
проходить/пройти
состояться
обвинять/обвинить
использовать

C.   Supply the verb in parentheses in the proper aspect and explain your reasoning. Underline the key words which determine the aspect.

1.   Каждый день стороны _______________ вопросы торговли.
                          (discussed)

2.   Президент Франции _______________ в следующий понедельник и
                        (will arrive)
     _______________ в среду.
        (will depart)

3.   За последние 4 года производство газа на Аляске _______________ в
                                                      (has increased)
     5 раз.

4.   Отношения между этими странами постоянно_______________________.
                                              (have been developing)

5.   К концу недели президент _______________ на родину.
                               (will depart)

6.   Во время переговоров стороны _______________ о будущей
                                   (talked)
     взаимопомощи.

7. Когда вы в первый раз_______________ о соглашении в Кэмп-Дэвиде?
(heard)

8. В 1933 году национал-социалисты начали _______________ Рейхстаг.
(control)

9. За 6 недель переговоров делегации _______________ широкий круг вопросов.
(discussed)

D. Choose and use the proper modifier in the sentences below.

в тот же день
весь день

Коммунисты продолжали говорить о международной напряженности.

каждый месяц
один раз

Переговоры прошли без успеха.

2 года
за 2 года

Нельзя быстро увеличить производство автомобилей.

E. Write ten sentences to illustrate the use of the imperfective and perfective aspect and translate them into English.

F. Translate the following sentences into Russian.

1. Soviet propaganda uses radio and television extensively.
2. It took them a week to discuss the plan of the meeting.
3. In the course of negotiations, both sides discussed the issue of bilateral relations and signed an agreement.
4. The world continues to talk about the energy crisis.
5. In the fifties many Americans were accused of collaboration with the Soviet Union.
6. Negotiations will start on Wednesday and will finish next week.
7. One is not allowed to inquire (ask) about issues of defense.
8. *Pravda* always writes about official visits to the Soviet Union.
9. How long were these Americans in POW camps?
10. The USSR has developed friendly relations with France over the last ten years.
11. He says that next year the socialists will nationalize everything.
12. By the end of the century scientific and technical cooperation will encompass new areas of industry.
13. For five years the salary (зарплата) was increasing.
14. Last year newspapers stopped talking about the energy crisis.
15. It is not allowed to use this TV set!

RENDERING

Render the following information into Russian. Do *NOT* translate word for word. Where you cannot express a word or phrase, edit it in such a way so that you use the Russian that you *do* know. Do *NOT* use a dictionary.

Remember, the purpose of this exercise is not to make you to restate what is given below, but rather to force you to communicate as much of the information as possible using the Russian you already know. Reviewing sentences from this chapter will help you find useful stock phrases.

The finance minister of Kowana arrived last week in Moscow for talks on developing trade contacts. Although Koana is just a small island in the Pacific Ocean, bilateral relations with Moscow have been developing rapidly under President Samut Legassa.

The meetings, which began a week ago and will end tomorrow, were highlighted by talks not only on trade, but on scientific and economic cooperation as well.

Political observers note that the Soviets have good reason to move quickly to take advantage of the poor state of relations between the U.S. and the Legassa regime. Last year the Koanian president accused the administration of skimping on foreign aid to his country.

Many believe that in time Legassa's negotiations with the men in the Kremlin will go beyond non-military trade and technology.

QUOTING SOURCES

ЛЮДИ	ГОВОРЯТ
а́втор	говори́т, что
представи́тель	о...
глава́	подчёркивает, что
ли́дер	заяви́л, что
президе́нт	объяви́л о...
журнали́ст	отмеча́ет, что
сове́тник по дела́м...	сказа́л в интервью́
заммини́стра	в переда́че по ра́дио
госсекрета́рь	по телеви́дению

Printed or broadcast formats:

в переда́че	говори́тся, что
в газе́те	о
в конститу́ции	говори́лось, что
в докуме́нте	о
в догово́ре	
в интервью́	
etc.	

SPEAKING EXERCISES

A.   Отве́тьте на сле́дующие вопро́сы по те́ксту.

1.   Где находи́лся президе́нт Фра́нции с неофициа́льным визи́том?
2.   Ме́жду кем состоя́лись бесе́ды о бу́дущем сове́тско-францу́зском сотру́дничестве?
3.   Каки́е вопро́сы обсуди́ли сто́роны?
4.   На како́й осно́ве стро́ятся отноше́ния ме́жду СССР и Фра́нцией?

B. 1)   Расскажи́те текст, испо́льзуя слова́рь Уро́ка 1.

    2)   Расскажи́те тот же текст, замени́в:
-уча́стников встре́чи
-ме́сто встре́чи
-те́му бесе́д
-хара́ктер отноше́ний

C.   Соста́вьте ситуа́цию, испо́льзуя сле́дующие выраже́ния.

this article deals with…, by invitation, on an official visit, issues of economic crisis, on the basis of mutual aid

D.   Опиши́те визи́т председа́теля Сове́та Мини́стров СССР во Фра́нции.

E.   Вы – представи́тель президе́нта Фра́нции. Проведи́те пресс-конфере́нцию по́сле его визи́та в СССР.

F.   Ваш преподава́тель – представи́тель сове́тского прави́тельства. Проведи́те пресс-конфере́нцию с ним по́сле визи́та президе́нта Фра́нции в СССР.

READING EXERCISES: INTRODUCTION

When you read a text, you have many tools at your disposal: your own background knowledge of the subject discussed, the context provided by the piece itself, and finally, cognates. Most likely you already know something about what the author is planning to say. Before you start to read a new text, ask yourself what you can expect to learn from it. What information are you *likely* to get? Then see if what you actually read meets your expectations. In other words, don't approach a passage as a set of hieroglyphics to be deciphered. Use what you actually know about the word, as well as the context provided to figure out what is likely to be said in advance.

For example, assume that you are reading a Soviet description about diplomatic contacts between Israel and South Africa. Would you expect the piece to characterize them as productive or suspicious?

After deciding what you suspect you might read, check to see if the context of what you are reading supports your conclusions. Use context and cognates to help you guess at the meanings of key words. Don't feel that you have to get the exact meaning of every word on your first run through. The purpose of reading expository prose is to get information, not decipher the meaning of individual words.

READING EXERCISE 1

PRE-TEXT:

Read the text with the following questions in mind. See if you can first guess at the information by taking a quick glance at the piece. Then go back and fill in the informational blank spots:

1.   What is this article about?
2.   When and where did the meeting described take place?
3.   What questions were discussed?
4.   The article says that there was an exchange of opinions; on which issues?
5.   How is the mood of the talks described?

Д Р У Ж Е С К А Я   В С Т Р Е Ч А

20 апреля в Берлине состоялась встреча Генерального секретаря ЦК КПСС М. С. Горбачева и Генерального секретаря ЦК СЕПГ, председателя Государственного совета ГДР Э. Хонеккера.

Были обсуждены вопросы дальнейшего укрепления сотрудничества между КПСС и СЕПГ, СССР и ГДР. Состоялся обмен мнениями по актуальным проблемам международного положения. Беседа прошла в сердечной атмосфере.

POST–TEXT (using sentence structure):

Extracting information quickly is important.   Often by using your knowledge of the world at large, context, and by knowing important key words, the sentences yield up their meanings quickly. On the other hand, information and opinions can be hidden in much denser prose, and sometimes a closer reading becomes necessary.

Russian with its developed inflectional system allows you to approach each sentence as a mathematical formula with several unknowns to be deduced from the context. In order to learn to read efficiently, you have to learn how to make those deductions.

First and foremost **never** look up a word in the dictionary before you have figured out the structure of the sentence. If you know the role each word plays, you have a good chance of guessing the meaning of the unknown word from context, or of deciding that you don't need an exact meaning to get at the information you want.

Here are some rules of reading more complicated prose in Russian.

Reading rule 1:   first of all, you should identify **the subject** – *the "doer" of the action in the nominative case.* If you fail to spot it right away, look for **the verb phrase** or **predicate** – *the "action" or "state" of the "doer".*

Verb phrases can be:

1)   *a verb*
       Они *обсудили* вопрос.
       Они *хотят обсуждать* вопрос.

2)   *a form of "to be" +   a full adjective*
                           a short adjective
                           a short past passive participle
                           a noun, numeral, a prepositional phrase

Это *будет невозможно сделать.*
Работа *была сделана. (passive predicate)*
На фронте *4 тысячи* танков.
Народу *нужна* свобода.

Remember that "to be" in the present tense is not obvious.

3)   *a part of an equation phrase (an "A is like B" sentence) used with the*
     instrumental case: "to be" (in past and future) + instrumental case
                           являться + instrumental case
                           оставаться + instrumental case

Он *будет членом* правительства.
Вопрос *остаётся открытым.*
Эти меры *являются незаконными.*

The grammatical structure verb phrase will indicate *the number and the gender* of the subject.   Some sentences consist of predicates without real subjects: *Нужно идти.*

There can be several subjects for one verb phrase or several verb phrases for one subject. *СССР и США готовы сотрудничать. Волков не должен и не может вам помочь.*

Note: enumeration of subjects or predicates, unless connected by «и», is separated by a comma.

Do the following exercises:

1.   In paragraph 1 find the verb phrase for the subject *встреча*.   It is... (mark the correct answer):
     a.   "to be"
     b.   *a verb*

     Translate these *subject-predicate pairs* into English.

2.   In paragraph 2 find the predicate for the subject *вопросы*.   It is... (mark the correct answer):
     a.   "to be" + a short adjective
     b.   "to be" + a short past passive participle

     Translate these *subject-predicate pairs* into English.

POST-TEXT (using context):

1. What sort of organization is the *СЕПГ*?
2. *Крепкий* means *strong*. What does *укрепление* mean? What other word could replace *укрепление* in this sentence?
3. Find the Russian for *exchange of opinions*.
4. *Актуальный* does not mean *actual* or *real*. What could it mean?
5. You may be able to figure out the word *сердечный* if you already know *сердце*. If you do not, figure out the meaning based on what you know about relations between these two countries. What other Russian words could have been substituted for *сердечный*?

READING EXERCISE 2

PRE-TEXT:

Read the text with these questions in mind:

1. What is the article about?
2. Where and when did the meeting take place?
3. Who hosted whom? What country was the visiting delegation from?
4. What was said about an exchange of opinions?
5. What countries are mentioned in the first column? What is said about them?
6. In the second column we read of support voiced for "new Soviet initiatives set forth by Gorbachev in Berlin." What general topic do these initiatives concern?
7. In the third column we read of "neo-Nazi tendencies." With which country are they associated?
8. Which two party congresses are mentioned in the third column?
9. How was the atmosphere of the talks described?

Беседа в ЦК КПСС

25 апреля член Политбюро ЦК КПСС, секретарь ЦК КПСС Е. К. Лигачев и секретарь ЦК КПСС В. А. Медведев приняли члена ЦК КПЧ, министра иностранных дел ЧССР Б. Хнеупека, находящегося в Советском Союзе с официальным дружественным визитом.

Состоялся обмен мнениями по актуальным вопросам международного положения. Указывалось, что ситуация в мире остается напряженной, острой. Продолжение ядерных взрывов, агрессивные действия США против Ливии еще более осложнили ее. В этих условиях страны социалистического содружества последовательно проводят свою принципиальную, ответственную внешнеполитическую линию, направленную на изменение к лучшему обстановки в Европе и мире.

Б. Хнеупек отметил, что руководство ЧССР активно поддерживает новые советские инициативы, с которыми выступил М. С. Горбачев в Берлине. Осуществление предложений, касающихся значительного сокращения всех компонентов сухопутных войск и тактической авиации европейских государств и соответствующих сил США и Канады, размещенных в Европе, а также инициатива в области запрещения химического оружия позволят понизить уровень военного противостояния. Важным условием оздоровления атмосферы в Европе является отказ от любых попыток ставить под сомнение основы послевоенного устройства и существующие границы, преодоление реваншистских тенденций, которые проявляются в политике ФРГ.

В ходе беседы подчеркивалось, что решения XXVII съезда КПСС и XVII съезда КПЧ открывают перспективы для углубления всестороннего сотрудничества обеих братских стран, их тесного взаимодействия на мировой арене. Выражено стремление и впредь совершенствовать практику координации внешнеполитических действий союзнических государств во имя обеспечения мира и безопасности народов.

Беседа прошла в сердечной, дружеской атмосфере.

(ТАСС).

POST-TEXT (using sentence structure):

Reading rule 2: Once you've found the subject and the predicate, look for **an object of the predicate.** It completes the meaning of the sentence.

Objects can be:

1) *direct – a noun or a pronoun in the accusative case. (only for active predicates)*
   Делегаты обсудили *доклад*

2) *indirect – nouns or pronouns in the dative, genitive or instrumental case.*
   Договор способствует *взаимопониманию.*
   Они добиваются *частичного разоружения.*
   Эта встреча станет *ключём* к договору.

3) *prepositional – objects with prepositions.*
   Большинство населения живёт в *центральной части России.*

4) *an object clause*
   Он сказал, *что переговоры закончились.*

Do the following exercises:

1. Find and classify objects for the following predicates:

paragraph 1	*dir. obj.*	*indir. obj.*	*prepos. obj*	*clause.*
приняли	__________	__________	__________	__________
paragraph 2				
осложнили	__________	__________	__________	__________
paragraph 3				
отметил	__________	__________	__________	__________
проявляются	__________	__________	__________	__________

2. Find and classify the following predicates:

paragraph 2	*verb.*	*"to be"*	*"A=B" + instrumental case*
остаётся	__________	__________	__________
проводят	__________	__________	__________
paragraph 3			
позволят	__________	__________	__________
является	__________	__________	__________
paragraph 4			
выражено	__________	__________	__________

POST-TEXT (using context):

1. *ССР* means *Советская Социалистическая Республика*, but here the first *С* stands for *Словацкая*. Which country does *ЧССР* stand for? (now: *ЧСР*)
2. What does *КПЧ* mean?
3. How are American actions characterized?
4. What is the Russian for *new Soviet initiatives*?
5. Find as many cognates as you can in the second column that allow you to guess at its content.

READING EXERCISE 3

PRE-TEXT:

Find out what the article is about, then read the text and determine which of the following statements the article contained:

1. President Alfonsin was invited by the Supreme Soviet Presidium, as well as by the government of the USSR.

2. At the time of this meeting Gromyko was still the Foreign Minister.
3. The following bodies were represented at the Argentine President's reception (true or false for each):
   a. Argentine Embassy in Moscow
   b. Council of Ministers
   c. Ministry of Trade
   d. Soviet Embassy in Argentina
   e. Supreme Soviet Presidium

4. Alfonsin's trip included a press conference.
5. The trip included a motorcade.

С ОФИЦИАЛЬНЫМ ВИЗИТОМ

По приглашению Президиума Верховного Совета СССР и Советского правительства 13 октября в Москву с официальным визитом прибыл Президент Аргентинской Республики Рауль Рикардо Альфонсин.

На Внуковском аэродроме у трапа самолета Р. Альфонсина встречал член Политбюро ЦК КПСС, Председатель Президиума Верховного Совета СССР А. А. Громыко.

Во встрече приняли участие заместитель Председателя Президиума Верховного Совета СССР Б. Язкулиев, первый заместитель Председателя Совета Министров СССР В. С. Мураховский, секретарь Президиума Верховного Совета СССР Т. Н. Ментешашвили, генеральный директор ТАСС С. А. Лосев, первые заместители министров СССР Н. П. Кудрявцев, П. Г. Лушев, заместители министров СССР В. В. Горлов, В. Г. Комплектов, посол СССР в Аргентине О. К. Квасов, другие официальные лица.

Среди встречавших находился посол Аргентины в СССР Ф. Браво.

На аэродроме были подняты государственные флаги Аргентины и Советского Союза, на летном поле выстроен почетный караул трех видов Вооруженных Сил СССР — Сухопутных войск, Военно-Воздушных Сил и Военно-Морского Флота. Оркестр исполнил государственные гимны двух стран.

А. А. Громыко и Р. Альфонсин обошли строй советских воинов.

Торжественная церемония встречи завершилась прохождением почетного караула.

На улицах и площадях столицы, по которым следовал с аэродрома кортеж автомашин в сопровождении почетного эскорта мотоциклистов, были вывешены государственные флаги Аргентины и СССР, приветственные транспаранты.

(ТАСС).

POST–TEXT (using sentence structure):

1. Find and classify the predicates and the objects for the following subjects:

	predicate(s)	*object(s)*
paragraph 1		
президент	__________	__________
paragraph 2		
член Политбюро	__________	__________
paragraph 5		
флаги	__________	__________
paragraph 7		
церемония	__________	__________

Translate these *subject-predicate-object* phrases into English.

POST–TEXT (using context):

1. Find the terminology in the text denoting these official positions:

president –
member of the Politburo –
Chairman of Supreme Soviet Presidium –
deputy chairman –
first deputy minister –
ambassador –

2.   This article describes an official reception and, therefore, contains
     a number of references to the accompanying military ceremonies. What
     does each of the following mean?

государственный флаг -
почётный караул -
государственный гимн -

PREPOSITIONAL CASE

MEANING:	PREPOSITION:	QUESTION:	VERBS:
About	О, ОБ, ОБО (about, concerning)	О КОМ? О ЧЁМ?	говори́ть расска́зывать чита́ть зна́ть спра́шивать мечта́ть и т.д.
Location	В, НА (in, on, at)	ГДЕ? в чём? на чём?	быть находи́ться рабо́тать учи́ться стро́ить лежа́ть стоя́ть висе́ть и т.д.
Period under a regime or government	ПРИ (under, during)	КОГДА? при ком? при чём?	

TIME-EXPRESSIONS: USEFUL IDIOMS:

в котóром часý?

в э́том мéсяце

в апрéлс

в прóшлом годý

в 1989-м годý
    (ordinal numeral)

в 20-м вéке
    (ordinal numeral)

в 40-х годáх
    (ordinal numeral)

на бýдущей недéле

éхать на машúне, пóезде, самолёте

говорúть на рýсском языкé
    (говорúть по-рýсски)

катáться на самолёте, кораблé

в хорóшем настроéнии
- to be in high spirits
в обстанóвке
- in the atmosphere of
в дýхе
- in the spirit of
в хóде
- in the course of
увéрен,-а,-о,-ы в полúтике
- confident in a policy
обвинять(ся) в рефóрмах
- to accuse of/to be accused of reforms
при поддéржке - with the support
при какúх услóвиях? - under what
                    conditions?
ни при какúх услóвиях - under no
                    circumstances
при услóвии, что...
  under the condition that...
при пóмощи - with the support

во-пéрвых, во-вторы́х

TABLE 3:

Imperfective aspect - emphasizes **process**

Denotes:

Repeated action	**A long-term action, an "on-going" action, a "state of being" action.**
Possible modifiers: ка́ждый день, раз в ме́сяц, всегда́, иногда́, ча́сто, ре́дко, обы́чно, по сре́дам, поро́й, вре́мя от вре́мени.	Possible modifiers: весь день, це́лую неде́лю, до́лго, 5 лет.
PAST Раз в неде́лю **прибыва́ли** иностра́нные делега́ции. Once a week foreign delegations **arrived**.	Перегово́ры **проходи́ли** в тёплой и дру́жеской обстано́вке. Negotiations **took place** in a warm and friendly atmosphere.
PRESENT Ка́ждый день **прибыва́ют** иностра́нные делега́ции. Every day foreign delegations **arrive**.	Сейча́с делега́ция **прибыва́ет** на Вну́ковский аэродро́м. At this moment, the delegation **is arriving** at Vnukov Airport.
FUTURE Делега́ции **бу́дут прибыва́ть** по сре́дам. Delegations **will arrive** every Wednesday.	У́ровень произво́дства **бу́дет увели́чиваться** 5 лет. The level of production **will be growing** for 5 years.

Imperfective aspect is used in the *infinitive* after:

1. начина́ться(ся), продолжа́ть(ся), конча́ть(ся) or any other verb indicating beginning or ending.
2. нельзя́ (not allowed)

У́тром **на́чали прибыва́ть** делега́ции.
   Delegations began to arrive in the morning.
Нельзя́ называ́ть те́му диску́ссии.
   The topic of discussion is not to be announced!

Perfective aspect - emphasises **result**.

Denotes :

**Specific one-time action;
A sequence of specific one-time actions;
Limited-term action**

Possible modifiers:
    то́лько что
    за 5 лет (unless used in present tense)
    к 1989-му го́ду

То́лько что **прибыла́** иностра́нная делега́ция.
A foreign delegation just **arrived.** (has arrived)

За 5 лет у́ровень произво́дства **увели́чился.**
Over five years, the level of production has increased.
(It took five years to increase the level of production)

P A S T

THERE IS **NO** PERFECTIVE IN THE PRESENT

P R E S E N T

Делега́ция **прибу́дет** в понеде́льник и **отбу́дет** во вто́рник.
The delegation **will arrive** on Monday and **leave** on Tuesday.
Строи́тели **сда́ду́т** пе́рвую о́чередь но́вой ГЭС **к** 1989-му го́ду
The builders **will have completed** the first section of a
new power station **by** 1989.

F U T U R E

Perfective aspect is also used in the *infinitive* after:

    1.   нельзя́ (not possible)

Нельзя́ бу́дет **обсуди́ть** прое́кт.
    It will not be possible to discuss the project.

CIRCLE ONE

LESSON TWO

AUDIO-COMPREHENSION EXERCISE

You are about to hear a text about the visit of a delegation to Washington. You will probably easily recognize the cognates given below. Look through the words and expressions listed below. Then listen to the text with the following questions in mind. Afterwards, listen to the text again, and write down the answers so as to be able to give the information to a non-Russian speaker.

1. What delegation visited Washington?
2. Who led the delegation? Was it official in nature?
3. Where did members of the administration meet their guests?
4. What questions were discussed?
5. How was the mood of meeting characterized?
6. What agreement was signed?

Cognates

департа́мент [stress!] (Госдепарта́мент is State Department)
делега́ция
премье́р-мини́стр
аэродро́м
гость
администра́ция
полити́ческий

WORDS AND EXPRESSIONS   (on the tape)

представи́тель Бе́лого до́ма
        администра́ции
        Госдепарта́мента
        республика́нского большинства́ Конгре́сса

официа́льное лицо́ – an official   официа́льные ли́ца – officials

(како́й?)	де́ятель	
ви́дный		prominent figure
отве́тственный		high-ranking, senior official
обще́ственный		public figure
полити́ческий		political figure
госуда́рственный		statesman

прошёл обмен мнениями   по вопросам америка́но-сове́тских отноше́ний
прошли бесе́ды   по вопро́сам двусторо́нних отноше́ний
       переговоры (plural only)   торго́вли
проходи́ть/про́йти
прохо́дят, пройду́т

(кака́я?)   делега́ция
прави́тельственная
парти́йная
парла́ментская
парти́йно-прави́тельственная
сена́тская

во главе́ с (кем?)
          премье́р-мини́стром
          Генера́льным секретарём
          ли́дером демократи́ческого меньшинства́ Конгре́сса
          республиканского большинства́ Сена́та

глава́ (m) – head, leader
глава́ (f) – chapter
                                   (где?)
встреча́ть/встре́тить   гостéй   на аэродро́ме
     -ют   -ят
провожа́ть/проводи́ть   делега́цию на вокза́ле
     -ют/прово́дят
встре́ча

устра́ивать/   (что?)   в честь (кого?)
      -ют   приём   высо́кого го́стя
устро́ить   за́втрак   главы́ делега́ции
      -ят   обе́д   ли́дера чёрного большинства́

обме́ниваться/   (чем?)   по вопро́сам двусторо́нних отноше́ний
      -ются   реча́ми   экономи́ческого кри́зиса
обменя́ться   мне́ниями   энергети́ческого кри́зиса
      -ются
обме́н   (чем?)

выступа́ть/   (с чем?)   по вопро́сам сотру́дничества
      -ют   с кра́ткой   ре́чью   по вопро́сам взаимопо́мощи
вы́ступить   с отве́тной   за разви́тие сотру́дничества
      -ят   с приве́тственной   про́тив режи́ма бе́лого меньшинства́
to make a... speech   in favor of (against)...

выступа́ть/   (где?)
вы́ступить   на приёме
                 на конфере́нции
                 на собра́нии
выступле́ние

подпи́сывать/	догово́р	(о чём?)
‑ют		о сотру́дничестве
подписа́ть		о взаимопо́мощи
подпи́шут	докуме́нт	о торго́вле
	соглаше́ние	об эконо́мике
	коммюнике́	об э́кспорте
	(no change)	
подписа́ние		

США, Соединённые Шта́ты Аме́рики, америка́нский, америка́нцы, Вашингто́н
Великобрита́ния, брита́нский, брита́нцы, англи́йский, англича́не, Ло́ндон, говори́ть
    по‑англи́йски
Шве́ция, шве́дский, шве́ды, Стокго́льм, говори́ть по‑шве́дски
Се́верная Аме́рика, североамерика́нский
Ю́жная Аме́рика, южноамерика́нский
Лати́нская Аме́рика, латиноамерика́нский
Центра́льная Аме́рика, центральноамерика́нский

TEXT: Read the following text; be able to translate it into English in written form.

Америка́но‑брита́нские перегово́ры

По приглаше́нию Бе́лого до́ма и Госдепарта́мента США в Вашингто́н с официа́льным визи́том прибыла́ прави́тельственная делега́ция Великобрита́нии во главе́ с премье́р‑мини́стром. На аэродро́ме госте́й встреча́ли отве́тственные представи́тели администра́ции и други́е ви́дные обще́ственные и полити́ческие де́ятели. В тот же день в честь высо́кого го́стя Бе́лый дом устро́ил прие́м, на кото́ром руководи́тели США и Великобрита́нии вы́ступили с кра́ткими приве́тственными реча́ми. На сле́дующий день начали́сь америка́но‑брита́нские перегово́ры.

В хо́де перегово́ров состоя́лся обме́н мне́ниями по вопро́сам двусторо́нних отноше́ний. Перегово́ры проходи́ли в тёплой, дру́жеской обстано́вке и в ду́хе взаимопонима́ния. Сто́роны подписа́ли догово́р о взаимопо́мощи.

VOCABULARY EXERCISES

Look through the vocabulary for the text «*Американо-британские переговоры*», then do the following exercises.

A. Give the plural for the following nouns. Mark the stress.

лицо́
премье́р-мини́стр
коммюнике́
речь

B. Give perfective forms for the following verbs. Conjugate the italicized ones. Mark the stress.

проходи́ть
устра́ивать
обме́ниваться
выступа́ть
подпи́сывать

C. Give derivative nouns for the following verbs.

подписа́ть
обменя́ться
вы́ступить
встреча́ть

D. Paraphrase the italicized words.

изве́стный де́ятель
ва́жный де́ятель
бесе́ды
состоя́лся обме́н мне́ниями
подписа́ть *догово́р*
ли́дер республика́нского меньшинства́

E. Give the opposite for the italicized words.

демократи́ческое *меньшинство́*
чёрное меньшинство́
дли́нная речь
вы́ступить *про́тив* культу́рного обме́на
провожа́ть

F. Fill in the blanks with the appropriate prepositions.

1. Прибыла́ делега́ция _____ главе́ _____ мини́стром торго́вли.
2. Состоя́лись перегово́ры _____ вопро́сам культу́ры.
3. _____ честь президе́нта устро́или приём.
4. Представи́тель администра́ции вы́ступил _____ кра́ткой ре́чью.
5. Гла́вы госуда́рств подписа́ли соглаше́ние _____ культу́рном обме́не.
6. _____ за́втраке сто́роны обменя́лись приве́тственными реча́ми.
7. Этот ви́дный де́ятель вы́ступил _____ обме́н мне́ниями с СССР.

G. Give Russian equivalents for the following English phrases.

- a White House spokesman
- a statesman
- negotiations have taken place
- delegation led by the Senate Republican majority leader
- reception in honor of the head of the delegation
- to exchange opinions on export
- to make a speech against white–minority rule
- to sign a mutual assistance treaty

H. Fill in the blanks with the appropriate words.

(каки́е?)   (чего́?)

1. ___________ де́ятели обменя́лись мне́ниями по вопро́сам ___________

    ___________   ___________

    ___________   ___________

(кака́я?)   (с кем?)

2. Прибыла́ ___________ делега́ция во главе́ с___________

    ___________   ___________

    ___________   ___________

(кого́?)

3. Бе́лый дом устро́ил приём в честь___________

    ____

    ____

I. Make several sentences using the following pattern. Use the words in the right-hand and left-hand columns.

1) (Кто?)   вы́ступил   (где?)

глава́ делега́ции	перегово́ры
высо́кий гость	приём
официа́льные ли́ца администра́ции	конфере́нция
госуда́рственные де́ятели	подписа́ние
премье́р-мини́стр М.Та́чер	обе́д

2)   (Кто?)   вы́ступил   (за что?)
                                                                      (про́тив чего́?)

     республика́нская па́ртия   торго́вля с СССР
     демократи́ческая па́ртия   поли́тика апартеида
     чёрное большинство́   отноше́ния с ЮАР
     бе́лое меньшинство́   раси́стский режи́м

3)   (Кто?)   подписа́л соглаше́ние   (о чём?)

     представи́тель госдепарта́мента   культу́рный обме́н
     мини́стр культу́ры   взаимопо́мощь
     делега́ция министе́рства торго́вли   двусторо́нние
                                                                          отноше́ния
     президе́нты   экономи́ческое
                                                                          сотру́дничество
     Великобрита́ния   э́кспорт
     ли́дер бе́лого меньшинства́   конфере́нция в
                                                                          Жене́ве

J.   Answer the following questions.   (on the tape)

1.   Где живу́т францу́зы?
2.   Кто живёт в Великобрита́нии?
3.   Как называ́ется столи́ца США?
4.   Кана́да – южноамерика́нская страна́?
5.   Аргенти́на – центральноамерика́нская страна́?
6.   На како́м контине́нте нахо́дится Никара́гуа?
7.   Что устра́ивают в честь высо́ких госте́й?
8.   Что подпи́сывают в результа́те перегово́ров?
9.   За что выступа́ют демокра́ты?
10.   За что выступа́ют республика́нцы?
11.   С каки́ми реча́ми выступа́ют на приёмах?

GRAMMAR: ACCUSATIVE CASE

The accusative case has the following basic uses:

1.   **Direct object to answer the question КОГО, ЧТО?**

    встречáть гостéй   to meet guests
    устрóить приём   to set up a reception

2.   **To answer the question КУДА? "where *to*" (direction) after the prepositions В "in, to", НА "on, at", ПОД "under", ЗА "behind."**

    прибы́ть в Вашингтóн   to arrive in Washington
          на конферéнцию   to a conference
    упáсть под лёд   to fall under the ice
    сесть за стол перегóворов   to sit down at the negotiating table

3.   **After the prepositions ЧЕРЕЗ "across" and СКВОЗЬ "through" to answer the questions ЧЕРЕЗ ЧТО?, СКВОЗЬ ЧТО?**

    чéрез мост   across the bridge
    сквóзь тумáн   through the fog

4.   **In time expressions:**

    WITHOUT prepositions to express duration КАК ДОЛГО?
    **   or frequency КАК ЧАСТО?**

    вестú переговóры 2 дня   to negotiate for two days
    вестú переговóры всю ночь   to negotiate all night (long)
    проходи́ть кáждый день   to take place every day

    WITH the prepositions: В "at, on" specifying a time or a date, ЧЕРЕЗ "in, after some period of time", ЗА "over a period of time."

    в суббóту   on Saturday
    в э́то врéмя   at this/that time
    чéрез час   in an hour
    за послéдние гóды   over the last years

See the reference chart at the end of Lesson 2 for additional time expressions using the accusative case.

GRAMMAR EXERCISES: ACCUSATIVE CASE

Read all the grammar related to accusative case; look through the reference chart and the end of Lesson 2 and the appendix.

A.   Find accusative case in the text. Explain its use.

B.   Answer the following questions using the preposition В or НА. Use the words beneath each set of questions. (Find the exercise on the tape)

Remember: choice of case does not affect the choice between В *and* НА.

1.   Куда́ прибыла́ делега́ция?   Где нахо́дится делега́ция?
         – Госуда́рственный департа́мент
         – большо́й приём

2.   Куда́ ты положи́л ка́рту СССР?   Где лежи́т ка́рта СССР?
         – край стола́
         – кни́жный шкаф

3.   Куда́ плывёт 5-й америка́нский флот?   Где нахо́дится 5-й
                                             америка́нский флот?
         – Средизе́мное мо́ре
         – юго-за́пад

4.   Куда́ е́дут э́ти солда́ты?   Где сейча́с э́ти солда́ты?
         – фронт
         – Центра́льная Евро́па

5.   Куда́ шли партиза́ны?   Где жи́ли партиза́ны?
         – густо́й лес
         – непроходи́мые джу́нгли

C.   Fill in the blanks below using one of the following prepositions: в, на, через, за, под, сквозь. Write Ø if no preposition is necessary.

1.   Делега́ты съезда ждали _____ видного партийного деятеля.
2.   Когда демократы вернутся _____ Белый дом?
3.   Война началась, когда армия перешла _____ границу.
4.   _____ конференции состоялась дискуссия по вопросу военной помощи.
5.   Студенты изучали _____ договоры ОСВ-1 и ОСВ-2.
6.   Советским гражданам трудно путешествовать _____ границу.
7.   Какие страны входят _____ НАТО?
8.   Словарь упал _____ пол. Достань мне его, пожалуйста!
9.   _____ дым ничего не было видно.
10. Отсюда ракета летит _____ Кубу 10 минут.

D. **Study Table 4 "The Measured..." which follows the accusative case chart at the end of Lesson 2.**

Fill in the missing parts with the appropriate numeral from the choices at the end of the exercise. Underline the noun in the sentence which is being measured. Translate these sentences into English.

1. База находилась на расстоянии в ___________ от города.
2. Он стал президентом на срок в ___________.
3. Африка получила помощь в ___________ от США.
4. Наш дефицит платёжного баланса в ___________ увеличивается.
5. Урожай в ___________ недостаточен для этой страны.
6. Уровень безработицы 1983 года в ___________ упал до 5%.
7. Венгрия - страна с населением в ___________.

($200,000,000,000; 3 километра; 110,000 тонн[1];   10%; 5 лет; $60,000,000; 4,000,000 человек)

E. **Write your own sentences expressing "the measured." Translate them into English.**

F. 1) **Form phrases using the words below according to the model—**

> $\underline{\text{numeral}}$ + раз(а) + в + $\underline{\text{noun}}$
> Acc. case   Acc. case

Example: 3 раза в год
 $\longrightarrow$ *Three times a year*

час
неделя
месяц
век
минута

2) **Be able to translate these phrases into English.**

Note: Nouns which have the same form for nominative singular and genitive plural are:
раз, человек, солдат, партизан

G. 1) **Consult idiomatic use of the accusative case in the chart at the end of Lesson 2. Give Russian equivalents for the following phrases.**

- to invite to a reception
- in response to a welcoming speech
- to enter a bloc

[1]trans. as metric tons = 2 200 lbs

  – to agree on trade with...
  – to resemble an economic crisis
  – the 6% rate of unemployment
  – to thank for economic assistance
  – 13 seat-majority in Parliament
  – to speak in favor of the proposal
  – to endanger

2) Make up sentences using these phrases.

H. Answer the following questions, using the words in the right-hand column. (Find the exercise on the tape)

1. Кого члены делегации увидят на приёме?
  – политические и государственные деятели
  – ответственные представители администрации
  – лидер чёрного большинства

2. Куда едет делегация Верховного Совета СССР?
  – Внуковский аэродром
  – Великобритания
  – Украина

3. Как (через что) летит этот самолёт?
  – Североамериканский континент
  – Аляска
  – государственная граница

4. Куда (за что) везут раненых?
  – линия фронта
  – Дон
  – граница

5. Сквозь что пробирается отряд партизан?
  – густой туман
  – тропический лес

6. Что обсуждают главы делегаций?
  – мирный договор
  – международная торговля
  – будущие соглашения

7. Куда (подо что) упала машина?
  – лёд
  – мост

8. Сколько времени проходили переговоры?
  – целая неделя
  – весь месяц
  – 4 года

9.   Как ча́сто они́ встреча́ются?
                              - ка́ждая пя́тница
                              - раз в неде́лю

J.   Write questions for the italicized words in the sentences below.

1.   Высокие гости прибыли в *столицу СССР*.
2.   Переговоры между СССР и Францией проходили *14 часов*.
3.   Стороны подписали *ряд важных соглашений*.
4.   Журналисты-международники часто ездят *за границу*.
5.   Наша группа прибыла в Вашингтон *в ответ на приглашение Госдепартамента*.
6.   Этот политический деятель всегда выступает за *хорошие отношения* между США и СССР.
7.   Грузовики переехали *через мост*.
8.   Президент встречается с прессой *раз в месяц*.
9.   *В субботу* состоится пресс-конференция с министром иностранных дел СССР.

K.   Review cardinal numerals in the accusative case.   Consult the appendix.

1)   Form phrases with the words below according to the model:

With animate masculine nouns and feminine nouns:

Example: знать/ 2/ ответственный деятель
                 ⟶ Мы знаем *двух ответственных деятелей*.

Use the following: (write out the numerals)

a)   встречать/ 4/ военная лётчица
b)   голосовать за/ 3/ генеральный секретарь
c)   видеть/ 5/ советский солдат
d)   при/ 2/ первый заместитель министра
e)   книга о/ 12/ американский президент

2)   Form phrases with the words below according to the model:

With inanimate masculine nouns and feminine nouns:

Example: через/ 2/ бетонный мост
                 ⟶ Танки прошли через *два бетонных моста*

Use the following: (write out the numerals)

a)   ехать на/ 6/ международная конференция
b)   подписать/ 11/ важный документ
c)   через/ 2/ огромный континент
d)   находиться на/ 1/ пресс-конференция
e)   обвиняться в/ 4/ авиационная катастрофа

I.   Review time expressions and idioms in the accusative case.   Translate the words in parentheses.

1.   Президент отвечал на вопросы (for 30 minutes) ___________.

2.   Кого они благодарят за (military aid) _________?

3.   (This very minute) __________ зазвонил телефон.

4.   Наша сторона не согласилась на (unilateral trade) ________.

5.   (Over the last 15 years) ___________ нефтяной рынок сократился.

6.   Ядерное оружие (endanger) __________ существование нашей планеты.

7.   Главы делегаций должны подписать договор (within two days) __________.

8.   (Every Wednesday) __________ они встречаются после работы.

9.   Он станет президентом на срок в (5 years) _________.

10.   Мы готовились к переговорам (for an entire summer) ________.

GRAMMAR EXERCISES: PREPOSITIONAL/ACCUSATIVE CASE

A.   Use the words in parentheses in the proper case.

1.   В сегодняшней газе́те говори́лось о (пятиле́тний план) _______.

2.   Самолёт лети́т че́рез (Украйна) _________.

3.   На́ши студе́нты изуча́ют (междунаро́дные соглаше́ния) _________.

4.   Каки́м был госуда́рственный долг США при (президе́нт Ка́ртер) ______?

5.   Отноше́ния ме́жду США и СССР стро́ятся на (взаймное недове́рие) _______.

6.   Делега́цию везу́т на (официа́льный приём) __________.

7. Сегодня на Внуковском аэродроме встречают (видный политический деятель) __________ Великобритании.

B. Translate the following sentences into Russian.

1. Newspapers today say that France responded to the aggression the very same day.
2. During this administration the 11% rate of inflation has dropped.
3. Both sides have been discussing issues of military cooperation for an entire month.
4. The Soviet Baltic Navy was sailing west.
5. The war began when the army crossed our frontier.
6. They were waiting for the black majority leader all afternoon.
7. On Monday the Democratic candidate received a 10-vote majority.
8. Great Britain does not look like "Old England" anymore.
9. These specialists know a lot about Central America.

GRAMMAR: REFLEXIVE VERBS

The particle –ся (–сь after a vowel), *itself*, attaches to the end of a verb and usually signals that *something has happened to the direct object*.

"СЯ"–verbs have the following meanings:

1. **Reflexive meaning:** direct object is deleted because it is the same as the subject.

    Местное население **обороняется** от партизан.
    The local population is defending itself against guerillas.

2. **Reciprocal meaning** ("each other"): direct object can either be included in the subject or expressed in a phrase with С + instrumental.

    Главы сверхдержав **встретились** в Женеве.
    The leaders of the superpowers met in Geneva.

    Глава США **встретился** *с советским главой* в Женеве.
    The US leader met the Soviet leader in Geneva.

    Главы делегаций ни о чём не **договорились.**
    The leaders of the delegations have not agreed upon anything.

    Глава делегации США ни о чём не **договорился** *с главой делегации СССР.*
    The leader of the US delegation has not agreed upon anything with the leader of the Soviet team.

3. **Passive meaning** (with imperfective verbs only): the direct object becomes
   the passive object, i.e. the action is done to it.

> (они) выполня́ют план в срок.
> План **выполня́ется** в срок.
> *The plan is (being) completed on time.*

If the doer of the action is expressed, it is in the instrumental case.

> Рабо́чие выполня́ют план в срок.
> План **выполня́ется** *рабо́чими* в срок.
> *The plan is (being) completed by workers on time.*

4. **After "change of state" transitive verbs with no direct object.** The direct
   object, "itself", is understood and expressed as –СЯ, as in verbs of
   beginning and *ending* which you learned in Lesson 1.   The following verbs
   belong to this group:

> начина́ться/нача́ться (see lesson 1)
> конча́ться/ко́нчиться (see lesson 1)
> продолжа́ться/продо́лжиться
> улучша́ться/улу́чшиться
> ухудша́ться/уху́дшиться
> увели́чиваться/увели́читься
> уменьша́ться/уме́ньшиться
> открыва́ться/откры́ться
> закрыва́ться/закры́ться

> Война́ **продолжа́ется**.   (reflexive because there is no d.o.)
> *The war goes on.*

> Прави́тельство продолжа́ет войну́.   (not refl. because there is d.o.)
> *The government continues the war.*

> Состоя́ние эконо́мики **улу́чшилось**.
> *The condition of the economy has improved.*

> Рефо́рмы улу́чшили состоя́ние эконо́мики.
> *The reforms have improved the condition of the economy.*

Certain verbs acquire a different meaning with "СЯ":

> находи́ть means *to find*, while находи́ться means *to take place or be
> located*.

Many verbs are not used without "СЯ":

> боя́ться (бои́шься), стара́ться, станови́ться, состоя́ться, явля́ться,
> остава́ться.

Note that "СЯ" particle "uses up" the verbs's ability to take a direct object.

GRAMMAR EXERCISES: –СЯ VERBS

Read all the grammar related to reflexive verbs. Consult Table 5 at the end
of Lesson 2.

1.   **FORMATION OF VERBS: CONJUGATION.** Review the conjugations of each of the
     reflexive verbs in this lesson. Translate the phrases below. Where
     context allows for both aspects, give both.

1.   Они ____.
              will defend themselves

2.   Они ____.
              were defending themseves

3.   Мы ____.
              are defending ourselves

4.   Заседание ______________________________.
                       closed

5.   Заседание ______________________________.
                     is closing

6.   Выставки ______________________________ завтра.
                     will open

7.   Они ______________________________________.
                   are meeting

8.   Они ______________________.
                 met

9.   Они ________________________________.
                  will meet

10. Доходы ________________________________.
                   are getting smaller

11. Доходы ________________________________.
                  were getting smaller

12. Доходы ________________________________.
                   have gotten larger

13. Доходы ________________________________.
                   will get larger

14. Собрание ______________________ в 16 часов.
                     was held

15.   В центре Москвы ________________ главные правительственные

      are located

учреждения.

16.   В это время министр иностранных дел ____________ за границей.

      was

17.   Стороны ________________ мнениями.

      exchanged

18.   Становится ясно, что генералы Пентагона __________ успешного

      fear

конца переговоров.

2.   RECIPROCAL MEANING

A.   Pick the correct verb.

1.   На аэродроме президента (встречали/встречались) тов. Маршаков и
     другие официальные лица.
2.   На приеме делегаты имели возможность (познакомить/
     познакомиться) друг с другом.
3.   После войны Сэмюэльсон часто (видел/виделся) с Петровым, но за
     последние 15 лет эти ветераны войны ни разу не
     (встретили/встретились).
4.   Председатель советской делегации (познакомил/познакомился)
     своего американского партнёра со своим заместителем и
     (договорил/договорился) с ним о следующей встрече.
5.   Мы таких случаев пока не (встречали/встречались).

B.   Verbs of meeting and acquaintanceship. Look at the following models. Then translate the phrases using the verbs below. Remember that Russian has different verbs for *meet (=get acquainted)* and *meet (=have a meeting with)*.

Познакомьтесь!
Познакомьте меня с заместителем!
Я вас с ним познакомлю с удовольствием!
Они уже познакомились!
Бизнесмена встретили на аэродроме.
С кем она встречалась?

1.   Два будущих лидера ____________________ ещё до войны.

     met

(Is there more than one meaning for "meet"?)

2.   Они ________________ неофициально.

     got together

3.   На пресс-конференции ___________________________________.
                                    they acquainted us with the facts

4.   Депутаты _______________ завтра.
                    will meet

5.   Конгрессмен ___________ одного из членов советской делегации в
                        met
коридоре и они договорились _______________ через неделю.
                                            to meet
Конгрессмен обещал _______________ Маркова со своими коллегами.
                            to introduce

C.   **Now translate the following sentences. Remember to keep an eye out for correct verbal aspect.**

1.   The minister met with the head of the delegation.
2.   The leaders of the superpowers agreed on nothing.
3.   Kennedy and Khrushchev met only once.
4.   The heads of the delegations often saw each other.
5.   Could you introduce me to Dr. Kissinger? I've never met him.
6.   The minister met with the American delegation yesterday.
7.   They agreed on the next meeting.

3. PASSIVE MEANING

A.   **Translate the following sentences. Then paraphrase them into active voice. You may have to insert a subject if one is not expressed, or you may resort to an *они* form verb without the *они* pronoun.**

Examples: Такие случаи часто встречаются.
                ——→*Мы часто встречаем такие случаи.*
          В газете сообщаются нужные факты.
                ——→ *В газете сообщают нужные факты.*
    OR ——→ *Газета сообщает нужные факты.*

1.   Из Вашингтона сообщается о решении Белого дома нарушить условия договора об ограничении стратегических вооружений (ОСВ-2).
2.   На Западе считается, что многие из принятых реформ окажутся безрезультатными.
3.   В документе говорится о необходимости продолжать поиски путей мирного урегулирования кризиса.
4.   Итоги конференции публикуются в печати.

B.   Rewrite the following sentences with a -ся verb in the passive meaning according to the model.

Examples: Наши ученые разрабатывают новые оборонные системы.

　　　　⟶ *Новые оборонные системы разрабатываются нашими ученами.*

　　　　Здесь строят микрорайон.

　　　　⟶ *Здесь строится микрорайон.*

1.   План выполняют в срок.
2.   Эти меры обсуждали на последнем заседании совета.
3.   Советские издательства не печатают антисоветской литературы.
4.   В газете пишут, что положение на Ближнем Востоке обостряется.
5.   Закон запрещает экспорт американских ЭВМ (электронно-вычислительных машин) в СССР.
6.   Передача «9-я студия» является форумом, на котором видные общественные деятели обсуждают важные текущие вопросы.

4.   "CHANGE OF STATE" VERBS

A.   Determine which sentences require reflexive meaning. Pick the correct verb. If the verb is unfamilar, figure out its meaning from context.

1.   В следующем году думают (увеличить/увеличиться) производство видеомагнитофонов и проигрывателей компактных дисков.
2.   За истекший период экономическая помощь странам данного региона (снизила/снизилась) более, чем на 28 процентов.
3.   Американская выставка в Москве (открывает/открывается) в июне этого года.
4.   Администрация США (продолжает/продолжается) поставлять силам реакции оружие разного рода.
5.   Принятые меры далеко не (улучшили/улучшились) экономическое положение в этом секторе. Напротив, ситуация значительно (ухудшила/ухудшилась).
6.   В Нью-Йорке (открыла/открылась) сессия Генеральной Асамблеи ООН. Сессия будет (продолжать/продолжаться) в течение трех недель.
7.   Средняя зарплата работников в этой области науки значительно (повысила/повысилась).
8.   В данный момент (разрабатывает/разрабатывается) план, который позволит крупным НИИ подключиться к некоторым компьютерным сетям, связывающим чуть ли ни все вузы западноевропейских стран.
9.   С появлением таких фильмов как «Рэмбо» и «Красный рассвет» американская кинопромышленность постепенно (превращает/превращается) в мощную антисоветскую пропагандистскую машину.

B.   Fill in the blank with the correct verb.   Determine whether -ся is needed.

1.   Экономические системы одних стран третьего мира ___________ по
develop
социалистическому пути, других – по капиталистическому.

2.   Председатель __________ заседание без окончательного решения.
closed

3.   Западные «советологи» забывают, что количество граждан, желающих уехать за границу, ________________.
has gone down

4.   До сих пор ___________ попытки спасти дискредитировавшую себя
continue
политику Белого дома относительно ЮАР.

5.   Было бы наивно предполагать, что Советский Союз не _____________
is developing
защитные средства от так называемой «стратегической оборонной
инициативы».

6.   С результатами соревнования вас _______________ наш
will acquaint
корреспондент в Лондоне.

7.   С запуском первого искусственного спутника Земли в 1957 году

_____________ новый век в истории человечества.
opened

8.   Из Бейрута сообщают, что армия _______________ аэродром.
has closed

5.   VERBS WHICH ARE ALWAYS REFLEXIVE.   Fill in the blanks.

1.   Завтра в Хельсинки _________________ собрание конференции «За
will take place
безъядерную Европу».

2.   _________________ ясно, что новая администрация действительно
It is becoming
_____________ найти выход из положения.
is trying

3.   Ответ американского госсекретаря ________ примером легкомысленного
is
отношения к серьезному предложению.   Но причина американского отказа

от серьезных переговоров ___________ пока неясной.
remains

6.   REVIEW EXERCISES

1.   В те дни в дискуссионом клубе университета студенты _______,
     met
     _____________________, ______________ текущие события.
     exchanged opinions   *discussed*
     _______________ и философские вопросы о взаимоотношении между
     Were discussed
     личностью   и   обществом.   В   конце   прошлого   года

     руководство университета, которое ____________ столь свободных
                                       was afraid of
     обсуждений, неожиданно дало приказ _____________ клуб.
                                        to close

2.   Кубинский кризис 1962 года _________ вскоре после того, как
                                ended
     представитель советского посольства в Вашингтоне ______ с одним
                                                       met
     американским   корреспондентом   в   китайском   ресторане.   Там

     они________, что американский корреспондент, ______________
         agreed   *would report*
     президенту о «неофициальном» советском предложении.

3.   В газете __________, что сегодня _______________ прием, после
              it says   *will take place*
     которого _______________ официальный обед.
              is being arranged

GRAMMAR EXERCISES: VERBAL ASPECT (Continued)

Review Table 3 at the end of Lesson 1.

A.   Pick the correct verb.   Justify to yourself the reason you picked it.   If the verb is unfamiliar, try to grasp its meaning from context.

1.   Конференция   организации   «Врачи   за   мир   и   безопасность»
     (завершáла/завершúла)   свою   работу.   Результаты   конференции
     публикуются в официальном документе.
2.   За   последнее   десятилетие   число   боеголовок   (увелúчивалось/
     увелúчилось) на пятьдесят процентов.
3.   Переговоры   по   развитию   сотрудничества   в   науке   и   технике
     (начинались/начались) еще в пятидесятых годах.   Но стороны начали
     (обмениваться/обменяться) опытом в большом маштабе только в начале
     шестидесятых годов.
4.   Советская сторона *не раз* [= больше, чем один раз, т.е. много раз]
     (выступáла/вúступила) за двусторонний обмен информацией по тому же
     вопросу.
5.   Вчера в Москву (прибывáла/прибылá) делегация из КНР.   Сегодня утром

заместитель министра иностранных дел СССР (устра́ивал/устро́ил) прием
в МИД СССР.

6. Переговоры в Женеве заверши́лись благополучно.   Главы делегаций
(подпи́сывали/подписа́ли) договор об экономической взаимопомощи.

7. Сначала премьер-министр (выступа́л/вы́ступил) с речью, а потом он
(соглаша́лся/согласи́лся) ответить на вопросы журналистов.

B.   Translate the words under the blanks.

1. Мы надеемся, что наши партнёры ______________ это немаловажное
                                      will sign

   соглашение.

2. Американские газеты *не раз* (= много раз) ______________ о
                                              have reported

   готовности Москвы регулярно ______________ опытом в этой области.
                                 to exchange

3. Обе стороны договорились ______________ два раза в год.
                               to meet

4. При этой администрации безработица ______________.   Еще к концу
                                        was declining

   прошлого года она ______________ на 1.6 (один и шесть десятых)
                        was reduced

   процента.

5. На будущей неделе мы ______________ вопрос эмиграции.
                          will be discussing

GRAMMAR: *ЛИ*, NOT *ЕСЛИ*

Watch the "ifs."

Consumers asked if that model is still being produced.	Потребители спроси́ли, произво́дится ли еще э́та моде́ль
The representative wants to know if the car can compete.	Представи́тель хоте́л бы зна́ть, бу́дет ли но́вая маши́на конкурентноспосо́бной.
The assistant manager has not found out if Bulgaria will supply the spare parts.	Замести́тель дире́ктора ещё не узна́л, бу́дет ли Болга́рия предоставля́ть запча́сти.
Ask if the refrigerators will be sold in all 35 countries.	Спроси́те, бу́дут ли продава́ться холоди́льники во всех тридцати́ пяти́ стра́нах.

When "if" means "whether," (and that is *most* of the time), use **ли**: invert the subject and predicate and make ли the *second* word in the clause.

When "if" is used in an "If A... then B..." sentence, use **е́сли**.

GRAMMAR EXERCISES: *ЛИ*, NOT *ЕСЛИ*

A. Determine which of the following English sentences will have ли in Russian.

1.   If you ask a stupid question, you get a stupid answer.
2.   Have you learned if the contracts have been signed?
3.   We'd like to find out if Kryukov has arrived yet.
4.   I'll agree to the conditions if you agree as well.

B. Translate the phrases below.

1.   Она нас спроси́ла, if the plant had opened.
2.   Мы забы́ли, if Bulgaria had supplied the spare parts.
3.   Председа́тель не узна́л, if his assistant has arrived.
4.   Потреби́тели всегда спра́шивают, if a new product costs more.
5.   Дава́йте спро́сим, if this shop works in the mornings.
6.   Мы не зна́ли, if Rumania buys raw materials from Mongolia.
7.   На́до спроси́ть, if the IMF will give credit to Poland.
8.   Мы бы хоте́ли узна́ть, if the President sent the General Secretary a telegram.

RENDERING

When you render, try not to think about the English phrasing. Don't try to say it all. Get out as much as you can muster. The point of an exercise such as this one is to teach you to say what you can, not what you can't. Look for simple ways to say difficult things. For example, you could render a sentence such as: *Zhadin made no bones about the fact that without a treaty the scare factor would increase dramatically...* into very manageable, albeit less than elegant Russian: *Жадин сказал, что без договора люди будут больше бояться.*

Render the following:

Yesterday the U.S. Academy of Sciences hosted a reception for a 25-person Soviet delegation which is been in the U.S. to work out details on plans for further cooperation in limiting pollution. In his opening remarks I.M. Chistonebov, head of the Soviet delegation, called for serious work on a number of issues which previously had not been at the top of the negotiating agenda. One such issue was the threat of acid rain.

Chistonebov noted that acid rain is no longer viewed solely as a North American problem. Over 70,000 square kilometers of lakes and rivers on Soviet territory are endangered. And while exact figures are hard to come by, Chistonebov ventured that that figure amounts to about a 200 percent increase over the last ten years. The Soviet scientist added that while Moscow has already appropriated over 300 million rubles towards clean-up and control of acid rain, that figure is just a drop in the bucket. Chistonebov was quick to point out that the effort has to be an international one. "Climate does not respect national borders," he said.

Both sides agreed that bilateral research and negotiations should continue. A number of delegates expressed the opinion that with the thaw in international relations, worldwide environmental efforts will increase. The question is if the situation can be turned around in time. Many fear that it is too late.

The Soviet delegation has so far spent two months in this country, much of it in northern states. The two delegations will be meeting in Moscow in six months.

Useful phrases:

acid rain – кислотный дождь (чего – кислотного дождя)
... are endangered – ... находятся под угрозой
environmental efforts – экологические меры
pollution – загрязнение окружающей среды
spend money (in order to do something) – тратить (трачу, тратишь) / потратить
    деньги, чтобы + infinitive

SPEAKING EXERCISES

A.   **Отве́тьте на сле́дующие вопро́сы по те́ксту.**

1. По чьему́ приглаше́нию в Вашингто́н прибыла́ прави́тельственная делега́ция Великобрита́нии?
2. Кто встреча́л делега́цию на аэродро́ме?
3. Где руководи́тели США и Великобрита́нии вы́ступили с приве́тственными реча́ми?
4. Как проходи́ли перегово́ры?
5. Како́й догово́р подписа́ли сто́роны?

B.   1)   **Расскажи́те текст, испо́льзуя слова́рь уро́ка 2.**

   2)   **Расскажи́те тот же текст, замени́в:**

- уча́стников перегово́ров
- ме́сто встре́чи
- атмосфе́ру приёма в честь госте́й
- те́му перегово́ров
- хара́ктер перегово́ров
- подпи́санный догово́р

C.   **Соста́вьте ситуа́цию, испо́льзуя сле́дующие выраже́ния.**

the spokeseman of... stated that.., led by ..., in honor of the important guest, to make a speech in favor of..., to sign an agreement on..., this document deals with...

D.   **Вы спи́кер пала́ты представи́телей Конгре́сса США (Speaker of the US Congress House of Representatives). Предста́вьте премье́р-мини́стра Великобрита́нии пе́ред объединённой се́ссией Конгре́сса США.**

E.   **Обсужде́ние америка́но-брита́нских отноше́ний по америка́нскому телеви́дению в програ́мме «Встре́ча с пре́ссой».**

F.   **Речь америка́нского президе́нта по́сле его́ визи́та в Великобрита́нию и его́ пресс-конфере́нция с америка́нскими журнали́стами.**

G.   **Вы чле́ны пала́ты о́бщин (брита́нский парла́мент). Зада́йте вопро́сы премье́р-мини́стру Великобрита́нии по́сле её (его́) возвраще́ния из США.**

READING EXERCISE 1

PRE-TEXT:

Read the text with the following questions in mind. Try to answer as many
as you can before you give the text a closer reading:

1.   What is this article about?
2.   Which two documents were signed?
3.   Who led the Soviet delegation?
4.   The article says that deep appreciation was expressed. To whom? For
     what?

Подписано соглашение

МАНАГУА, 8. (ТАСС). 6 ноября здесь подписано соглашение о сотрудничестве между Коммунистической партией Советского Союза и Сандинистским фронтом национального освобождения на 1986—1990 годы и план связей между КПСС и СФНО на 1986—1987 гг.

По поручению ЦК КПСС документы были подписаны членом ЦК КПСС, заместителем Председателя Совета Министров СССР В. М. Каменцевым. Возглавляемая им делегация КПСС принимает участие в торжествах, посвященных 25-й годовщине основания СФНО.

От Сандинистского фронта документы подписал заместитель координатора исполнительной комиссии Национального руководства СФНО Байардо Арсе. На состоявшейся в этой связи церемонии он выразил глубокую признательность народу и правительству СССР за помощь и поддержку, оказываемые никарагуанской революции.

POST-TEXT (using sentence structure):

Review Reading rules as presented in Lesson 1 and do the following exercise:

Find and classify the predicate(s) for the following subjects and the
objects(s) to these predicates:

	predicate(s)	*object(s)*
paragraph 1 соглашение	_____________	_____________
paragraph 2 документы	_____________	_____________
paragraph 3 заместитель	_____________	_____________

Translate these *subject-predicate-object* phrases into English.

POST–TEXT   (using context):

1. What does *СФНО* stand for?
2. Find the Russian for *deputy*.
3. How many times is the word used in the text?
4. What related words do you know for *помощь* and *поддержка*?
5. The name of the country is *Никарагуа*. How do you say *the people of Nicaragua*?
6. Make a list of words that you can use to talk about signing agreements.

READING EXERCISE 2

PRE–TEXT:

Read the text with the following questions in mind:

1. What is said in this article?
2. What congress is reported on?
3. What report did the delegates discuss and approve?
4. How many five-year plans for economic development did the country have prior to the congress?

Завершил
работу

ТИРАНА. Сегодня здесь завершил работу IX съезд Албанской партии труда. Как сообщает агентство АТА, делегаты обсудили и одобрили доклад «О деятельности Центрального Комитета АПТ и ее предстоящих задачах», доклад Центральной контрольно - ревизионной комиссии партии и директивы относительно восьмого пятилетнего плана развития экономики и культуры нСРА в 1986—1990 гг., избрали руководящие органы партии.

Первым секретарем ЦК АПТ вновь избран Рамиз Алия.

(ТАСС, 8).

POST-TEXT   (using sentence structure):

Reading rule 3:   Now, look for words **which modify other words** and therefore clarify their meaning.

A noun modifier can be:

1)   *an adjective (in the same gender, number and case as the noun it modifies.)*
        Директивы *восьмого пятилетнего* плана

2)   *a pronoun or a numeral*
        её задачи
        четыре плана

3)   *a noun or a noun phrase*
        соглашение *о сотрудничестве*
        заместитель *координатора*

Do the following exercises:

1.   Find and classify the modifiers for the following words in the first paragraph: съезд, задачи, доклад, план, органы
2.   Translate these nouns with their modifiers into English.

POST-TEXT   (using context):

1.   What does АПТ stand for? What about HCPA?
2.   In what city does the action take place?
3.   The people of this country *говорят по–...*?
4.   *Предстоящий* means *forthcoming*. How can you guess its meaning without a dictionary?
5.   What is the Russian for *to elect leading party organs*?
6.   Make a list of words that you can use to talk about conferences.

READING EXERCISE 3

PRE-TEXT:

Read the text with the following questions in mind:

1.   What is the story about?
2.   Who visited where?
3.   How many Chinese officials are identified by name?
4.   What questions were discussed during the exchange of opinion?

5.   In the second column we read about *the necessity to continue the dialogue* between... (true or false for each item):
       a.   China and the USSR
       b.   Japan and China
       c.   China and the USSR
       d.   the USSR and the USA

6.   On what basis did the delegations agree on the necessity to continue the dialogue?

Завершение визита

ПЕКИН, 9. (ТАСС). Сегодня завершился визит в Китай премьер-министра Японии Я. Накасонэ. Он провел переговоры с Генеральным секретарем ЦК КПК Ху Яобаном, премьером Госсовета КНР Чжао Цзыяном, председателем центральной комиссии советников КПК Дэн Сяопином. Обсуждались вопросы двусторонних отношений, состоялся обмен мнениями по проблемам международной обстановки.

В ходе рассмотрения итогов советско-американской встречи на высшем уровне в Рейкьявике, отметил выступивший здесь на пресс-конференции японский премьер-министр, стороны подчеркнули необходимость продолжения диалога между СССР и США на основе достигнутого в Рейкьявике определенного прогресса в интересах мира во всем мире.

POST-TEXT   (using sentence structure):

1.   Find and classify the subject, predicate, object(s) for the predicate and all modifiers for nouns in all four sentences of the text.
2.   Translate them into English.

POST-TEXT   (using context):

1.   What does КПК stand for?
2.   How do we call people who live in China?
3.   What language do they speak?
4.   *Горсовет* is an example of a common type of contraction in modern Russian. Of what two words? Do you know any derivatives for the word *совет*? What word is related to *совет*?
5.   Make a list of words that you can use to talk about negotiations.

READING EXERCISE 4

PRE-TEXT:

Read the text with the following questions in mind:

1.   What is the article about?
2.   Who met with George Shultz?

3. Where did he go for the meeting?
4. What questions were given special consideration?

Встреча с Дж. Шульцем

ВЕНА, 5. (ТАСС). Член Политбюро ЦК КПСС, министр иностранных дел СССР Э. А. Шеварднадзе, прибывший сюда для участия в венской встрече государств—участников Совещания по безопасности и сотрудничеству в Европе, имел встречу с государственным секретарем США Дж. Шульцем.

В ходе беседы были рассмотрены вопросы, относящиеся к тематике венской встречи, а также к области советско-американских отношений. Особое внимание было удслоно вопросам безопасности в контексте результатов, достигнутых на встрече Генерального секретаря ЦК КПСС М. С. Горбачева с президентом США Р. Рейганом в Рейкьявике.

POST-TEXT   (using sentence structure):

Reading rule 3:   Modifiers (continued)

Noun modifiers can also be:

1)   *participles*
     читающее население

2)   *participial phrases*
     армия, *выходящая* из страны

3)   *adjectival phrase*
     оружие, *способное* уничтожить цель

They all agree with the noun they modify in *number, gender and case.*

Do the following exercises:

1. Find the subject and the predicate in the first sentence.
2. Find a modifier for the subject. It is... (pick the correct answer):
    a.   an adjective
    b.   an adjectival phrase
    c.   a participal
    d.   a participial phrase

3. Find an object for the predicate.   It is... (pick the correct answer):
    a.   a direct object
    b.   an indirect object
    c.   a prepositional object

4. Translate this sentence into English.

5.   In the first sentence of the second paragraph, find the subject and
     the predicate. The predicate is... (pick the correct answer):
     a.   "to be" + short adjective
     b.   "to be" + short past passive participle

6.   Find a modifier or modifiers for the subject. It is... (pick the
     correct answer):
     a.   an adjective
     b.   an adjectival phrase
     c.   a participal
     d.   a participial phrase

7.   Translate this sentence into English.
8.   In the second sentence of the same paragraph, find an object for the
     predicate. It is... (pick the correct answer):
     a.   a direct object
     b.   an indirect object
     c.   a prepositional object

9.   Find a modifier for the word «результатов». It is... (pick the
     correct answer):
     a.   an adjective or adjectival phrase
     b.   a participle or a participial phrase

10. Translate the sentence into English.

POST-TEXT (using context):

1.   What is the Russian for "Secretary of State"? What is the equivalent
     of this position in the USSR? In Europe?
2.   Find the Russian for "member-countries." Are both Russian words in
     the same case? Why? Put them them into nominative case.
3.   Find cognates in the second column.
4.   Make a list of vocabulary that you can use to talk about conferences
     and talks.

READING EXERCISE 5

PRE-TEXT:

Read the text with the following questions in mind:

1.   What is the main idea of the article?
2.   Who held the press-conference?
3.   What visit of the French President was discussed?   (check the right
     answer):
     a.   a forthcoming visit
     b.   a current visit
     c.   a past visit
     d.   a postponed visit

4. The minister referred to three areas of Soviet–French relations. What were they?
5. Name two forums for discussion of Soviet–French relations.
6. How can the tone of the report be characterized?   (check the right answer):
   a.   positive
   b.   neutral
   c.   hostile
   d.   emotional

ПРЕСС-КОНФЕРЕНЦИЯ МИНИСТРА

ПАРИЖ. [Соб. корр. «Известий»]. Отвечая на вопросы вашего корреспондента на состоявшейся в Париже встрече с журналистами Ассоциации дипломатической печати, министр иностранных дел Франции Жан-Бернар Рэмон заявил:

Предстоящий визит президента Франции Франсуа Миттерана в Советский Союз даст возможность рассмотреть важнейшие международные проблемы, в том числе вопросы разоружения и контроля над вооружениями, а также положение в различных регионах мира.

Министр особо отметил успешное развитие франко-советских отношений. В этой связи он подчеркнул, что Советский Союз и Франция проводят консультации в рамках различных международных форумов, в том числе и на стокгольмской Конференции по мерам укрепления доверия, безопасности и разоружению в Европе. Остановившись на двусторонних отношениях в торгово-экономической области, он заявил, что в ходе состоявшихся в 1985/1986 годах сессий советско-французской «Большой комиссии». были достигнуты договоренности, предусматривающие заключение крупных контрактов.

Министр также отметил важность франко-советского сотрудничества в области науки, техники и культуры, высказался за его расширение. Предстоящие франко-советские переговоры на высшем уровне в Москве, подчеркнул Ж.-Б. Рэмон, будут чрезвычайно полезными как в международном плане, так и для развития двусторонних связей.

Президент Франции, продолжал далее Ж.-Б. Рэмон, выступает за дальнейшее развитие франко-советского диалога. Этой цели и служит встреча руководителей двух стран. Министр также выразил надежду на то, что визит Ф. Миттерана в СССР даст новый импульс двусторонним консультациям по проблеме разоружения, будет содействовать углублению франко-советских экономических и торговых связей.

POST-TEXT (using the sentence structure):

Reading rule 3:   Modifiers (continued)

A verb modifier can be:

1)   *an adverb.*   Adverbs answer the questions *where, when, how,* and *why,* but
not *which one* or *what kind of.*
его выступление было встречено *холодно. (How?)*

2)   *an adverbial phrase*
делегация прибыла *в Москву. (Where?)*
3)   *a verbal adverb and a verbal adverbial phrase*
понимая ситуацию, он не задавал вопросов. *(Why?)*

Note: A verbal adverbial phrase is always separated by a comma.

Do the following exercises:

1.   In paragraph 1 find a modifier (modifiers) for the predicate *заявил.*
It is (they are)...(mark the correct answer):
a.   an adverb
b.   an adverbial phrase
c.   a verbal adverb
d.   a verbal adverbial phrase

2.   Translate the entire sentence into English.
3.   In paragraph 3 find a modifier for the predicates *подчеркнул* and
(further down) *заявил.*   They are... (mark the correct answer):
a.   an adverb
b.   an adverbial phrase
c.   a verbal adverb
d.   a verbal adverbial phrase

4.   Translate both sentences into English.

POST-TEXT   (using context):

1.   Find the Russian for *summit.*   Give a synonym.
2.   What does *соб. корр.* stand for?   What does it mean?
3.   There are two degrees of comparison: *comparative* and *superlative.*
Which one is *важнейшие?*   Transform it into the other kind of
comparison.   What is the basic form of the adjective?
4.   In *на высшем уровне,* you find another adjective in a degree of
comparison.   Determine the degree and the basic form of the
adjective.
5.   Find the word *регион* in the text.   It is used in a geopolitical or
in a domestic sense?   Give a synonym.
6.   *Этой цели служит встреча руководителей двух стран.* Find the subject
of this sentence.   Does *и* mean *and?*

7. One often finds in Russian *конференция по.*   What is its English equivalent?

8. What derivative noun and verb do you know of the Russian word *торговый?*

9. Make a list of words that you will use to talk about visits and talks.

READING EXERCISE 6

PRE-TEXT:

Read the text with the following questions in mind.   Check to see how many you can answer before you have read the text carefully.   Then go back and see if you were correct:

1. What is the main idea of the article?
2. Which of the following statements is true:
    a. The General Secretary of the CC CPSU met with the President of South Africa.
    b. The General Secretary of the CC CPSU met with the President of the African National Congress.
    c. The Chairman of the Supreme Soviet met with the Prime-Minister of South Africa.
3. The Soviet Union views the ANC as...(true or false for each item):
    a. a spokesman for the legitimate interests of the people of South Africa.
    b. the sole representative of the national liberation movement in South Africa.
    c. a recognized leader of the national liberation movement in South Africa.
    d. a recognized leader of the national liberation movement in the south of Africa.

4. The President of the ANC...(true or false for each item):
    a. thanked the Soviet people for their support.
    b. stated that the goal of the ANC is to create a unified democratic state.
    c. requested aid from the Soviet Union.
    d. welcomed Soviet efforts for the improvement of international relations.

5.   It will be impossible to reach a just political settlement in South
     Africa if...(true or false for each item):
     a.   independence is guaranteed to Namibia.
     b.   an embargo is placed on all South African goods.
     c.   an end is put to Pretoria's aggression against its neighbors
     d.   the United States stops its support of the South African regime.
     e.   the apartheid regime in South Africa is eliminated.

6.   Which US policies did the participants of the talks condemn?
7.   Which of the following African states are mentioned in this article:
     Botswana, Zimbabwe, Swaziland, Namibia, Mozambique, Lesotho?

Встреча в Кремле

4 ноября состоялась встреча Генерального секретаря ЦК КПСС М. С. Горбачева с Президентом Африканского национального конгресса Южной Африки (АНК) О. Тамбо, прибывшим в СССР во главе делегации АНК.

Приветствуя Президента АНК, М. С. Горбачев выразил солидарность с мужественной борьбой южноафриканских патриотов против бесчеловечной системы апартеида, сказал, что в Советском Союзе рассматривают АНК как выразителя подлинных интересов народа Южной Африки, признанного руководителя национально - освободительного движения в этой стране.

Президент АНК сердечно поблагодарил КПСС, советский народ за неизменную поддержку борющегося народа Южной Африки. Он рассказал о положении в ЮАР, характеризующемся глубоким кризисом режима апартеида. Отметив небывалый подъём массовых антирасистских выступлений, он подчеркнул, что патриотические силы Южной Африки во главе с АНК ставят перед собой цель создания единого демократического государства, в котором не останется места расизму и будут гарантированы равные права всем гражданам, независимо от цвета кожи. Генеральный секретарь ЦК КПСС заявил, что такая позиция встречает в Советском Союзе полное понимание.

О. Тамбо приветствовал усилия СССР, направленные на радикальное оздоровление международной обстановки, высоко оценил ответственную и принципиальную позицию советского руководства на встрече в Рейкьявике.

Руководители КПСС и АНК высказали общее мнение, что справедливое политическое урегулирование на Юге Африки может быть достигнуто. Для этого необходимо положить конец агрессивным действиям Претории против независимых африканских государств, обеспечить предоставление независимости Намибии в соответствии с известными решениями ООН, устранить режим апартеида в ЮАР, который является первопричиной конфликтной ситуации в регионе. Они призвали всех, кто заинтересован в мирном и свободном будущем народов Юга Африки, внести свой вклад в коллективные поиски путей решения этих задач.

Участники встречи подтвердили свою солидарность с «прифронтовыми» африканскими государствами и СВАПО, осудили так называемое конструктивное сотрудничество администрации США с южноафриканскими расистами, ее вмешательство во внутренние дела Анголы путем поддержки марионеточных банд УНИТА.

М. С. Горбачев и О. Тамбо чувством глубокой скорби отдали дань светлой памяти Саморы Машела — видного деятеля национально-освободительного движения, Председателя Партии Фрелимо, президента Народной Республики Мозамбик.

В заключение беседы М. С. Горбачев просил О. Тамбо передать привет и чувства солидарности Н. Манделе и другим политическим заключенным, томящимся в расистских застенках. Он пожелал АНК новых успехов в его справедливой борьбе.

(ТАСС).

POST–TEXT   (using sentence structure):

Reading rule 3: Modifiers: (continued)

Both noun and verb can be modified by a subordinate clause, a sentence which contains its own subject and predicate.

Встреча посвящена книге, *о которой говорит весь мир.*

Когда главы государств встретились, они подписали договор.

Note: «Который» reflects *the number and the gender* of the noun it modifies.

Reading rule 1: (continued from lesson 1)

Sometimes the **subject**, the "doer" in the nominative case, is missing in the sentence.   However, the **predicate** will indicate the reason for its absence.   Here are two of such reasons:

a)   A predicate in the third person plural indicates that «они» is omitted, a commonly used construction in Russian.

Говорят, что скоро будет война.

b)   A predicate "to be" + важно, нужно, необходимо, надо indicates the use of *Impersonal construction,* where the "doer" is either missing (in a general statement) or is used in the dative case.

(Нам) нужно развивать торговлю.

Do the following exercises:

1.   In paragraph 2   the subject has two predicates.   Find them and determine their objects.   They are...(check the right answer):
     a.   a direct object
     b.   an indirect object
     c.   a prepositional object
     d.   a clause

2.   Find a modifier for the first predicate.   It is...(check the correct answer):
     a.   an adverb
     b.   an adverbial phrase
     c.   a verbal adverbial phrase
     d.   a clause

3.   In the subordinate *что*-clause find the subject and the predicate. The subject is...(check the correct answer):
     a.   the "doer" in the nominative case
     b.   the *они*-construction
     c.   an impersonal construction

4. Find and classify an object for the predicate.
5. Find a modifier for that object.   It is.... (check the correct answer):
    a.   a word
    b.   a phrase
    c.   a clause

6. Translate paragraph 2 into English.
7. In paragraph 5, sentence 2, find the subject and the predicate.   The subject is... (check the correct answer):
    a.   the "doer" in the nominative case
    b.   the *они*-construction
    c.   an impersonal construction

8. A comma in front of *обеспечить* and *устранить* separates... (check the correct answer):
    a.   a clause
    b.   a phrase
    c.   an enumeration

9. Find a modifier for «режим».   It is...(check the correct answer):
    a.   a word
    b.   a phrase
    c.   a clause

10. Translate this sentence into English.

POST-TEXT   (using context):

1. Break the word *небывалый* into component parts.
2. What is the Russian for *to guarantee equal rights to all citizens regardless of color*?
3. *СВАПО* = Народная организация Юго-Западной Африки.   What is its English equivalent?
4. Find the name of the geopolitical region where this country is located.
5. What derivatives can you name for the word *расист*?
6. Make a list of words that you can use to talk about a conference on apartheid.

ACCUSATIVE CASE

USES:	PREPOSITIONS:	QUESTION:	VERBS:
Direct Object	--	Кого? Что?	**transitive verbs** понимáть ждáть обсуждáть провожáть и т.д.
Direction of movement	В,НА (in,on,at) ЗА,ПОД (behind, under)	Кудá? За что? Подо что?	прибывáть идти́ éхать плы́ть летéть класть стáвить пáдать везти́ вести́ верну́ться сади́ться и т.д.
From one side to the other	ЧЕРЕЗ (across) СКВОЗЬ (through)	Чéрез что? Сквозь что?	
About	ПРО	Про кого? Про что?	говори́ть расскáзывать спрáшивать ду́мать и т.д.

TIME-EXPRESSIONS:

в какой день недели?
в этот день

But: **на** следующий день

в среду
в этот момент
в эту минуту, секунду
в это время
в 2 часа

в первый (последний) раз

раз в неделю, год, месяц

через час - in an hour
             an hour later

год назад - a year ago
             a year before

за эту неделю (within a week)
за последние 20 лет

сколько времени?
как долго?
    - всю ночь
    - целое лето
    - два века
    - одну минуту
    - весь месяц
    - неделю (for a week)

как часто?
    - каждый день
    - каждую среду
    - раз в год
    - пять раз в год

USEFUL IDIOMS:

отвечать на агрессию
в ответ на агрессию
-in response to agression

соглашаться на экспорт
согласен,-а,-о,-ы на реформы
- to agree to reforms
похож,а,е,и на кризис
- to resemble a crisis
приглашать на встречу
- to invite to a meeting
входить в блок
- to be a member of a block
расстояние в 7 километров
 a 7-kilometer distance
выступать за предложение
- to take a stand in favor of...
благодарить за помощь
- to thank for assistance
голосовать за соглашение
- to vote for the agreement
ответственность за поражение
- responsibility for defeat
брать под контроль
- to take under control
ставить под угрозу
- to threaten

TABLE 4:   "THE MEASURED..."

If you want to be able to say in Russian:

The ten percent rate of inflation is dropping.
Уровень инфляции в 10 процёнтов пáдает.
or
The capital is at the distance of 70 miles from...to...
Столйца нахóдится на расстоянии в 70 миль от... до...

In other words, if you have to express **the amount** of something, or **measure** something, use this:

THE MEASURED *(make sure you have it)*	B *(preposition)*	NUMBER *(in accusative case)*
дефицйт - deficit	в	130,000,000,000
ýровень инфляции - rate of inflation	в	5%
ýровень безрабóтицы - rate of unemployment	в	4%
экономйческая пóмощь - economic aid	в	73,000,000
государственный долг - national debt	в	360,000,000,000
расстояние - distance	в	12,000
гранйца - frontier	в	100
большинствó - majority	в	3
срок - term	в	4
перйод - period	в	19
урожáй - crop, yield	в	700
вес - weight	в	2
населéние - population	в	350,000,000

NOTE: This construction is **an attribute** to "**the measured**".
It is **NEVER** a part of the predicate.

Уровень инфляции 10 процéнтов.   *The rate of inflation is 10%*
Уровень инфляции увелйчился   *The rate of inflation*
(умéньшился) на 10 процéнтов.   *increased (dropped) by 10%.*

человéк, -а, человéк
гóд, -а, лет
тóнна, -ы, тонн
цéна, -ы, цен
франк, -а, фрáнков
фунт, -а, фýнтов
дóллар, -а, дóлларов
рýбль, -я, рублéй
километр, -а, киломéтров
мúля, -и, миль
процéнт, -а, процéнтов
мéсто, -а, мест
гóлос, -а, голосóв

UNIT OF MEASURE (case depends on the final digit)	MEASURED IN:
миллиáрдов	дóлларов
	процéнтов - per cent процéнта
миллиóна	фýнтов - pounds
миллиáрдов	рублéй
тýсяч	киломéтров
сто	миль - miles
	местá, голосá - seat, votes
	гóда
	лет
семьсóт	тонн
	тóнны (metric tons)
миллиóнов	человéк

TABLE 5:   REFLEXIVE VERBS

1.   Reflexive meaning:

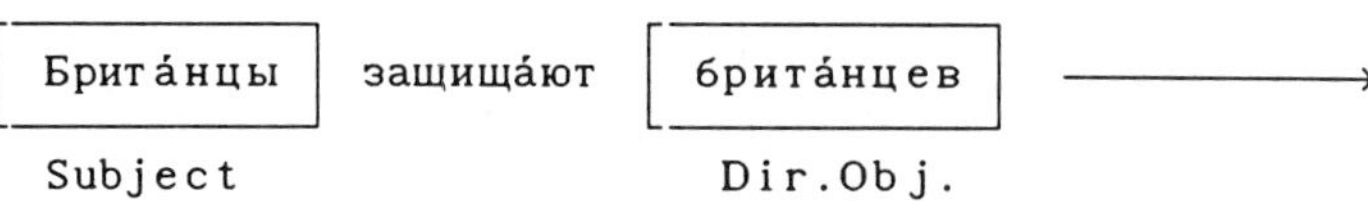

2.   Reciprocal meaning:

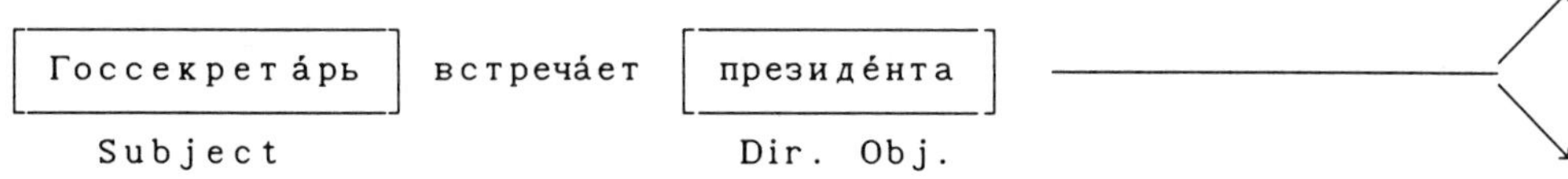

3.   Passive meaning: (with imperfective verbs only)

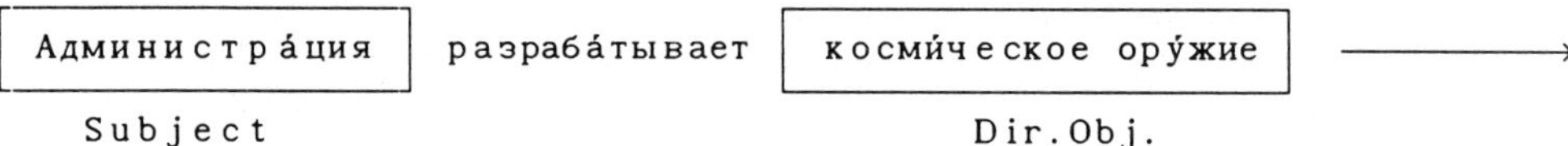

4. After "change of state" transitive verbs with no direct object:

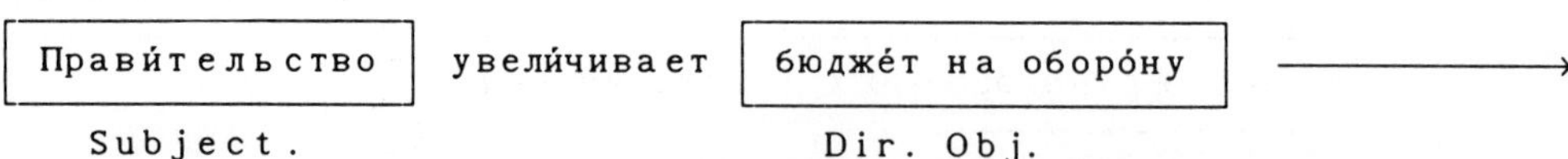

"The British defend themselves"

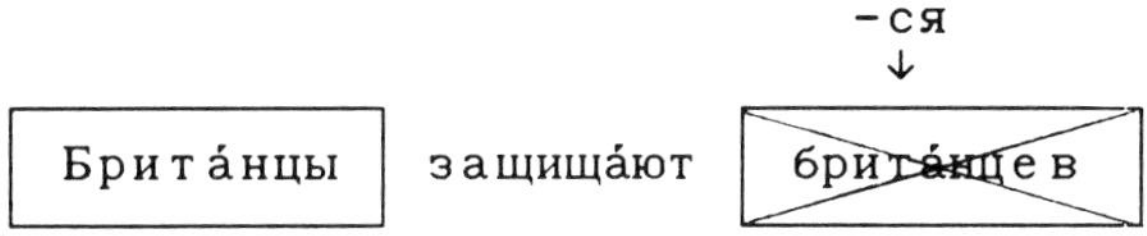

"The Secretary of State and the President meet (each other)"

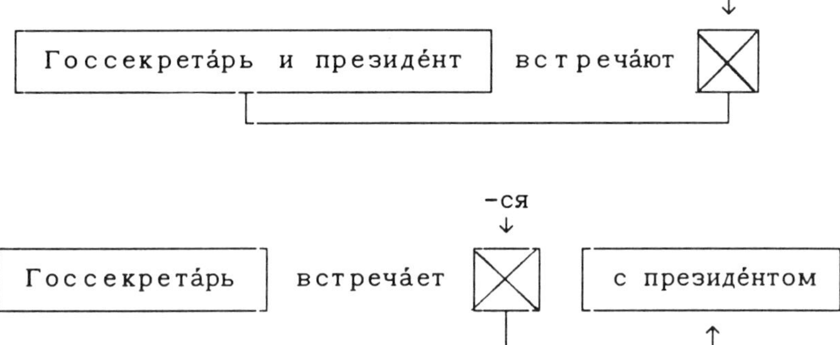

"The Administration is developing space weapons."

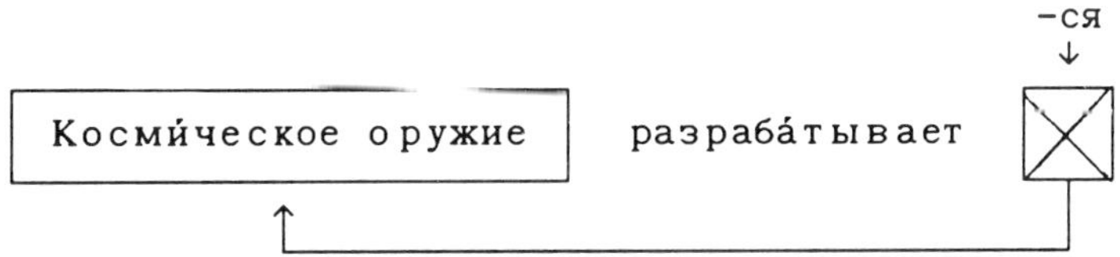

"Defense budget is increasing (itself)"

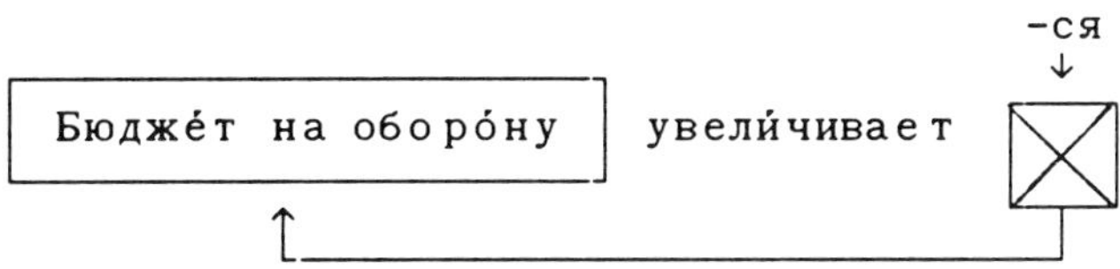

CIRCLE ONE

LESSON THREE

AUDIO-COMPREHENSION EXERCISE

You are about to hear a text about an economic agreement between the Soviet Union and West Germany. You will probably easily recognize the cognates given below. Look through words and expressions listed after the cognates. Before you listen for content, ask yourself whether this item is likely to report new economic ties or Western economic pressure. Then listen to the text with the following questions in mind. Afterwards, listen to the text again, and write down the answers.

1. This meeting had to do with the use of natural resources. Whose? What geographical areas were specifically mentioned?
2. Who led the Soviet delegation?
3. What intergovernmental protocol was signed? For what does it provide?
4. What, according to the report, is the attitude of the West German business community toward trade with the USSR?
5. Two West German officials commented favorably on the new agreement. Name one of them.

Cognates

ресу́рсы
протоко́л
э́кспортно-и́мпортный банк
ба́нковский креди́т
эконо́мика
интере́с
эта́п

WORDS AND EXPRESSIONS (on the tape)

разраба́тывать/разрабо́тать   план – to develop a plan
        -ют   -ют   програ́мму
                    приро́дные ресу́рсы – to develop natural resources
                    ко́смос – to explore space
разрабо́тка приро́дных ресу́рсов
        сырья́ (no plural) – raw materials
        пла́нов
        програ́мм

проводи́ть/провести́   (что?)   (с кем?)
прово́дят проведу́т   переговóры   с ЕЭС
                       бесéды   с СЭВ
                       обмéн мнéниями   с ФРГ
                       разрабóтку кóсмоса
                                  прогрáммы
проведéние

возглавля́ть/возгла́вить   (что?)
      -ют   -ят   делегáцию
                               прави́тельство

      замести́тель   мини́стра внéшней торгóвли

пéрвый замести́тель госсекретаря́ – Deputy Secretary of State
замести́тель госсекретаря́ – Undersecretary
помóщник госсекретаря́ – Assistant Secretary of State

предоставля́ть/предоста́вить   (что?)   (кому?)
      -ют   -ят   креди́т   Совéтскому Сою́зу
                                пóмощь   Изрáилю
предоставлéние креди́та – granting of credit

получа́ть/получи́ть   (что?)   (от кого?)
      -ют полу́чат   креди́т   от Соединённых Шта́тов Амéрики
                      пóмощь   от Изрáиля
получéние пóмощи

(какóй?)   креди́т
долгосрóчный
краткосрóчный
бáнковский
коммéрческий

в соотвéтствии (с чем?)
                с протокóлом
                с договóром
                с заявлéнием

(какие?)   круги́
деловы́е
полити́ческие

закла́дывать/заложи́ть оснóву
      -ют зало́жат

покупа́ть/купи́ть   (что?)   (у кого́?)
   –ют ку́пят   сырьё   у США
                 пшени́цу   у стран Общего ры́нка
                 нефть
поку́пка (no plur) – purchase, purchases

продава́ть/прода́ть   (что?)   (кому?)
продаю́т   продаду́т   стратеги́чески ва́жное обору́дование   ЕЭС
                     сырьё   Еги́пту
                     сверхсовреме́нную те́хнику   hi-tech

прода́жа (no plur) – sale, sales

ЕЭС, Европе́йское экономи́ческое сообщество   EEC
СЭВ, Сове́т экономи́ческой взаимопо́мощи   COMECON
                                           CMEA or
                                           CEMA
                        (in Soviet publications in English)

Междунаро́дный валю́тный фонд – International Monetary Fund
Всеми́рный банк разви́тия и реконстру́кции – The World Bank
ФРГ, Федерати́вная Респу́блика Герма́ния, не́мцы, немецкий, Берли́н, Бонн,
    говори́ть по-неме́цки
Норве́гия, норве́жский, норве́жцы, Осло, говори́ть по-норве́жски
Еги́пет, еги́петский, египта́не, ара́бский, Каир, говори́ть по-ара́бски
Изра́иль, изра́ильский, израильта́не, иври́т (говори́ть на иври́те only), Иерусали́м
Бли́жний Восто́к, ближневосто́чный
Да́льний Восто́к, дальневосто́чный

Стра́ны-чле́ны СЭВ (ceased to exist in 1990):
    [страна́, pl. стра́ны]

НРБ, Наро́дная Респу́блика Болга́рия, болга́рский, Софи́я, говори́ть по-болга́рски
ВР, Венге́рская Респу́блика, Ве́нгрия, венге́рский, Будапе́шт, говори́ть
    по-венге́рски
СРВ, Социалисти́ческая Респу́блика Вьетна́м, вьетна́мский, Хано́й, говори́ть
    по-вьетна́мски
Респу́блика Ку́ба, куби́нский, Гава́на
МНР, Монго́льская Наро́дная Респу́блика, Монго́лия, монгольский, Ула́н-Ба́тор,
    говори́ть по-монго́льски
ПР, По́льская Респу́блика, По́льша, по́льский, Варша́ва, говори́ть по-по́льски
Румы́ния, румы́нский, Бухаре́ст, говори́ть по-румы́нски
ЧСФР, Чехо-Слова́цкая Федерати́вная Респу́блика, Чехослова́кия, че́шский, словацкий,
    Пра́га, говори́ть по-че́шски, Братисла́ва, говори́ть по-слова́цки.

TEXT: Read the following text; be able to translate it into English in written form.

Соглашéние об экономи́ческом сотрýдничестве мéжду СССР и ФРГ

В Бóнне состоя́лись переговóры по совéтско-западногермáнскому сотрýдничеству в разрабóтке прирóдных ресýрсов Сиби́ри и Дáльнего Востóка. С совéтской стороны́ переговóры вели́сь прави́тельственной делегáцией, возглавля́вшейся замести́телем мини́стра внéшней торгóвли. Глáвы делегáций подписáли межправи́тельственный протокóл о предоставлéнии Совéтскому Сою́зу долгосрóчного бáнковского креди́та. В соотвéтствии с подпи́санным протокóлом креди́т предостáвит западногермáнский экспортно-и́мпортный банк.

Деловы́е круги́ ФРГ, ведýщие торгóвлю с СССР, с интерéсом подошли́ к нóвому совéтско-западногермáнскому соглашéнию. Президéнт экспортно-и́мпортного бáнка заяви́л при подписáнии протокóла, что тем сáмым «заклáдываются твёрдые оснóвы совéтско-западногермáнского экономи́ческого сотрýдничества». Мини́стр экономики ФРГ вы́разил надéжду, что совéтская готóвность начáть переговóры с ЕЭС открывáет двéри нóвому этáпу в экономи́ческих свя́зях между Востóком и Зáпадом.

VOCABULARY EXERCISES

Look through the vocabulary for the text *«Соглашéние об экономи́ческом сотрýдничестве мéжду СССР и ФРГ»*, **then do the following exercises.**

A.   Give the plural forms for the following nouns.   Mark the stress.

сообщество
продáжа
креди́т
сырьё
лицó
странá

B. Give perfective forms for the following verbs. Conjugate them in both perfective and imperfective. Mark the stress.

проводи́ть
продава́ть
закла́дывать

C. Give derivative nouns for the following verbs.

продава́ть
покупа́ть
получа́ть
предоставля́ть
проводи́ть
разраба́тывать

D. Give the opposite for the italicized words.

- *краткосро́чный* креди́т
- *покупа́ть* пшени́цу у Еги́пта
- *предоставле́ние* по́мощи
- *бли́жне*восто́чный
- республика́нское *меньшинство́*

E. Fill in the blanks with the appropriate prepositions.

1. В соотве́тствии ____ э́тим заявле́нием мы не бу́дем покупа́ть стратеги́чески ва́жное сырьё ___ Ю́жной А́фрики.
2. ___ бу́дущем ме́сяце делега́ция госдепарта́мента США проведёт перегово́ры ___ представи́телями СЭВ.
3. Приём ___ честь высо́кого го́стя состои́тся ___ четве́рг.
4. ___ после́дние 38 лет Изра́иль получа́ет по́мощь от Соединённых Шта́тов Аме́рики.
5. Сове́тский Сою́з нахо́дится ___ двух контине́нтах.
6. ___ 1978 году́ делега́ция Верхо́вного Сове́та СССР во главе́ Л. Бре́жневым прибыла́ ___ Ве́нгрию.

F. Give Russian equivalents for the following English phrases.

- development of natural resources
- Deputy Secretary of State
- to grant long-term credits to Poland
- to buy raw materials from Mongolia
- sales of hi-tech to Bulgaria
- the World Bank
- EEC
- COMECON

G. Fill in the blanks with appropriate words.

                      (чего?)

1. разрабо́тка _________________
                      ____
                      ____

                      (како́й?)

2. По́льша получи́ла _______________ креди́т
                      ____
                      ____

                      (с чем?)

3. в соотве́тствии с _______________
                      ____
                      ____

                      (что?)   (с чем?)

4. ЧСФР прово́дит _______________ с _______________
                      _______________   _______________
                      _______________   _______________

H. Make sentences with appropriate words from the list in the right hand column.

1)

(Кто?) предоставля́ет	(что?)	(кому́?)
СССР	вое́нную по́мощь	Бли́жний Восто́к
США	экономи́ческую помощь	Чехослова́кия
Великобрита́ния		Вьетна́м
Фра́нция		
ФРГ		
Норве́гия		

2)

(Кто?) покупа́ет	(что?)	(у кого́?)
За́падная Герма́ния		
Изра́иль	сырьё	За́падная Евро́па
Еги́пет	пшени́ца	СССР
Румы́ния	стратеги́чески	Великобрита́ния
Ку́ба	ва́жное обору́до-вание	США
Шве́ция	сверхсовреме́нная те́хника	Еги́пет
		Изра́иль

3)

(Кто?) продаёт	(что?)	(кому́?)
Великобрита́ния	пшени́ца	Восто́чная Герма́ния
Фра́нция	компью́торы	Ве́нгрия
Сове́тский Сою́з	нефть	Монго́лия

I.   Answer the following questions.   (on the tape)

1. Какие заместители есть у госсекретаря?
2. Какую помощь предоставляет СССР Кубе?
3. Какие страны получали военную помощь от СССР?
4. Какие страны получают экономическую помощь от США?
5. Что покупает Израиль у Египта?
6. Где находится самый богатый нефтяной район мира?
7. Что разрабатывает СССР в Сибири?
8. Какие кредиты предоставляет Международный валютный фонд?
9. Какие страны продают стратегически важное сырьё?
10. Что такое ЕЭС?
11. Что такое СЭВ?
12. Назовите страны-члены СЭВ.
13. Что такое ЧСР?
14. Где живут египтяне?
15. На каком континенте находится Израиль?
16. На каком языке говорят в ФРГ?
17. Кто живёт в ГДР?
18. Как называется столица Венгрии?
19. Куба - дальневосточная страна?
20. Где находится Осло?

GRAMMAR: DATIVE CASE

In this chapter we see three of the uses of the dative case: (1) as an indirect object, (2) after the preposition **к**, and (3) after preposition **по**.

1.   Indirect object

An indirect object denotes a person or a thing which receives something from a subject to answer the question **кому́, чему́**.

The pact gives | *us* | new opportunities. (=gives *to us*)
            i.o.   d.o.
Догово́р даёт | *нам* | но́вые возмо́жности.

Sometimes where Russian uses dative, English uses "for" or "to":

The new constitution guarantees   rights | *for all citizens.*
               d.o. | i.o.
Но́вая конститу́ция гаранти́рует   права́ | *всем гра́жданам*

A number of verbs such as **говори́ть/сказа́ть** or **пока́зывать/показа́ть** *naturally* take indirect objects (*to tell* or *show* something *to* someone).   For a more complete list, see the table.

2.   Dative after the preposition K

At last a rule with no exceptions: **к** always takes dative.   K has three basic meanings:

     a.   *towards; up to* (answers *куда, к чему* with verbs of motion):

Прави́тельственная маши́на | The government car pulled
подъе́хала *ко Дворцу́ Съе́здов.* | *up to the Palace of Congresses.*

     b.   *to (a person)* = English *to go to see someone* (answers *к кому́* with verbs of motion):

Они пошли́ *к мини́стру.* | They went *to see the minister.*

Ара́бы то́лько прибегу́т | The Arabs will just run
к ру́сским за креди́тами. | *to the Russians* for credits.

     c.   *by* (plus a time expression):

к концу́ го́да. | *By the end* of the year.

3. Dative after ПО

At first glance **по** appears to be an all-purpose preposition. For the time being learn these set phrases:

a.   *by (a communications medium):*

по телефо́ну, по телеви́зору, по ра́дио, по телегра́фу

b.   *according to; following (a set scale or pattern):*

по Це́льсию, по Фаренге́йту, по слова́м а́втора, по зако́ну

c.   *on (a topic)*

по вопро́су: заявле́ние по вопро́су экономи́ческого разви́тия
по исто́рии: уче́бник по исто́рии КПСС
по сотру́дничеству: перегово́ры по сотру́дничеству

По is also used in pluralized time expressions: *по утра́м – in the mornings*; *по вечера́м, по ноча́м, по понеде́льникам, по вто́рникам,* etc.

GRAMMAR EXERCISES: DATIVE CASE

Read through the material on the dative case. Look through the reference chart at the end of Lesson 3 and the appendix.

A.   Find the forms of the dative in the text. Explain their use.

B.   Answer the following questions using the words in the right-hand column. (Find the exercise on the tape)

1.   По каки́м вопро́сам
     при́няли реше́ние?

   – но́вые торго́вые конта́кты
   – незако́нченный проéкт
   – дальне́йшая рабо́та конфере́нции
   – разрабо́тка ко́смоса

2.   К како́му числу́ сдаду́т
     пе́рвую часть пла́на?

   – нача́ло го́да
   – коне́ц ме́сяца
   – пе́рвое декабря́
   – середи́на кварта́ла

3.   Кому́ сообщи́ли о
     но́вом пла́не?

   – Генера́льная Ассамбле́я ООН
   – все делега́ты конгре́сса
   – то́лько э́ти чле́ны парла́мента
   – изра́ильская делега́ция

4.   Куда́ (к кому́) уе́хал
     наш секрета́рь?

   – свои́ родны́е
   – своя́ семья́
   – глава́ делега́ции
   – пе́рвый замгоссекретаря́
   – помо́щник госсекретаря́

5.   Как сообщи́ли о сме́рти
     космона́втов?

   – телеви́дение
   – телегра́ф
   – телефо́н
   – ра́дио

C.   Answer the questions using dative and accusative where needed according to the model. Be able to translate the answers. (Find the exercise on the tape)

Example: Куда́ они́ при́были?   – мы, на́ша ро́дина
       ⟶ Они́ при́были **к нам** на *на́шу ро́дину.*

1.   Куда́ идёт заммини́стра?   – мини́стр, МИД
2.   Куда́ пое́хали эмигра́нты?   – ро́дственники, Изра́иль
3.   Куда́ прие́хал председа́тель   – Нью-Йо́рк, мэр *(mayor)*
     исполко́ма Москвы́?

4. Куда́ идёт э́та делега́ция?   – Генера́льный секрета́рь,
                                         Центра́льный Комите́т

5. Куда́ при́был глава́   – Сена́т, но́вый ли́дер демокра-
    оппози́ции?   ти́ческого большинства́

**D. Write five sentences to illustrate the use of dative versus accusative
with verbs of motion.**

**E. Fill in the blanks with the correct preposition. Mark Ø if no preposition
is needed.**

1. В своем заявлении ____ корреспондентам ____ вопросу о расширении
    торговых контактов между СЭВ и ЕЭС советский представитель сказал,
    что принятые меры должны войти в силу ____ началу второго
    квартала.

2. ____ вашим словам можно подумать, что вы полностью против нашей
    инициативы ____ урегулированию положения.

3. Представитель Всемирного банка развития и реконструкции сообщил ____
    делегатам, что в настоящих условиях ____ латино-американским
    странам-должникам не может быть предоставлен долгосрочный кредит.

4. В своем выступлении ____ телевизору Генеральный Секретарь
    неоднократно упоминал о только что подписанной договоренности ____
    созданию самостоятельных торговых предприятий.

5. Участники конференции должны прибыть ____ нам в Москву ____ первому
    марта.

6. Мы с ними обычно встречаемся ____ понедельникам и средам.

F. Direct objects versus indirect objects. Fill in the blanks.

1. США отказались продать ___________ _______________.
                              Poland   *raw material*

2. Заместитель министра торговли сообщил _________________ о провале
                                              correspondents
    переговоров.

3. Я _______ коротко расскажу _____________ наших торговых отношений, а
        you   *the history*

    потом попрошу _______ задать ______ вопросы.
                    you   *me*

4. Мы уверены, что ______ окажут __________.
                      us   *support*

5. Президент отправил _______________________ _____________.
                         the General Secretary   *a telegram*

G. Write five sentences to illustrate the use of indirect object versus direct object.

H. Asking and answering. Remember:

спрашивать/спросить – *кого-то о чём-то* (not dative, and cannot add *вопрос*)
but
задавать/задать *кому-то* вопрос
отвечать/ответить *кому-то* на вопрос

Now fill in the blanks.

1. Мы спросили ________________ о предстоящих переговорах, но он
        the chairman

    ______ не ответил ______________.
      us   *the question*

2. Премьер-министр сделал краткое заявление, а потом журналисты

    задавали ______ вопросы.
        him

3. ____________ делегации попросили рассказать ____________ ЦК об
      the head   *members*

    успехах встречи.

4. Ключевые вопросы задавали ________________________ уже после
                            the General Secretary

    пресс-конференции. Интересно, о чём ________ спрашивали?
                                          him

5. По-моему, вы не точно ответили ______________.
                                    our question

I. Review idiomatic uses and time expressions in the dative case chart at the end of Lesson 3. Give Russian equivalents for the following expressions:

- By April 15
- In the President's opinion
- On Thursdays
- They sell raw materials to CMEA

- In the evenings
- Willingness to answer questions
- In his statement to the press
- On Tuesdays
- In his address to the people of Czechoslovakia
- According to the text of the speech
- We will sell raw materials to CMEA.

J.   Write questions for the italicized words below.

1.   Мы не раз доказывали *всем народам* свои добрые намерения.
2.   Прокурор не поколебался: он сразу пошел *к вышестоящим органам.*
3.   Строители выполнят план *к двадцатому декабря.*
4.   Вы должны спросить *Веру Цветкову* о планах комитета.
5.   Вы должны задать этот вопрос *Вере Цветковой.*
6.   Мы пришли *к вам на консультацию.*
7.   В министерстве иностранных дел брифинги обычно бывают *по утрам.*

**K.   Consult the appendix to review cardinal numbers in dative.   Form phrases
with the words below according to the model.   (Write out the numerals!)**

Example: объяснить/ это/ 3/ общественные деятели
$\longrightarrow$ Объясните это трём общественным деятелям.

1.   по/ 2/ важный вопрос
2.   подойти к/ 5/ ракетная система
3.   приказывать / 20/ изранльский солдат
4.   показывать / 40/ официальное лицо

L.   Translate the sentences below.

1.   We asked the economics minister many questions.
2.   We asked him about the next round of negotiations.
3.   The IMF informed Bulgaria that it will extend short-term credit by
     the beginning of next month.
4.   The president's statement to the workers was broadcast on television.
5.   In his speech the deputy minister promised security to the people of
     the United States and Canada.
6.   The Soviet willingness to answer questions about Chernobyl opens the
     door to scientific cooperation.
7.   The undersecretary described for us what happened at the negotiations
     in Geneva.
8.   In my opinion we will be selling raw materials to the CMEA countries.
9.   We came to Moscow to see the head of Gosteleradio.
10. By the beginning of next year we will be meeting three times a week:
     on Mondays, Wednesdays, and Fridays.

GRAMMAR: RUSSIAN PARTICIPLES - INTRODUCTION

Russian participles are a cross between a verb and an adjective. Therefore, they have a double nature – they retain some characteristics of both verbs (tense, voice, case government, reflexive СЯ-ending, etc), and adjectives (gender, number and case).

Look at the phrases below:

	Verb (stem)		Adj. (ending)	
1. Человéк, всегдá	говор	**я́щ**	и й	прáвду
2. Мéры,	принимá	**ем**	ы е	кабинéтом
3. На мостý,	постр ó	**енн**	о м	год назáд
4. Без специалúста,	знак ó ми	**вш**	е го ся	с проблéмой
			(verb)	

1. A man always *telling* the truth.
2. Measures, *adopted* by the cabinet.
3. On the bridge *built* a year ago.
4. Without a specialist, *familiarized* with the problem.

All participles can be substituted with КОТОРЫЙ-clauses.

Человéк, всегдá *говоря́щий* прáвду.
Человéк, *котóрый* всегдá *говорúт* прáвду.

PRESENT ACTIVE PARTICIPLES

Now look at the following sentences and their translations:

Достúгли соглашéния, *предусмáтривающего* (котóрое предусмáтривает) частúчное сокращéние вооружéний.
The reached an agreement providing (which provides) for a partial reduction of weapons.

Это журналúст, *проводя́щий* (котóрый провóдит) расслéдование скандáла с продáжей орýжия Ирáну.
This is a journalist *conducting* (who is conducting) an investigation of the scandal in connection with the weapons sales to Iran.

Гостя́щая в Москвé францýзская делегáция отбывáет зáвтра. (Делегáция, котóрая гостúт)...
The French delegation *staying* (that is staying) in Moscow departs tomorrow.

These are present active participles. They always function as adjectives, and like adjectives, they must agree in gender, number and case with the noun they modify.

These participles modify their antecedents in terms of action in the present and as such they correspond to –**КОТОРЫЙ** clauses with the verb in the present tense. They can be placed before or after the noun they modify.

Это наруше́ние мо́жет име́ть *выходя́щие* за у́зкие ра́мки догово́ра после́дствия.

Это наруше́ние мо́жет име́ть после́дствия, *выходя́щие* за у́зкие ра́мки догово́ра.

This violation may have consequences *exceeding* beyond the narrow limits
    of the treaty.

In English a participle with a modifying phrase comes after the noun as above. Note that in Russian such a participial phrase may precede or follow the noun: (~= the ⟨*exceedng* beyond the narrow limits of the treaty⟩ consequences)

Present active participles are formed only from imperfective verbs and often (but not always!) correspond to the –ing form in English. They can also be rendered by means of pronouns who, which and that.

Some participles are used as adjectival nouns and therefore stand alone.

На́ша па́ртия защища́ет права́ всех *трудя́щихся.*
Our party defends the rights of all the *workers.*

You can identify present active participles by the Щ suffix: *гостя́щая.*

PAST ACTIVE PARTICIPLES

Now look at these sentences and their translations:

    Экспе́рты задава́ли друг дру́гу вопро́сы во вре́мя *дли́вшейся* всю ночь дискуссии.
    Experts were asking each other questions during the discussion, *which
went* all night long.

    В све́те слов и дел, *после́довавших* по́сле встре́чи, появи́лись но́вые вопро́сы.
    New issues have emerged in light of the words and deeds *that followed* the meeting.

The forms you have just seen are **past active participles.** They also agree in gender, number and case with the noun they modify and can stand either before or after that noun.

These participles modify their antecedents in terms of actions in the past and as such, they correspond to **КОТОРЫЙ** clauses with the verb in the past tense.

Эксперты задавали друг другу вопросы во время дискуссии, *которая длилась* всю ночь.

В свете слов и дел, *которые последовали* после встречи, появились новые вопросы.

Past active participles can be formed from both perfective and imperfective verbs. Notice the difference in translation of the verbal aspect in the sentences below:

Вот американский критик, *отмечавший* этот факт.
Here is the American critic, *who was emphasizing* that fact.

Вот американский критик, *отметивший* этот факт.
Here is the American critic, *who had emphasized* that fact.

Past active participles are most often rendered into English by **who**, **which** and **that** clauses.

You can identify past active participles by the ВШ suffix: длившийся.

TABLE 6: ACTIVE PARTICIPLES

	Imperfective	Present Tense	Past Tense
t r a n s i t i v e	**обсужда́ть** to discuss **провожа́ть** to see off	обсужда́ющий discussing провожа́ющий seeing off	обсужда́вший who discussed провожа́вший who saw off
	Perfective		
	обсуди́ть to discuss (to have discussed) **проводи́ть** to have seen off	no present form	обсуди́вший who discussed проводи́вший who saw off

	Imperfective	Present Tense	Past Tense
i n t r a n s i t i v e	**прибыва́ть** to arrive	прибыва́ющий arriving	прибыва́вший who arrived
	Perfective		
	прибы́ть to arrive (to have arrived)	no present form	прибы́вший who arrived

GRAMMAR EXERCISES: PRESENT ACTIVE AND PAST ACTIVE PARTICIPLES

A. **Read all the grammar on active participles. Review their formation. Study Table 6 on the previous page. Find active participles in the text. State their aspect and tense of these participles, as well as their gender, number, and case.**

B. 1) **Make present active participles using the verbs in parentheses below.**

Example: гостить ⟶ они гост **ят** ⟶ гост **ящий**

(предоставлять/предоставить,   продавать/продать,   констатировать, находиться, покупать/купить, состояться)

2) **Now Make perfective and imperfective forms of past active participles out of the same verbs.**

Examples: читать ⟶ чита **л** ⟶ чита **вший**
прочитать ⟶ прочита **л** ⟶ прочита **вший**

C. **Complete the sentences below with the noun and the participle in the proper case. Determine the type of participle. Be able to translate them into English.**

1. Невозможно начать важный диалог между Востоком и Западом

при ____.
(отношения, строящиеся на недоверии)

2. Западной Европе необходимо покупать нефть у_____________________
(страны Ближнего Востока,
____.
продающие её по довольно высоким ценам)

3. Представитель Пентагона ничего не сказал о___________
(встреча,
_____________________________________.
состоявшаяся две недели тому назад в Вашингтоне)

4. Администрация не ответила на ________________________
(перемены, происходившие в
___________________.
Советском Союзе)

5. Деловые круги Японии с интересом подошли к ______________
(предложения,
_____________________________________.
обсуждающиеся в министерствах торговли двух стран)

D. Determine the type of participle in the sentences below. Replace participial constructions with relative clauses. Be able to translate them.

Example: То и дело *подъезжавшие* и *отъезжавшие* от здания Конгресса США машины тормозили движение.

    —→ Машины, *которые* то и дело *подъезжали* и *отъезжали* от здания Конгресса, тормозили движение.

1. Уже *ставшие* достоянием гласности законодательные планы демократов указывают на будущие конфликты между ними и республиканцами.
2. Разве можно замаскировать милитаристскую лихорадку, *охватившую* администрацию США?
3. Вновь прозвучал призыв к плодотворному сотрудничеству, *отвечающему* интересам народов СССР и США.
4. Главы делегаций произнесли речи на *состоявшемся* здесь приёме.
5. Он рассказывал об *осуществляющихся* в СССР мерах по охране окружающей среды.
6. Новые лишения сулит народу *наступающий* год.
7. Среди делегаций, *прибывших* на заседание СЭВ, был наблюдатель от СФРЮ.
8. Штат Белого дома, *устраивавший* приём, не присутствовал на нём.
9. Все газеты писали о канцлере ФРГ, *находящемся* с официальным визитом в Москве.
10. Закон, *избавляющий* население от налогов на машины, вступит в силу в январе.

E. Replace relative clauses in the sentences below with participial constructions. Be able to translate the latter into English.

1. Демократы добились успехов, которые сильно *впечатляют*.
2. Кандидаты, которые *проиграли* на ноябрьских выборах, уезжали.
3. Мы хотим избежать ошибок стран, которые *начали* развиваться раньше.
4. Законодателям придётся заняться проблемами транспорта и окружающей среды, которые постоянно *обостряются*.
5. Советско-американской встрече на высшем уровне, которая *стала* событием международной жизни, посвящён документальный фильм «Трудовой диалог».
6. «Самой успешной встречей» назвал глава американской делегации сессию, которая только что *завершилась*.
7. Председатель Совета Министров СССР, который *находится* здесь по приглашению Президента Финляндской республики, посетил сегодня дом, в котором в августе 1917 года жил В.И. Ленин.
8. Господин Шмидт был главой делегации, которая *находилась* в Москве.
9. Наблюдается явление взаимного обогащения верхушки и корпораций, которые *работают* на войну.
10. Приоритеты, которые *определялись* президентом, неизменно становились национальными приоритетами.
11. Первая сессия Конгресса США 100-ого созыва, которая *начала* свою работу 4 ноября, являет собой «неизвестную величину».

G. Translate the following sentences using participles or participial constructions.

1. According to the radio report, the agreement was signed between banks (which) extend long-term and short-term credits to Egypt.
2. Talks were conducted by the Deputy Secretary of State, who led the American delegation.
3. Among senior officials who were seeing off guests of honor at the airport were First and Second Secretaries of the Moscow City Party Committee. (Московский Горком партии)
4. Departing passengers ought to be on board the plane.
5. You can find this information in the article dealing with Soviet natural resources in the 90's.
6. There was good cooperation among participants, who were exchanging opinions on how to improve relations between the two countries.
7. The session which has now been going on for seven hours will probably come to an end at 8:00 p.m.
8. A demonstration of Moscow workers is in Red Square.
9. According to the author of this article, important agreements were signed at the meeting which took place in the French capital.
10. An important topic of the conference was trade cooperation satisfying the interests of both peoples.

RENDERING

Render. Be careful of where you use ли **and** если. **Remember that as a rule** если **is the wrong word.**

COMECON spokesperson Valentin Somov announced yesterday that COMECON members will jointly produce a new front-wheel drive automobile. According to the announcement, the car, christened the "Sevmobile," will be produced under a complicated arrangement in plants in five countries.

The main assembly plant is to be located in East Germany. The plant will buy parts from other COMECON suppliers. The East Germans will buy basic parts, such as wheels and windshields, from the USSR and Poland, where they are already being manufactured. High tech components, such as computer chips, will be manufactured in Bulgaria and traded for Czech beer. The Czechs will then sell the chips to East Germany.

East Germany plans to put the Sevmobile into production by the beginning of the year. By the end of 1992 production is expected to reach 200,000 units annually. East Germany has already concluded agreements to export the Sevmobile to over 35 countries, both socialist and capitalist.

After the opening statement, Mr. Somov answered questions from consumer group members, who had been invited to participate.

Asked if the car will be competitive with Japanese and German models, Mr. Somov answered that he expects that nearly everyone considering a new car will give the Sevmobile a serious look.

Consumers, of course, want to know how much the car will cost. Somov indicated that Western consumers can expect to pay about $5000 for a basic 90-horsepower model. One participant asked Somov about the availability of spare parts. Somov emphasized that those countries that manufacture parts will supply large shipments of spare parts to any city in which the car is to be sold.

Useful words:
front-wheel drive automobile – автомобиль с передними приводными колёсами
wheel – колесо́; wheels – колеса́
windshield – лобово́вое стекло́; windshields – стёкла
computer chips – микросхе́мы
to be competitive – конкури́ровать
basic model – ба́зовая моде́ль
ninety horsepower – девяносто лошади́ных сил
spare parts – запча́сти
shipment – партия

QUOTING SOURCES:

Media:

по ра́дио

                                сообща́лось, что...

по телеви́дению   о....

                                передава́лось, что...

                                      о ...

According to:

по слова́м а́втора кни́ги ....

по мне́нию а́втора статьи́...

по конститу́ции....

по зако́ну...

SPEAKING EXERCISES

A.   Отве́тьте на сле́дующие вопро́сы по те́ксту уро́ка.

1.   Каки́е перегово́ры состоя́лись в Бо́нне?
2.   Кто вёл перегово́ры с сове́тской стороны́?
3.   Како́й протоко́л подписа́ли гла́вы делега́ций?
4.   Каки́е круги́ ФРГ с интере́сом подошли́ к но́вому соглаше́нию?
5.   Что заяви́л президе́нт э́кспортно-и́мпортного ба́нка?
6.   Чему́ открыва́ет дверь сове́тская гото́вность нача́ть перегово́ры с ЕЭС, по слова́м мини́стра эконо́мики ФРГ?

B.   1)   Расскажи́те текст, испо́льзуя слова́рь Уро́ка 3.

2)   Расскажи́те тот же текст, замени́в:
- уча́стников встре́чи
- ме́сто встре́чи
- те́му бесе́д
- хара́ктер отноше́ний

C.   Соста́вьте ситуа́цию, испо́льзуя сле́дующие выраже́ния.

according to the author of..., International Monetary Fund, to grant a $300 000 000 credit to..., to buy.... from Egypt, development of...., to sell...to..., to lay the foundation for...

D.   Опиши́те докла́д сове́тского замминистра вне́шней торго́вли на заседа́нии Сове́та. Мини́стров о результа́тах его пое́здки в ФРГ.

E.   Происхо́дит заседа́ние директоро́в западногерма́нского э́кспорто-и́мпортного ба́нка. Каки́е аргуме́нты приво́дятся в по́льзу предоставле́ния долгосро́чного креди́та Сове́тскому Сою́зу и про́тив э́того?

F.   Пресс-конфере́нция ка́нцлера ФРГ по́сле подписа́ния догово́ра о предоста́влении креди́та СССР. Вопро́сы либера́льных и консервати́вных журнали́стов.

G.   Речь представи́теля прави́тельства СССР на заседа́нии Верхо́вного Сове́та о перспекти́вах экономи́ческого сотру́дничества ме́жду СССР и ЕЭС. Вопро́сы сове́тских парламента́риев.

READING EXERCISE 1

PRE-TEXT:

Read the text with the following questions in mind:

1.   What is the main idea of the article?
2.   The level of the COMECON meeting in Bucharest was...(check the correct answer):
     a.   heads of state
     b.   heads of government
     c.   ministers of trade
     d.   deputy ministers of trade

3.   Which countries participated?
4.   The People's Republic of Poland was not present at the meeting. Why?
5.   According to the agreement, what conditions will be created for the development of direct relations and effective cooperation of joint enterprises, associations and organizations?
6.   The completion of what kind of program is emphasized in the agreements?
7.   COMECON countries will cooperate in...(true or false for each):
     a.   modernization of productive capacities
     b.   creation of a joint space program
     c.   construction of a new gas pipeline
     d.   economy of resources

Подписаны соглашения

Во время работы 42-й сессии Совета Экономической Взаимопомощи в Бухаресте состоялось подписание на уровне глав правительств двусторонних межправительственных соглашений по вопросам развития прямых производственных и научно-технических связей между хозяйственными организациями СССР и НРБ, ВНР, ГДР и ЧССР, а также о создании совместных предприятий, международных объединений и организаций.

С советской стороны соглашения подписал Председатель Совета Министров СССР Н. И. Рыжков.

Соглашения с правительством ПНР заключены ранее.

Подписанными соглашениями предусматривается создание в странах благоприятных экономических, организационных и правовых условий для развития прямых связей и эффективной деятельности совместных предприятий, объединений и организаций. Определены меры, стимулирующие инициативу хозрасчетных звеньев в развитии между ними научно-технической и производственной кооперации, прежде всего по выполнению заданий Комплексной программы научно-технического прогресса стран—членов СЭВ до 2000 года. Предприятия братских стран будут активно сотрудничать в модернизации и более полном использовании производственных мощностей, экономии ресурсов, увеличении выпуска продукции, отвечающей высшим мировым достижениям.

Достигнута договоренность продолжить работу по дальнейшему вовлечению в эти прогрессивные формы сотрудничества новых предприятий и объединений.

Подписание соглашений знаменует крупный практический шаг в реализации курса XXVII съезда КПСС и съездов других братских партий на развитие новых прогрессивных форм сотрудничества как важного резерва интенсификации прогресса социалистической экономической интеграции.

При подписании присутствовали член Политбюро, секретарь ЦК КПСС Л. Н. Зайков, кандидат в члены Политбюро ЦК КПСС, первый заместитель Председателя Совета Министров СССР Н. В. Талызин, заместитель Председателя Совета Министров СССР, постоянный представитель СССР в СЭВ А. К. Антонов, президент Академии наук СССР Г. И. Марчук.

(ТАСС).

POST-TEXT   (using sentence structure):

Commas can give you clues as to which parts of the sentence are doing what, especially because the use of commas is far more rigid in Russian than in English.

A comma can separate:

1) an enumeration of nouns, adjectives, verbs, abverbs, numerals, prepositional phrases, clauses etc.

Он говорил *долго, медленно, скучно.*

2)   nouns, adjectives, verbs, adverbs, prepositional phrases, etc after: *а,
но, или, ни...ни.., как..., так и...* etc

    Он говорил *медленно,* **но** *интересно.*

3)   independent clauses after *а, но, и, или* etc.

    Промышленность загрязняет воздух, **а** люди им дышат.

4)   subordinate clauses after conjunctions *кто, что, куда, когда, который,
чем, если, хотя, с тех пор, как* etc.

    Речь, *о которой* писали все газеты, произвела сенсацию.

5)   detached words such as:

a)   noun phrases, adjectival phrases, participial phrases which follow a
noun or a pronoun and reflect its number, gender and case.

    Они говорили о Устинове, *новом главе....*
    Мы увидели политика, *знаменитого своей дружбой...*
    В коммюнике, *подписанном вчера,* говорилось о...

b)   adverbal modifiers

    Встретив делегацию, мы повезли её на приём.

6)   author's words

    Соединённые Штаты, *утверждает автор,* не пойдут на уступки.

Do the following exercises:

1. Explain several uses of comma in the first paragraph.
2. Translate the paragraph into English.
3. In the second sentence of paragraph 4, explain the use of the comma after:
   1) *меры*. It is used to separate: (check the correct answer)
      a. an enumeration
      b. a modifier

   2) *кооперации*. It is used : (check the correct answer)
      a. to mark the beginning of a new modifier
      b. to mark the end of a previous modifier

4. Translate the sentence into English.

POST-TEXT   (using context):

1. In paragraph 6 *как* is used in the meaning of...(check the correct answer):
   a. like, similar (comparative)
   b. as, in the quality of.

2. What is the Russian for *COMECON*?
3. What does the Russian abbreviation stand for?
4. Explain the difference between *экономический* and *экономный*. What are the related nouns for each adjective?
5. Find the Russian for *scientific-technological relations*. What are their related nouns?
6. Explain the composition of the word *хозрасчёт*. What is its English equivalent?
7. Make a list of words that you can use to talk about economic cooperation.

READING EXERCISE 2

PRE-TEXT

Read the text with the following questions in mind:

Section 1

1. What is said in this article?
2. Which meeting did the Executive Committee of COMECON convene? (check the correct answer)
   a. 42nd
   b. 121st

3.   The level of participation was...(true or false for each item):
     a.   heads of government
     b.   deputy heads of government
     c.   permanent representatives of the Council
     d.   temporary representatives of the Council

4.   What question did the Executive Committee examine?
5.   How is the mood of the meeting described?

Section 2

1.   What is Section 2 about?
2.   Which of the following statements does the article contain?   (yes –
     no for each)
     a.   Today's regular meeting of the COMECON Committee dealt with
          issues of cooperation in planning.
     b.   Heads of governments participated in this session.
     c.   A representative of the Socialist Federal Republic of Yugoslavia
          was an observer.
     d.   All COMECON member-countries are to take part in the Krivorog
          ore-enriching (ore-refining) facility.

Заседание органов СЭВ

БУХАРЕСТ, 5. (ТАСС). Здесь сегодня состоялось 121-е заседание Исполнительного комитета Совета Экономической Взаимопомощи.

В заседании приняли участие заместители глав правительств, постоянные представители стран в Исполнительном комитете, секретарь Совета.

В заседании участвовал член Союзного исполнительного веча СФРЮ.

Исполнительный комитет рассмотрел вопросы, связанные с организацией работы по реализации постановлений, принятых сессией Совета на 42-м заседании.

Работа Исполнительного комитета проходила в обстановке дружбы и товарищеского сотрудничества.

◇

БУХАРЕСТ, 5. (ТАСС). Здесь сегодня состоялось очередное заседание Комитета СЭВ по сотрудничеству в области плановой деятельности. В его работе приняли участие представители стран — членов СЭВ в комитете, председатели центральных плановых органов стран — членов СЭВ.

В заседании участвовал представитель СФРЮ. В качестве наблюдателя присутствовал представитель НДРЙ.

Комитет рассмотрел вопросы и принял решения по обеспечению выполнения постановлений, принятых на 42-м заседании сессии Совета и на 120-м и 121-м заседаниях Исполнительного комитета СЭВ, по проблемам, входящим в его компетенцию.

На заседании комитета были также обсуждены вопросы реализации мероприятий по сотрудничеству в области экономного и рационального использования топлива и энергии и рассмотрена информация о ходе реализации многостороннего соглашения о сооружении совместными усилиями заинтересованных стран — членов СЭВ Криворожского горно-обогатительного комбината.

(ТАСС).

POST-TEXT (using sentence structure):

1.   Explain how commas are used in paragraph 8.   They are used to mark...
(check the correct answer):
a.   an enumeration
b.   a modifier

2.   Translate this paragraph into English.

POST-TEXT: (using context)

1.   What is the Russian for *executive committee*?   Form the verb for the
Russian adjective.
2.   What does *НДРЙ* stand for?
3.   Point out the cognates in the phrase *председатели центральных
плановых органов.*
4.   What two meaning does the word *глава* have?   Since they are of
different genders, use an adjective with each word.   What is the
derivation of this word?
5.   Paraphrase the italicized word in: «в качестве *наблюдателя*».
6.   What is the English equivalent for ......*обогатительный комбинат*?
What other phrases can you form following this pattern?
7.   Make a list of words that you will need to talk about conferences on
economic cooperation.

READING EXERCISE 3

PRE-TEXT:

Read the text with the following questions in mind:

1.   What is the main idea of the article?
2.   The Chinese Premier's report at the Fourth All-Chinese Congress was
on...(true or false for each item):
a.   a draft of the next five-year plan
b.   results of the previous five-year plan
c.   state of the current plan
d.   change to seven-year pattern

3.   How large was GNP growth for 1980-85?
4.   China has used $10.3 billion.   Where did this money come from?
5.   What are the areas of basic achievement?
6.   Pursuit of super-high rates in production had an effect on...(true
or false for each item):
a.   the general standard of living
b.   the quality of production
c.   the quantity of production
d.   the efficiency of production

7. China will have to lay the foundation for...(true or false for each item):
    a. a new economic system
    b. a new political system
    c. a Chinese-style socialist economic system

8. Can the reorganization be completed within one plan period?
9. China ought to take into account the experience in operative economic management of...(true or false for each item):
    a. countries of the entire world
    b. socialist-bloc countries
    c. the Soviet Union
    d. capitalist countries

Выступление Чжао Цзыяна

ПЕКИН, 29. (ТАСС). На проходящей здесь 4-й сессии Всекитайского собрания народных представителей шестого созыва с докладом о проекте седьмого пятилетнего плана экономического и социального развития КНР (1986—1990 годы) выступил Премьер Госсовета КНР Чжао Цзыян. Подводя итоги минувшего пятилетия, он сообщил, что среднегодовой прирост валового промышленного и сельскохозяйственного производства составил 11 процентов. Удалось остановить сокращение доходной части госбюджета, а в 1985 году — сбалансировать доходы и расходы. За этот период КНР использовала иностранные инвестиции на сумму 10,3 млрд. долларов.

В числе основных достижений Чжао Цзыян отметил осуществление самообеспечения КНР зерном и хлопком, улучшение снабжения населения товарами повседневного спроса, изменение серьезной диспропорции между сельским хозяйством, легкой и тяжелой промышленностью. Это позволило отменить талоны на ряд промышленных товаров, однако по-прежнему сохраняется нормированное распределение муки, круп и растительного масла. Премьер Госсовета указал, что погоня за сверхвысокими темпами в промышленности привела к возникновению факторов нестабильности, сказалась на эффективности производства и качестве продукции.

В течение нынешнего пятилетия или более длительного срока, сказал Чжао Цзыян, предстоит «заложить фундамент социалистической хозяйственной системы нового типа, имеющей китайскую специфику». Проект пятилетнего плана предусматривает увеличение валовой продукции промышленности и сельского хозяйства на 33 процента. Будет подготовлено около 5 миллионов специалистов с высшим образованием, начнется введение обязательного девятилетнего обучения.

Глава правительства КНР подчеркнул, что в силу чрезвычайной сложности задач перестройки хозяйственной системы ее реформа не может быть завершена в течение начавшейся седьмой пятилетки. Будет создан только «каркас новой хозяйственной системы». В этой связи он призвал «серьезно изучать и учитывать весь передовой опыт оперативно-хозяйственного управления, накопленный странами мира, в том числе и развитыми капиталистическими государствами».

Чжао Цзыян отметил необходимость в области внешнеэкономических связей Китая «поставить во главу угла увеличение притока иностранной валюты за счет расширения экспорта».

POST–TEXT (using sentence structure):

Reading rule 1: (continued from lessons 1 and 2)

Here are two more situations when "the doer" in the nominative case is missing:

c) Such verbs as *удаваться, хотеться, предстоять* + **infinitive** require the use of *Impersonal construction*, where the "doer" is either missing or is used in the dative case.

> Никому *не хотелось воевать.*

d) Sometimes the demands of Russian grammar *disguise* the "doer" in genitive clothing. The predicate in such sentences is in the singular.

> *Большинство военнопленных* вернулось домой.

Do the following exercises:

1. Explain uses of comma in the second sentence of paragraph one.   Now, look at the picture below. This is the table of your sentence.

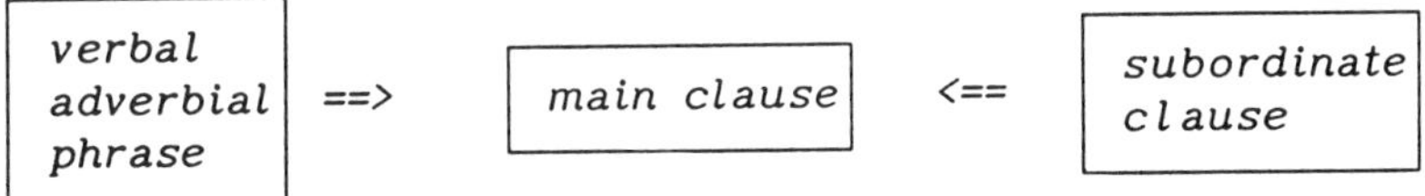

   a. Above the arrow to the left of the main clause write the word which is modified by the verbal adverbial phrase.

   b. Above the arrow to the right of the main clause write the word which....(check the correct answer):
     1. is modified by the subordinate clause.
     2. to which the subordinate clause is an object.

2. Translate the sentence into English.

3. There are three "no subject" sentences in this article. Find them and explain why the "doer" is missing. There is no "doer" in the nominative case because....(check the correct answer):
   a. *они–*construction is used.
   b. this is a "disguised" subject.
   c. this is an impersonal construction.

4. Translate these sentences into English.

POST–TEXT (using context):

1. What is the English for *Всекитайское собрание*? Break the adjective down to its parts. What other phrases can you form following this pattern?
2. Find the Russian for *profit and expenses*. What do these nouns have in common? Can you think of other derivatives for these Russian words?
3. Find a synonym for *товары широкого употребления* in the article.
4. What two types of industries are mentioned in the article? What is the difference between them?
5. *За счёт* means (a) *through* and (b) *at the expense of*. Which meaning does it have in the text?
6. Make a list of words that you will use to talk about various branches of economy and economic planning.

READING EXERCISE 4

PRE–TEXT:

Read the text with the following questions in mind:

1. What is the main point in this story?
2. Soviet Foreign Minister Schevardnadze was in Afghanistan for...(check the correct answer):
    a.   an official visit
    b.   an unofficial visit
    c.   a working visit
    d.   a secret visit

3. Whom did he meet there?
4. The meeting participants discussed practical issues of Soviet–Afghanistan relations at the stage of...(check the correct answer):
    a.   national reconciliation
    b.   escalation of the war
    c.   Soviet troop withdrawal
    d.   civil war

5. Which political line put forth by the Afghanistan government did the Soviets fully support?

6.   What is the role of the UN General Secretary's representative in Afghanistan?
7.   Hope was expressed that all forces involved in the conflict will.... (true or false for each):
     a.   solve the problem by political means
     b.   form a joint national government
     c.   realistically approach the Afghan proposal
     d.   create the conditions for an open dialogue

8.   Which kinds of economic cooperation with the USSR were emphasized?
9.   Among urgent international problems discussed at the meeting were... (true or false for each item):
     a.   an end to the arms race
     b.   non-proliferation of the arms race in space
     c.   creation of a general security system
     d.   the US–USSR summit

10. How did the Soviet side explain the end of the nuclear detonations moratorium?

ВИЗИТ В ДРА

По приглашению ЦК НДПА и правительства ДРА 5—7 января в Демократической Республике Афганистан находились с рабочим визитом член Политбюро ЦК КПСС, министр иностранных дел СССР Э. А. Шеварднадзе и секретарь ЦК КПСС А. Ф. Добрынин. Они имели беседы с Генеральным секретарем ЦК НДПА Наджибом, членом Политбюро ЦК НДПА, Председателем Совета Министров ДРА С. А. Кештмандом, членом Политбюро ЦК НДПА, министром иностранных дел ДРА А. Вакилем, другими афганскими руководителями.

В развитие принципиальных договоренностей, достигнутых между М. С. Горбачевым и товарищем Наджибом на встрече в Москве, были обсуждены практические вопросы советско-афганских отношений на этапе национального примирения в Афганистане. С советской стороны была дана высокая оценка решениям чрезвычайного расширенного пленума ЦК НДПА, выражена полная поддержка политическому курсу афганского руководства, его далеко идущим шагам, направленным на создание условий для начала открытого общеафганского диалога с целью установления мира в стране и образования правительства национального единства. Было подтверждено, что советское руководство всецело одобряет линию ЦК НДПА и правительства ДРА на скорейшее достижение через личного представителя генерального секретаря ООН политического урегулирования положения вокруг Афганистана, в рамках которого будет согласован и вопрос о сроке вывода советских войск. Афганская сторона может рассчитывать на конструктивное сотрудничество Советского Союза в деле выработки и осуществления такого соглашения о политическом урегулировании, которое отвечает интересам афганского народа и будет способствовать установлению прочного мира и общенационального согласия в Афганистане. Была выражена надежда, что все силы, вовлеченные в борьбу внутри Афганистана, и все круги, причастные к вмешательству извне в дела ДРА, серьезно и реалистически подойдут к предложению афганского правительства о прекращении огня и воспользуются предоставленной им возможностью политическими средствами в условиях национального примирения решить интересующие их вопросы. Тот, кто не сделает этого, возьмет на себя ответственность за продолжение кровопролития, за страдания афганского народа и за обострение международной обстановки.

В ходе переговоров в Кабуле состоялся обмен мнениями о путях интенсификации советско-афганского сотрудничества в различных сферах. Было подчеркнуто стремление к расширению экономических связей, увеличению товарооборота между двумя странами, использованию новых перспективных форм сотрудничества, в частности путем создания смешанных предприятий с участием афганского частного сектора. Достигнута договоренность о развитии взаимных обменов в области науки, техники и культуры, а также об углублении дружественных разносторонних связей между КПСС и НДПА.

Были рассмотрены актуальные международные проблемы, прежде всего касающиеся прекращения гонки вооружений и недопущения ее распространения на космос, создания всеобъемлющей системы международной безопасности, формирования системы безопасности на Азиатском континенте. При этом отмечалось, что конструктивной основой для борьбы миролюбивых сил за ликвидацию ядерных и других видов оружия массового уничтожения является программа действий, изложенная М. С. Горбачевым в Заявлении от 15 января 1986 года.

Информируя товарища Наджиба о решении СССР прекратить односторонний мораторий на ядерные взрывы после первого ядерного взрыва в США, советские представители подчеркнули, что эта мера является вынужденной, продиктованной интересами безопасности СССР и его союзников. Они подтвердили готовность Советского Союза добиваться достижения договоренностей о прекращении ядерных испытаний.

С афганской стороны было выражено понимание мотивов, побудивших Советское правительство принять это решение, дана высокая оценка советским мирным инициативам, конструктивной и ответственной линии Советского Союза в международных делах.

Встречи и беседы прошли в атмосфере полного взаимопонимания и товарищества.

POST–TEXT (using sentence structure):

1. Explain the uses of comma in the second sentence of the second paragraph. Draw a table of this sentence.(see **Reading exercise 3** above.)
2. Translate it into English.
3. In the third sentence find the word which is modified by a *который* clause.
4. Translate the sentence into English.
5. In the *что-*clause (sentence 5):
   a. find a predicate (predicates) for the subject *«силы»*.
   b. find the words, modified by *вовлечённые* and *причастные.*

6. Translate the sentence into English.

POST–TEXT (using context):

1. What are the inhabitants of Afghanistan called?
2. What derivatives does the word *примирение* have?
3. *Рамка* means *frame*. What is the English for *в рамках...?*
4. Explain the use of the preposition *от* in *заявление от 15 января.*
5. Make a list of words that you can use to talk about an intensification of cooperation.

DATIVE CASE

USES:	PREPOSITIONS:	QUESTION:	VERBS:
Indirect Object	---	Кому́? Чему́?	Natural indirect object: давáть покáзывать покупáть сказáть объяснять и т.д.
"Dative Objects"			Dative objects: помогáть спосóбствовать мешáть принадлежáть прикáзывать угрожáть и т.д.
Direction of Movement	К (towards, in the direction of)	Куда́? К чему́? К кому́?	verbs of motion
Location	ПО (along)	Где? Вдоль чего́?	

TIME-EXPRESSIONS:	USEFUL IDIOMS:

TIME-EXPRESSIONS:

к концу́ го́да
к нача́лу января́
к середи́не фина́нсового
     го́да

к пе́рвому кварта́лу

по суббо́там
по сре́дам
по утра́м
по вечера́м

USEFUL IDIOMS:

Impersonal construction:

1) на́до, ну́жно

2) мо́жно, невозмо́жно
    нельзя́ - forbidden
             - impossible

3) ну́жно, интере́сно, ску́чно,
    неудо́бно и т.д.

4) каза́ться, удава́ться - to succeed
    хоте́ться, нра́виться и т.д.

ПО телефо́ну, телеви́зору, ра́дио
    по́чте
ПО вопро́су..., исто́рии, фи́зике
    эконо́мике - on economics
ПО Це́льсию, Фаренге́йту, пра́вилу,
    зако́ну, конститу́ции
    - according to the constitution
ПО слова́м (а́втора)
    - according to the author
е́здить ПО стране́
    - travel around the country

отвеча́ть кому́-то на вопро́с
- to answer somebody's question
обраща́ться к... - to make an
                  address to
обраще́ние к... - an address to

гото́виться к... - to get ready for

призыва́ть к... - to call for

Learn also:

по-мо́ему, по-тво́ему,
    по-ва́шему

but

по его́ мне́нию, по её мне́нию,
    по их мне́нию

CIRCLE ONE

LESSON FOUR

AUDIO-COMPREHENSION EXERCISE

You are about to hear a text about an economic summit in Tokyo. You will probably easily recognize the cognates given below. Look through words and expressions listed after the cognates. Then listen to the text with the following questions in mind. Afterwards, listen to the text again, and write down the answers.

1. Economic summit meetings of the heads of the Western industrialized powers were initiated in the early seventies and have become a yearly fixture on presidential agendas. What do you already know about such meetings? What questions are usually discussed?
2. Which heads of government met in Tokyo?
3. What issue on the agenda was mentioned first?
4. On other issues the report said that a number of agreements were reached. What agreement was reached to improve the world trade balance?
5. What proposals did the U.S. make?
6. How was the meeting characterized?

Cognates

програ́мма
конкре́тные ме́ры
террори́зм
ли́дер
капиталисти́ческий
фина́нсовая систе́ма
реалисти́ческий курс
бала́нс
протекциони́зм
партнёр
техни́ческий
стратеги́ческая инициати́ва
пробле́ма
констру́ктивный хара́ктер

WORDS AND EXPRESSIONS (on the tape)

завершѝлись переговóры глав государств и правѝтельств
                         ведýщих стран Зáпада
                         ближневостóчных стран
завершáть/завершѝть
    –ют   –áт
завершéние
   (conclusion)

выражáть/   решѝмость   разрабóтать прогрáмму
    –ют   укрепѝть международную финáнсовую систéму
вы́разить
    –ят
выражéние

мéры по борьбé   (с чем?) – measures against
                  с террорѝзмом
                  с протекционѝзмом
                  с энергетѝческим крѝзисом

уделять/ внимáние   (чему?)
    –ют   проблéме экономѝческого сотрýдничества
уделѝть   укреплéнию международной финáнсовой систéмы
   –ят   сокращéнию учётных стáвок – reduction of interest
                                     rates

ряд вáжных договорённостей (о чем?)
                  о бóлее реалистѝческом кýрсе обмéна валю́т
                       – hard-currency exchange
                  о дальнéйшем сокращéнии учётных стáвок
                  об искýсственном поощрéнии э́кспорта
                     – artificial export encouragement

(какое?)   сотрýдничество
торгóвое
технѝческое
наýчно-технѝческое
торгóво-экономѝческое

наýка и тéхника
тéхника (no plural)
наýчный
технѝческий

приводи́ть/привести́   (к чему?)
приво́дят/приведу́т   к выра́вниванию торго́вого бала́нса –the leveling up of
                                                  the trade balance

                           к протекциони́стским ме́рам

                           к экономи́ческому кри́зису

экспорти́ровать   (что?)   (куда́?)
        -уют   нефть(fem)   в Япо́нию
(no perf.form)   у́голь(masc)   в Кита́й
                      ура́н   в ФРГ
                      пшени́цу   в Еги́пет
э́кспорт (no plur) – export, exports

импорти́ровать   (что?)   (откуда?)
        -уют   обору́дование   из Великобрита́нии
(no perf. form)   алма́зы   из Юго-восто́чной Азии
и́мпорт (no plur) – import, imports

в ра́мках програ́ммы СОИ (стратеги́ческой оборо́нной инициати́вы)
                                                 – in the framework of SDI

        Общего ры́нка
        СЭВ

носи́ть   (какой?)   хара́ктер
но́сят   делово́й
          конструкти́вный
          дру́жеский
          форма́льный
(no perf. form)

Япо́ния, япо́нский, япо́нцы, говори́ть по-япо́нски, на япо́нском языке́, То́кио
Кита́й, кита́йский, кита́йцы, говори́ть по-кита́йски, на кита́йском языке́, Пеки́н
Да́льний Восто́к, дальневосто́чный
Индия, инди́йский, инди́йцы, говори́ть на хи́нди (only), Де́ли
Южная Азия, южноазиа́тский
Юго-Восто́чная Азия

Стра́ны-чле́ны ЕЭС:

Бе́льгия, бельги́йцы, говори́ть по-флама́ндски, Брюссе́ль
Великобрита́ния, Ло́ндон (Lesson 2)
Голла́ндия, голла́ндский, голла́ндцы, говори́ть по-голла́ндски, Гаа́га
Гре́ция, гре́ческий, гре́ки, говори́ть по-гре́чески, Афи́ны
Да́ния, да́тский, датча́не, говори́ть по-да́тски, Копенга́ген
Ита́лия, италья́нский, италья́нцы, говори́ть по-италья́нски, Рим
Испа́ния, испа́нский, испа́нцы, говори́ть по-испа́нски, Мадри́д
Ирла́ндия, ирла́ндский, ирла́ндцы, говори́ть по-гэ́льски, Ду́блин

Люксембу́рг, люксембу́ржцы, Люксембу́рг
Португа́лия, португа́льский, португа́льцы, говори́ть по-португа́льски, Лисабо́н
    (Лиссабо́н)
Фра́нция, Пари́ж (Lesson 1)
ФРГ, Бонн (Lesson 3)

TEXT: Read the following text; be able to translate it into English in written form.

Встре́ча в То́кио

В То́кио заверши́лись перегово́ры глав госуда́рств и прави́тельств веду́щих стран За́пада. Высо́кие догова́ривающиеся сто́роны вы́разили реши́мость разрабо́тать програ́мму конкре́тных мер по борьбе́ с расту́щим в ми́ре террори́змом.

Гла́вное внима́ние ли́деры капиталисти́ческого ми́ра удели́ли пробле́ме экономи́ческого сотру́дничества. Уча́стникам перегово́ров удало́сь заключи́ть ряд ва́жных соглаше́ний по вопро́сам торго́вли и укрепле́ния междунаро́дной фина́нсовой систе́мы. В ча́стности, была́ дости́гнута договорённость о дальне́йшем сокраще́нии учётных ста́вок и бо́лее реалисти́ческом ку́рсе обме́на валю́т стран-уча́стников перегово́ров. Это, в свою́ о́чередь, должно́ привести́ к выра́вниванию торго́вого бала́нса. Соотве́тственно, отпадёт необходи́мость как в протекциони́зме, так и в иску́сственном поощре́нии э́кспорта, проводи́мых администра́цией.

Администра́ция США та́кже обрати́лась к партнёрам по перегово́рам с предложе́нием расши́рить програ́мму нау́чного и техни́ческого сотру́дничества в ра́мках стратеги́ческой оборо́нной инициати́вы.

По оце́нкам обозрева́телей, перегово́ры, хотя́ и не реши́ли мно́гих пробле́м, спосо́бствовали взаимопонима́нию по ключевы́м вопро́сам междунаро́дной торго́вли. Встре́ча носи́ла дру́жеский и конструкти́вный хара́ктер.

VOCABULARY EXERCISES

Look through the vocabulary for the text «Встре́ча в То́кио», then do the following exercises.

A.   Give the plural forms for the following nouns. Mark the stress.

глава́
страна́
нау́ка
те́хника
систе́ма
э́кспорт
и́мпорт
ры́нок

B.   Give perfective forms for the following verbs. Conjugate them. Mark the stress.

импорти́ровать
носи́ть (хара́ктер)
выража́ть
уделя́ть

C.   Give derivatives of the following words.

заверше́ние
экспо́рт и и́мпорт
выраже́ние
нау́ка и те́хника
делово́й
дру́жеский
торго́вый
договорённость
экономи́ческий

D.   Paraphrase the italicized words.

переговоры *окончились*
ЕЭС
ме́ры *против* террори́зма
уменьше́ние э́кспорта
вывози́ть нефть
програ́мма «*звёздные во́йны*»
носи́ть *делово́й* хара́ктер

E.   Give the opposite for the italicized words.

импортировать
увеличение учётных ставок
естественное поощрение
начать переговоры
ослабить финансовую систему

F.   Fill in the blanks with the appropriate prepositions.

1.   В СССР были приняты строгие меры ＿＿ борьбе с алкоголизмом.
2.   Срок договорённости ＿＿ научно-техническом сотрудничестве истекает ＿＿ следующем месяце.
3.   ＿＿ чему приводит политика протекционизма?
4.   Какие страны находятся ＿＿ рамках Варшавского договора?
5.   Многие западноевропейские страны импортируют нефть ＿＿ стран Ближнего Востока.
6.   Кто покупает стратегически важное сырьё ＿＿ СССР?

G.   Give Russian equivalents of the following English phrases.

- further reduction of interest rates
- artificial export encouragement
- science and technology
- to be of a business like character
- leveling up of a trade balance
- to import uranium
- within the framework of SDI
- leading capitalist countries

H.   Fill in the blanks with appropriate words.

(чему?)
1.   Стороны уделили внимание ＿＿＿＿＿＿＿
＿＿＿＿＿＿＿
＿＿＿＿＿＿＿

(какое?)
2.   ＿＿＿＿＿＿＿ сотрудничество успешно развивается
＿＿＿＿＿＿＿
＿＿＿＿＿＿＿

(чего?)
3.   Важно расширить программу в рамках ＿＿＿＿＿＿＿
＿＿＿＿＿＿＿
＿＿＿＿＿＿＿

4. Переговóры носи́ли _____________ (какóй?) хара́ктер
    ____
    ____

5. Уча́стники обсуди́ли ряд _____________ (чегó?)
    ____
    ____

I. Make sentences with appropriate words from the list in the right-hand column.

1) протекциони́зм   мóжет привести́   (к чему́?)

поощре́ние поли́тики Ира́на
сокраще́ние учётных ста́вок
разрабóтка СОИ
высóкие це́ны на нефть
выра́внивание торгóвого бала́нса
экономи́чское сотру́дничество
продáжа ору́жия
разрабóтка кóсмоса

дальне́йший прогре́сс нау́ки
    и те́хники
экономи́ческий кри́зис
укрепле́ние междунарóдной
финáнсовой систе́мы
мировáя войнá
междунарóдный террори́зм
дру́жеские отноше́ния в ми́ре

2) ФРГ   импорти́рует   (что?)   (отку́да?)

США   импорти́руют   сырьё   Сове́тский Сою́з
Пóльша   высокосовреме́нная   Бли́жний Востóк
Изра́иль   те́хника   Южная АФрика
СССР   нефть   Ку́ба
Шве́ция   алма́зы   Соединённые
    пшени́ца   Штáты Аме́рики
    стратеги́чески   Еги́пет
    вáжное обору́дование
    са́харный тростни́к

J. Answer the following questions.   (on the tape)

1. Что такóе ЕЭС?
2. Каки́е стрáны-чле́ны ЕЭС вы знáете?
3. Каки́е ви́ды сотру́дничества существу́ют ме́жду э́тими стрáнами?
4. Каки́е ви́ды сотру́дничества существу́ют между США и СССР?
5. К чему́ привóдит разв́итие нау́ки и те́хники?
6. К чему́ привóдит поощре́ние террори́зма?
7. Что импорти́рует Индия? Отку́да?
8. Что экспорти́руют США в Китáй?
9. Что импорти́рует Зáпадная Еврóпа из СССР?

10.   В ра́мках чего́ прохо́дит экономи́ческое сотру́дничество ме́жду СССР и стра́нами наро́дной демокра́тии?
11.   Что тако́е СОИ?
12.   Како́й хара́ктер но́сят америка́но-сове́тские отноше́ния?
13.   Како́й хара́ктер но́сят отноше́ния ме́жду стра́нами-чле́нами СЭВ?
14.   Како́й хара́ктер но́сят отноше́ния ме́жду стра́нами-чле́нами ЕЭС?
15.   Кто живёт в Индии?
16.   На како́м языке́ они́ говоря́т?
17.   Кто живёт в Бе́льгии?
18.   На како́м языке́ они́ говоря́т?
19.   Как называ́ется столи́ца Гре́ции?
20.   Кита́й нахо́дится в Юго-Восто́чной Азии?
21.   На како́м контине́нте нахо́дится Португа́лия?
22.   Шве́ция нахо́дится на ю́ге Евро́пы?

GRAMMAR: DATIVE CASE (Continued)

In this lesson we see more uses of the dative:

1.   **In impersonal constructions where "the doer" is either missing, a general statement, or in the dative case.**

Impersonal constructions can express:

a.   Need:

Нам **ну́жно** поду́мать об э́том.	We have to think this over.
Нам **на́до** поду́мать об э́том.	(Lit.: To us is necessary to think this over.)

Note that *на́до* is restricted to infinitives: **на́до поду́мать** – It is necessary *to think*. **Ну́жно** can change gender to allow "needing" for nouns.

b.   "Permitted/possible"   and   "forbidden/impossible."   Look   at   the following sentences:

Вам **мо́жно** позвони́ть домо́й.	You can call home. (To you is permitted/possible to call home.)
Вам **нельзя́** звони́ть домо́й.	You must not call home.
Вам **нельзя́** позвони́ть домо́й.	You can not call home. (physically impossible)

To sum up:
мо́жно – permitted *or* possible; takes both aspects
невозмо́жно – physically impossible; takes both aspects, it is always
     a general statement and is never usedwith dative.
нельзя́ + imperfective – forbidden
нельзя́ + perfective – impossible

c.   Physical or emotional states of being. Note these sentences:

Ему́ **ску́чно**.	He's bored (Lit.: To him
Ему́ бы́ло **ску́чно**	is/was boring.)
Ей **интере́сно**.	She's interested.
Ей бы́ло **интере́сно**.	She was interested.
Нам **неудо́бно**.	We're uncomfortable.
Нам бы́ло **неудо́бно**.	We were embarrassed.

Всем **ясно**.	It's clear to all.
Всем бы́ло **ясно**.	It was clear to all.
Всем **изве́стно**	Everyone is aware (that...)

As you can see impersonal constructions often refer to physical or mental states and are formed with a dative plus an adverbial form ending in −o.

Where the context is clear, impersonal constructions usually stand alone, as a general statement without a dative:

Ну́жно поду́мать.	It is necessary to think things over.
Ску́чно слу́шать.	It's boring to listen.

d.   Constructions with verbs. Learn the following set phrases:

кому́...

    хо́чется (де́лать что-то) – feels like (doing smthng)
    хоте́лось (де́лать что-то) – felt like (doing smthng)
    ка́жется, что... – seems that...
    каза́лось, что... – seemed that...
    уда́стся (сде́лать что-то) – will manage
    удаётся (сде́лать что-то) – manages (to do smthng)
    удало́сь (сде́лать что-то) – managed

2. **The following verbs take dative objects:**

помога́ть/помо́чь:помогу́, помо́жешь, помо́гут, помо́г, помогли́
спосо́бствовать: спосо́бствую
меша́ть/помеша́ть (кому́-то) де́лать (что-то)
принадлежа́ть: принадлежу́, принадлежи́шь, принадлежа́т
прика́зывать/приказа́ть: прикажу́, прика́жешь, прика́жут
угрожа́ть

3. Idioms:

обраща́ться/обрати́ться к (кому́-то, чему́-то) – to turn (to someone)

Конгре́сс обрати́лся
к мирово́й обще́ственности.

The Congress turned *to the world public at large.*

гото́виться/подгото́виться к (чему́-то) – to prepare for

Страна́ гото́вится к вы́борам.

The country is preparing *for elections.*

призыва́ть/призва́ть (призовёшь) к (чему́-то) – to call for

СССР призва́л к созда́нию
комите́та по э́тому вопро́су.

The USSR called *for the creation* of a committee on this issue.

приводи́ть/привести́ (приведу́, приведёшь, привёл, привела́) к (чему́-то) –
to lead to, to bring about

Это приведёт к расшире́нию
конта́ктов.

That will bring about a
broadening of contacts

GRAMMAR: *ASKING* AND **ASKING** – QUESTIONS *VERSUS* REQUESTS

Consider the following sentence and its translation:

Она *попросила* меня *спросить*   She *asked* me to *ask* you about it.
вас об э́том.

The verb for "request" is **проси́ть** (прошу́, про́сишь, про́сят) / **попроси́ть**, while "inquire" is **спра́шивать** / **спроси́ть** (спрошу́, спро́сишь, спро́сят).   Both verbs take accusative, not dative.

GRAMMAR EXERCISES: DATIVE CASE (Continued)

A. Read over the grammar on dative case in this lesson.   Review the dative case chart at the end of Lesson 3.   Then read over the text.   Find all the places where dative is used and determine the reason for each occurence.

B. Answer the questions using the words in the right-hand column. (Find the exercise on the tape)

1.   Кому́ ну́жен про́чный мир?

   –Все лю́ди на плане́те
   –европе́йцы
   –жи́тели двух стран
   –Индия и Пакиста́н
   –ва́ша страна́

2.   Кому́ нельзя́ критикова́ть прави́тельство в э́той стране́?

   –любо́й ле́вый писа́тель
   –изве́стные диссиде́нты
   –люба́я неофициа́льная организа́ция

3.   Кому́ бу́дет неудо́бно пе́ред на́ми?

   –чле́ны профсою́за, обеща́вшие не бастова́ть.
   –на́ши конкуре́нты
   –люба́я сторона́, нару́шившая догово́р

4.   Кому́ удало́сь заключи́ть ряд соглаше́ний?

   –уча́стники делега́ции, проводи́вшие переговоры всю ночь.
   –ли́деры двух стран
   –премье́р-мини́стр Индии и президе́нт Фра́нции
   –госсекрета́рь и мини́стр иностра́нных дел

5. К кому́ обрати́лся глава́
делега́ции?

—все, жела́ющие ми́ра на плане́те
—мирова́я обще́ственность
—обще́ственные организа́ции

6. Чему́ спосо́бствует
перестро́йка?

—нау́чно-техни́ческий прогре́сс
—увеличе́ние конта́ктов ме́жду людьми́
—техни́ческий прогре́сс
—экономи́ческое разви́тие
—дальне́йшая реконстру́кция

7. Чему́ угрожа́ет догово́р?

—о́бщее взаимопонима́ние ме́жду
       на́шими наро́дами
—расшире́ние торго́вых свя́зей
—разрабо́тка ко́смоса

8. Кому́ принадлежа́т э́ти а́кции?

—ча́стные компа́нии
—госуда́рство
—за́падногерма́нская фи́рма

9. К чему́ приво́дит
протекциони́зм?

—ни́зкое ка́чество проду́кции
—иску́сственное поощре́ние э́кспорта
—выра́внивание торго́вого бала́нса.

10. Кому́ э́то изве́стно?

—все, живу́щие на плане́те
—америка́нские учёные
—ли́деры всех стран

**C. Change the following должен expressions to надо expressions.   Study
Table 9 at the end of Lesson 4. Pay close attention to tense.**

Example: Мы должны были приготовить лекцию.
  $\longrightarrow$ *Нам надо было приготовить лекцию.*

1. Сотрудники данных предприятий должны принимать меры для повышения
качества обслуживания.
2. Лица, проживающие за границей, все равно должны платить налоги.
3. Представитель ЕЭС должен был прочитать доклад на заседании СЭВ.
4. Эти корреспонденты должны будут изучать новый иностранный язык.
5. Председатель комиссии должен был признаться в некоторых ошибках.

D. Translate the sentences below.

1. Our country needs a new economic policy.
2. We will have to work out a program of measures on terrorism.
3. The Irish living in Northern Ireland have to negotiate with the
English who live there.
4. Third World leaders will have to turn to the Soviet Union.

5.   Our people needed an effective financial system.
6.   Everyone will need schools and universities.

E.   Review the use of мочь, должен, нужно, нельзя.   Translate the sentences below expressing various nuances of "permitted/possible" and "forbidden/impossible."   Leave out the dative object where it is not absolutely necessary.

1.   We musn't pay too much attention to the question of protectionism.
2.   We can reach an agreement on imports this year.
3.   Members of the delegation must not forget about our problems.
4.   Oil must not be exported to that country.
5.   We were not allowed to meet with representatives of trade organizations.
6.   The congressmen were allowed to talk to everyone at the embassy.

F.   Translate the following impersonal expressions.

1.   Who is interested in it?
2.   The ambassador will be bored.
3.   It was clear to all.
4.   I feel embarrassed.
5.   We all feel bad.
6.   All were aware (that...)

G.   Fill in the blanks.

1.   _________________ заключить договор с вами, если только
     We would like

     _________________ договориться о некоторых оставшихся деталях. Лично
     we can manage

     _________________, что это не должно быть трудно.
     it seems to me

2.   В своём _________ _______________________ Генеральный секретарь
              address   *to the people of the US*

     _______________________ в науке и технике.
     called for cooperation

3.   _________________ правительство данной страны может
     In our opinion

     _________________ прекратить свою деятельность в любой момент.
     order the terrorists

     _________________ это сделать?
     What prevents them

4. Пока _________________________, _________________________ военные базы.
       it isn't clear to us   *to whom belong*

5. Советские люди сейчас _________________________________ в жизни своей
                              are preparing for changes

страны.

II. **Translate the impersonal phrases, avoiding a dative object where one is given or where context is clear.**

1. It appears that artificial encouragement of exports is not needed.
2. It was interesting to note that the new policy began last week.
3. We would like to look at the proposal by the beginning of the month.
4. The members of our delegation were not allowed to speak at the conference.
5. We'll have to turn to our partners in the Common Market.
6. I'm interested in finding out what information can be received on the situation in Romania.
7. As everyone is aware, tensions in the region are growing.

I. **Write ten sentences to illustrate the uses of impersonal constructions you have seen in this lesson.**

J. **Render the following sentences. Do not translate word for word. Rather give the idea expressed. But be on the lookout for tricky verbs for inquiring, requesting and answering:**

просить/попросить кого-то – чего-то
                           – о чём-то
спрашивать/спросить кого-то о чём-то;
задавать/задать вопрос кому-то (о чём-то);
отвечать/ответить (кому-то на вопрос);

1. If you're *asking* about economic aid to Ethiopia, I can't *answer your question* right now. However, we are ready to extend all the aid they *have asked for.*
2. I *will ask* you one more time: why *haven't* you *inquired* about the negotiations?
3. Reporters usually *ask* the Foreign Ministry spokesman *many questions* about human rights in the USSR, *which* he always *answers.* But when they *ask* him to talk about changes at the top, he doesn't always *answer.*
4. "*Ask* the reporter *to ask* about liberalization."
    "No, he *won't ask* such a *question.* He's afraid."
5. Brazil *is asking* the IMF to extend long-term credit.

K. Translate the sentences below.

1.   If the US won't sell the Soviet Union wheat, it will turn to Argentina.
2.   Artificial prices lead to inflation.
3.   This program promotes mutual understanding.
4.   Gorbachev addressed the American people.
5.   Cuba says that it is aiding Angola.
6.   You must prepare for the conference.
7.   The Danish proposal led to further negotiations.
8.   What's preventing you from working?
9.   It seems to us that Libya is threatening the West.
10.   This territory once belonged to Germany. It now belongs to Poland.
11.   The ambassador ordered his assistant to offer aid.
12.   We call on all nations to observe the conditions of the treaty.
13.   This agreement will lead to an artificial increase in the price of grain.
14.   What will they order the trade minister to do?

GRAMMAR: PAST PASSIVE PARTICIPLES - SHORT FORMS

Now look at these sentences and their translations.

В хо́де перегово́ров *бы́ли обсуждены́* вопро́сы двусторо́нних отноше́ний.
Issues of bilateral relations *were discussed* in the course of negotiations.

В тече́ние 10 лет *бу́дет ликвиди́ровано* всё я́дерное ору́жие.
All nuclear weapons *will be liquidated* over ten years.

Бо́мба *спря́тана* в чемода́не.
The bomb *is hidden* in the suitcase.

These are short forms of past passive participles. Like short adjectives, they can be used only as predicate components after the verb "to be."

Note that short form past passive participle constructions have active voice equivalents with the verb in the third person plural, where the passive subject becomes the direct object.

В хо́де перегово́ров *обсуди́ли* вопро́сы двусторо́нних отноше́ний.
В тече́ние 10 лет *ликвиди́руют* всё я́дерное ору́жие.
Бо́мбу *спря́тали* в чемода́не.

Past passive participles are formed from perfective transitive verbs only!

GRAMMAR: PAST PASSIVE PARTICIPLES – LONG FORMS

Look at these sentences and their translations. Compare the long form past passive participles used here with the short forms above.

Вопро́сы, *обсуждённые* в хо́де перегово́ров, включа́ют пробле́му «прове́рки на
    ме́сте».
or
Вопро́сы, *кото́рые бы́ли обсуждены́* (or *кото́рые обсуди́ли*) в хо́де перегово́ров,
    включа́ют пробле́му «прове́рки на ме́сте».

Issues *discussed* in the course of negotiations include the problem of "on site
    inspection".
or
Issues *which were discussed* in the course of negotiations include the problem
    of "on site inspection".

Отку́да вы зна́ете о бо́мбе, *спря́танной* в чемода́не?
or
Отку́да вы зна́ете о бо́мбе, *кото́рая спря́тана* (or *кото́рую спря́тали*) в
    чемода́не?...

How do you know about the bomb *hidden* in the suitcase?
or
How do you know about the bomb, *which is hidden* in the suitcase?

    Long form participles function like long form adjectives. They agree with
the noun they modify in gender, number and case.
    Like their short form counterparts, long form participles are derived only
from perfective verbs and formed only from transitive verbs. No –"**СЯ**" verbs
are transitive.

You can identify past passive participle by the –Н– suffix: обсуждена́

GRAMMAR: PRESENT PASSIVE PARTICIPLES

Look at the following sentences and their translations.

Чем отлича́ется нефть, *экспорти́руемая* с Бли́жнего Восто́ка, от не́фти из Се́верного
    мо́ря?
or
Чем отлича́ется нефть, *кото́рую экспорти́руют* с Бли́жнего Восто́ка, от не́фти из
    Се́верного мо́ря?

What is the difference between the oil, *exported* from the Middle East and the
oil from the North Sea?
or
What is the difference between the oil, *which is being exported* from the
Middle East and the oil from the North Sea?

Present passive participles are rare outside scientific or technical
writing. However, because they are formed only from imperfective verbs, they
are used to convey the idea of repeated action in the passive voice, whereas
past passive participles, which are always perfective, give the idea of a
one-time action.

Ме́ры, *употреблённые* здесь, неуме́стны.
Measures *used* here (at this time) are out of place.

Ме́ры, *употребля́емые* здесь, неуме́стны.
Measures *used* here (all the time) are out of place.
Measures *which are being used* here (process) are out of place.

Present passive participles are formed only from transitive verbs. No
-"СЯ" verbs are transitive.

You can identify present passive participles by the -M- suffix:
экспорти́руемая.

TABLE 7: PASSIVE PARTICIPLES

	Imperfective	Present Tense	Past Tense
t r a n s i t i v e	**обсужда́ть** to discuss **провожа́ть** to see off	**обсужда́ ем ый** being dicussed **провожа́ ем ый** being seen off	no past form (for most transitive imperfective verbs)
	Perfective		
	обсуди́ть to discuss (to have discussed)	no present form	**обсужд ённ ый** discussed
	Imperfective	Present Tense	Past Tense
i n t r a n s i t i v e	**прибыва́ть** to arrive	no present form	no past form
	Perfective		
	прибы́ть to arrive (to have arrived)	no present form	no past form

Here is a list of some verbs from chapters 1-4 and their forms as past passive
participles. Note that only perfective transitive verbs can be used.

Infinitive	Long participle	Short participle
возгла́вить	возгла́вленный	возгла́влен
встре́тить	встре́ченный	встре́чен
вы́разить	вы́раженный	вы́ражен
да́ть	да́нный	дан
заверши́ть	завершённый	завершён
заложи́ть	зало́женный	зало́жен
купи́ть	ку́пленный	куплен
обсудить	обсуждённый	обсуждён
подписа́ть	подпи́санный	подпи́сан
получи́ть	полу́ченный	полу́чен
провести́ (to conduct)	проведённый	проведён
предоста́вить	предоста́вленный	предоста́влен
прода́ть	про́данный	про́дан
разрабо́тать	разрабо́танный	разрабо́тан
постро́ить	постро́енный	постро́ен

TABLE 8:   PASSIVE CONSTRUCTIONS - SUMMARY

ASPECT	GRAMMATICAL FORM
Imperfective *Ongoing or repeated action*	**Imperfective -ся Verbs:** Кни́ги (ча́сто) чита́ются здесь *Books are (often) read here.* Кни́ги (ча́сто) чита́лись здесь. *Books were (often) read here.* Кни́ги (ча́сто) бу́дут чита́ться здесь. *Books will (often) be read here.*
Perfective *One-time action, NO repetition*	**Perfective verb past passive participles:** Кни́ги уже́ прочи́таны. *The books are already read.* (OR) *The books have already been read.* Кни́ги уже́ бы́ли прочи́таны. *The books were already read.* Кни́ги бу́дут прочи́таны. *The books will already be read.*

GRAMMAR EXERCISES: PAST PASSIVE AND PRESENT PASSIVE PARTICIPLES

A. Read all the grammar on passive participles. Review their formation.
Study Tables 7 and 8 above. Find passive participles in the text. State
their aspect and the tense as well as their gender, number and in the case
of long forms, their case.

B. 1)   Make past passive participles out of the verbs below:

покупать/купить   выражать/выразить
проводить/провести   завершáть/завершѝть
получать/получить   встречать/встретить
подпѝсывать/подписáть   разрабатывать/разработать
экспортировать (-овать verbs   давать/дать
    made of foreign words   обсуждáть/обсудить
    usually have only an
    imperfective form)

2)   Now make present passive participles out of the same verbs.

C.   Find the participle in the sentences below. Determine the original form of the verb. Change the following sentences with short past passive participles as a predicate into their equivalent form – "ОНИ" (omitted) + verb in third person plural.

Examples: Бомба *найдена*.   Бомбу *нашли*.
    ⟶ The bomb *was found*.   ⟶ *They found* the bomb.

1.   Этот закон *был встречен* с энтузиазмом.
2.   *Заложены* основы добрососедских отношений.
3.   Программа реформ наконец *будет разработана*.
4.   Особое внимание *уделено* проблеме алкоголизма.
5.   В законопроект *была внесена* ещё одна поправка.
6.   *Обоснована* такая позиция или нет?
7.   Высокая оценка *была дана* решениям пленума.
8.   *Отменены* многие рейсы авиакомпаний и *заблокированы* порты.
9.   *Были отмечены* традиционные связи между СССР и АРЕ.

D.   Explain the difference between the participles in each pair of sentences below. Determine the original form of the verb. Be able to translate both variants into English.

1)   Вот ряд вопросов, *рассмотренных* на сессии СЭВ.
    Вот ряд вопросов, *рассматриваемых* на сессии СЭВ.

2)   Помощь, *полученная* от развитых стран, недостаточна.
    Помощь, *получаемая* от развитых стран, недостаточна.

3)   Они встретились на *проводимых* сейчас переговорах.
    Они встретились на только что *проведённых* переговорах.

4)   *Подписанный* меморандум намечает направление совместных советско-
    американских усилий в освоении космоса.
    Подписываемый меморандум намечает направление совместных советско-
    американских усилий в освоении космоса.

E. **Complete the sentences below with the noun and the participle in the proper case. Be able to translate these sentences into English.**

1. Они не думают о _______________ (возможности, предоставляемые им).

2. Мы подошли к _____________ (вопрос, согласованный на вчерашней сессии).

3. Рассмотрим _____________ (программа, изложенная Горбачёвым в заявлении от 15 января 1989 года).

4. Это произошло при _____________ (руководство, созданное ещё в 50-ых годах).

5. Вот – _______________ (документ, обсуждаемый советскими и американскими экспертами).

F. **Replace participial constructions in the sentences below with relative clauses.**

Example: Он остановился на конкретных проектах, *намеченных* к претворению в жизнь.

——→ Он остановился на конкретных проектах, которые *намечены* к претворению в жизнь.

1. Выражена полная поддержка курсу, *направленному* на создание условий для диалога.
2. Силы, *вовлечённые* в борьбу, реалистически подойдут к предложениям о прекращении огня.
3. Среди вопросов, *связанных* со встречей в Рейкьявике, один вызывает особый интерес.
4. Доклад, *одобренный* на очередном заседании, появился на первых страницах «Правды».

G. **Translate the following sentences into Russian. Note the difference in English between participial constructions and passive predicates. Check the list of past passive participles.**

1. At the negotiations completed yesterday a number of important agreements was concluded.
2. This plan of mutual assistance was developed in the 70s.
3. The decision of the committee will be discussed at the meeting in June.
4. Which raw materials currently exported from South Africa do we really need?
5. Is the interest expressed at the conference in London truly genuine?
6. The delegation will be met at the airport.
7. The facts which are being stated right now are quite remarkable.

RENDERING

Write a paragraph in *simple* Russian using the grammar and vocabulary you have learned so far to convey the following facts. Do *not* translate word for word. Use what you know to *render* all the information you can:

> *Trade officials* of a country which we will call Bukustan (so as not to offend anyone) have just returned from Latvia where they were *conducting negotiations with the representatives* of the huge VEF electronics complex in Riga.
>
> Taking advantage of the Soviets' *new policy encouraging* direct enterprise-to-enterprise *negotiations* which by-pass the central ministerial level, VEF has *reached an agreement* with BNE (Bukustan National Electronics), Ltd. whereby VEF will *export* semi-conductors to BNE. BNE will assemble the parts into cheap walkman-style tape recorders for use both at home and *for sale* back to the Soviet Union.
>
> Such an *agreement was impossible under Brezhnev,* and it appears that current *conditions could lead to* other such arrangements as Soviet enterprises *turn to* companies outside the USSR. At the same time *it is clear that* such a *policy* might *lead to* a relationship between Soviet enterprises and enterprises in neighboring countries, particularly to the south, where workers are paid less and work harder.

Useful words and phrases:

assemble parts into something – собирáть (что-то) из детáлей
BNE – фирма БНЭ («Букистáн нэшнл электрóникс лúмитед»)
enterprise (= "company" in socialist countries) – предприя́тие
semi-conductor – полупроводнúк
tape recorder – магнитофóн
VEF Electronics Complex – объединéние ВЭФ
Walkman-style cassette player – плéйер

SPEAKING EXERCISES

A.   Ответьте на следующие вопросы по тексту урока.

1.   Какие переговоры завершились в Токио?
2.   С чем высокие договаривающиеся стороны выразили желание бороться?
3.   По каким вопросам участникам переговоров удалось заключить важные соглашения?
4.   Что должно привести к выравниванию торгового баланса?
5.   В рамках какой программы администрация предлагает расширить научное и техническое сотрудничество?
6.   Чему способствуют эти переговоры?

B.   1)   Расскажите текст, используя словарь урока 4.

   2)   Расскажите тот же текст, заменив:
            – участников встречи
            – место встречи
            – тему бесед
            – характер отношений

C.   Составьте ситуацию, используя следующие выражения.

according to the radio reports,.., in the framework of.., leading capitalist countries, measures against..., the reduction of interest rates, the leveling up of trade balance, to result in...

D.   Проведите заседание глав ведущих стран Запада, на котором обсуждаются вопросы укрепления международной финансовой системы.

E.   Пресс-конференция министра финансов США о мерах по сокращению дефицита платёжного баланса.

F.   Речь министра финансов о причинах, по которым американские товары мало поступают на японские рынки.

G.   Почему администрация Рейгана выступала против протекционистских мер во внешней торговле?

READING EXERCISE 1

PRE-TEXT:

Read the text with the following questions in mind:

1.   What is this article about?
2.   Which body decided to raise the EEC budget?
3.   Which political factions expressed discontent with EEC agricultural policy?
4.   What are the consequences of this policy, according to the author?
5.   Which EEC bodies must present their policy recommendations next January?

Бельгия

«Общий рынок» без бюджета

БРЮССЕЛЬ, 13. Вопрос о бюджете ЕЭС на 1987 год по-прежнему остается открытым. Европейский парламент, заседающий в Страсбурге, большинством голосов постановил увеличить общую сумму бюджета, превысив тем самым максимальную цифру, установленную советом министров «Общего рынка». Депутаты от левых партий, к которым присоединились христианские демократы, своим голосованием выразили недовольство совместной сельскохозяйственной политикой ЕЭС, которая приводит к падению доходов мелких и средних крестьянских хозяйств.

Комиссия европейских сообществ и совет министров ЕЭС должны будут представить свои соображения по бюджету на очередной сессии Европарламента, которая состоится в январе будущего года.

Ю. ХАРЛАНОВ.

POST-TEXT (using context and structure):

Review all the reading rules that we have studied so far.

1. Find the object for the predicate in the first sentence.   It is....
    (check the correct answer):
    a.   direct
    b.   indirect
    c.   prepositional

2. The subject in the second sentence is modified by...(check the
    correct answer):
    a.   an adjectival phrase
    b.   a participial phrase
    c.   by a subordinate clause

3. The predicate *постановил* has several modifiers.   They are... (check
    the correct answer):
    a.   adverbs
    b.   an adverbial phrase
    c.   a verbal adverbial phrase
    d.   a subordinate clause

4. Find the word modified by a participial phrase starting with
    установленную.

5. There are two *который* clauses in the third sentence.   Find the word
    they modify.

6. In the second paragraph determine the type of predicate in the main
    clause.   It is...(check the correct answer):
    a.   verb
    b.   "to be"
    b.   "A=B"

7. Find the word modified by the *который* clause.

8. Find *по-прежнему* in the text. How do you say it in English? Explain
    the ending *-ему*. Form an antonym for *по-прежнему* following the same
    pattern.

9. Find the Russian for "next January."   Form other time-expressions
    using this pattern.

10. Translate this article into English.

11. Make a list of words dealing with economic issues.

READING EXERCISE 2

PRE-TEXT:

Read the text with the following questions in mind:

1. What is the main idea of the article?
2. Whom did the Soviet Chairman receive, according to the report?
3. What purpose does the Soviet-Italian dialogue serve?
4. According to the Chairman, what intentions of the Soviet Union did the January Plenum of the CC CPSU confirm?
5. What new possibilities for Soviet-Italian economic cooperation has perestoika produced, according to the Chairman?
6. What was the Italian's response to the Chairman's remarks?
7. Who else was at the meeting?

Беседа в Кремле

3 февраля Председатель Совета Министров СССР Н. И. Рыжков принял находящегося в Москве министра внешней торговли Италии С. Формику.

С обеих сторон было выражено удовлетворение развитием советско-итальянского политического диалога, который отвечает интересам укрепления доверия и оздоровления обстановки в Европе и в целом в мире.

Н. И. Рыжков подчеркнул, что взятый в Советском Союзе курс на ускорение социально-экономического развития страны, подтвержденный январским Пленумом ЦК КПСС, убедительно свидетельствует о мирной направленности планов Советского Союза, о его стремлении положить конец гонке вооружений, устранить угрозу ядерного конфликта.

Было отмечено, что проводимая в СССР перестройка, которая распространяется и на внешнеэкономическую деятельность, открывает новые возможности для развития взаимовыгодного экономического сотрудничества между советскими организациями и итальянскими фирмами с использованием как традиционных связей, так и новых форм взаимодействия, в том числе производственной кооперации и создания совместных предприятий.

С. Формика, отметив живой интерес в Италии к происходящим в Советском Союзе преобразованиям в различных областях социально-экономической жизни, высказался за расширение советско-итальянских экономических связей на взаимовыгодной основе.

В беседе, проходившей в атмосфере взаимопонимания, приняли участие заместитель Председателя Совета Министров СССР В. М. Каменцев, министр внешней торговли СССР Б. И. Аристов, а также посол Италии в СССР С. Романо.

(ТАСС).

POST-TEXT (using context and structure):

1. In the first sentence of the third paragraph the predicate *подчеркнул* is completed by...(pick the correct answer):
   a.   a direct object
   b.   an indirect object
   c.   a prepositional object
   d.   an object clause

2. In the same sentence find the predicate(s) for *курс.*
3. Explain the use of a comma before *о его стремлении.*   It separates... (pick the correct answer):
   a.   a clause
   b.   detached words
   c.   an enumeration.

Translate the entire paragraph into English.

4. Explain the uses of commas in the next sentence.   Find the predicate in the *что* clause.   What is the subject of the *которая* clause? Translate this sentence-paragraph into English.
5. In paragraph five the predicate is modified by...(mark the correct answer):
   a.   an adverb
   b.   an adverbial phrase
   c.   a verbal adverbial phrase

6. Explain the difference between *министр торговли* and *министр внешней торговли* in the Soviet context.
7. Find the Russian for *to meet the interests of...* and *to put an end to* in the text.
8. Find three uses of *взаимо...* in the article.   Be able to translate them.   What other word of this type do you know?
9. What is the Russian for *company, firm, business*?
10. Find the construction *как..., так и....*   What is its English equivalent?
11. Make a list of vocabulary dealing with the subject of economic cooperation.

READING EXERCISE 3

PRE-TEXT:

Read the text with the following questions in mind:

1.   What is the main idea of the article?
2.   The regular session of the joint Soviet-US committee on environmental protection adopted a report on the period... (true or false for each item):
     a.   since 72
     b.   from Dec. 85 to Dec.86
     c.   1987
     d.   five future years

3.   Who led the US delegation?
4.   Who led the Soviet group?
5.   The meeting included... (check the right answer):
     a.   a reception
     b.   a press-conference
     c.   an exchange of farewell speeches
     d.   a dinner party

Заседает комиссия по окружающей среде

ВАШИНГТОН, 19 декабря. (ТАСС). С 15 по 18 декабря здесь проходила X сессия смешанной советско-американской комиссии по сотрудничеству в области охраны окружающей среды.

Эта комиссия была создана в соответствии с заключенным между СССР и США в 1972 году соглашением о сотрудничестве в области охраны окружающей среды. На очередном заседании был одобрен доклад о выполнении этого соглашения в период с декабря 1985 по декабрь 1986 года.

Смешанная советско-американская комиссия также подтвердила намерение обеих сторон продолжать усилия по развитию сотрудничества в этой области, которое, как отмечалось на заседании, может внести полезный вклад в дело улучшения отношений между Советским Союзом и США. На сессии был принят меморандум, в котором намечаются планы совместных работ на 1987 год по 38 проектам. Было также принято решение продлить действие советско-американского соглашения о сотрудничестве в области охраны окружающей среды еще на пять лет.

«Самой успешной встречей» назвал завершившуюся сессию глава американской делегации директор агентства по охране окружающей среды Ли Томас. Он отметил, что подписанный по ее итогам меморандум «намечает направления совместных исследований по широкому спектру проблем». Двустороннее научное сотрудничество в этой области приносит большую пользу не только нашим странам, но и всему миру, подчеркнул американский представитель на состоявшейся здесь пресс-конференции.

Руководитель советской делегации председатель Государственного комитета СССР по гидрометеорологии и контролю природной среды Ю. А. Израэль подробно остановился на конкретных проектах и совместных программах, которые осуществляются или намечены к претворению в жизнь. Он подчеркнул, что это взаимовыгодное сотрудничество, от которого одинаково выигрывают обе стороны. Отвечая на многочисленные вопросы, советский представитель рассказал об осуществляющихся в СССР мерах по охране окружающей среды.

POST-TEXT (using context and structure):

1. Find *c 15 по 18 декабря...* in the text. Note that *no* in this phrase does not require dative, but accusative case. It means *up to* (*including*). The session lasted... (check the correct answer):
   a.   3 days
   b.   4 days

2. There are two uses of *который* clauses in the second paragraph. Determine:
   a.   which words are modified by these clauses.
   b.   the subject in both of *который* clauses.

   Translate this paragraph into English.

3. Find two more *который* clauses in the last paragraph of the article. Which words do they modify? Find the subject in each of them. Translate this paragraph into English.
4. What is the Russian for *joint committee*?
5. Find the Russian equivalent for *environmental protection*.

READING EXERCISE 4

PRE-TEXT:

Read the text with the following questions in mind. If you are familiar with the history of OPEC, you may be able to predict many of the answers. See if what the text says matches your expectations of what you expect to read:

1. What is the main idea of the article?
2. By how many barrels of oil per day will OPEC reduce production after February 1?
3. Oil prices caused a shock in the 70s and in 1986 for... (Check the correct answer):
   a. the same reason.
   b. a different reason.

4. What influenced OPEC in 1985 to abandon price fixing?
5. Low oil prices led to... (true or false for each item):
   a. an economic recovery
   b. an increase in unemployment
   c. an increase in the production rate
   d. a decrease in the production rate

6. What was the effect of low oil prices on oil-producing countries?
7. List the oil-producing countries mentioned in the article who are not members of OPEC.

ОПЕК: возврат к базисным ценам

На днях на конференции в Женеве страны ОПЕК приняли план повышения цен на нефть до уровня 18 долларов за баррель (159 литров).

Этот план предусматривает сокращение с 1 февраля будущего года добычи «черного золота» членами организации на один миллион баррелей в день. Принятие плана означает возврат к системе базисных твердых цен на нефть, существовавшей на рынке до конца прошлого года.

Как известно, в конце 1985 года базисные цены ОПЕК составляли 28 долларов за баррель. Однако под воздействием западных стран и их нефтяных монополий ОПЕК вынуждена была отказаться от фиксированных цен. По этой причине положение на мировом рынке нефти довольно быстро вышло из-под контроля, и к лету текущего года цены снизились до 9 долларов за баррель.

В связи с трехкратным падением цен на нефть в первом полугодии 1986 года приходят на память события 70-х годов, когда многократное повышение цен на «черное золото» вызвало шок в странах-импортерах. В этом году шок вызвало значительное падение цен. Это произошло не в результате избытка нефти в мире, а вследствие искусственного перенасыщения ею рынка.

Правящие круги Вашингтона и ряда других западных стран исходили из того, что низкие цены на нефть приведут к оживлению экономики, а они, вопреки ожиданиям, способствовали увеличению безработицы, усилению неуверенности деловых кругов и сокращению темпов роста производства. В США, например, была закрыта почти половина буровых вышек, значительно сократились инвестиции в разведку и добычу нефти.

Падение цен на нефть вызвало шок и в самих странах ОПЕК. Когда в конце 1985 года принималось решение об отказе от базисных цен на нефть, большинство ее членов исходило из возможности понижения цен на несколько долларов за баррель, но никто не рассчитывал, что цены упадут ниже 20 долларов за баррель.

Пытаясь найти выход из создавшегося положения, многие нефтедобывающие страны стали свертывать строительство важных экономических объектов, урезать импорт продовольственных и промышленных товаров, вновь были вынуждены прибегнуть к иностранным займам на еще более жестких условиях.

Даже такие страны, как Саудовская Аравия, Кувейт, Ливия, ОАЭ, Катар, оказались в довольно затруднительном положении. Они резко сократили импорт, заморозили строительство многих объектов, выслали сотни тысяч иностранных рабочих и отказались от ряда финансовых обязательств в отношении других стран. Потери только арабских нефтедобывающих стран от реализации нефти уже превысили в этом году 100 миллиардов долларов.

Нефтедобывающие страны, не являющиеся членами ОПЕК, такие, как Мексика, Египет, Малайзия, Оман, Ангола, Норвегия, поддерживают усилия ОПЕК по урегулированию цен на нефть. Представители многих из этих стран принимали участие в работе 80-й конференции ОПЕК в качестве наблюдателей. Советский Союз также не остается в стороне от усилий по стабилизации и выравниванию цен на мировом рынке нефти. Он был и остается поборником установления справедливых, стабильных и предсказуемых цен.

Решение, принятое на конференции в Женеве, свидетельствует о том, что страны ОПЕК, несмотря на существующие между ними разногласия, сумели сделать важный шаг на пути установления стабильных цен. Зарубежные средства массовой информации сообщают, что за последние две недели цены на нефть поднялись до 17,5—18 долларов.

И. ЕРМАЧЕНКОВ,
кандидат экономических наук.

POST-TEXT   (using context and structure):

1.   In the second sentence of the third paragraph the predicate is...
     (mark the correct answer):
     a.   verb
     b.   "to be"

     Underline all three components of the predicate.

2. In the third sentence of the same paragraph a comma separates... (mark the correct answer):
   a. a subordinate clause
   b. an independent clause

Translate this paragraph into English.

3. In the first sentence of the fourth paragraph, which word does the *когда* clause modify? Translate this sentence into English.
4. In the first sentence of paragraph five, analyze the uses of commas. Translate it into English.
5. In paragraph eight analyze the uses of commas. Underline all the predicates. Translate this paragraph into English.
6. In the last sentence of paragraph ten, the predicate is... (mark the correct answer):
   a. verb
   b. "to be"
   c. "A=B"

Translate this sentence into English.

7. What part of speech is *нефтедобывающий*? Explain its composition.
8. The word *цены* occurs in the text with six different adjectives. Find them and be able to translate them. On the basis of this exercise, determine the Russian for *floating prices*.
9. What is the English for *цена на нефть*? What case does *цена на...* require? Form four other phrases following this pattern.
10. Find the English for *падение цены на ... долларов за баррель*. What is the opposite for **падение** *цены...*? Note that *баррель* is masculine.
11. What is *чёрное золото*?
12. Make a list of words dealing with the subject of oil production and sales.

READING EXERCISE 5

PRE-TEXT:

Read the text with the following questions in mind:

1. What is the main idea of the text?
2. Non-official consultations of ten Western countries were held at... (check the right answer):
   a. Common Market headquaters
   b. Geneva
   c. FAO headquaters
   d. UNESCO headquaters

3. The topic of the meeting was...(check the right answer):
    a.   lumber policy
    b.   texile policy
    c.   agricultural policy
    d.   consumer goods policy

4. What was the central issue of the original meeting?
5. The trade war was prompted by a... (check the right answer):
    a.   reduction of Spanish imports of feed grain from the US
    b.   reduction of US imports of fodder from Spain
    c.   increase of US exports of feed grain to Spain
    d.   increase of Spanish exports of feed grain to the US

6. New tariffs on European goods are intended to... (check the correct
    answer):
    a.   reduce the US trade deficit
    b.   give more incentive to American production
    c.   undermine European competition

7. Which countries have already been hit by the trade war?
8. According to *Pravda*, why is France the main target of the proposed
    200% increase in tariffs?

Заметки по поводу

ТРАНСАТЛАНТИЧЕСКАЯ ДУЭЛЬ

ЖЕНЕВА. (Соб. корр. «Известий»). В рамках генерального соглашения о тарифах и торговле (ГАТТ) здесь проходят неофициальные консультации десяти делегаций западных стран по вопросам сельскохозяйственной политики.

Они — продолжение состоявшейся в Женеве встречи представителей администрации Рейгана и штаб-квартиры «Общего рынка». Центральным вопросом переговоров стала угроза Белого дома повысить до 200 процентов пошлину на отдельные товары традиционного экспорта стран ЕЭС в США.

Напомним, что в «торговой войне» первыми открыли огонь Соединенные Штаты, потребовав от ЕЭС значительных уступок.

Это наступление мотивировалось тем, что принятие Испании в «Общий рынок» нанесло урон сельскохозяйственным экспортерам США и что, в частности, ежегодные потери от снижения экспорта кормов в Испанию находятся на уровне 500—600 миллионов долларов. Сославшись на этот факт, администрация Рейгана не нашла ничего лучшего, как компенсировать свои неудачи в конкурентной борьбе за рынки сбыта массированным нажимом на штаб-квартиру ЕЭС. В Брюсселе согласились на частичную и временную компенсацию американских потерь, но не более. Тогда сорвавшаяся на крик вашингтонская администрация объявила о своем намерении с конца января увеличить пошлины и заставить ЕЭС выкладывать американской таможне дополнительно 400 миллионов долларов в год.

Новое наступление Соединенных Штатов на торговую практику ЕЭС объясняется серьезным обострением политических отношений между партнерами, недовольством Брюсселя отказом США учитывать национальные интересы западноевропейских стран.

Перенос торговой войны в систему ГАТТ, подчеркивают в кругах делегаций, означает интернационализацию торговых и политических разногласий между США и ЕЭС. За последнее время США усилили нажим на партнеров по ГАТТ, стремясь заставить их добровольно оплачивать огромный торговый дефицит США, который в прошлом году составил 170 миллиардов долларов. США, опираясь на статью договора ГАТТ о «возможном добровольном ограничении экспорта», уже выкрутили руки Сингапуру и Южной Корее, добившись одностороннего сокращения текстильного экспорта, и принудили Японию сократить свой экспорт в США. Подобные же попытки были приняты в отношении Швейцарии и Западной Германии.

Угроза о 200-процентном повышении пошлин показывает, что удар заокеанских стратегов направлен против тех стран ЕЭС, которые выступают в ГАТТ с осуждением американского диктата в международной торговле. Так, например, основной удар Вашингтон планирует нанести Франции, которая должна дополнительно платить за свой экспорт 250 миллионов долларов ежегодной пошлины.

«Удастся ли остановить торговую войну или в Женеве события выйдут из-под контроля?» — тревожится «Уолл-стрит джорнэл». Встреча в Женеве — очередная попытка остановить трансатлантическую дуэль. Но независимо от женевских переговоров уже сейчас ясно: Соединенные Штаты потерпели моральное поражение, нанесен удар престижу администрации Рейгана, ее попыткам диктата в международной торговой практике.

В. КУЗНЕЦОВ.

POST-TEXT (using context and structure):

1. Find the Russian for *agricultural policy*. Explain the composition of the adjective.
2. In the first sentence of the second paragraph, what does *они* stand for?
3. Explain the meaning of *штаб-квартира*. In what other context can the word be used?
4. In the second sentence of the second paragraph the object of *стала* is... (mark the correct answer):
   a. a direct object
   b. a indirect object
   c. an "A=B" phrase

   Translate this paragraph into English.

5. The third paragraph contains...(mark the correct answer):
   a. a reason for the problem
   b. a solution to the problem

6. Analyze the use of commas in the third sentence of paragraph three. Find the Russian equivalent for *to find nothing better than* + infinitive. Translate the sentence into English.
7. In sentence five of the third paragraph, find modifiers for the subject *администрация*.
8. In sentence three of paragraph five, analyze the use of commas. There are two predicates and two verbal adverbial phrases in this sentence. The phrases modify...(mark the correct answer):
   a. the first predicate
   b. the second predicate
   c. both predicates

   Translate this sentence into English.

9. What is the Russian for *to harm agricultural exporters*? Explain the use of cases in this expression. Following this pattern, how would you say *to bring defeat to the oil importers*?
10. Find *to suffer defeat* in the last paragraph.
11. Form other expressions following the pattern **партнёры** *по* **ГАТТ**. Be able to translate them into English.
12. Find *заокеанские стратеги* in the text. Does it have a neutral or derogatory flavor?
13. Make a list of words dealing with the subject of trade.

TABLE 9:   TENSES IN IMPERSONAL CONSTRUCTIONS

НУЖНО

PRESENT
мне   **ну́жен** план (masc)
тебе **нужна́** ка́рта (fem)
ей   **ну́жно** вре́мя (neut)
ему   **нужны́** де́ньги (plur)
им   **ну́жно** рабо́тать (inf)

PAST
нам   **был ну́жен** план (masc)
вам   **была́ нужна́** ка́рта (fem)
им   **бы́ло ну́жно** вре́мя (neut)
ему   **бы́ли нужны́** де́ньги (plur)
ей   **бы́ло ну́жно** рабо́тать (inf)

FUTURE
им   **бу́дет ну́жен** план (masc)
нам   **бу́дет нужна́** ка́рта (fem)
вам   **бу́дет ну́жно** вре́мя (neut)
мне   **бу́дут нужны́** де́ньги (plur)
тебе **бу́дет ну́жно** рабо́тать (inf)

НА́ДО, МО́ЖНО, НЕЛЬЗЯ́

PRESENT		
ей	на́до	рабо́тать
мне	мо́жно	рабо́тать
ему	нельзя́	рабо́тать

PAST		
ему	на́до бы́ло	рабо́тать
тебе	мо́жно бы́ло	рабо́тать
ей	нельзя́ бы́ло	рабо́тать

FUTURE		
нам	на́до бу́дет	рабо́тать
вам	мо́жно бу́дет	рабо́тать
им	нельзя́ бу́дет	рабо́тать

CIRCLE ONE

LESSON FIVE

AUDIO-COMPREHENSION EXERCISE

You are about to hear a text about the Kremlin's willingness to negotiate with the U.S. You will probably easily recognize the cognates given below. Look through words and expressions listed after the cognates. Then listen to the text with the following questions in mind. Afterwards, listen to the text again, and write down the answers.

1. What sorts of negotiations did the Soviet Union say it was ready to conduct with the United States?
2. What is the negotiating agenda?
3. What did the Soviets announce?

Cognates

космический
перспективы
раунд
позиция
реализм

WORDS AND EXPRESSIONS (on the tape)

сокращать/сократить стратегические вооружения
    -ют   -ят   тактические
                 обычные
сокращённый
сокращение

                                            (куда?)
включать/включить широкий круг вопросов   в дискуссию
    -ют   -ат   договор об ОСВ-2 (SALT-2)   в переговоры
                 программу СОИ (SDI)   в повестку дня
включённый

   (где?)
на повестке дня   были перспективы очередного раунда бесед
– on the agenda   была безопасность в Центральной Европе
                был   контроль над вооружениями – arms control
                было расширение экспорта сырья

контро́ль (no plural)

                                             (куда?)

ста́вить/поста́вить вопро́с безопа́сности   на пове́стку дня
  -ят   -ят   - to put the question of ... on the agenda
                        обме́на информа́цией
                        Общего ры́нка
                        уда́рного косми́ческого ору́жия - space strike weapons

поста́вленный

ору́жие (no plural)

информа́ция (no plural)

на восто́ке   восто́чный
на за́паде   за́падный
на ю́ге   ю́жный
на се́вере   се́верный

на Сре́днем За́паде
на Бли́жнем Восто́ке
на Да́льнем Восто́ке

заявля́ть/заяви́ть   (о чём?)
    -ют заявят   о свое́й гото́вности торгова́ть - to announce one's readiness
                                       to conduct trade
                  об опа́сности настоя́щей ситуа́ции
                  о сокраще́нии стратеги́ческих вооруже́ний

зая́вленный
заявле́ние

добива́ться/доби́ться   (чего?)
    -ются добью́тся   разря́дки междунаро́дной напряжённости
                    успе́ха на предстоя́щих перегово́рах
                    предотвраще́ния угро́зы но́вой войны́

проявля́ть/прояви́ть   реали́зм   на предстоя́щих перегово́рах
    -ют проя́вят   до́брую во́лю   на проше́дших
                  гото́вность - to show, manifest one's readiness

проя́вленный

спосо́бствовать   (чему?)
    -уют   улучше́нию междунаро́дной обстано́вки
(no perfective)   упроче́нию ми́ра
                  безопа́сности для всего́ челове́чества
                  междунаро́дной напряжённости

Ли́вия, ливи́йский, ливи́йцы, Три́поли
Лива́н, лива́нский, лива́нцы, Бейру́т
Ниге́рия, нигери́йский, нигери́йцы, Ла́гос
ЮАР, Южно-Африка́нская респу́блика, южноафрика́нский, африка́анеры, негритя́нское
    населе́ние, граждани́н ЮАР, Прето́рия, говори́ть на языке́ африка́анер
Африка, африка́нский, африка́нцы
Центра́льная Африка, центральноафрика́нский
Се́верная Африка, североафрика́нский
Южная Африка, южноафрика́нский

TEXT: Read the following text; be able to translate it into English in written form.

Гото́вность Москвы́

Сове́тский Сою́з вы́разил гото́вность провести́ перегово́ры с Соединёнными Шта́тами на у́ровне мини́стров иностра́нных дел по широ́кому кру́гу вопро́сов, представля́ющих взаи́мный интере́с. Осо́бое внима́ние бы́ло предло́жено удели́ть пробле́ме сокраще́ния стратеги́ческих вооруже́ний, включа́я я́дерное косми́ческое ору́жие.

Кро́ме того, на пове́стке дня бу́дут перспекти́вы очередно́го ра́унда Совеща́ния по безопа́сности и сотру́дничеству в Евро́пе, а та́кже проходя́щие в Ве́не перегово́ры о сокраще́нии обы́чных вооруже́ний в Центра́льной Евро́пе. Положе́ние на Бли́жнем Восто́ке, на ю́ге Африки и в Центра́льной Аме́рике бу́дет то́же обсужда́ться во вре́мя встре́чи.

Сове́тский Сою́з заяви́л о свое́й гото́вности укрепля́ть междунаро́дную безопа́сность и добива́ться разря́дки междунаро́дной напряжённости во и́мя предотвраще́ния угро́зы но́вой войны́.

Советский Союз подчёркивает недопустимость действий с позиции силы в международных отношениях. Проявив реализм и добрую волю на предстоящих переговорах, американская сторона сможет, по словам советского представителя, способствовать улучшению международной обстановки, упрочению мира и безопасности для всего человечества.

VOCABULARY EXERCISES

Look through the vocabulary for the text «Готовность Москвы». Do the following exercises.

A. Give the plural forms for the following nouns. Mark the stress.

вооружение
оружие
день
контроль
экспорт
заявление
ситуация
сырьё
успех

B. Give perfective forms for the following verbs. Conjugate the italicized words in both perfective and imperfective. Mark the stress.

способствовать
уделять
включать
заявлять
добиваться
проявлять

C. Give derivatives for the following words.

сократи́ть
гото́вность
включа́ть
контроли́ровать
угро́за
торгова́ть
заявле́ние

D. Paraphrase the italicized words.

настоя́щее *положе́ние*
ору́жие
ЕЭС
бу́дущие переговоры
безопа́сность *для всего́ ми́ра*

E. Give the opposite for the italicized words.

стратеги́ческие вооруже́ния
опа́сность
широ́кий круг вопро́сов
на *Бли́жнем* Восто́ке
сокраще́ние э́кспорта
ухудше́ние междунаро́дной обстано́вки

F. Fill in the blanks with the appropriate prepositions.

1. ___ пове́стке дня был контро́ль ___ вооруже́ниями.
2. Конфере́нция удели́ла осо́бое внима́ние ___ безопа́сности в Евро́пе.
3. ___ предстоя́щих перегово́рах сове́тская делега́ция зая́вит об опа́сности настоя́щей ситуа́ции ___ ми́ре.
4. Встре́ча ___ вы́сшем у́ровне мо́жет спосо́бствовать улучше́нию междунаро́дной обстано́вки.
5. Бу́дет тру́дно добива́ться стаби́льности ___ африка́нском контине́нте.

G. Give Russian equivalents for the following English phrases.

- to put the question of space strike weapons on the agenda
- to pay attention to conventional weapons
- to include arms contol
- announce one's readiness to conduct trade
- to achieve success in forthcoming negotiations
- to add to international tension

H.   Find cognates in the text.

I.   Fill in the blanks with the appropriate words.

          (что?)   (где?)

1.   США проявили ___________ на___________

         ___________   ___________

         ___________   ___________

              (чего?)

2.   СССР проводит сокращение ___________

            ____

            ____

             (о чём?)

3.   Бе́лый дом заявил о ___________

          ____

          ____

            (чему́?)

4.   Эта ситуа́ция спосо́бствует ___________

            ____

            ____

            (чему́?)

5.   Сто́роны удели́ли внима́ние ___________

            ____

            ____

J.   1)   Make sentences with appropriate words from the list in the middle.

СССР поста́вил вопро́с	(чего́?)	(куда́?)
США	контро́ль над вооруже́ниями	на пове́стку дня
Ку́ба	стратеги́чески ва́жное сырьё	
Великобрита́ния	стратеги́ческие вооруже́ния	
Кита́й	програ́мма СОИ	
ЮАР	очередно́й ра́унд бесе́д	
Чехослова́кия	обме́н информа́цией	
	уда́рное косми́ческое ору́жие	
	настоя́щая ситуа́ция на ...	

2)   Change your sentences following the model.

Вопро́с   (чего́?)   был   (где?)

                                    на пове́стке дня

K. 1)   Make sentences with appropriate words from the list in the middle.

Стóроны включáют вопрóс   (чегó?)   в переговóры.

стратегúческая оборóнная инициатúва
обмéн информáцией
продáжа сверхсовремéнной тéхники
покýпка пшенúцы
протекционúзм
сокращéние учётных стáвок

2)   Change your sentences following the model.

Вопрóс   (чегó?)   включáется в переговóры.

L.   Answer the following questions.   (on the tape)

1.   На какúх ýровнях провóдятся переговóры?
2.   Кто провóдит переговóры на вы́сшем ýровне?
3.   Какúм проблéмам уделя́ют внимáние на переговóрах на ýровне минúстров инострáнных дел?
4.   Какúм проблéмам уделя́ют внимáние на ýровне минúстров торгóвли?
5.   Какúе вопрóсы обсуждáет Совещáние по безопáсности и сотрýдничеству в Еврóпе?
6.   Что на повéстке дня переговóров в Вéне?
7.   Что бы́ло на повéстке дня на недáвней встрéче в верхах?
8.   Какúе райóны мúра чáще всегó обсуждáются на встрéчах по междунарóдной безопáсности?
9.   Чегó пытáется добúться американская сторонá на переговóрах в Женéве?
10.   Какúе дéйствия спосóбствуют улучшéнию междунарóдной обстанóвки?
11.   Какúе дéйствия спосóбствуют её ухудшéнию?
12.   На какóм континéнте нахóдится Аргентúна?
13.   Кто живёт в Лúвии?
14.   Кто живёт в Ливáне?
15.   На какóм языкé говоря́т в э́тих странах?

GRAMMAR: GENITIVE CASE

The genitive is used as follows:

1. **Possession ("of").**   Угро́за я́дерной войны́ – threat *of* nuclear war; прое́кт призиде́нт**а** – the president*'s* project; группиро́вка сепарати́ст**ов** – factions *of* separatists.

2. **"Have" constructions.**   У учёных уже́ есть нау́чные да́нные – The scientists already have the necessary data.   *Lit: At the researchers already is the necessary data.*   In other words those who "have" are in *genitive*; the object "had" is *in nominative.*

3. **Absence: НЕТ constructions for "doesn't have" and "isn't there."**   Note these sentences:

   Нет (не́ бы́ло) догово́ра.   There is/was no treaty.

   У нас **нет (не бу́дет)**   We don't/won't have the
   средств.   means. (Lit.: At us aren't/
                                                  won't be the means.)

4. **After prepositions.**

   A.   **"From"** (ОТКУ́ДА): ИЗ, С, ОТ.   These words are not interchangeable:

   из (*used with nouns that use* **в** *for* куда́)
      Отку́да? – Из библиоте́ки   Куда́ – в библиоте́ку

   с (*used with nouns that use* **на** *for* куда́)
      Отку́да? – С рабо́ты   Куда́ – на рабо́ту

   от (*used with nouns that use* **к** *for* куда́, *usually people*)
      Отку́да? – От дру́га   Куда́ – к дру́гу

   B.   **Other prepositions.**

      у – next to, by: Стоя́ли у окна́.
      о́коло – near, apporoximately: О́коло Москвы́ – near Moscow; о́коло ста
         челове́к – around (approximately) 100 people.
      ми́мо – past: Мы е́хали ми́мо Бе́лого до́ма – We drove by the White House.
      вокру́г – around (in a circle) – вокру́г Земли́ – around the Earth.
      среди́ – among: Среди́ специали́стов
      вдоль – along down (a river): вдоль реки́
      внутри́, вне – inside, outside: внутри́ (вне) Сове́тского Сою́за.
      без – without: без по́мощи

кро́ме – besides, in addition to: кро́ме того́ – besides that

для – for (the benefit of) – Для всех и ка́ждого – for each and every person.

до – up to, as far as: Ехали до Ми́нска – They rode as far as Minsk.

про́тив – against: Проте́сты про́тив го́нки вооруже́ний

посреди́ – in the middle of: посреди́ зимы́

поми́мо – in addition to: поми́мо того́ – in addition to that

C.   **Time.**

во вре́мя – during: во вре́мя войны́

до – before, up till, as far as: до войны́ – before the war, up until the war. по́сле – after: по́сле войны́

с – from, since: с девяти́ до пяти́ – from nine to five (o'clock); с про́шлого го́да – since last year

от + date – from (a date, e.g. "In a March 6 article..."): в статье́ от шесто́го ма́рта...

5.   **Dates, months, years.**   Note where genitive is used (and just as importantly where it is *not* used in dates, months, and years.

Use genitive:

a.   **"On a date":** Это случи́лось **пе́рвого** мая. – This happened *on* May 1. (*NO preposition in Russian!*)

b.   **"On a date of a month":** Это случи́лось пе́рвого **мая.** – This happened on *May* 1.

c.   **"On a date (or in a month) of a year":** Это случи́лось в ма́е **шестьдеся́т пе́рвого го́да.** – This happened in May of *1961.*

Do NOT use genitive:

a.   **To "announce" a date "Yesterday was..."** Вчера́ бы́ло **пе́рвое мая.** (*Note that all dates are neuter adjectival "ordinal" numbers.*)

b.   **"In a (*certain*) month"** (without a date): Это случи́лось **в а́вгусте** (in August) во́семьдесят седьмо́го го́да. (**В** + *prepositional*).

c.   **"In a (*certain*) year"** (without a preceding month or date): Это случи́лось **в се́мьдесят седьмо́м году́.** – It happened in 1977. (**В** + *prepositional.*)

d.   **"On a day" (as opposed to a date):** Это случи́лось **в сре́ду,** восьмо́го апре́ля. (**В** + *accusative.*)

GRAMMAR: -ТО AND -НИБУДЬ AND НИ- ... НЕ CONSTRUCTIONS

Look at the following sentences and their translations:

Она́ что-нибу́дь пишет?　　　　　　　Is she writing something?

Да, она́ что-то пишет.　　　　　　　Yes, she's writing something.

Нет, она́ ничего́ не пишет.　　　　　No, she's not writing anything.

As you can see there is *no direct correspondence* between **-то, -нибу́дь,** and **ни...не** on the one hand, and *some-, any-* and *-no-* on the other.   Follow the rules below:

1.   Use **ни...не(т)** in all negative constructions:

У нас **нет ничего́** - We don't have anything.   Она **никуда́ не** идёт - She's going nowhere.

2.   Use **-нибу́дь:**

    a.　　Questions:　　Они **кого́-нибу́дь** зна́ют?
    b.　　Future tense: Мы **что-нибу́дь** сде́лаем.
    c.　　Imperatives:　Сде́лайте **что-нибу́дь!**
    d.　　Sentences adverbs of repetition (всегда́, всё вре́мя, ка́ждый день, etc.):　Они всегда́ **что-нибу́дь** чита́ли. - They were always reading something (or another).

3.   Use **-то** in all other present and past tense sentences:

Он как-то вы́шел из положе́ния - He got out of that situation somehow.
Мы где-то встреча́лись - We've met somewhere.

TABLE 10:   POSSESSION AND PRESENCE

	"possession" construction	"presence" construction

positive	У Кана́ды **есть** догово́р.
	(gen) **был** (nom)
	       бу́дет
	
	Canada **has** a treaty.
	Canada **had** a treaty.
	Canada **will have** a treaty.
		В По́льше **есть** свобо́да.
		(prep) **была́** (nom)
		          бу́дет
		
		There **is** freedom in Poland.
		There **was** freedom in Poland.
		There **will be** freedom
		   in Poland.

negative	У Кана́ды **нет** догово́ра.
	    не́ было (gen)
	    не бу́дет
	
	Canada **has no** treaty.
	
	Canada **had no** treaty.
	
	Canada **will not have** a
	   treaty.
		В По́льше **нет** свобо́ды.
		     не́ было (gen)
		     не бу́дет
		
		There **is no** freedom in
		   Poland.
		There **was no** freedom in
		   Poland.
		There **will be no** freedom
		   Poland.

Synonym: «**име́ть**»	Кана́да **име́ет** догово́р.
	          (acc)
	Кана́да **не име́ет** догово́ра.
	              (gen)
		Synonym: «**существова́ть**»
		
		В По́льше **существу́ет** свобо́да.
		                     (nom)
		В По́льше **не существу́ет**
		   свобо́ды. (gen)

TABLE 11: Куда? Где? Откуда?

КУДА?	ГДЕ?	ОТКУДА?
В Европу (accusative) to Europe	В Европе (locative) in Europe	ИЗ Европы (genitive) from Europe
НА конференцию (accusative) to the conference	НА конференции (locative) at the conference	С конференции (genitive) from the conference
К границе (dative) towards the border	У границы (genitive) at the border	ОТ границы (genitive) from the border
К советнику (dative) to the adviser	У советника (genitive) at the adviser's	ОТ советника (genitive) from the adviser

GRAMMAR EXERCISES: GENITIVE CASE

A. Read over the grammar on genitive case for Lesson 5. Study Tables 10 and 11 above, as well as the chart and Table 13 at the end of Lesson 5. Then review the reading text. Find all the places where genitive is used and determine the reason for each occurence.

B. Translate the following "of" and "-'s" phrases.

1.   American president's position
2.   the head of your delegation
3.   conditions of war
4.   the desire of the Soviet people
5.   the issue of peace in the Middle East
6.   the danger of nuclear proliferation
7.   exports of raw material
8.   position of strength
9.   round of wideranging questions

C. Russian often uses genitive "of" constructions in place of compressed English *noun-noun* constructions (e.g. "peace issue" ---> "issue of peace" *вопрос мира*). How would you expand the following phrases in Russian?

1.   third world countries
2.   medium-range weapons
3.   The Reagan doctrine
4.   Warsaw Pact meeting
5.   White House policy statement
6.   Congressional approval
7.   delegation members
8.   security issues
9.   information exchange
10. deputy defense minister
11. export expansion
12. conventional weapons reduction

D. **Review Table 11. Answer the questions using the words in the right-hand column. (Find the exercise on the tape)**

1.   Чего явно не было на
     переговорах?

     –добрая воля
     –добрые намерения
     –желание достичь договорённости
     –настоящее понимание вопроса
     –бурные дискуссии

2.   Откуда этот текст?   -ваша конференция
     (из, с, от)   -американские газеты
                                          -программа «Время»
                                          -глава делегации
                                          -сегодняшнее выступление

3.   Кроме чего?   -американские предложения
                                          -советские инициативы
                                          -неотложные вопросы
                                          -инспекция на месте
                                          -стратегические вооружения

4.   Без чего?   -участие Организации
                                              освобождения Палестины
                                          -ядерные боеголовки
                                          -сверхсовременная техника
                                          -поддержка администрации

5.   Против чего?   -всё человечество
                                          -расизм и дискриминация
                                          -распространение ядерного оружия
                                          -расширение влияния военно-
                                              промышленного комплекса

E.   Combine the prepositions given below with each of the noun phrases in the blanks to complete the sentences. Use as many prepositions with each noun phrase as make sense.

до, после, у, около, мимо, вокруг, среди, вдоль, внутри, вне, для, против, кроме, помимо, посреди

1.   Спутник «Венера-2» вышел на орбиту _____ ___________.
                                                      планета

2.   Такое мнение сейчас распространяется _____ ___________.
                                                      молодежь

3.   Ничего не сказав, заведующий отделом прошел _____ ______________.
                                                           лаборатория

4.   Средний советский гражданин зарабатывает _____ ________________
                                                         двести пятьдесят

     рублей в месяц.

5.   Демонстранты выступили _____ _________________.
                                      ядерные испытания

6. Что входит в договоренность ______ _________________________

портативные вычислительные

________?

машины

7. Такую технику можно увидеть лишь в США ______ __________________ вы ее

Советский Союз

не увидите.

8. Все это случилось еще ______ ________ .

война

9. Ошибка была обнаружена только ______ _________ _________.

запуск   ракета

10. ______ _________________________ военный бюджет в миллиард долларов

такая маленькая страна

в год нереален.

F. Review time-expressions from previous lessons and from the genitive case chart at the end of Lesson 5.   Translate these time expressions. (Write out all numbers)

1.   On Wednesday, April 3, 1989
2.   Yesterday was October 23, 1987.
3.   Yesterday was Saturday.
4.   In March, 1981
5.   In 1966
6.   By the beginning of next year
7.   By thc end of the month
8.   Tomorrow will be January 22, 1988.
9.   This happened June 22, 1941.
10. In June and July of this year
11. From November 12 until December 29, 1990
12. From two o'clock until four
13. Since 1974
14. From 1961 to 1983
15. Since last week
16. From 11 until 12
17. From fall until spring
18. Since the October Revolution
19. This month
20. Next week
21. During the war
22. Next year
23. On Sunday at 2:00pm
24. Until 1979
25. Before August 16, 1986

G. Fill in the blanks. Watch for absence or presence. Study Table 10.

1. Где вы нашли эти ______________? Ведь ______ __________ в
    documents   *they   weren't*

    библиотеке. Нет, ________ ________ там, только не в том отделе.
                 they   were

2. Где ______ ______________________? Почему ______ ________ на
    was   the deputy minister   *he   wasn't*

    выступлении министра?

3. У США ______ ____________________ с Кубой до шестьдесят первого
    had   diplomatic relations

    года.

4. Жена Горбачёва часто сопровождает его в поездках за границу, но на

    предстоящей встрече ______ ____________________.
                        she   will not be present

5. У Никсона ______ ______________, чтобы положить конец войне во
    had   a secret plan

    Вьетнаме? Многие обозреватели считают, что у него ____________
                                                       didn't have

    ______________.
    such a plan

6. У СССР ______________ ______________________.
    has no   space offensive weapons

**H. TO BE OR NOT TO BE. Translate the sentences. Then give their opposites
("There was" --> "There wasn't" and vice-versa.) (This exercise may
involve engaging in some wishful thinking.)**

1. The minister's statement was in the newspaper.
2. There was an exchange of information until 1975.
3. This question is on the agenda.
4. There can be a summit meeting under those conditions.
5. Many believe that there is parity between the US and USSR.
6. There was an article in the paper about SDI.
7. There will be no verification.
8. There was no conference on the Central African issue.
9. There are no citizens of Vietnam in the U.S.
10. There is no serious trade between the EEC and Albania.
11. There can be no agreement on the situation in Lebanon.
12. There was no improvement in the Nigerian economy.

I. HAVING: У + КОГО VERSUS В + ЧЕМ. So far "having" has been expressed only with an у + кого construction. That works nicely for people and for countries, which are often personified. But *things* often "have" with a в + чём construction.

У **москвичей** есть метро.   *BUT*   В **Москве** есть метро.
Moscovites have a metro.   Moscow has a metro.

With this in mind translate the sentences below.

1. The delegates have a new agreement.
2. The agreement had conditions for information exchange.
3. The embassy has no hidden microphones.
4. China has a people's army.
5. The Lenin Library has publications on U.S. weaponry.
6. The deputy minister had a new proposal.
7. Japan has no natural resources.
8. The paper had an article on national security.
9. The President had an interesting statement.
10. The magazine has an interesting editorial.

J. TO HAVE AND TO HAVE NOT. Study Table 10 above and Table 13 at the end of Lesson 5. Translate the sentences. Then restate them in the affirmative (engaging in occasional wishful thinking or unbridled pessimism).

1. We have no diplomatic relations with North Korea.
2. The black population of South Africa does not have the right to vote.
3. We do not have time to negotiate a settlement.
4. Libya does not have good relations with the U.S.
5. Our armed forces do not have chemical weapons.
6. Brezhnev did not have new ideas about the Soviet economy.
7. Your group will not have the opportunity to visit NATO headquarters.
8. Moscow did not have an air defense system.
9. The laboratory does not have modern equipment.
10. The Nicaraguan government has no communists.

K. Put the numbers and nouns into the correct form. Consult the appendix.

1. На конференцию приехали делегаты более, чем из _____________________.
                                                                        thirty-five countries

2. Средний рабочий работает с ____________ утра до ____________.
                                                nine o'clock   *five o'clock*

3.   Годовая экономическая эффективность проекта может дойти до

______________.
6,500 rubles

4.   В демонстрации приняло участие около ______________ из
54,000   people

______________ ______________.
twenty-nine   countries

5.   От решений всего лишь ______ ________ зависят судьбы __________
two   people   *of millions*

______________.
of Africans

6.   Около ______ __________ земли данной страны находится в руках
80   percent

______ __________.
of 41   families

7.   На острове Диксон завершена работа группы ______ __________ из
52   geologists

______________. Учёные перезимовали на острове, где температура
12 countries

ночью доходит до ______ __________ мороза.
65   degrees

8.   Согласно данным США «ограниченный» советский военный контингент в

Афганистане состоял из __________ __________.
95,000   troops

9.   В ядерных арсеналах обеих стран находится около ________ __________.
100,000   warheads

10.   УПДК обслуживает сотрудников ______ __________.
238   embassies

GRAMMAR EXERCISE: –ТО, –НИБУДЬ AND НИ– ... НЕ CONSTRUCTIONS

Fill in the blank with **–то, –нибу́дь,** or **–ни...не** constructions.   Use the
following words: **что-то, кто-то, как-то, почему́-то, где-то, куда́-то, когда́-то**
or their **–нибу́дь** or **ни–...не** equivalents.   Remember that the **что-** and **кто-**
parts of these words decline.

1.   Корреспонденты спрашивали __________ об этом?
someone

2. Блейк __________ был в Кремле.
         never

3. По-моему, ______________ сообщили об изменении в повестке дня, но
         (to) someone

    ______________ __________ из нашей группы не знал об этом.
    for some reason *no one*

4. Вы ________ видели такое выступление?
         ever

5. У нас ______________ были нерешённые вопросы.
         at one time

6. Не волнуйтесь, мы __________ решим этот вопрос.
         somehow

7. В договоре есть ______________ об обменах студентами?
         something

8. Вы ищете нашего партнёра? Он ______________ не ушёл. Вот он сейчас
         anywhere

    идёт.

9. В договоре ________________________________ необходимых условий.
         nowhere (are there to be found)

10. Напишите __________ о нашем проекте!
         something

GRAMMAR: VERBAL ADVERBS - INTRODUCTION

Verbal adverbs are a cross between a verb and an adverb. Therefore, they have some characteristics of both verbs (transitive/intransitive, case government, reflexive СЯ-ending, aspect), and adverb (no change for gender, number and case; it modifies the predicate verb).

Look at the phrases below:

| Слу́ша | я | |

лекцию, они делали пометки.

Listening to the lecture, they were making notes.

| Интересу́ | я | сь |

политикой, он регулярно читает газеты.

Taking interest in politics, he regularly reads newspapers.

| Подписа́ | в |

договор, стороны откроют новую эру в советско-китайских отношениях.

(By) signing the treaty, both sides will open a new stage in Soviet-Chinese relations.

Verbal adverbs do not express tense. They indicate the *circumstances of action of the predicate*: when когда́, why почему́, under what circumstances при како́м усло́вии.

Слу́шая ле́кцию, они́ де́лали поме́тки.
Когда́ они́ де́лали поме́тки? Когда́ они́ *слу́шали* ле́кцию.

Интересу́ясь поли́тикой, он регуля́рно чита́ет газе́ты.
Почему́ он регуля́рно чита́ет? Потому́ что он *интересу́ется* поли́тикой.

Подписа́в догово́р, сто́роны откро́ют но́вую э́ру в сове́тско-кита́йских отноше́ниях.
При како́м усло́вии сто́роны откро́ют но́вую э́ру в сове́тско-кита́йских отноше́ниях? Если они́ *подпи́шут* догово́р.

IMPERFECTIVE VERBAL ADVERBS

Now look at the following sentences and their translations:

Отвеча́я на многочи́сленные вопро́сы, сове́тский представи́тель рассказа́л о существу́ющих ме́рах по охра́не окружа́ющей среды́.	*While answering* numerous questions, the Soviet spokesman recounted existing measures for environmental protection.
Не понима́я су́ти перестро́йки, невозмо́жно её провести́ в жизнь.	It is impossible to implement "perestroika" *without understanding* its meaning.
Рассчи́тывая на пост в но́вой администра́ции, он заи́грывает с демокра́тами.	*Hoping* to get a position in the new administration, he flirts with Democrats.

Note that "without doing something" is always rendered with a verbal adverb as above.

These are **imperfective verbal adverbs**. They are made of imperfective verbs and denote *an action simultaneous with the action of the predicate*.

You can replace verbal adverbs by clauses of time: когда́, в то вре́мя как..., cause: потому́ что, так как..., and condition: е́сли, etc.

В то вре́мя, как (когда́) сове́тский представитель отвеча́л на многочи́сленные вопро́сы, он рассказа́л о существу́ющих ме́рах по охра́не окружа́ющей среды́.

Если не понима́ть су́ти перестро́йки, её невозмо́жно провести́ в жизнь.

Он заигрывает с демокра́тами, *так как* (*потому́ что*) он рассчи́тывает на пост в но́вой администра́ции.

As you can see, both active participles (discussed in lesson 3) and imperfective verbal adverbs usually correspond to the -ing participles in English.

You can identify imperfective verbal adverbs by the - А, Я   ending: сокраща́я, добива́ясь, слы́ша.

PERFECTIVE VERBAL ADVERBS

Now look at the following sentences and their translations.

В «торго́вой войне́» пе́рвыми откры́ли ого́нь США, *потре́бовав* от ЕЭС значи́тельных усту́пок.	In the trade war the US was the first to open fire, *(by) requesting/ having requested* considerable concessions from EEC.
Размести́в необходи́мые си́лы вдоль грани́цы, партиза́ны смо́гут контроли́ровать ситуа́цию.	*Once* necessary forces *are deployed* along the border, guerrillas will be able to control the situation.

These are **perfective verbal adverbs.** They are made of perfective verbs and denote *an action prior to the action of the predicate.* They frequently correspond to "having done," "after..., upon..., once..." constructions in English.

However, Russian is usually more exact that English. Hence perfective verbal adverbs are more frequent in Russian than such English constructions as "having done." English often uses an -ing form even when the action described precedes the action of the predicate.

Отказа́вшись от морато́рия на испыта́ния я́дерного ору́жия, США по́лностью разоблачи́ли себя́.	The US has shown its true nature *by turning down* the moratorium on nuclear testing.

You can replace verbal adverbs by clauses of time: **когда́, после того́, как...,** cause **потому́ что..., так как...** , and condition: **е́сли,** etc.

В «торго́вой войне́» пе́рвыми откры́ли ого́нь США *после того́, как* они́ *потре́бовали* от ЕЭС значи́тельных усту́пок.

США по́лностью разоблачи́ли себя́, *когда́* они́ *отказа́лись* от морато́рия на испыта́ния я́дерного ору́жия.

or (depending on the context)

США по́лностью разоблачи́ли себя́, *так как* они *отказа́лись* от морато́рия на испыта́ния я́дерного ору́жия.

Партиза́ны смо́гут контроли́ровать грани́цу, *е́сли* они́ *разместя́т* вдоль неё необходи́мые си́лы.

You can identify perfective verbal adverbs by the – В(ШИ) ending: сыгра́в, заинтересова́вшись.

TABLE 12:   VERBAL ADVERBS

denote an action...

	...simultaneous with action of the predicate	...preceding the action of the predicate
i m p e r f e c t i v e	**ЧИТАТЬ** (они) ЧИТА ЮТ ЧИТА Я (while reading) **ПОЛЬЗОВАТЬСЯ** (они) ПОЛЬЗУ ЮТ СЯ ПОЛЬЗУ Я СЬ (while using) *BUT*: дава́ть ⟶ дава́я признава́ть ⟶ признава́я	NONE
p e r f e c t i v e	NONE	**ПРОЧИТА ТЬ** ПРОЧИТА В(ШИ) (having read) **ВОСПОЛЬЗОВА ТЬ СЯ** ВОСПОЛЬЗОВА ВШИ СЬ (having used) *BUT*: провести́ ⟶ проведя́ пройти́ ⟶ пройдя́ помо́чь ⟶ помо́гши

GRAMMAR EXERCISES: VERBAL ADVERBS

A.   Read all the grammar on verbal adverbs.   Review their formation.   Find verbal adverbs in the text and determine the reason for their occurrence.

B.   1)   Make imperfective verbal adverbs out of the verbs in the right-hand column.

сокращать/сократить
включать/включить
ставить/поставить
заявлять/заявить
добиваться/добиться

2)   Now make perfective verbal adverbs out of the same verbs.

проявлять/проявить
способствовать
покупать/купить
продавать/продать
предоставлять/предоставить

C.   Make one sentence out of two by forming a verbal adverb out of the italicized verb; make necessary changes.   Be able to translate your sentence.

Example: Великобритания *начала* сокращать свои стратегические силы.   Тем самым она поставила под угрозу безопасность своей территории.

— → *Начав* сокращать свои стратегические силы, Великобритания поставила под угрозу безопасность своей территории.

1.   В «торговой войне» первыми открыли огонь Соединённые Штаты.   Они *потребовали* от ЕЭС значительных уступок.

2.   За последнее время США усилили нажим на партнёров по ГАТТ.   Они *стремятся* заставить их добровольно оплачивать свой огромный торговый дефицит.

3.   Япония уже выкрутила руки Сингапуру.   Она *добилась* «добровольного» сокращения текстильного экспорта.

4.   Дж. Шульц *рассказывал* об исландской встрече.   Он сказал, что обе стороны искренне стремились к успешному завершению её.

5.   Т. Трентон *говорил* об отношении Англии к вопросам обороны.   Он отметил, что позиция Англии к ним не изменилась.

6.   Сначала ОПЕК *отказалась* от фиксированных цен на нефть.   Вскоре же она была вынуждена снизить цены до 9 долларов за баррель.

D. **Replace adverbial clauses in the sentences below with verbal adverbial constructions. Be able to translate the latter into English.**

Example: *В то время, как нефтедобывающие страны пытаются найти выход из* создавшегося положения, они переходят к займам на ещё более жестких условиях.
       ——→ *Пытаясь* найти выход из создавшегося положения, нефтедобывающие страны переходят к займам на ещё более жёстких условиях.

1. Переговоры он ведёт «спустя рукава», т.е плохо, *так как* он не *собирается* заключать соглашения.
2. *После того как* администрация *сослалась* на этот факт, она решила компенсировать свои неудачи нажимом на штаб-квартиру ЕЭС.
3. *В то время как* президент *подчёркивал* мирное назначение этих противоракетных космических станций, он сказал, что он готов поделиться новой техникой с русскими.
4. *Когда* военные-учёные *возражали* президенту, они говорили о наступательном потенциале «звёздных войн».
5. *Так как* мы *предполагаем*, что это заявление верно отражает позицию президента, мы хотели бы задать три вопроса.
6. *В то время как* Р.Рейган *оценивал* общие результаты встречи, он сказал, что в Рейкьявике был достигнут значительный прогресс.

E. **Fill in the blanks. Be able to translate these sentences into English.**

1. _____________ на повестку дня вопрос о контроле над вооружениями, СССР
   (putting)

   продемонстрировал свою решимость бороться за мир.

2. _______________________________ СССР в переговоры, США исключили
   (having failed to include)

   возможность решения ближневосточной проблемы.

3. Во время обмена мнениями стороны, ____________________ о своей
                       (having announced)

   заинтересованности подписать соглашение, назначили дату следующей

   встречи.

4. _________________ с приветственной речью, президент отметил недавний
   (giving a speech)

   прогресс в американо-советских отношениях.

5.   Мы ставим под угрозу нашу национальную безопасность, постоянно

_______________ высокосовременную технику из Японии.
(importing)

G.   Translation.

1.   Addressing a session of European Parliament, the French representative paid special attention to the new EEC agricultural policy.
2.   By not having paid attention to the energy problem in the 70's, we now have to buy much foreign oil.
3.   Having reduced its nuclear arsenal, the US will increase its conventional forces.
4.   Will the Department of Commerce demonstrate its good will by granting long-term credits to China?
5.   Ambassador Lawrence can contribute to the improvement of the political climate only by achieving success in the forthcoming negotiations.

RENDERING

A. *Render* **the following sentences. Do not translate word for word. Rather, give the idea expressed.**

1. The Soviet Union has agreed to open trade negotiations with South Korea, although the future relationship is as yet unclear.
2. Before Reagan's announcement of SDI in 1983, political observers from the third world had hoped for better U.S.–Soviet relations, leading to a reduction in world tension.
3. From 1972 to 1978 there existed a relaxation of tensions between the US and the USSR. During detente trade contacts were broadened. American firms such as IBM and Holiday Inn were negotiating major trade deals with the Soviets.
4. The international situation sharpened considerably after the events of 1979, when the Soviet Army entered Afghanistan.
5. Among other issues of the period were the situation in Poland, the matter of Jewish emigration from the Soviet Union, and the boycott of the Olympic Games of 1980.

B. **Write a paragraph or two in** *simple* **Russian using the grammar and vocabulary you have learned so far to convey the following facts. Do** *not* **translate word for word. Use what you know to** *render* **all the information you can.**

The Chernenian People's Democratic Republic, closed off from both CMEA and the Western economic community (IMF, World Bank, EEC, etc.) for nearly four decades, has suddenly and unexpectedly announced its willingness to talk trade -- with its neighbors in the immediate future, and with other countries perhaps several years down the road. Specifically, Leonarz Melijtyz, general secretary of the Chernenian United Workers' Party, has invited the prime minister of the largest neighboring country (you make up the name) to come to the capital, Pustovilja, for the first-ever talks on trade and mutual security.

The landmark negotiations are unprecedented; the CPDR has no diplomatic relations with its neighbors; for that matter, most diplomats scratch their heads when asked to name any other country with an embassy in Pustovilja.

Nevertheless, the two heads of state remain undaunted. On the agenda are dozens of trade issues; the PDR's possible export of raw materials, the expansion of tourism (now non-existent), and scientific-technical exchanges are included in the agenda.   Even the possibility of setting up joint ventures is not out of the question.

Mutual security is also to play a significant role in the talks. General Secretary Melijtyz is thought to be toying with the idea of relaxing his country's strict border control. He is likely to propose a reduction of the troops facing each other on both sides of the border. He would also like his neighbor to join with him in a mutual call to both superpowers to reduce the number of nuclear weapons in Europe.

While outsiders can only guess at the motivations for Chernenia's about-face, few doubt that the mere fact that some contacts are now at last taking place is sure to promote the development of mutually beneficial relations with other countries as well.

QUOTING SOURCES:

In English "sources" can speak:

Well informed sources said yesterday that...

In Russian «источники» can not «говори́ть»:

ИЗ   журнали́стских

ИЗ   вое́нных

ИЗ   секре́тных   исто́чников ста́ло изве́стно, что...

ИЗ   америка́нских   о...

ИЗ   исто́чников   Пентаго́на

                   Бе́лого до́ма   ста́ло изве́стно, что...

                   ЦРУ   о...

SPEAKING EXERCISES

A.   Отве́тьте на сле́дующие вопро́сы по те́ксту уро́ка.

1.   Како́й пробле́ме бы́ло предло́жено удели́ть наибо́льшее внима́ние на встре́че мини́стров иностра́нных дел СССР и США?
2.   Каки́е други́е вопро́сы бу́дут обсужда́ться на э́той встре́че?
3.   Во и́мя чего́ Сове́тский Сою́з гото́в добива́ться разря́дки междунаро́дной напряжённости?
4.   Как америка́нская сторона́ смо́жет, по слова́м сове́тского представи́теля, спосо́бствовать улучше́нию междунаро́дной обстано́вки?

B.   1)   Расскажи́те текст, испо́льзуя слова́рь уро́ка 5.

2)   Измени́те расска́з, испо́льзуя слова́рь уро́ка.

C. **Соста́вьте ситуа́цию, испо́льзуя сле́дующие выраже́ния.**

...sources said that..., to put the question of...on the agenda, to achieve ... in forthcoming negotiations, prevention of a threat of a new war, to contribute to...in international relations

D. **Опиши́те пресс-конфере́нцию М. Горбачёва об ограниче́нии стратеги́ческих вооруже́ний.**

E. **Расскажи́те, каки́е разногла́сия сохрани́лись ме́жду США и СССР на после́дней встре́че в верха́х.**

F. **Речь главы́ америка́нской делега́ции на перегово́рах по сокраще́нию обы́чных вооруже́ний в Центра́льной Евро́пе.**

G. **Заседа́ние изра́ильского кабине́та мини́стров. Приведи́те аргуме́нты премье́р-мини́стра Изра́иля про́тив предоставле́ния СССР ро́ли в ближневосто́чном ми́рном урегули́ровании.**

READING EXERCISE 1

PRE-TEXT:

Read the text with the following questions in mind:

TEXT 1

1. What is the text about?
2. Did Marshal Kulikov preside over the Military Council or over the Political Consultative Committee of the Warsaw Pact?
3. Which officials participated in this event?
4. Which of the following was emphasised at the meeting...(true or false for each):
    a. liquidation of nuclear weapons.
    b. reduction of nuclear weapons.
    c. liquidation of conventional weapons
    d. reduction of conventional weapons

5. According to what was said, what level of Warsaw Pact forces should be maintained?
6. What types of military readiness were discussed at the meeting?
7. Who hosted the reception?

TEXT 2

Which of the following statements is true?

1. The initiative to reduce joint forces by 5% was approved by referendum in Rumania.
2. The Military Council of the Warsaw Pact countries met on June 10–11.
3. The members of the Warsaw Pact proposed a substantial bilateral reduction of forces *vis-a-vis* NATO.
4. Land forces together with strategic missiles systems would be reduced by 25%.
5. The U.S. and its allies have not yet responded to this proposal.

Об итогах очередного заседания Военного совета Объединенных вооруженных сил государств—участников Варшавского Договора

С 12 по 14 ноября 1986 года в столице Социалистической Республики Румынии г. Бухаресте под председательством главнокомандующего Объединенными вооруженными силами Маршала Советского Союза Куликова В. Г. состоялось очередное заседание Военного совета Объединенных вооруженных сил государств — участников Варшавского Договора.

В его работе приняли участие члены Военного совета, а также ответственные должностные лица министерств обороны государств — участников Варшавского Договора и органов управления Объединенными вооруженными силами.

Военный совет обсудил вопрос об итогах и выводах, вытекающих из встречи Генерального секретаря ЦК КПСС М. С. Горбачева с президентом США Р. Рейганом в Рейкьявике. Отмечен важный вклад союзных социалистических государств в обеспечение мира, подчеркнута необходимость наращивания совместных усилий в интересах борьбы за ликвидацию ядерных и сокращение обычных вооружений, за укрепление международной безопасности.

Намечены конкретные меры по поддержанию войск и сил флотов, выделенных от союзных армий в состав Объединенных вооруженных сил, на уровне, обеспечивающем сохранение военного паритета между Варшавским Договором и блоком НАТО.

На заседании были подведены также итоги оперативной и боевой подготовки Объединенных вооруженных сил государств — участников Варшавского Договора за истекший год, определены задачи на новый учебный год и рассмотрены другие вопросы текущей деятельности Объединенных вооруженных сил.

По мнению всех участников заседания, была подтверждена необходимость дальнейшего расширения и углубления боевого содружества между союзными армиями.

Военный совет по обсуждавшимся вопросам принял согласованные рекомендации и предложения.

Заседание прошло в деловой обстановке, в духе дружбы и взаимопонимания.

Участников заседания принял Генеральный секретарь Румынской коммунистической партии, Президент СРР Н. Чаушеску.

Референдум в Румынии

БУХАРЕСТ, 25. (ТАСС). В ходе состоявшегося 23 ноября в СРР референдума была одобрена инициатива о сокращении на 5 процентов вооружений, войск и военных расходов Румынии.

Как известно, на совещании Политического консультативного комитета в Будапеште 10—11 июня 1986 года государства — участники Варшавского Договора предложили значительные взаимные сокращения вооруженных сил и вооружений противостоящих друг другу военно-политических союзов в Европе. В случае реализации этих предложений сухопутные войска вместе с тактической ударной авиацией обоих союзов были бы сокращены приблизительно на 25 процентов по сравнению с сегодняшним уровнем, т. е. на полмиллиона человек с каждой стороны. Сокращения сопровождались бы соответствующим снижением военных расходов государств. США и их союзники по НАТО до сих пор не дали ответы на эту инициативу, как и на предложение организовать контакты рабочих групп двух военно-политических союзов для конкретного рассмотрения вопросов взаимных сокращений вооруженных сил и вооружений в Центральной Европе.

POST–TEXT (using sentence structure):

Reference words: Sometimes a sentence contains words, often pronouns or conjunctions, which point to things or events from the previous sentence or paragraph. These words signal that you should look back to find out what is being **referred** to.

1. Find the word(s) in the first paragraph to which *в его работе* in the second paragraph refers.
2. Paragraph three contains...(mark the correct answer):
    a.   an illustration for paragraphs 1 and 2
    b.   a comparison with facts in paragraphs 1 and 2.
3. In paragraph four, find the word modified by a participial phrase.
4. Translate this sentence into English.

POST–TEXT (using context):

1. What are the English words for *очередной* and *внеочередной?*
2. Find the Russian equivalent for *joint forces.* Note the use of a different adjective in *смешанная комиссия.*
3. Find the Russian for *commander-in-chief of the armed forces.* Note the use of instrumental for English *of.*
4. Find a synonym for *военный баланс* in the text.
5. The Warsaw Pact is termed a *военно-политический союз.* Find the names in the text for the bodies which are responsible for respective parts of the alliance.
6. What is the opposite of *взаимные сокращения?*
7. What are the English equivalents for *сухопутные войска* and *ударная авиация?*
8. Make a list of words that you can use to talk about armed forces.

READING EXERCISE 2

PRE-TEXT:

Read the text with the following
questions in mind:

1.   What is the article about?
2.   Where was the briefing held?
3.   Who was the spokesman?
4.   How many subjects did he
     touch upon?
5.   What were they?
6.   Did the briefing include a
     question and answer period?

В пресс-центре МИД СССР

27 ноября в пресс-центре МИД СССР состоялся брифинг для советских и иностранных журналистов.

Выступивший на нем первый заместитель начальника управления информации МИД СССР Б. Д. Пядышев сконцентрировал внимание собравшихся на официальном дружественном визите Генерального секретаря ЦК КПСС М. С. Горбачева в Индию. Он подчеркнул, что Делийская декларация, подписанная М. С. Горбачевым и Премьер-Министром Индии Р. Ганди, является добрым примером, которому могли бы последовать другие государства. Этот документ несомненно оставит заметный след в истории международных отношений наряду с принципами «Панча шила», Бандунга.

Касаясь вскрывшихся фактов передачи администрацией США никарагуанским «контрас» крупных финансовых средств, заработанных на поставках оружия Ирану, представитель МИД подчеркнул, что это еще больше обострило кризис внешнеполитического курса США.

Напомнив, что Первый комитет Генеральной Ассамблеи ООН одобрил внушительным большинством голосов проект резолюции по внесенному группой социалистических стран вопросу о создании всеобъемлющей системы международного мира и безопасности, представитель МИД СССР отметил, что сделан важный шаг на пути к разработке и претворению на практике концепции обеспечения всеобщей безопасности на равной основе для всех государств. Смысл этого предложения заключается в том, чтобы материализовать новое политическое мышление в конкретных действиях.

Было подчеркнуто, что политика доверия должна стать одной из гарантий безопасности. Именно на это должно быть сконцентрировано усилие всего мирового сообщества.

Были даны ответы на вопросы журналистов.

(ТАСС)

POST-TEXT (using sentence structure):

1. Find the word in the first paragraph to which *на нём* in the second paragraph refers.
2. Find the words which modify the subject of the first sentence in the first paragraph.
3. In the second sentence of the first paragraph, circle the word to which *которому* refers.
4. Translate this sentence into English.
5. In the third paragraph, what two phrases preceed the subject? What do they modify? What follows the subject?
6. Translate the sentence into English.

POST-TEXT (using context):

1. Which words in the first sentence are not of Russian origin?
2. What is the English for *сконцентрировать внимание на официальном визите*? Is the verb perfective or imperfective?

   Conjugate *сконцентрировать* in the future tense. This verb is used one more time in the text. In what form?

3. Find the Russian equivalent for "to follow somebody's example." Note the use of dative in this expression.
4. Translate the sentence starting with *касаясь вскрывшихся фактов....* Note the use of genitive with this verb.
5. Find the Russian for "General Assembly." Is the word "general" a noun or an adjective? What other expressions do you know which use this word?
6. Explain the composition of the word *всеобъемлющий*.
7. The article starts with *27 ноября*. Spell out the numeral. What case is it in? Why? What is the English equivalent?
8. Make a list of words that you can use to talk about national security.

READING EXERCISE 3

PRE-TEXT. Read the text with the following questions in mind:

1. What is the main idea of this text?
2. What organization held a meeting in Vienna?
3. The participants discussed a proposal for the next session of which conference...(check the right answer):
   a. Helsinki
   b. Stockholm
   c. Madrid
   d. Geneva

4.   Which document outlines a joint position of the socialist countries on reduction of forces and conventional weapons in Europe?

5.   The reduction plan would permit reduction of... (true or false for each):

a.   the level of military confrontation
b.   the intensity of the arms race
c.   the danger of a sudden attack
d.   military-strategic instability

6.   Which countries should the negotiations include?

7.   What methods does the Soviet spokesman suggest for dealing with the issues of disarmament?

На общеевропейской встрече в Вене

ВЕНА, 4. (ТАСС). Венская встреча представителей государств — участников Совещания по безопасности и сотрудничеству в Европе вступила в новый важный этап своей работы. Началось рассмотрение вносимых делегациями предложений по всем направлениям общеевропейского процесса.

Активно обсуждается предложение Польши о том, чтобы на последующем этапе стокгольмской конференции обсуждались параллельно меры укрепления доверия и практические вопросы сокращения вооруженных сил и обычных вооружений в Европе.

Делегация СССР сегодня на пленарном заседании изложила принципиальный подход Советского Союза ко всему комплексу этих вопросов. Что касается содержания будущих переговоров по сокращению вооруженных сил и обычных вооружений, заявил глава советской делегации Ю. Б. Кашлев, то совместная позиция социалистических стран четко изложена в будапештском обращении государств — участников Варшавского Договора, принятом на совещании ПКК в июне 1986 года. Она представляет собой детально разработанную, сбалансированную программу европейского разоружения в широкой географической зоне — от Атлантики до Урала. В ней предлагается такой порядок сокращений, при котором понижался бы уровень военного противостояния в Европе, уменьшалась опасность внезапного нападения, укреплялась военно-стратегическая стабильность.

Проблема сокращения вооруженных сил и обычных вооружений в масштабе всей Европы должна рассматриваться на общеевропейской основе с участием всех 35 государств — участников СБСЕ. Такой подход предполагает, что в переговорах должны участвовать — в приемлемой форме — нейтральные и неприсоединившиеся государства.

Советский представитель отметил, что принципиальная позиция Советского Союза не исключает, что в целях ускорения перехода к предметному рассмотрению вопросов разоружения в Европе можно было бы использовать любые формы работы, включая неофициальные контакты — как двусторонние, так и в более широком кругу.

POST-TEXT   (using sentence structure):

1. Find *она* in sentence 3 of paragraph 3.   Now look at sentence 2 in paragraph 3.   To what does *она* refer?
2. The third and fourth sentences contain...   (mark the correct answer):
    a.   a solution to the problem
    b.   a description of the problem

3. Translate these sentences into English.

POST-TEXT   (using context):

1. Names of capitals often serve as names of the conferences held in them.   Find the names of four capitals in adjectival form which serve this role.   Transform them back into nouns.
2. What is the Russian for *The Conference on the European Security and Cooperation?*
3. *Что касается..., то...* is *as far as something is concerned, (then)...* Give several examples to illustrate the use of this phrase.
4. Proposals are usually *submitted*, then *discussed* and finally, *adopted.* Find the Russian equivalents for these verbs.
5. Find the Russian for *neutral* and *non-aligned states.*
6. Find the sentence with *в целях ускорения...* Rephrase it avoiding *в целях.*
7. Make a list of words that you can use to talk about national security.

READING EXERCISE 4

PRE-TEXT.   Read the text with the following questions in mind:

1. What is the article about?
2. The article discusses US violation of the...   (true or false for each):
    a.   ABM Treaty
    b.   SALT Treaty
    c.   INF Treaty
    d.   IRBM Treaty

3. What US action constitutes a violation of this treaty?
4. The treaty provides for a total number of 1,320...   (true or false for each):
    a.   intermediate-range missiles
    b.   bombers with cruise-missiles
    c.   total number of strategic bombers

5.   Why did anonymous administration sources acknowledge a violation had taken place?

6.   According to the treaty, when should bombers and missiles be counted?

США нарушили положения ОСВ-2

ВАШИНГТОН, 18. (ТАСС). Рейгановская администрация, твердо встав на путь торпедирования важнейших договорных обязательств в области контроля над ядерными вооружениями, уже нарушила краеугольные положения советско-американского Договора ОСВ-2.

В этом прямо обвинил официальный Вашингтон заместитель директора авторитетной общественной организации Ассоциация сторонников контроля над вооружениями Джеймс Рубин. Он заявил сегодня в Вашингтоне, что «вывод из ангаров на вспомогательной военно-воздушной базе в Сан-Антонио (штат Техас) 131-го оснащенного крылатыми ракетами с ядерными боеголовками стратегического бомбардировщика В-52 свидетельствует о том что США уже превысили ключевые ограничения в рамках Договора ОСВ-2». Бомбардировщик был переоборудован под носителя крылатых ракет и выведен на летное поле 12 ноября. Договором ОСВ-2, как известно, предусматривается ограничение 1.320 единицами числа стратегических ракет с боеголовками индивидуального наведения и бомбардировщиков с крылатыми ракетами.

Как указывает сегодня газета «Вашингтон пост», «ряд высших представителей администрации, которые просили не называть их имен, также полагают, что нарушение договора уже произошло, поскольку модифицированный бомбардировщик уже может быть зарегистрирован советскими техническими средствами наблюдения». Газета напоминает, что в соответствии с положениями договора ракеты и бомбардировщики с крылатыми ракетами подлежат зачету, после «вывода из цехов, заводов или других объектов».

POST–TEXT (using sentence structure):

1.   Look at the beginning of the second paragraph. Find the word(s) in the first paragraph to which *в этом прямо...* refers.
2.   Translate both the first paragraph and the first sentence of the second paragraph.
3.   In the first sentence of paragraph three, find the word(s) to which *которые* refers.
4.   Translate the first sentence of paragraph 3 into English.

POST–TEXT   (using context):

1.   What do you think is the difference in style between *Рейгановская администрация* and *администрация Рейгана*?
2.   What does *ОСВ* stand for?
3.   Find the Russian equivalent for *arms control* in the text.

4. Make a list of cognates used in the text. Give Russian equivalents
    for: to torpedo, hangar, base, strategic bomber, modified bomber, to
    register.
5. Describe the characteristics of the B-52 bomber using the vocabulary
    of this article.
6. There is an abundance of military and arms control terminology here.
    Make a list of useful expressions. Give Russian equivalents for:
    air-force base, cruise-missile, nuclear warheads with MIRVs, carrier.
7. What is the English for *ключевой*? Explain its composition.
8. Translate the word *носитель* and explain its composition.
9. What are the English equivalents for *превысить ограничения* and
    предусматривать ограничения?

READING EXERCISE 5

PRE-TEXT.   Read the text with the following questions in mind:

1. Skim the article for the main idea.
2. The proposal was submitted to a committee of the UN General Assembly
    by... (check the correct answer):
    a. neutral countries
    b. non-aligned countries
    c. socialist countries
    d. NATO countries

3. What would **a universal system of security** provided by this proposal
    entail?
4. Representatives of which two countries are quoted as being in favor
    of this proposal?

5. A US delegate called this proposal... (check the correct answer):
    a. promising
    b. dangerous
    c. amorphous
    d. futile

6. On what is the initiative based, according to the Soviet Deputy
    Foreign Minister?

ДИАЛОГ БУДЕТ ПРОДОЛЖЕН

НЬЮ-ЙОРК. [Соб. корр. «Известий»] В Первом комитете Генеральной Ассамблеи ООН закончилась дискуссия по проблемам укрепления международной безопасности.

Социалистические страны внесли предложение о создании всеобъемлющей системы международного мира и безопасности. Инициатива эта была в центре внимания делегатов. В ходе прений указывалось, что это предложение предусматривает создание целостной структуры безопасности, основу которой составляют военно-политические и международно-правовые, экономические и морально-психологические, прямые и косвенные гарантии того, что мир не будет разрушен, что стоящие перед человечеством задачи созидания в условиях свободы будут решаться совместными усилиями государств и народов.

Делегаты многих государств поддержали предложение социалистических государств. «Я рад, что ряд стран внес предложение о создании всеобъемлющей системы международного мира и безопасности», — заявил представитель Буркина Фасо О. Манса. «Предложение о создании всеобъемлющей системы международного мира и безопасности,— сказал представитель Шри Ланки Т. Фернандо,— предполагает широкий и продуктивный диалог по широкому кругу вопросов, относящихся к стоящим перед человечеством проблемам».

Противниками инициативы социалистических стран оказались в основном лишь несколько натовских стран. Главным из них, как всегда, были Соединенные Штаты. Американский делегат Р. Иммерман заявил, что предложение о создании всеобъемлющей системы международного мира и безопасности — это некая «аморфная система», цель которой «переписать Устав ООН».

В ходе дискуссии возражения против инициативы социалистических стран были убедительно опровергнуты. Делегаты говорили, что за 41 год существования ООН мир во многом изменился, и это требует учета новых реальностей. Совместная инициатива социалистических стран, заявил заместитель министра иностранных дел СССР В. Ф. Петровский, полностью основывается на Уставе ООН, берет из него свое начало. Она направлена на претворение в жизнь целей и принципов ООН, на реализацию всех заложенных в Уставе возможностей поддержания и укрепления международного мира и безопасности в современных условиях, с учетом реалий ядерно-космической эры, с учетом открываемых ею беспрецедентных опасностей для всех народов и государств и одновременно небывалых перспектив их развития.

Проект резолюции, призывающей к продолжению диалога о создании всеобъемлющей системы международной безопасности, был поставлен на голосование. Вот итоги:

● «За» проголосовали 82 страны.

● «Против» только Соединенные Штаты и Франция.

● 35 стран воздержались.

В. СОЛДАТОВ.

POST-TEXT   (using sentence structure):

1. Find in the text the paragraph(s) which contain(s):
   a. a problem.
   b. a solution
   c. a description

2. Find *она* in sentence 4 of paragraph 4.   To what word does it refer?
3. Translate both sentences into English.

POST-TEXT   (using context):

1. Find the Russian for *in the course of debates*.
2. What is a good English equivalent for *перед миром стоят серьёзные проблемы*?
3. What is the difference in style between *страны НАТО* and *натовские страны*? Which similar usage did you recently come across? Formulate the rule. Try it on *the UN Charter*.
4. List UN terminology which you find in the text.
5. Find two uses of the word *учёт* in the text. What is the Russian for *taking into consideration the realities of nuclear era* and for *this requires (taking into) consideration of new realities*?
6. What is the Russian for *to vote against (in favor of)*? What is the Russian for *to abstain*?

GENITIVE CASE

USES	PREPOSITIONS:	QUESTION:
Ownership	English "of", "-'s"	Кого́? Чего́?
"have"	у	У кого́? У чего́?
Absence	у	У кого́ нет? У чего́ нет? Кого́ нет? Чего́ нет?
From a place	ИЗ С ОТ	Отку́да?

Other prepositions	во вре́мя
	 до - till
	    - as far as
	 по́сле
	 у
	 о́коло - near
	    + a number
	 =approximately
	 ми́мо
	 вокру́г
	 среди́
	 вдоль
	 внутри́
	 вне
	 без
	 кро́ме
	 для
	 про́тив
	 посреди́
	 поми́мо
	 вме́сто
		Во вре́мя чего́?
		
		 Без кого́?

TIME-EXPRESSIONS:	OTHER USES:

TIME-EXPRESSIONS:

второе мая

второго мая

с середины года

до конца квартала

статья от первого
декабря

OTHER USES:

1.   after numerals:

2(3,4) крылатых ракеты
5(6-20) крылатых ракет
            - cruise missiles

2.   after simple comparatives:

больше нашей армии
меньше ваших расходов

3.   Genitive plural after:

сколько, много, мало,
столько, достаточно,
большинство, один из,
одна из, одно из, одни из

4.   after:

достигать - to achieve
бояться - to fear
требовать - to demand
ждать (with inanimate)
ожидать (with inanimate)
избегать - to avoid

TABLE 13: CONSTRUCTION OF POSSESSION

Affirmative

Present:

У	меня́		план
	нас	есть	ка́рта
			вре́мя
	них		де́ньги

possessor in genitive	possession in nominative

Past:

У	меня́		
	нас	был	план (masc)
		была́	ка́рта (fem)
		бы́ло	вре́мя (neut)
	них	бы́ли	де́ньги (plur)

the VERB is in the gender of the possession.

Future:

У	меня́		вре́мя (sing)
		бу́дет	план (sing)
	нас		ка́рта (sing)
	них	бу́дут	де́ньги (plur)

the VERB is in the number of the possession.

Negative

У	тебя вас неё	нет	пла́на ка́рты вре́мени де́нег
	possessor **in** **genitive**		**possession** **in** **genitive**

У	тебя́ вас него́	не́ было	пла́на ка́рты вре́мени де́нег
	the VERB is always neuter		

У	тебя́ вас них	не бу́дет	де́нег пла́на ка́рты вре́мени
	the VERB is always singular		

CIRCLE ONE

LESSON SIX

AUDIO-COMPREHENSION EXERCISE

You are about to hear a text about the World Peace Council, a Soviet dominated international organization. You will probably easily recognize the cognates given below. Look through words and expressions listed after the cognates. Then listen to the text with the following questions in mind. Afterwards, listen to the text again, and write down the answers.

1. What do you already know about the World Peace Council? What in your view can they be expected to say about American and Soviet nuclear weapons? What is the official Soviet attitute towards such an organization likely to be?
2. To which country did the WPC appeal?
3. What kinds of weapons were mentioned?
4. To which body of the government was the appeal directed?
5. The WPC referred to a disarmament proposal already on the table. Whose?
6. And now, exactly what does the WPC want?
7. Which American politician commented on the WPC statement? What did he say?
8. Did his statement match your expectations of what a person in his position could have said?

Cognates

конгре́сс
хими́ческий
биологи́ческий
рекомендова́ть
центра́льный
специа́льный мемора́ндум
ко́мплекс
реакцио́нный
комменти́ровать
республика́нский
сена́т
сена́тор
контроли́роваться
критикова́ть
агресси́вный блок

WORDS AND EXPRESSIONS (on the tape)

	(к кому?)	
обраща́ться/обрати́ться	к Конгре́ссу	ратифици́ровать догово́р
-ются -я́тся	к Сове́тскому Сою́зу	добива́ться разря́дки
	к президе́нту	оказа́ть по́мощь
обращённый		
обраще́ние		

запреща́ть/запрети́ть	а́томное	ору́жие
-ют -ят	я́дерное	
	хими́ческое	
	биологи́ческое	
	обы́чное	
	уда́рное косми́ческое	
запрещённый		
запреще́ние		

оказывать/	влия́ние (на что/кого?)	
-ют	на администра́цию	приня́ть предложе́ние СССР
оказа́ть	на Соединённые Шта́ты	обрати́ться к ООН
ока́жут	на сове́тскую сто́рону	заключи́ть соглаше́ние
ока́занный		
оказа́ние		

принима́ть/	предложе́ние	прекрати́ть все испыта́ния я́дерного ору́жия
-ют		запрети́ть хими́ческое ору́жие
приня́ть		сократи́ть стратеги́ческие вооруже́ния
при́мут		обы́чные вооружённые си́лы в ФРГ
при́нятый		

в призы́ве	говори́тся о... (о чём?)
в мемора́ндуме	говори́тся, что...
в протоко́ле	

	(imperfective)
прекраща́ть/прекрати́ть	нагнета́ть междунаро́дную обстано́вку
-ют -ят	развя́зывать го́нку вооруже́ний - to unleash
	the arms race
	испо́льзование я́дерной эне́ргии
прекращённый	
прекраще́ние	

комменти́ровать	мемора́ндум - to comment upon the memorandum
-уют	догово́р
прокомменти́ровать	

по́длинная   незави́симость – genuine independence
полити́ческая
экономи́ческая

подде́рживать/поддержа́ть   Варша́вский догово́р
       -ют подде́ржат   Североатланти́ческий сою́з/НАТО
подде́ржанный

подрыва́ть/подорва́ть   еди́нство За́пада
     -ют   -ут   вое́нный сою́з
                             ми́рный догово́р
подо́рванный
подры́в

Аргенти́на, аргенти́нский, аргенти́нцы, Буэ́нос-А́йрес
Брази́лия, брази́льский, брази́льцы, Брази́лия
Ме́ксика, мексика́нский, мексика́нцы, Ме́хико
Сомали́, сомали́йский, сомали́йцы, Могади́шо
Вьетна́м, вьетна́мский, вьетна́мцы, Хано́й, говори́ть по-вьетна́мски
Австра́лия, австрали́йский, австрали́йцы, Ка́нберра
Но́вая Зела́ндия, новозела́ндский, новозела́ндцы, Веллингто́н

TEXT: Read the following text; be able to translate it into English in written form.

Призы́в Сове́та ми́ра

Всеми́рный сове́т ми́ра обрати́лся к Конгре́ссу США с призы́вом добива́ться запреще́ния а́томного, хими́ческого и биологи́ческого ору́жия. Сове́т ми́ра та́кже рекоменду́ет, чтобы Конгре́сс оказа́л влия́ние на америка́нскую администра́цию приня́ть сове́тское предложе́ние прекрати́ть все испыта́ния я́дерного ору́жия, а та́кже пойти́ навстре́чу сове́тскому предложе́нию о сокраще́нии обы́чных (нея́дерных) вооружённых сил в Центра́льной Евро́пе. В призы́ве Сове́та ми́ра, заключа́вшемся в специа́льном меморандуме на и́мя Конгре́сса США, говори́тся: «необходи́мо, чтобы вое́нно-промы́шленный ко́мплекс и други́е «реакцио́нные» круги́ Аме́рики прекрати́ли нагнета́ть междунаро́дную обстано́вку и развя́зывать го́нку вооруже́ний».

Комменти́руя мемора́ндум, ли́дер республика́нского большинства́ в сена́те подчеркну́л, что «у Всеми́рного сове́та нет по́длинной незави́симости и он по́лностью контроли́руется сове́тским прави́тельством». «Сове́т ми́ра, -- сказа́л сена́тор, -- всегда́ критику́ет НАТО, называ́я его агресси́вным бло́ком, и по́лностью подде́рживает Варша́вский догово́р. Одна́ из его це́лей, соотве́тственно, не затормози́ть го́нку вооруже́ний, а помеша́ть США идти́ на необходи́мые ме́ры по укрепле́нию свое́й оборо́ны. Сове́т ми́ра, -- по мне́нию сена́тора,-- стреми́тся к тому́, чтобы подорва́ть еди́нство За́пада».

VOCABULARY EXERCISES

Look through the vocabulary for the text «*Призы́в Сове́та ми́ра*». Do the following exercises.

A. Give perfective forms for the following verbs. Conjugate the italicized ones. Mark the stress.

подде́рживать
прекраща́ть
подрыва́ть
принима́ть
запреща́ть
обраща́ться
ока́зывать

B. Give derivative forms for the following words.

подрыва́ть
коммента́рий
прекраще́ние
влия́ние
оказа́ть
обраще́ние
заключи́ть

C. Paraphrase the italicized words.

поддéрживать Варшáвский договóр
оказáть пóмощь
ухудшáть междунарóдную обстанóвку
влиять на администрáцию
остановúть все испытáния
настоящая незавúсимость
начáть гóнку вооружéний

D. Give the opposite for the italicized words.

увелúчить стратегúческие вооружéния
ядерные сúлы
начáть гóнку вооружéний
укрепúть едúнство Зáпада

E. Give Russian equivalents for the following English phrases.

- to address the US Congress to ratify the treaty
- to reduce conventional forces
- to cease all nuclear testing
- to exert influence on the administration to sign the treaty
- to unleash the arms race
- to comment on the memorandum
- to increase international tension
- to undermine the unity of the West
- to support the Warsaw pact

F. Fill in the blanks with the appropriate prepositions.   Write Ø if no preposition is necessary.

1. Конгрéсс обратúлся ___ президéнту с предложéнием оказáть пóмощь жéртвам землетрясéния.
2. ___ призыве говорúтся, что необходúмо добивáться разрядки.
3. ___ повéстку дня постáвили вопрóс ___ стратегúческих вооружéний ___ европéйском континéнте.
4. Мировáя общéственность пытáется оказáть влияние ___ сверхдержáвы, чтóбы остановúть ___ гóнку вооружéний.
5. Осóбое внимáние уделúли ___ запрещéнию химúческого орýжия.

G. List cognates from the text of lesson 6.

H.   Fill in the blanks with the appropriate words.

                            (како́е?)

1.   Догово́р запреща́ет ___________ ору́жие

                     ____

                     ____

                            (сде́лать что?)

2.   Сове́т ми́ра при́нял предложе́ние ____________

                              ____

                              ____

                           (что?)

3.   Обще́ственность подде́рживает __________

                           ____

                           ____

                           ____

                           (что?)

4.   Го́нка вооруже́ний подрыва́ет __________

                           ____

                           ____

I.   Make several sentences following the pattern below.   Be able to translate your sentences.

1.   (кто?)   обрати́лся   (к кому́?)   (сде́лать что?)

2.   (кто?)   ока́зывает влия́ние   (на кого́?)   (сде́лать что?)

3.   (кто?)   комменти́рует   (что?)

K.   Answer the following questions.   (on the tape)

1.   К каки́м о́рганам вла́сти америка́нского прави́тельства ча́сто обраща́ется президе́нт?
2.   Како́й о́рган вла́сти ратифици́рует догово́ры в США?
3.   Како́й о́рган вла́сти ратифици́рует догово́ры в Великобрита́нии?
4.   Како́й о́рган вла́сти ратифици́рует догово́ры во Фра́нции?
5.   Како́й о́рган вла́сти ратифици́рует догово́ры в СССР?
6.   На что обще́ственное мне́ние мо́жет ока́зывать влия́ние в демократи́ческих стра́нах?
7.   Каки́е ви́ды ору́жия пыта́ются сократи́ть на переговóрах в Ве́не?
8.   Каки́е ви́ды ору́жия пыта́ются запрети́ть на переговóрах в Жене́ве?
9.   Каки́е а́кции мо́гут нагнета́ть междунаро́дную обстано́вку?
10.   Како́й незави́симости добива́ются стра́ны тре́тьего ми́ра?
11.   Что включа́ет в себя́ по́длинная незави́симость?
12.   Каки́е де́йствия подрыва́ют еди́нство За́пада?

13. Брази́лия нахо́дится на североамерика́нском контине́нте?
14. Сомали́ - это азиа́тская стра́на?
15. На како́м контине́нте нахо́дится Австра́лия?
16. На како́м языке́ говоря́т в Но́вой Зела́ндии?
17. В Аргенти́не говоря́т по-аргенти́нски?
18. Как называ́ется столи́ца э́той страны́?

GRAMMAR: COMPARATIVE AND SUPERLATIVE DEGREES OF ADJECTIVES

Note: Only *qualitative* adjectives have degrees of comparison.

Look at the sentences below and their translations:

Ваш вопро́с тру́дный.	Your question is hard.

Comparative:
Её вопро́с трудне́е.	Her question is hard*er*.

Superlative:
Их вопро́с **са́мый тру́дный**.	Their question is the hard*est*.

Comparisons are made by using **чем** separated by a comma:

Этот план эконо́мн**ее, чем**   This plan is more economical
тот план.   than that plan.

Она говори́т быстр**ее, чем** он.   She speaks faster than he does.

Important note: The *short-form* comparatives you have seen so far cannot decline.   Therefore they may be adverbs, or they may occur only *after some form of the verb "to be."*   In other words they must be predicate adjectives:

Adverb:

Во́лков писа́л ме́дленее.   Volkov wrote more slowly.

Predicate adjective:

Её отве́т **про́ще**.   Her answer *is* simpler.
Её отве́т был **про́ще**.   Her answer *was* simpler.
Её отве́т бу́дет **про́ще**.   Her answer *will be* simpler.

But what if you want to say: "She gave a simpler answer"?   Look at the sentences below:

Она дала́ **бо́лее просто́й** отве́т.
Мы говори́ли о **бо́лее ва́жных** дела́х.
Вопро́с был решён **бо́лее жёсткими** ме́тодами.
Это **бо́лее серьёзный** вопро́с.

In other words, when a comparative is placed in a *declinable position* (that is, anywhere *not* immediately after a "to be" verb), you must use the *long-form* construction **бо́лее + regular adjective + correct ending for gender, number and case.**

Now check yourself to see that you have understood the difference between *short form* and *long form* comparatives. Look at the English sentences below and determine which in Russian would require long-form comparatives (**бóлее**):

1.   These terms are *more difficult* than the ones we we had hoped for.

2.   We have to take a *more positive* attitute in the future.

If you said that #1 takes a short form, while #2 requires the long form **бóлее** construction, you were right.

Replacement of ЧЕМ + nominative with genitive case:

Look at the two synonymous sentences below:

Сегóдняшние обстоятельства
сложнéе, чем вчерáшние.

Today's circumstances are
more complicated than yesterday's.

Сегóдняшние обстоятельства
сложнéе вчерáшних.

As you can see, the comparative **чем** + nominative can be replaced by a genitive without **чем**.

Comparisons with numbers

Look at the sentences below and their translations:

Эта дорóга **на пять**
киломéтров длиннéе той.

This road is longer than
that one *by five kilometers.*

Он **на два гóда молóже** её.

He's two years younger than she
is.

Этот план **в пять раз лýчше.**

This plan is five times better.

Note that in comparisons the numerical expressions are expressed by **на** + numerical expression. The exception is *x number of times (better, cheaper, taller, etc.):* **в два рáза (в пять раз) лýчше, дешéвле, вы́ше,** etc.

Formation of the superlative

Superlative adjectives ("the most...") are formed by the construction **са́мый** + an adjective. Both **самый** and the adjective decline in gender, number, and case:

Это са́мая сканда́льная програ́мма.
Одна́ из са́мых сканда́льных програ́мм...
О са́мой сканда́льной програ́мме...

Superlative adverbs (e.g. "She works the fastest") are formed by means of the comparative plus **всех:**

Она́ рабо́тает **быстре́е всех.**   She worked the fastest.
Мы говори́ли **ме́дленнее всех.**   We talked the slowest.

GRAMMAR: GENITIVE CASE (Continued)

1. QUANTITIES

After **мно́го, ма́ло, не́сколько, ско́лько, сто́лько, доста́точно, большинство́, оди́н (одна́, одно́, одни́) из.., ряд..**

> *ско́лько догово́ров, большинство́ вое́нных сою́зов, доста́точно я́дерного оружия.*

BUT!

мно́гие (немно́гие) ду́мают (счита́ют, говоря́т, пи́шут, etc.) – Many (fewer)
    believe (think, say, write, etc.)
Не́которые ду́мают... – Some believe..., etc.

2. NUMBERS:

A.   Look at the model:

тридцать **два** интере́сных сообще́ния

The formula is: Numbers ending in...
    два
    две **три четы́ре** + gen. pl. adj. + gen. sg. noun

Note: **два** + masculine or neuter nouns: **два** вопро́са
             две + feminine nouns: **две** пробле́мы

B.   Look at the model:

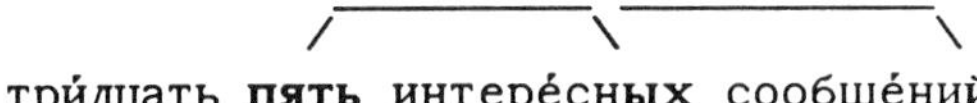

тридцать **пять** интере́сных сообще́ний

Numbers ending in **пять, шесть, семь, во́семь, де́вять,** as well as zero-digit numbers (**два́дцать, три́дцать,** etc.) and teens (**оди́ннадцать, двена́дцать**) take both adjectives and nouns in genitive plural.

C.   *BUT!*

If the number itself is not in nominative (or a form of accusative which looks like nominative), then the thing being counted reverts to the plural form of whatever case would be expected in that particular construction.   Compare:

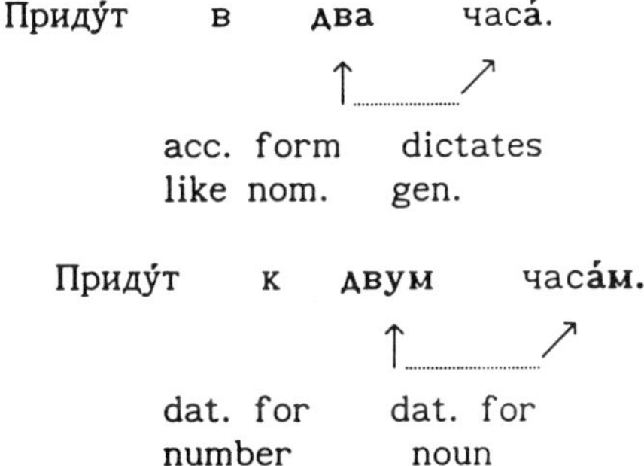

Приду́т   в   **два**   часа́.

acc. form   dictates
like nom.   gen.

Приду́т   к   **двум**   часа́м.

dat. for   dat. for
number   noun

D.   **Numbers ending in "one" are more like adjectives.**   They always take *singular* adjective-noun combinations:

В делега́ции два́дцать **оди́н** челове́к.
Была́ одна́ проблема́.   Без одно́й проблемы́...
Бы́ло одно́ сообще́ние.   В одно́м сообще́нии...

3.   **After comparatives as a synonym for чем + nominative: бо́льше, чем Сове́тский Сою́з = бо́льше Сове́тского Сою́за.**

4.   **After certain verbs: боя́ться** *to fear,* **достига́ть/дости́гнуть** *to achieve,* **добива́ться/доби́ться** *to strive for/to accomplish,* **тре́бовать/потре́бовать** *to demand.*

Ждать *to await* and **ожида́ть** *to expect* take masculine inanimate objects in genitive; feminine in accusative: **ждать отве́та** but **ожида́ть програ́мму.**

GRAMMAR EXERCISES: COMPARATIVES AND SUPERLATIVES

A. Read grammar on comparitives and superlatives.   Change comparative genitive constructions into comparative чем + nominative constructions.

1.   больше нас
2.   ниже положенной суммы
3.   выше нормы
4.   громче других
5.   хуже обычного результата
6.   моложе нашего президента
7.   старше него
8.   лучше других
9.   старее той церкви
10.   легче того разговора

B. Now use the phrases above in complete sentences.

C. Make the following into comparitives and superlatives following the model.

Example: Эти цены... низкие... объявленные цены
      ——→ *Эти цены ниже объявленных цен.*
      ——→ *Эти цены самые низкие.*
      ——→ *Я никогда не слышал о более низких ценах.*

1.   Москва...старая...Ленинград
2.   Наши цифры... точные... эти
3.   Связи с КНР... крепкие... обычные
4.   Это решение... хорошее... ваше решение
5.   Наша программа... плохая... ваша программа
6.   ВВС... сильные... пехота
7.   Этот обзор... широкий... тот обзор
8.   Ваш план... простой... данный проект.

D. Review genitive forms of numbers in the appendix.   Then change the following чем-type comparisons into genitive constructions according to the model.

Example: меньше, чем четыре человека ——→ меньше *четырёх человек*

1.   Больше, чем 25 предприятий
2.   Меньше, чем 4 солдата
3.   Больше, чем 1200 рублей
4.   Меньше, чем 12 сантиметров
5.   Больше, чем 24000 километров

6.   Больше, чем 125 видных деятелей
7.   Чуть меньше, чем 2200 боеголовок
8.   Свыше, чем 362 рабочих дня
9.   Больше, чем 45 лет
10.   Меньше, чем 3 месяца

E.   Translate the following sentences.

1.   This building is 25 meters taller than that one.
2.   This plan is 200 pages longer than that one.
3.   This plant is a million rubles more expensive than that one.
4.   This formula is ten times stronger than that one.
5.   Our plane flies three times faster than theirs.

GRAMMAR EXERCISES: GENITIVE CASE (Continued)

Review the grammar on the genitive case. Look over the genitive case chart at the end of Lesson 5. Then complete the exercises below.

A.   Put the words in parentheses into the correct form according to the model.

Example: На собрании (был... много... москвич)
           ——→ *На собрании было много москвичей.*

Remember the difference between countable nouns and uncountable nouns.

1.   Такой план (поддерживал... большинство... население).
2.   На приёме в посольстве (находился... несколько... представитель...) вашей страны.
3.   Уже (опубликован... немало... интересная статья) о будущих космических станциях.
4.   К концу года (будет принят... много... необходимая мера) по укреплению обороны.
5.   В статье говорится, что обе стороны проводят слишком (много... ненужное испытание).
6.   Нефтяные месторождения Кавказа дают (много... высококачественная нефть).
7.   Пока сдана только первая очередь новой станции, и поэтому она даёт (меньше... газ), чем планировалось.
8.   В Москве (был подписан... несколько... многообещающая договорённость) об использовании космоса в мирных целях.
9.   В Варшавский договор (входить... меньшинство... страна..., находящаяся) в Центральной Европе.
10.   СССР издаёт (больше... научная публикация), чем любая другая страна мира.

B.   Fill in the blanks.

1.   На съезде ________________________________ из США.
         there were many delegates

2.   С тех пор ________________________________.
         there have been achieved few agreements

3.   После провала на переговорах в верхах ________________________.
                                             there was little hope

4.   ________________________________ за этот законопроект?
         How many Congressmen

5.   Этой теме посвящён ________________________.
                          a number of articles

C.   Unlike other quantities весь, вся, всё (*all of* + singular) and все (*all* plus plural) do *not* take genitive.   Rather they function like adjectives. With that in mind, change the sentences below according to the model.

Examples: Там было мало студентов. ⟶ Там *были все студенты.*
               Мы продали мало водки. ⟶ Мы продали *всю водку.*

1.   В Ленинской библиотеке мало зарубежных изданий.
2.   Мы заметили меньше перемен.
3.   Мы осмотрели три научно-исследовательских института.
4.   На пленуме присутствовало несколько членов зарубежных компартий.
5.   На съезде было принято много важных решений.
6.   СССР покупает у Кубы много сахара.
7.   Большинство молодёжи поддерживает перестройку.
8.   Договор запрещает ряд испытаний ядерного оружия.

D.   Translate the following phrases using все, многие, немногие, некоторые, as well as the grammatically singular forms большинство, ряд and никто не, as appropriate.

1.   Everyone thought that...
2.   Many believe that...
3.   No one would say that...
4.   Few would say that...
5.   A number of people consider...
6.   Nearly all agree that...
7.   Some continue to say that...
8.   No one thinks that...
9.   The majority says that ...
10.   Certain people might say that...
11.   Most feel that...

E. **Write out the forms of the numbers along with the phrase that follows. Watch for the correct form of два/две.**

Reminder: No number has more than one ь. In teens the ь is at the end. In "-ties" it is in the middle: **пятнадцать** *but* **пятьдесят.**

1.   2... важный вопрос
2.   12... обещающая область
3.   116... известная фирма
4.   242... золотая монета
5.   351... подписанное соглашение
6.   490... убеждённый коммунист
7.   502... маленькая деревня
8.   644... серьёзный ответ
9.   782... открытое место
10.   821... советский учёный
11.   900... тяжёлый день

F. **Put each of the phrases above into genitive, dative, and prepositional case. Consult the appendix.**

G. **Write out the prices and percentages.**

1.	$2,530,000.00	2.	R.110.82	3.	$2,200.00
4.	R.2,534	5.	$0.22	6.	R.52,000.00
7.	$454.00	8.	R.1,229.45	9.	$180,000
10.	R.119.90	11.	22%	12.	50%
13.	76%	14.	91%	15.	100%

H. **Fill in the blanks.**

1.   В Австралии примерно __________________.
        16 million inhabitants

2.   Договорённость предусматривает ______________.
        2000 warheads

3.   Выступление Генсека продолжалось всего ___________.
        22 minutes

4.   В СССР до сих пор было ___ __________ ______________.
        7   general   secretaries

I. Decide whether the numbers and nouns below follow the "number plus genitive" pattern, or whether the entire expression declines. Fill in the blanks.

1. Мы знаем всего о ________ _______ _______.
   два/две   такие   случай

2. На совещании было ____ ______ _______.
   32   видные   ученые

3. В конференции принимали участие представители ____ __________
   8   африканские
   ________.
   страны

4. У нас нет ни __ ________ на чужой территории.
   1   солдат

5. Выступление президента было передано по всем ____ __________
   4   программы
   телевидения.

6. Мы познакомились с делегатами из _____ _________ _______.
   35   крупные   города

7. На собрании было около _____ _______ президента.
   250   гости

8. Наши успехи полностью зависят от ____ пока __________
   2   неизвестные
   ________.
   факторы

J. Make up sentences, each with one of the following verbs.

*бояться, достигать/достигнуть, добиваться/добиться
требовать/потребовать, ждать, ожидать*

Where both aspects are given make up a sentence for each aspect.

GRAMMAR: SUBJUNCTIVE AND CONDITIONAL

Subjunctive indicates that the action is viewed not as a real fact but as something possible or desirable.

I wish I *were* an ambassador!	*Была бы* я послом!
It is important that he *go* to the conference.	Важно, чтобы он *поехал* на конференцию.
If we *had worked* hard, we *might have resolved* these problems.	Если *бы* мы *поработали* как следует, мы *бы могли* разрешить эти проблемы.

As you see, English subjunctive has many forms.

Russian subjunctive has only one form: the verb in the past and either **БЫ** or **ЧТОБЫ**, depending on context.

Subjunctive is used in "ЧТОБЫ" Clauses:

1. **After the following impersonal phrases expressing desirability of action:**

> **надо, нужно** – it is necessary,
> **важно** – it is important,
> **необходимо** – it is vital,
> **желательно** – it is desirable.
> **пора** – it is time.

Было *важно, чтобы* стороны *подписали* договор.	It was important that the sides sign the treary.
	or
	It was important for the sides to sign the treaty.
Будет *желательно, чтобы* лидеры стран Запада регулярно *встречались*.	It will be desirable that the leaders of western countries get together on a regular basis.

Note that that the tense in the main clause has no effect on subjunctive.

2.   **After the following verbs expressing order, demand or suggestion:**

> **хотéть** – to want,
> **трéбовать** – to demand,
> **рекомендовáть** – to recommend,
> **предпочитáть** – to prefer.

Президéнт *хóчет, чтóбы* Конгрéсс *ратифицúровал* договóр.	The President wants the Congress to ratify the treaty.
Мы *хотúм, чтóбы* сверхдержáвы в Женéве *достúгли* какóго-нибýдь прогрéсса.	We want the superpowers to achieve some progress in Geneva.

хотéть + **чтóбы** Subjunctive is translated into English as **"to want somebody to do something"**

Мировáя обществéнность *трéбует, чтóбы* СССР *вы́вел* войскá из Афганистáна.	World public demands that the USSR withdraw its troops from Afganistan

Note that subjunctive is necessary after these verbs only when the doer in the main clause is different from the doer in the "ЧТОБЫ" clause.   Otherwise, there is no need for a subordinate clause.

Мировáя обществéнность *трéбует вы́вода* совéтских войск из Афганистáна.

The world public demands Soviet troops' withdrawal from Afganistan.

3.   **In clauses of purpose when the doer of the main clause has the doer of the "ЧТОБЫ" clause do something.**

Эту попрáвку ввелú для тогó, *чтóбы* эмигрáция из Совéтского Союза *продолжáлась*.	This ammendment was introduced so that emigration from the USSR would continue.

Note that if the doer in both clauses is the same, a **"ЧТОБЫ"** + infinitive phrase is sufficient.

Эту попрáвку ввелú для тогó, *чтóбы продóлжить* эмигрáцию из Совéтского Союза.	This ammendment was introduced to prolong the emigration from the Soviet Union.

Conditional indicates:

1. **An action which may take place under certain circumstances in "ЕСЛИ" clauses.**

Если бы X. ..., то Y. бы....

Телесéрия «Амéрика» *моглá бы* нанестú вред, *éсли бы* лю́ди *воспринимáли* её серьёзно.

The TV series "Amerika" could have been harmful if people had taken it seriously.

А *éсли бы* президéнт *подписáл* что-нибýдь, как *бы* хозя́ева Амéрики *поступúли* с договóром?

And if the President were to sign something, how would the bosses of America treat the agreement?

English clauses with indirect speech in the past ought not to be confused with unreal condition.

Indirect speech:

The White House spokesman *said that* if Secretary of State *went* to Moscow, he *would talk* about Jewish emigration as well.

Direct speech:

The White House spokesman said: "If Secretary of State goes to Moscow, he will talk about Jewish emigration."

Russian translation of "false subjunctive":

Представúтель Бéлого дóма сказáл, что, éсли Госсекретáрь поéдет в Москвý, то он бýдет говорúть о «еврéйской эмигрáции».

Now look at the same sentence with "true subjunctive":

Представúтель Бéлого дóма сказáл, что, éсли бы Госсекретáрь *поéхал* в Москвý, то он *говорúл бы* о «еврéйской эмигрáции».

The White House spokesman said that if the Secretary of State *were to go* to Moscow, he *would talk* about Jewish emigration as well.

2. **An action which is desired or planned or to express request without "ЕСЛИ".**

Бы́ло бы жела́тельно встре́титься
в ближа́йшем бу́дущем.

It would be desirable to get
together in the very near furure.

В програ́мме предлага́ется тако́й
поря́док, при кото́ром понижа́лся
бы у́ровень вое́нного
противостоя́ния.

Under the arrangements provided
by the program, the level of
military confrontation would
decrease.

GRAMMAR EXERCISES: SUBJUNCTIVE AND CONDITIONAL

A. **Read over the grammar on subjunctive in this lesson. Then review the
text. Find all the places where subjunctive is used and determine the
reason for each occurrence.**

Subjunctive after impersonals:

B. **Put the verbs in the infinitive into a proper form. Be able to translate
these sentences into English.**

1. Ва́жно, чтобы наши экономические отношения________________ быстрее.
    (развиваться)

2. Было желательно, чтобы банки ____________ долгосрочный кредит
    (предоставить)
    Польше.

3. Надо, чтобы США ______________ меньше нефти.
    (импортировать)

4. Будет нужно, чтобы наш представитель _________ об опасности
    (заявить)
    настоящей ситуации.

5. Пора, чтобы переговоры _________ более конструктивный характер.
    (носить)

C. **Fill in the blanks using subjunctive.**

1. Надо, _______________________________ по этому животрепещущему вопросу.
    that we exchange opinions

2.   Будет важно, _______________________________________
that the memorandum indicate our determination

укреплять международную финансовую систему.

3.   Было бы желательно,_________________________________
that the US and the USSR would develop space

в мирных целях.

4.   Пора, ___________________________________ на основе доверия.
that relations between allies be built

Subjunctive after verbs expressing order:

D.   Fill in the blanks using subjunctive.   Be able to translate these sentences into English.

1.   Госсекретарь не захочет, _____________________ в Хельсинки.
the meeting to take place

_________________________ из ЮАР.
US firms to import diamonds

_________________________ Китаю.
West-Europeans to sell hi-tech

2.   Меморандум требует, _____________________________
that members of IMF pay more attention

более реалистическому курсу обмена валют.

____
that representatives of both sides

_________________ как можно скорее.
conduct negotiations

____
that superpowers show some good-will

на предстоящих переговорах.

3.   Доклад рекомендовал,

____

that the Congress exert its influence

на настоящую администрацию.

____

the new treaty ban the development

биологического оружия.

____

socialist countries open the door

новому этапу в отношениях между Востоком и Западом.

Subjunctive in "ЧТОБЫ" clauses:

E. Change the following sentences using subjunctive.   Make necessary adjustments. Translate these sentences into English.

Пример: Министр обороны *сказал* своему помощнику *подготовить* доклад.
———→ Министр обороны *сказал, чтобы* его помощник *подготовил* доклад.

1.   Глава советской делегации попросил представителя Болгарии принять участие в переговорах.
2.   Главнокомандующий приказал войскам прекратить наступление.
3.   Президент обратился к Конгрессу ратифицировать договор об ОСВ-2.
4.   Пресса оказала влияние на администрацию принять предложение СССР.

F. Translate the following sentences into English.

1.   Нужно продолжать осуществление «стратегической оборонной инициативы», чтобы русские нас не обогнали.
2.   Важно, чтобы высказанные идеи были развиты дальше.
3.   Мы хотели бы, чтобы на переговорах в Женеве был достигнут прогресс.
4.   Необходимо, чтобы существующие соглашения были подписаны не позднее 1987-го года.
5.   Важно, чтобы эти вопросы были вынесены на более видное место.
6.   Комитет настаивает на том, чтобы Госдепартамент немедленно отозвал наших дипломатов.
7.   Надо, чтобы в Европе не оставалось ни советских, ни американских ракет средней дальности.
8.   Министры иностранных дел арабских стран встретились на конференции, чтобы мировая общественность признала важность урегулирования в этой части мира.

9. Мы ожидаем существенного сокращения в обычных вооружениях, чтобы имеющаяся ныне диспропорция в пользу Организации Варшавского договора была ликвидирована.
10. Они настаивали на том, чтобы был достигнут «тотальный пакет».
11. Договаривающиеся заявили о своей заинтересованности в том, чтобы обе стороны соблюдали ОСВ-2.
12. На повестку дня поставили предложение Польши о том, чтобы на последнем этапе Стокгольмской конференции обсуждались меры укрепления доверия.
13. Не существует ни одной проблемы в мире, которая стоила бы того, чтобы из-за неё началась ядерная война.

Subjunctive in clauses of unreal condition and to express wish or probability.

G. Change the following sentences in the indicative into subjunctive. Be able to translate both.

1. Если найдут новые источники энергии, можно будет улучшить состояние платёжного баланса.
2. В целях ускорения процесса можно использовать любые формы работы.
3. Если эта страна достигнет более высокого уровня экономического развития, она не позволит проникновение иностранного капитала в свою экономику.
4. Если Великобритания признает этот режим белого меньшинства, она предаст тем самым дело освобождения Чёрной Африки от колониализма.
5. Если администрация не окажет поддержку нашим союзникам по блоку, мы встанем перед лицом реальной возможности локальной войны в этом стратегически важном районе мира.
6. Если удастся договориться по процедурам контроля и инспекции, это будет важным шагом вперёд.
7. Мы против перенесения СС-20 по другую сторону Урала, откуда они могут быть возвращены обратно.

H. Write ten sentences to illustrate the use of subjunctive.

I. Translate the following sentences into Russian.

1. It is important that Latin American governments carry out agrarian (аграрный) reforms in their countries.
2. Brazil wants western banks to extend long-term credits to it.
3. If they reached an agreement on further reductions of interest rates, that would strengthen the world monetary system.
4. This report would include a variety of issues.
5. Israel announced its readiness to negotiate with the PLO so that Arab moderates (умеренные) would attend the conference.

6. The Soviet Union prefers for the NATO members themselves to undermine the unity of the alliance.
7. It would be essential that our negotiating team achieve success at the forthcoming arms control talks.
8. Would the US be ready to sell strategically important equipment to the Soviet Union if Moscow opened its doors to emigration?
9. Would he take a stand on the issue of apartheid? (апартеид)
10. The Soviets demand that the US drop the development of SDI.
11. President Truman supported the Marshall Plan so that post-war Europe could rebuild (восстановить) its economy.
12. It is desirable that current changes contribute to the relaxation of international tension.
13. The Secretary of Commerce demanded that our trading partners put an end to the artificial export encouragement so that our economy would get stronger.
14. Several members of Congress addressed the President so that he would put the Soviet arms control violations on the agenda.

RENDERING

Use what you know to render, not translate, the following information as best you can. If you find you cannot say something, edit it down to some thing you are capable of. You should review this chapter but you should *not* use a dictionary.

> *President Haglund is expecting a victory in Congress on the issue of the ratification of the ABM-2 Treaty, which the previous Congress voted down in 1982. While American conservatives are optimistic that Hagland cannot get Congressional approval, many feel that the grass-roots demand for passage is growing.*
>
> *Support for the treaty is stronger in Europe. Many there feel that that issue is more important than all others. Just last week more than 200,000 West Germans took part in a massive demonstration urging the Haglund administration and the American Congress to approve the treaty and get on with negotiating SALT III, whose success depends on the continuation of ABM.*
>
> *Most observers believe that a succesful SALT III negotiation would reduce the total number of warheads by 85%.*

SPEAKING EXERCISES

A.   Отве́тьте на сле́дующие вопро́сы по те́ксту уро́ка.

1.   С каки́м призы́вом обрати́лся Сове́т ми́ра к америка́нскому конгре́ссу?
2.   Что рекоменду́ет америка́нскому конгре́ссу Сове́т ми́ра?
3.   Почему́ у Сове́та ми́ра, по слова́м ли́дера республика́нского большинства́ в сена́те, нет по́длинной незави́симости?
4.   Что явля́ется це́лью э́той организа́ции, по мне́нию америка́нского сена́тора?

B.   1)   Расскажи́те текст, испо́льзуя слова́рь уро́ка 6.

2)   Измени́те текст, испо́льзуя слова́рь уро́ка.

C.   Соста́вьте ситуа́цию, испо́льзуя сле́дующие выраже́ния.

according to... sources; to exert influnce on...; to undermine the unity of; a ban on...; to address...to support...; to increase international tension; to comment on the treaty

D.   Расскажи́те, когда́ и при каки́х обстоя́тельствах был со́здан Се́веро-атланти́ческий сою́з (НАТО).

E.   Вы – главы́ америка́нской и сове́тской делега́ций на перегово́рах по я́дерным и косми́ческим вооруже́ниям в Жене́ве.   Обсуди́те пробле́му продле́ния де́йствия догово́ра ПРО.

F.   Происхо́дит очередна́я се́ссия перегово́ров об ограниче́нии обы́чных и нея́дерных вооруже́ний в Ве́не. Изложи́те пози́ции сторо́н относи́тельно чи́сленности войск НАТО и Варша́вского догово́ра в Евро́пе.

G.   Вы сове́тский мини́стр иностра́нных дел и америка́нский госсекрета́рь. Обменя́йтесь мне́ниями относи́тельно прекраще́ния испыта́ний я́дерного ору́жия.

READING EXERCISE 1

PRE-TEXT:

Read the text with the following questions in mind:

1. What is the main idea of the article?
2. How many countries signed the Helsinki Final Act?
3. What was the good of the practical steps which these countries pledged to take?
4. In what three areas do the socialist countries ignore the principles of the Final Act, according to President Reagan?
5. According to the article, which US actions violate the Final Act?

Не в ладах с деиствительностью

ФАКТЫ И РИТОРИКА

ВАШИНГТОН, 2. (ТАСС). «Одиннадцать лет назад США, Канада и тридцать три европейские страны подписали в Хельсинки Заключительный акт Совещания по безопасности и сотрудничеству в Европе. Те, кто подписал этот акт, обязались соблюдать важные нормы международного поведения и предпринимать практические шаги, чтобы снизить барьеры, разделяющие Европу на Восток и Запад». Так начинается заявление президента Рейгана по случаю одиннадцатой годовщины хельсинкского совещания. И на этих двух фразах заканчивается его соответствие действительности. Далее идут утверждения, будто социалистические страны игнорируют положения Заключительного акта, а вот США якобы скрупулезно соблюдают их — и в области прав человека, и в деле обеспечения европейской безопасности, и в экономической сфере.

Никак не вяжутся с действительностью, например, утверждения президента, будто США выполняют положения Заключительного акта об укреплении безопасности и ослаблении напряженности в Европе. Не США ли уже после подписания этого документа начиняли и продолжают начинять Европейский континент все новыми видами вооружений, в том числе ядерными ракетами «Першинг-2» и крылатыми ракетами? Не с территории ли Европы Вашингтон, игнорируя не только Заключительный акт, но все другие нормы международного права, осуществляет опасные, дестабилизирующие международную обстановку акции государственного терроризма, о чем, в частности, свидетельствует использование США аэродромов в Англии для нанесения бомбового удара по Ливии? Видимо, как «вклад» в европейскую безопасность рассматривают американские руководители и недавнее решение администрации начать производство новейшего варварского химического оружия — бинарных боеприпасов, которые в случае «чрезвычайных обстоятельств» планируется перебросить в Западную Европу, превращенную в хранилище американской «химической смерти». При этом США демонстративно отвергают поддерживаемые многими западноевропейскими странами советские инициативы, направленные на избавление Европы, да и всего мира от ядерного и химического оружия.

Не выдерживают критики и содержащиеся в заявлении Рейгана утверждения насчет заботы США о соблюдении положений Заключительного акта в экономической сфере.

POST–TEXT   (using sentence structure):

Comment – Topic: You already have learned to analyze sentences grammatically in terms of subject and predicate.   But sentences can also be looked at from a "thematic" point of view.   Nearly all Russian sentences contain two parts: a **topic** and a **comment** on that topic (when, where, why, how, etc:)

topic	*comment*
Лететь самолётом	всегда удобно

In purely *neutral* style topic precedes comment.   Topic usually represents **known information**, something that the reader either already knows about or has read about in a previous sentence:

topic	*comment*
В Тибет	введена армия.
topic	*comment*
Армия	будет работать, чтобы обеспечить...

Nevertheless, word order is never a sure thing.   Therefore you should learn to find topic and comment to keep track of who is doing what to whom when, how, and why.

Do the following exercises:

1.   Underline the topic and the statement in the third sentence of paragraph one.
2.   Rewrite the third sentence in paragraph 1 into sentence following the pattern:

subject-(modifiers)-predicate-(modifiers)-object(s)-(modifiers)

Spell out any reference words. (see **Reading rule 4** in lesson 5.

3.   Translate this sentence into English.
4.   Rewrite the first sentence of paragraph two using direct word order (see assignment 2, above)
5.   Translate it into English.
6.   Rewrite the first sentence of the last paragraph using direct word order.
7.   Translate it into English.

POST–TEXT   (using context):

1.   What is the Russian for *Final Act*?
2.   Find two different verbs to say *to observe principles*.
3.   In the sentence begining with *далее...* find two words indicating the author's skeptical attitude towards the statement.
4.   What is the English equivalent for *начинять Европу ракетами*? Note the use of instrumental with the verb.
5.   Make a list of useful military terminology in the text. Include the Russian equivalents for: to strike Libya, binary weapons, to transfer (lift) weapons to...
6.   Find the sentence beginning with *Не США ли....* Explain the word order.
7.   Find in the text:
     – problem
     – description

READING EXERCISE 2

PRE–TEXT:

Read the text with the following questions in mind:

1.   What is this article about?
2.   Which measure of the UN General Assembly might resolve a conflict situation in the Middle East?
3.   Which countries supported this resolution?
4.   What is the Soviet position on the resolution of the situation in the Middle East?
5.   According to the article, the people of the Middle East ought to have a guarantee of... (true or false for each):
     a.   peace
     b.   a right to national sovereignty
     c.   security
     d.   a political system of their choice

ЗАЯВЛЕНИЕ МИД СССР

Генеральная Ассамблея ООН приняла резолюцию 41/43 D, в которой не только подтверждается необходимость безотлагательного созыва международной мирной конференции по Ближнему Востоку, но и впервые одобрен призыв к созданию в рамках Совета Безопасности подготовительного комитета с участием всех постоянных членов СБ ООН для принятия необходимых мер по созыву такой конференции. Таким образом, сделан шаг, открывающий путь к практическому разблокированию конфликтной ситуации на Ближнем Востоке коллективными усилиями, за что неизменно и последовательно выступал Советский Союз и другие миролюбивые страны.

В Советском Союзе, который вместе с 122 другими странами—членами ООН проголосовал за эту резолюцию, особое удовлетворение вызывает тот факт, что международное сообщество подавляющим большинством одобрило выдвинутое СССР предложение о создании подготовительного комитета по созыву конференции. Широкая поддержка этого предложения в ООН, равно как на VIII Конференции глав государств и правительств неприсоединившихся стран в Хараре, свидетельствует о том, что борьба за справедливое и всеобъемлющее ближневосточное урегулирование, за созыв международной мирной конференции по Ближнему Востоку вступает в качественно новый этап.

Позиция СССР о необходимости без промедления начать подготовительную работу по созыву международной конференции по Ближнему Востоку и создать с этой целью в рамках Совета Безопасности подготовительный комитет была недавно вновь подтверждена Генеральным секретарем ЦК КПСС М. С. Горбачевым.

Советский Союз далек от того, чтобы навязывать какой-то заранее заготовленный жесткий регламент работы по подготовке конференции. Это — дело коллективное, которое должно быть предметом двусторонних контактов и многосторонних обсуждений, в том числе в рамках подготовительного комитета, когда он будет создан.

Главное сейчас — это начать движение к тому, чтобы наконец-то развязать опасный для всех узел напряженности на Ближнем Востоке.

Народам Ближнего Востока должны быть обеспечены долгожданный мир, надежно гарантированное право на национальный суверенитет, безопасное существование и развитие. Для этого необходимо на практике проявить готовность к новому политическому мышлению, строить свою политику с учетом взаимных интересов, на основе принципа равенства и одинаковой безопасности. Только таким образом окажется возможным сдвинуть с мертвой точки дело ближневосточного урегулирования.

POST–TEXT (using sentence structure):

1. Find the word(s) in the first sentence of paragraph four to which *Это* – ... in the second sentence refers.

2. Translate the sentences you found above into English.

3. Rewrite the first sentence of the last paragraph using direct word order. (see **Reading exercise 1** in this lesson)
4. Translate the sentence you rewrote above into English.

POST-TEXT (using context):

1. Explain the composition of the following words: *безотлагательный, разблокирование, долгожданный.*
2. Look at the participles in the following three set expressions: *подавляющее большинство, неприсоединившиеся страны, всеобъемлющее урегулирование.* Analyze their structure and find their English equivalents.
3. What is the English for *сдвинуть с мёртвой точки?*
4. What type of committee is mentioned in the text? What other kinds do you remember?
5. Make a list of words that you can use to talk about national security.

READING EXERCISE 3

PRE-TEXT:

Read the text with the following questions in mind:

1. What is said in this article?
2. What prompted the Soviet Embassy statement to the Italian Foreign Ministry?
3. What are the consequences of a shift in military-strategic parity?
4. Which previous actions by the Italian government are contradicted by its recent decision?
5. When does the ABM Treaty expire?
6. What hope is expressed in the Soviet Embassy statement?

Заявление посольства СССР в Италии

Посольство СССР в Риме сделало министерству иностранных дел Италии заявление в связи с принятым правительством Италии решением, позволяющим итальянским фирмам участвовать в программе осуществления СОИ. Такой шаг, отмечается в заявлении, не может рассматриваться иначе как постепенное втягивание Италии в реализацию планов США, направленных на милитаризацию космического пространства. Итальянское правительство не может не сознавать, что претворение в жизнь этих планов, целью которых является ломка сложившегося военно-стратегического равновесия и достижение военного превосходства над СССР, неизбежно означает перенесение гонки вооружений в космос, дестабилизацию стратегической обстановки, а также противоречит положениям бессрочного Договора по ПРО 1972 года, являющегося фундаментом процесса ограничения и сокращения ядерных вооружений.

Вышеупомянутые действия итальянского правительства идут явно вразрез с его неоднократными заверениями о готовности способствовать прекращению гонки вооружений, снижению уровня военного противостояния в мире и в Европе и содействовать успешному ходу и позитивному завершению советско-американских переговоров в Женеве по ядерным и космическим вооружениям. Они вряд ли согласуются и с заявлениями правительства Италии в пользу строгого соблюдения Договора по ПРО 1972 года. Нынешняя переломная обстановка в мире, как было подчеркнуто в заявлении, требует неотложных усилий по предотвращению перенесения гонки вооружений в космос, ее обузданию на Земле, и каждое государство должно с повышенной ответственностью относиться к своим практическим шагам и решениям.

Была выражена надежда, что итальянское правительство с должным пониманием отнесется к этому заявлению и сделает выводы, действительно свидетельствующие о подлинной приверженности Италии делу ограничения и сокращения ядерных вооружений, предотвращения гонки вооружений в космосе. Такая позиция вполне отвечала бы жизненным интересам всех государств Европы, в том числе и Италии.

(ТАСС).

POST–TEXT: (using sentence structure):

1. In sentence three of the first paragraph, make a list of predicates connected with **претворение в жизнь**.
2. Which word does a *который* clause modify?
3. Find the word modified by the *являющегося* phrase.
4. Translate the sentence you found in #3, above, into English.

POST–TEXT (using context):

1. Explain the the composition of the word *бессрочный*.
2. Newspaper Russian often uses the word *сложившийся* which means something that has already taken shape.   It can be translated as *existing* or *current*.   Think of at least five nouns it can modify.
3. Find the expression *идти в разрез с....*   What is its English equivalent?   Note the use of instrumental after the preposition с.
4. Find the Russian for *aforementioned*.
5. Make a list of words that you can use to talk about arms control.

READING EXERCISE 4

PRE-TEXT:

Read the text with the following questions in mind:

1. According to the article, why did the list of issues on the agenda of the Geneva Conference on Disarmament never change?
2. What did the UN General Secretary emphasize in his telegram to the conference?
3. What program did the Soviet Union prepare a year ago?
4. According to the article, joint efforts of the participants are necessary in order to... (true or false for each):
   a.   get out of a procedural rut
   b.   develop a new work procedure
   c.   find constructive compromises
   d.   prevent abuses
5. According to the Soviet spokesman, what should the conference do regarding chemical weapons?

НА КОНФЕРЕНЦИИ ПО РАЗОРУЖЕНИЮ

ЖЕНЕВА, 3 февраля. (ТАСС). Сегодня в Зале совета женевского Дворца наций вновь собрались делегации 40 государств, участников Конференции по разоружению.

На повестке дня—широкий круг вопросов, относящихся к ограничению гонки вооружений и разоружению. Этот список остается почти неизменным многие годы, поскольку большой переговорный потенциал многостороннего женевского форума все эти годы использовался далеко не в полной мере прежде всего из-за позиции США и их ближайших союзников по НАТО.

Необходимость активизировать работу конференции, сосредоточить усилия на выработке конкретных мер разоружения в соответствии с рекомендациями Генеральной Ассамблеи ООН вновь подчеркнул генеральный секретарь ООН X. Перес де Куэльяр в телеграмме, направленной в адрес участников.

Работа конференции имеет жизненно важное значение для всего человечества, указывает генеральный секретарь ООН. Поэтому мировое сообщество будет пристально следить за ходом переговоров в Женеве в надежде на успех в деле уменьшения опасностей, нависших над миром в результате неограниченной гонки вооружений.

С большим вниманием было встречено выступление прибывшего в Женеву первого заместителя министра иностранных дел СССР Ю. М. Воронцова. Обеспечение надежной безопасности для всех — это общая ответственность всех членов мирового сообщества, сказал он. Советский Союз в полной мере осознает свою долю ответственности. Год назад он выступил с небывалой по масштабам и целям программой создания безъядерного мира до конца нынешнего столетия. Эта программа стала ядром выдвинутой XXVII съездом КПСС концепции формирования всеобъемлющей системы международной безопасности. Безопасность неделима. Ни одна страна не добьется ее только для себя, действуя в одиночку или вместе с узкой группой своих союзников, опираясь лишь на военно-технические средства, будь то на Земле или в космосе.

Сейчас как никогда необходимо результативное взаимодействие государств, больших и малых, для дальнейшей жизни и прогресса человечества. Общие усилия нужны и для того, чтобы вырвать конференцию по разоружению из «процедурной трясины», выйти на поиск конструктивных решений и ведущих вперед компромиссов.

Как заявил представитель СССР, первоочередной мерой на пути к свертыванию ядерных вооружений и их последующей ликвидации является запрещение испытаний ядерного оружия. В центре внимания Конференции по разоружению должна находиться программа ликвидации ядерного оружия к 2000 году. С этими вопросами связано и предотвращение гонки вооружений в космосе. Необходимо приложить также все усилия, чтобы завершить разработку конвенции по запрещению и ликвидации химического оружия уже в этом году.

В заключение Ю. М. Воронцов выразил надежду, что на сессии этого года дело реального разоружения двинется наконец вперед.

POST–TEXT (using context):

1. What is the English for *опасности, нависшие над миром*?
2. Find the Russian for *to act alone, on one's own.*
3. The sentence that you found in #2, above, contains the phrase *relying on military-technological means.* Find it. Note the use of accusative after *на.*
4. Write out *к 2000 году.*
5. What does *первоочередной* mean? Explain its composition.

AUDIO-COMPREHENSION EXERCISE

You are about to hear a text about U.S. elections. You will probably easily recognize the cognates given below. Look through words and expressions listed after the cognates. Then listen to the text with the following questions in mind. Afterwards, listen to the text again, and write down the answers.

1. Soviet audiences have only a primitive understanding of the American electoral system. How would you explain the significance of a midterm election as opposed to a full blown presidential and congressional campaign? How would you characterize the Democratic and Republican positions on main issues of economic and foreign policy?
2. Who is up for re-election? Is this a presidential race or a midterm one?
3. What does the author say about the connection between the Senate races and the presidential election?
4. According to the report, what is the main issue in this campaign? Is it the only issue?
5. Which party now controls the White House?
6. What is the main complaint of the opposition party?

Cognates

па́ртия
губерна́тор
муниципа́льный о́рган
шанс
центр
диску́ссия
кандида́т
пози́ции
авторите́т
либера́льный
авторита́рный режи́м
платфо́рма
ассигнова́ние
социа́льный

WORDS AND EXPRESSIONS (on the tape)

(какáя?)   пáртия
республикáнская
демократи́ческая
социалисти́ческая
социáл-демократи́ческая
коммунисти́ческая
лейбори́стская
пáртия трудá (трудовáя пáртия)

готóвится/подготóвиться (к чему?)
    -ятся   к предстоя́щим вы́борам - forthcoming elections
                          к президéнтским
                          к муниципáльным
                          к областны́м
                          к провинциáльным
                          к губернáторским
                          к перви́чным - primaries
подготóвленный
подготóвка к вы́борам

вы́боры - elections, вы́бор - choice
избрáние

вы́боры   (куда?)
кандидáт   в палáту представи́телей
                в сенáт от республикáнской пáртии
                в парлáмент от лейбори́стской пáртии
                в Верхóвный Совéт
                в óрганы мéстного управлéния - local government
                в óрганы влáсти
                в Конгрéсс

вы́боры   (на какýю дóлжность?)
кандидáт   в сýдьи (судья́ - sing.)
                           в губернáторы - gubernatorial candidate
                           в члéны палáты представи́телей
                           в конгрессмéны

выбирáть/вы́брать кандидáта на срок в 5 лет/4 гóда/1 год
    -ют вы́берут
вы́бранный

исхóд вы́боров
     дискýссии
     переговóров

определя́ть/определи́ть   расстано́вку полити́ческих сил
      -ют   -я́т   исхо́д президе́нтских вы́боров
                           результа́ты встре́чи
определённый

показа́тель   ша́нсов па́ртии на вы́борах
              экономи́ческого положе́ния

восстана́вливать/восстанови́ть междунаро́дные пози́ции
            -ют восстано́вят авторите́т администра́ции
восстано́вленный

затра́чивать/затра́тить   (что?)   (на что?)
      -ют   -ят
                          сре́дства   на оборо́ну
                          де́ньги   на социа́льное обеспе́чение
затра́ченный

за счёт нужда́ющихся
        избира́телей
        разли́чных програ́мм
        ассигнова́ний на подде́ржку пра́вых режи́мов

либера́льные круги́
консервати́вные

предвы́борная платфо́рма - election platform
             кампа́ния
             програ́мма

выража́ть/вы́разить интере́сы свои́х сторо́нников
      -ют   -ят   избира́телей - electorate
                                    америка́нского наро́да
                                    демократи́ческой па́ртии
вы́раженный
выраже́ние

всео́бщие вы́боры - general elections

та́йное голосова́ние - secret ballot

Швейца́рия, швейца́рский, швейца́рцы, Берн
Финля́ндия, фи́нский, фи́нны, говори́ть по-фи́нски, Хе́льсинки (indecl.)
Кана́да, кана́дский, кана́дцы, Отта́ва
Пакиста́н, пакиста́нский, пакиста́нцы, Исламаба́д
Зимба́бве (indecl.), зимбабви́йский, зимбабви́йцы, Хара́ре (indecl.)
Никара́гуа (indecl.), никарагуа́нский, никарагуа́нцы, Мана́гуа indecl.)
Антаркти́да
анта́рктика, ю́жная поля́рная о́бласть земли́, ю́жный поля́рный круг, антаркти́ческий
а́рктика, се́верная поля́рная о́бласть земли́, се́верный поля́рный круг, аркти́ческий

TEXT: Read the following text; be able to translate it into English in written form.

Предстоя́щие в США вы́боры

Республика́нская и демократи́ческая па́ртии гото́вятся к предстоя́щим вы́борам. Переи́збраны бу́дут одна́ треть чле́нов сена́та, все чле́ны пала́ты представи́телей, а также мно́гие губерна́торы, су́дьи и руково́дство муниципа́льных о́рганов вла́сти.

Полити́ческие обозрева́тели отмеча́ют, что исхо́д вы́боров, кото́рые определя́т, кака́я па́ртия бу́дет контроли́ровать сена́т США, неизбе́жно ока́жет влия́ние не то́лько на ны́нешнюю расстано́вку полити́ческих сил в Аме́рике, но и бу́дет явля́ться показа́телем ша́нсов обе́их па́ртий на сле́дующих президе́нтских вы́борах.

Очеви́дно, что це́нтром полити́ческой диску́ссии бу́дет экономи́ческое положе́ние в стране́. В си́лу того́, что оно́ явля́ется весьма́ неопределённым, вопро́сы вне́шней поли́тики приобрету́т осо́бое значе́ние.

Кандида́ты в Конгре́сс от республика́нской па́ртии подчёркивают, что и́менно реши́мость их администра́ции помогла́ восстанови́ть междунаро́дные пози́ции и авторите́т Аме́рики. Мно́гие же представи́тели демократи́ческой па́ртии говоря́т, что сли́шком мно́го средств бы́ло затра́чено на оборо́ну за счёт нужда́ющихся в сами́х Соединённых Шта́тах. Либера́льные круги́ та́кже критику́ют подде́ржку республика́нской администра́цией пра́вых авторита́рных режи́мов в ми́ре.

Предвы́борная платфо́рма демокра́тов обеща́ет незамедли́тельное соглаше́ние с СССР об ограниче́нии я́дерных вооруже́ний. Кро́ме того, выража́я интере́сы свои́х сторо́нников, демокра́ты обеща́ют расши́рить ассигнова́ния на разли́чные програ́ммы социа́льного обеспе́чения.

VOCABULARY EXERCISES

Look through the vocabulary for the text «*Предстоящие в США выборы*». Do the following exercises.

A. Give the plural forms for the following nouns. Mark the stress.

па́ртия, представи́тель, судья́, пози́ция, оборо́на, нужда́ющийся, обеспече́ние

B. Give perfective forms for the following verbs. Conjugate the italicized ones both in perfective and imperfective. Mark the stress.

выбира́ть
определя́ть
восстана́вливать
выража́ть
гото́виться

C. Give related forms for the following words.

нужда́ющиеся
подгото́вка
расстано́вка
исхо́д
сре́дства
вы́боры
обеспече́ние
голосова́ние
показа́тель

D. Explain the following words through their composition.

предстоя́щий
самоуправле́ние
представи́тель
всео́бщий

E. Paraphrase the italicized words.

результа́ты перегово́ров
выбира́ть на *перио́д* в 5 лет
вы́боры в *пала́ту представи́телей*
бе́дные
сре́дства

F. Give the opposite for the italicized words.

проти́вники
откры́тое голосова́ние
либера́льный
состоя́вшиеся вы́боры

G. Give Russian equivalents for the following English phrases.

- an election campaign
- to determine the balance of power
- at the expense of the needy
- a senatorial candidate (2 variants)
- to spend the allocation for social welfare
- secret ballot
- to prepare for primaries
- elections for local government
- support of rightist regimes

H. Fill in the blanks with the appropriate prepositions.

1. Этот кандида́т ____ Конгре́сс обеща́ет увели́чить ассигнова́ния в подде́ржку «ко́нтрас».
2. Америка́нский президе́нт избира́ется ____ срок ____ 4 го́да.
3. Ско́лько волонтёров занима́ется подгото́вкой ____ вы́борам?
4. Но́вые кандида́ты ____ демократи́ческой па́ртии име́ют ша́нсы победи́ть.
5. Но́вые смертоно́сные систе́мы стро́ятся ____ счёт програ́мм социа́льного обеспече́ния.

I. Write sentences following the patterns below. Be able to translate your sentences.

1. Населе́ние гото́вится   (к чему́?)

    ____
    ____
    ____

2. Пора́ затра́тить бо́льше средств   (на что?)

    ____
    ____
    ____

3. Опро́с обще́ственного мне́ния определи́т   (что?)

    ____
    ____
    ____

4.   Справедли́в ли прогре́сс   (за счёт кого́?)

____________________?
____________________?
____________________?

5.   В соотве́тствии   (с кем? с чем?)   (что произошло́?)

_____________   _____________
_____________   _____________
_____________   _____________

J.   Answer the following questions. (on the tape)

1.   Каки́е разли́чные ти́пы вы́боров вы зна́ете? Объясни́те, кого́ избира́ют на них.
2.   Как ча́сто происхо́дят вы́боры в сена́т США?
3.   Кака́я часть пала́ты представи́телей переизбира́ется на вы́борах?
4.   На како́й срок избира́ется президе́нт в США?
5.   Когда́ президе́нт не мо́жет контроли́ровать Конгре́сс?
6.   Каки́е фа́кторы ча́сто влия́ют на исхо́д вы́боров?
7.   Каки́е вопро́сы обы́чно явля́ются це́нтром полити́ческой дискус́сии во вре́мя предвы́борной кампа́нии?
8.   Каку́ю традицио́нную платфо́рму занима́ют республика́нцы по вну́тренней поли́тике?
9.   За что обы́чно выступа́ет демократи́ческая па́ртия по вопро́сам вне́шней поли́тики?
10.   На что обеща́ют демокра́ты затра́чивать бо́льшую часть средств?
11.   Каки́е кру́пные европе́йские па́ртии вы зна́ете? Что вы зна́ете о них?
12.   В каки́х стра́нах па́ртию труда́ называ́ют лейбори́стской? Почему́?
13.   На како́м языке́ говоря́т в Кана́де?
14.   Пакиста́н нахо́дится в Юго-Восто́чной Азии?
15.   Как называ́ются жи́тели Зимба́бве?
16.   На како́м контине́нте нахо́дится э́та страна́?
17.   Кто живёт в Антаркти́де?
18.   В како́м го́роде нахо́дится столи́ца Никара́гуа?
19.   Где живу́т фи́нны?
20.   Швейца́рия нахо́дится на се́вере Евро́пы?
21.   Перечи́слите назва́ния существу́ющих контине́нтов.
22.   Чем отлича́ется а́рктика от анта́рктики?

GRAMMAR: INSTRUMENTAL CASE

Instrumental case has the following uses:

1. To denote **a tool**, a means by or with which the action is performed. It answers the question "**кем?, чем?**" and takes no preposition. (English **"by", with"**)

   стреля́ть катю́шами — to shoot with Katushas

2. After the preposition **C "together with"** to answer the question "**с кем? с чем?**"

   сове́товаться с судьёй — to consult with a judge

Note: **C "since, from"** requires genetive case.

3. After the prepositions **над** "above", **под** "under", **за** "behind", **пе́ред** "before", **ме́жду** "between" to answer the question "**где?**"

   проводи́ть испыта́ния под землёй. — to conduct tests under the ground.

Note: **за** "behind", "beyond" requires accusative case to answer the question "**куда́?**"

4. As a part of a predicate to answer the question "**кем?, чем?**" after "**быть**" in the past, future or infinitive form, "**стать**", "**явля́ться**", "**счита́ться**", "**называ́ться**" etc.

   Одно́й из пробле́м явля́ется го́нка вооруже́ний. — The arms race is one of the problems.

5. After some verbs which indicate the object which "keeps the subject busy". (see the table)

   руководи́ть вы́борами — To run the elections.
   занима́ться эконо́микой. — To study economics.

6. To indicate the "doer" of the action in a passive type construction.

   Они́ вы́браны гра́жданами. (past passive participle) — They are elected by citizens.
   Они́ выбыра́ются гра́жданами. ("СЯ" verb) — They are elected by citizens.

GRAMMAR EXERCISES: INSTRUMENTAL CASE

Read through the materials on instrumental case. Look through the reference chart at the end of Lesson 7 and the appendix.

A. Find the forms of the instrumental in the text. Explain their use.

B. Answer the following questions using the words given below each question. (Find the exercise on the tape)

1. С кем говори́т губерна́тор?

- э́ти обще́ственные де́ятели
- тот республика́нский ли́дер
- все, жела́ющие ми́ра на земле́
- не́которые официа́льные ли́ца
- пе́рвый замести́тель мини́стра

2. Чем обстреля́ли э́ту диви́зию?

- пу́ли
- раке́ты
- снаря́ды
- артилле́рия

3. Пе́ред кем вы́ступил представи́тель комите́та?

- но́вые гра́ждане
- журнали́сты из ра́зных аге́нств
- лю́ди, потеря́вшие ро́дственников на войне́
- те англи́йские либера́лы

4. Кем был и́збран президе́нт Ре́йган?

- америка́нский наро́д
- консервати́вные элеме́нты
- вся Аме́рика
- подавля́ющее большинство́

5. Како́й стано́вится лейбори́стская па́ртия?

- па́ртия национа́льного освобожде́ния
- бо́лее либера́льная па́ртия
- бо́лее консервати́вная па́ртия
- веду́щий представи́тель трудя́щихся

6. Чем определи́тся исхо́д голосова́ния?

- влия́ние пре́ссы
- коли́чество избира́телей
- вре́мя и де́ньги
- нажи́м, ока́зываемый Сове́тским Сою́зом

7. Над чем летит снаряд?

- огромная толпа
- южноамериканская территория
- столица Ливии
- идущий в Персидский залив фрегат

8. С кем советуется президент?

- Папа Римский
- свой советник
- директор ЦРУ
- жена
- японский министр торговли

9. Чем торгует Португалия?

- сельскохозяйственные продукты
- красная рыба
- жизнь своих заложников

10. С какими странами она торгует?

- Никарагуа
- Мексика
- Ливия
- Вьетнам

C. Substitute the italicized words with the appropriate question word.

1. Лейбористская партия стала *крайне левой*.
2. Встреча в верхах состоится *осенью*.
3. Выборы в той стране контролируются *партией*.
4. ЮАР считается *самой расистской страной на африканском континенте*.
5. Этот план поддержан *общественными организациями*.
6. Такие перемены ещё недавно казались *невозможными*.
7. Встретившись *с дипломатами*, премьер-министр ушел на приём.
8. Переговоры продолжались *неделями*.
9. Партнёры по переговорам сидели за *столом*.
10. Теперь Хрущёв сам стал *объектом критики*.
11. Будучи Генеральным секретарём, Брежнев обладал *почти неограниченной властью*.

D. Fill in the blanks with the correct prepositions. Write Ø if no preposition is needed.

1. Рейган встречал ______ высокопоставленных гостей в аэропорту.
2. Рейган встречался ______ Горбачёвым в Белом доме.
3. Деревня обстреливалась ______ катюшами.
4. ______ сторонами состоялась двухчасовая встреча.
5. Делегация во главе ______ замминистра прибыла в Афины на переговоры.
6. Отношения ______ этими странами обострились.

7. Нацисты остались ответственными _______ народом.

8. Коммунисты и прогрессивная общественность _______ рубежом также отрицательно оценили эти акции со стороны США.

9. Сообщение было встречено _______ негодованием.

E. Instrumental case versus genitive after *C*. Fill in the blanks.

1. Сколько времени прошло с _____________ в Рейкьявике?
   the summit

2. Журналисты познакомились с _______________ от партии Ликуд.
   the candidates

3. С _______________ правительство начало репрессии.
   its first days

4. Город был окружён с _______________.
   all sides

5. Он поздравил их с ___________________ в экономике страны.
   the new phase

6. Именно с _______ Горбачёв связывал престиж Советского Союза.
   this

7. Страны третьего мира никак не могут согласиться с___________________.
   such a position

8. Конституцию надо было перевести с __________ на языки всех
   Russian
   народов СССР.

9. Новая программа реформ осуществляется с___________ года.
   the end

F. Instrumental case versus accusative after *ПОД* and *ЗА*. Fill in the blanks.

1. В конце концов микроплёнка была найдена под_________ около двери.
   the snow

2. Самолет с официальными лицами на борту упал под___________.
   the ice

3. Вся армия находится под _____________ иностранных советников.
   the influence

4. Мать послала его стоять в очереди за _____________.
   groceries

5. В печати открылась кампания за ________________ к требованиям

                                   more attention

трудящихся.

6. Самолет полетел за __________________ .

                            the Berlin Wall

7. Партизаны стояли за ________________ .

                        the truck

8. Этим заявлением канцлер поставил весь народ под ______ .

                                   threat

G. Write your own sentences to illustrate the use of instrumental versus genitive and accusative.

H. Change each sentence below following the pattern.

Example: *Он представитель* американского народа.
        ⟶ *Он* был *представителем* американского народа.
        ⟶ *Он* будет *представителем* американского народа.
        ⟶ *Он* должен быть *представителем* американского народа.
        ⟶ *Он* является *представителем* американского народа.

1. Хрущёв - Генеральный секретарь.
2. М. Тачер - премьер-министр Великобритании.
3. М. С. Горбачёв - глава КПСС.
4. Этот человек - гость МИД.
5. Члены делегации - трудящиеся СССР.

I. Review the use of Russian passive construction.   Consult Table 8 in Lesson 4. Change each sentence below following the pattern.

Example: *Народ переизбирает* президента.
        ⟶ Президент переизбирается *народом.*
        Исход дискуссии *определит* результаты встречи.
        ⟶ Результаты встречи *будут определены исходом* дискуссии.

1. Представители демократической партии готовят этот законопроект.
2. Министр торговли затратит большие средства на закупку новейшей техники.
3. Американские учёные разрабатывают программу СОИ.
4. Французский дипломат выразил позицию всех стран-членов ЕЭС.
5. Лейбористская партия поддерживает политику гласности.
6. Зимбабвийские танки открыли огонь по столице.

J. **Review cardinal numerals in the instrumental case. Consult the appendix.
Form phrases according to the model. (Write out all numerals)**

Example: перед/ 5/ английский парламентарий
⟶ перед пятью английскими парламентариями

1. руководить/ 3/ сенатский комитет
2. встречаться/ с/ 254/ иностранный гость
3. быть довольным/ 2/ новое соглашение
4. видеться с/ 16/ политический деятель
5. интересоваться/ 1/ партийный представитель

K. **Review idomatic uses and time expressions in the instrumental case chart
at the end of Lesson 7. Give Russian equivalents for the following
expressions.**

-from time to time
-to work on the SDI program
-to be rich in natural resources
-in that way
-to confer with the workers on the outcome of the talks
-to direct the further development of the country's economy
-at night
-in the winter
-to be involved with the upcoming elections
-to be considered the best candidate for the Supreme Soviet

L. **Translate the sentences.**

1. The election [избрание] of Kaifu by the majority of the population greatly changed the configuration of political forces in Japan.
2. The publication of all materials was controlled by GLAVLIT.
3. The Minister of Defense was dissatisfied that the issue of ICBMs in Antarctica had not even been placed on the agenda.
4. Although that region is not rich in oil, the situation with natural gas is quite different.
5. At first it seemed that those two candidates represented different points of view [точки зрения], but in the spring it became clear that the difference between them was only slight.
6. The Social Democratic Party tried to restore its authority in Parliament by means of reforms.
7. Allocations for social welfare programs were reduced by the Congress for a period of 5-1/2 years.
8. In his nationwide televised announcement, the dictator announced that elections would not be held in the winter as planned.
9. As a result of the administration's work on agricultural policies, the old laws assume new importance.

GRAMMAR: SUBORDINATE CLAUSES

A note on clauses:

Much of the grammar of this chapter has to do with the concept of clauses. Before going on, make sure you know the difference between a clause and a phrase:

A *phrase* is *any* group of words:

flying high   *beyond the pale*   *greetings all*   *after dinner*

A *clause* is any group of words with both a subject and predicate:

Clause 1:	*Clause 2:*
subj. predicate	subj. predicate
They went back to the apartment	after they killed him.

In English prepositions may begin entire *clauses*. For example:

They told me **about** *how the doctors cured her.*
We cannot agree **with** *what you said.*

However, in Russian prepositions may NOT precede entire clauses! Therein lies the problem.

"Before," "after," and "since" plus a clause:
«До того́, как» «пе́ред тем, как» «по́сле того, как» «с тех пор, как»

Note what happens to **до, пе́ред,** and **по́сле** when they combine with clauses:

NO CLAUSE BOUNDARY	CLAUSE BOUNDARY
До войны́ всё бы́ло споко́йно.	До **того́, как** начала́сь война́, всё бы́ло споко́йно.
Пе́ред войно́й всё бы́ло споко́йно.	Пе́ред **тем, как** начала́сь война́, всё бы́ло споко́йно.
Everything was calm before the war.	*Everything was calm before the war began.*
Everything was calm right before the war.	*Everything was calm right before the war began.*

После войны́ всё бы́ло споко́йно.

После того́, как начала́сь война́, всё бы́ло споко́йно.

Everything was calm after the war.

Everything was calm after the war began.

План де́йствует с про́шлого го́да.

План де́йствует с тех пор, как он был одо́брен.

The plan has been in effect since last year.

The plan has been in effecl ever since it was approved.

In short, when *before*, *after*, and *since* precede clauses, use

до того́, как	*before*
пе́ред тем, как	*immediately before*
после того, как	*after*
с тех пор, как	*since*

Note the comma preceding **как**.   In Russian, all clauses within sentences are set off by commas.

Note that **после того, как** can usually be replaced by **когда́** plus perfective:

После того́, как всё ста́нет я́сно, мы начнём принима́ть ме́ры.

After everything becomes clear, we'll start taking measures.

Когда́ всё ста́нет я́сно, мы начнём принима́ть ме́ры.

Once everything becomes clear, we'll start taking measures.

ТО, ЧТО ("that which") Constructions

Now look at this sentence:

We cannot agree with what you said.

Notice that *what* has two functions.   It is the object of the preposition *with*, but it is also the direct object of *you said*.   What is its case?

By now you may have guessed that the *what* in this sentence is really a contract form for the formal *that which:*

We cannot agree with that which you have said.

Now look at how Russian divides up these two clauses, using **то, что** to straddle the clause boundary.

	obj. of *prep.* **с**	*dir. obj.* *of* "*сказáли*"
Мы не соглáсны **с**	**тем,**	**что** вы сказáли.

Now look at these Russian sentences and their English equivalents. See if the Russian now makes grammatical sense to you:

1. Вы увéрены **в том, что** вы дéлаете? — *Are you sure of what you're doing?*

2. Мы не боúмся **того́, чего́** боúтесь вы. — *We don't fear what you fear.*

3. Вы не довóльны **тем, что** я вам показáл? — *Are you not satisfied with what I've showed you?*

4. Мы уважáем **то, к чему́** вы стремúтесь. — *We respect what you're striving for.*

5. Все гото́вятся **к тому́, что** произойдёт зáвтра. — *Everyone is preparing for what will happen tomorrow.*

ТО, КАК Constructions

Look at the following sentences:

Избирáтели ничего́ не знáют **о том, как** фунционúруют «первúчные» вы́боры. — *The voters know nothing about how the primaries work.*

As you can see, when "how" straddles a clause, Russian uses **то, как**. Just as in **то, что** clause-straddlers the **то** declines according to its position in its own clause. **Как** of course is indeclinable.

Subordinate clauses and tense

Look at the following sentences. Pay attention to the tense used in the subordinate clause (**Когда́...** or **Если...**)

Если республика́нцы **вы́играют** в обе́их пала́тах, на́ша фина́нсовая поли́тика ре́зко **изме́нится**.	If the Republicans win in both houses, our budgetary policy will change drastically.
Что **произойдёт** в СССР, **когда́** Горбачёв **уйдёт** в отста́вку?	What will happen in the USSR when Gorbachev leaves office?

Notice that English uses *present* tense in subordinate clauses, even when future events are referred to ("What *will* happen when Gorbachev *leaves*..."). In Russian, if the main clause is in the future, then the subordinate clause is also nearly always in the future tense.

GRAMMAR EXERCISES: SUBORDINATE CLAUSES

Read through the material on subordinate clauses. Then do the exercises below.

A. Translate the clauses below using *до того, как; перед тем, как; после того, как;* and *с тех пор, как.*

1. Right before Gorbachev spoke [вы́ступил]...,
2. Ever since we helped to restore the authority of the U.S...,
3. Before the polls began to influence election outcomes...,
4. After Congress increased appropriations...,
5. Before the Republicans won the Senate...,

B. Replace после того, как clauses with когда clauses.

1. Сенат будет решать этот вопрос после того, как президент вернётся из Пакистана.
2. Американцы смогут ездить в Северную Корею только после того, как Конгресс одобрит соответствующий законопроект.
3. Мы узнаем результаты выборов только после того, как об этом сообщат средства массовой информации.
4. Избиратели решат, за кого голосовать после того, как выступят все кандидаты.

C. Fill in the blanks with the verbs below. Pay attention to tense.

1. Если _________________________ отношения между США и СССР, то
    улучша́ться / улу́чшиться

    следует ожидать победу республиканцев в ноябре.

2. Если Конгресс США _________________________ законопроект о торговле
    одобря́ть / одо́брить

    с СССР, тогда увеличатся возможности для совместных советско-

    американских предприятий.

3. Когда средства массовой информации_________________________
    переставать / перестать

    публиковать результаты опросов общественного мнения, у нас резко

    изменится стиль предвыборных кампаний.

4. Женщина будет избрана президентом США, только если

    _________________________ система первичных выборов.
    изменяться / измениться

5. Если президент США открыто _________________________, что он думает
    высказывать / высказать

    по этому вопросу, он вряд ли будет переизбран.

D. Rewrite the sentences following the models below.

Example: Социалистическая партия провела много перемен. Консерваторы
этим недовольны.
    ——→ The Socialist Party made many changes. The conservatives are
disturbed by that.
    Консерваторы недовольны тем, что сделала социалистическая партия.
    ——→ The conservatives are disturbed by what the Socialist Party
did.

1. Наши лидеры обещают слишком много. Мы беспокоимся об этом.
2. Консерваторы утверждали, что налоги нанесут ущерб экономическому
    балансу страны. Либерали не согласны с этим.
3. Избиратели были против космической программы. Кандидат голосовал за
    неё.
4. Конгрессмен высказывал свою позицию. Он был в ней уверен.

5. Лектор обсуждал неприятные вопросы. Никто не хотел думать о них.
6. Стороны не достигли взаимопонимания. Договор не подписали из-за этого.
7. Он выступил за ратификацию. Потом его все обвинили в этом.
8. Как люди будут жить без войн? Он не мог этого понять.
9. Избирательная кампания будет трудной. Мы готовы к этому.
10. Администрация Рейгана пришла к власти в 1980 году. США восстановили свои международные позиции с тех пор.
11. Расстановка политических сил определится в ходе кампании. Шансы Демократической партии вырастут после этого.
12. Кандидат в президенты получил необходимое большинство. Его друзья и соратники поздравляют его с этим.

RENDERING

Exercise 1:

Imagine that you are describing the second Eisenhower-Stevenson election to a Soviet analyst. Be sure to mention the following facts. You may, of course, add any extra information you wish, as well as your own interpretation:

> *Dwight D. Eisenhower had returned from postwar Europe a hero. Both Democrats and Republicans had courted him as their presidential nominee for the 1952 election. Eisenhower's first term had seen the end of the Korean War, the rise and fall of McCarthyism, as well as the expansion of the American peacetime economy. In 1956, the year after polio was conquered, the country felt good about itself.*
>
> *In 1956, the Democrats nominated their previous standard-bearer, Adlai Stevenson. Stevenson was a hero to liberal intellectuals, but Eisenhower was hero to the mass of voters. Stevenson's issues, racial discrimination, poverty, and social injustice, simply failed to attract the attention of voters who, after two and a half tumultuous decades, spanning the Depression, World War II, and the Korean War, wanted a breather to feel good about living in a country that for once appeared to be economically and militarily secure. The issues that the Democrats raised in 1956 would not come to have an impact on the voting public for another four years.*

Exercise 2:

Describe any other election campaign with which you are thoroughly familiar. Give a short chronology of the campaign, and state why you think the victorious candidate won.

QUOTING SOURCES

ЛЮ́ДИ:

в соотве́тствии с

áвтором статьи́

представи́телем Бе́лого до́ма

ли́дером бе́лого меньшинства́

главо́й делега́ции

сове́тником по дела́м...

госсекретарём

ANY SOURCES:

в соотве́тствии с

журнали́стскими исто́чниками

переда́чей радиоста́нции
«Го́лос Аме́рики»

сове́тской конститу́цией

догово́ром о
нераспростране́нии...

вчера́шней передови́цей

выступле́нием заммини́стра

те́кстом коммюнике́

зако́ном о тунея́дстве

SPEAKING EXERCISES

A. Отве́тьте на сле́дующие вопро́сы по те́ксту.

1. К каки́м вы́борам гото́вятся о́бе па́ртии?
2. Что определи́т исхо́д вы́боров?

3. Показа́телем чего́ я́вится исхо́д вы́боров?
4. К чему́ приведёт неопределённое экономи́ческое положе́ние в стране́?
5. Что восстанови́ло междунаро́дные пози́ции и авторите́т Аме́рики?
6. За чей счёт э́тот авторите́т был восстано́влен?
7. Чем отлича́ется платфо́рма демокра́тов от платфо́рмы республика́нцев?

B. 1) Расскажи́те текст, испо́льзуя слова́рь Уро́ка 7.

    2) Расскажи́те тот же текст, замени́в страну́ вы́боров.

C. Соста́вьте ситуа́цию, испо́льзуя сле́дующие выраже́ния.

according to the spokesman for the Democratic election campaign...;
to be preparing for...; an outcome; a pre-election platform; to
spend...for...; at the expense of; a candidate to...for the term of...

D. Опиши́те аргуме́нты республика́нской администра́ции про́тив предложе́ния
демократи́ческого большинства́ конгре́сса ре́зко сократи́ть вое́нный бюдже́т
США.

E. Проведи́те деба́ты ме́жду республика́нским и демократи́ческим кандида́том о
внутриполити́ческих приорите́тах США.

F. Расскажи́те, почему́ Дже́си Дже́ксон, да́же не бу́дучи кандида́том в
президе́нты, мо́жет оказа́ть большо́е влия́ние на предвы́борную платфо́рму
демокра́тов.

G. Расскажи́те о секре́тном докла́де сове́тских экспе́ртов Горбачёву, о том, чья
побе́да – республика́нцев или демокра́тов – бу́дет бо́льше способ́ствовать
сове́тским интере́сам.

READING EXERCISE 1

PRE-TEXT:

Read the text with the following questions in mind:

1. What is the article about?
2. Brazil held elections for... (true or false for each):
   a. deputies to the National Constituent Assembly
   b. members of State Assemblies
   c. governors
   d. judges

3. How many people participated in Brazil's elections?
4. Which parties received the majority of votes in the National Constituent Assembly?
5. When will the Assembly act as a parliament?
6. Why has the Brazilian Communist Party not voted for a long time?
7. In what way does the BCP support the president?
8. What were the president's comments on the elections?

Этап демократизации

БРАЗИЛИА, 18. (ТАСС). В Бразилии продолжается подсчет голосов, поданных на выборах депутатов Национального учредительного собрания, губернаторов и членов законодательных собраний штатов, которые состоялись 15 ноября. Сообщается, что в выборах приняло участие 95 процентов из почти 70 миллионов избирателей.

Согласно опубликованным здесь предварительным данным, правительственная коалиция Демократический союз, куда входят партия бразильского демократического движения и либеральный фронт, получила большинство голосов в Национальном учредительном собрании, которое должно принять в 1987 году новую конституцию Бразилии, а затем будет исполнять функции парламента.

Впервые в выборах принимала участие Бразильская компартия (БКП), которая в течение многих лет при военном режиме действовала в условиях подполья и только при гражданском правительстве добилась права на легальную политическую деятельность. БКП поддерживает правительство президента Жозе Сарнея в усилиях, направленных на углубление процесса демократической перестройки общества с учетом требований трудящихся масс. По предварительным данным, представители БКП войдут в состав Национального учредительного собрания.

Президент Ж. Сарней в беседе с журналистами подчеркнул, что выборы 15 ноября стали первым этапом демократизации страны.

POST–TEXT (using sentence structure):

1. In the first sentence of paragraph one, circle the word to which the *которые* clause refers.
2. Translate the first paragraph into English.

POST–TEXT (using context):

1. Explain the composition of the word *законодательный*.
2. Find the English for *according to the preliminary data*.
3. Find two uses of *при* in the text. Translate them into English. Form your own examples following this pattern.
4. What is the English for *действовать в условиях подполья*?
5. Explain the word *подполье* through its composition.
6. Make a list of words that you can use to talk about elections.

READING EXERCISE 2

PRE–TEXT:

Read the text with the following questions in mind:

1. What is the article about?
2. With whom did the special presidential envoy meet?
3. What was the purpose of this meeting?
4. On which of Corazon Aquino's plans did President Marcos comment?
5. What is the tone of the TASS report of events in the Philippines? (check the correct answer):
   a. positive
   b. hostile
   c. negative
   d. neutral

6. What reaction to events in the Philippines has there been on the part of the American press and US political figures?
7. What did the Pope support?

После выборов

Обстановка на Филиппинах и «миротворчество» Вашингтона

МАНИЛА, 17. (ТАСС). Сегодня в условиях секретности состоялась встреча президента Ф. Маркоса с находящимся здесь специальным представителем президента США Ф. Хабибом. Позже эмиссар Вашингтона провел переговоры с лидером оппозиции К. Акино и главой католической церкви кардиналом Сином. Печать считает, что цель миссии Хабиба — примирить противоборствующие стороны и добиться создания коалиционного правительства, дезавуировав тем самым итоги выборов.

Выступая здесь перед филиппинскими и иностранными журналистами, Ф. Маркос заявил, что возглавляемая им администрация готова рассмотреть любые предложения оппозиции относительно выработки разумного политического компромисса. Проявляя выдержку и терпение, указал президент, правительство, однако, будет пресекать все попытки оппозиции прибегнуть к «политическому насилию». Комментируя планы К. Акино провозгласить себя главой государства и сформировать «временное правительство», Ф. Маркос отметил, что подобные действия будут носить антиконституционный характер.

ВАШИНГТОН, 17. (ТАСС). В США развернута оголтелая антифилиппинская кампания. Многие влиятельные газеты продолжают публикацию тенденциозных, а порой и откровенно провокационных комментариев о положении на Филиппинах. Вернувшиеся из поездки по Филиппинам сенаторы-демократы Д. Борен, К. Левин и Д. Прайор призвали президента Р. Рейгана «действовать незамедлительно» и «заставить Маркоса уйти в отставку».

РИМ, 17. (ТАСС). К развязанной Соединенными Штатами кампании вмешательства во внутренние дела Филиппин подключился и глава римско-католической церкви Иоанн Павел II. По сообщению газеты «Стампа», он одобрил решение руководства филиппинской католической церкви поддержать оппозицию в противоборстве с правящей коалицией.

POST-TEXT (using sentence structure):

1. Re-write the first sentence using direct word order. (see **Reading exercise 1, lesson 6**)
2. Translate the first paragraph into English.
3. Re-write the first sentence of the last paragraph using direct word order. (see **Reading exercise 1** of lesson 6)
4. Translate this paragraph into English.

POST–TEXT (using context):

1. Find the Russian for *to reconcile opposing sides.*
2. Explain the composition of the word *противоборствующий.*
3. What is the English equivalent for *тем самым?*
4. List the cognates used in the first paragraph.
5. Paraphrase the words in italics in the phrase below:
   пресекать все попытки оппозиции *прибегнуть* к «политическому урегулированию».
6. What is the English for *развёрнута оголтелая антифиллипинская кампания?*
7. What is another way of saying *глава римско-католической церкви?*
8. Make a list of words that you will need to talk about a government crisis.

READING EXERCISE 3

PRE–TEXT:

Read the text with the following questions in mind:

1. What is the main idea of the article?
2. How many parties qualified for the elections?
3. How many parties will have seats in Parliament?
4. Changes will favor the... (true or false for each):
   a. CDU/CSU
   b. SPD
   c. FDP
   d. the Greens

5. Which party considerably strengthened its position?
6. Which issues were of primary importance for the Greens in the pre-election campaign?
7. Why couldn't the Christian Democrats achieve their secret goal?
8. What was Strauss's reaction to the outcome of the elections?
9. The Social Democrats suceeded in... (true or false for each):
   a. consolidation of the party base after the defeat in elections in Hamburg.
   b. giving the FRG a new chancellor.
   c. stopping the "victory march" of the CDU/CSU
   d. strengthening the "ost politik".

БЛОК ХДС-ХСС ТЕРЯЕТ ГОЛОСА

БОНН. (Соб. корр. «Известий»). Когда на мониторах и телевизорах, установленных в залах Дома Конрада Аденауэра — партийной «диспетчерской» ХДС — вечером минувшего воскресенья появились первые предварительные цифры, хозяевам и гостям — многочисленным журналистам нетрудно было увидеть окончательный итог голосования.

Как и предполагалось, из шестнадцати политических партий, допущенных к участию в выборах в парламент, прошли пять: христианско-демократический и христианско-социальный союзы (ХДС и ХСС), свободная демократическая (СвДП), социал-демократическая (СДПГ) и «зеленые».

Большинство осталось за правящей коалицией. Изменение произойдет лишь при распределении мандатов, причем не в пользу консерваторов. Блок ХДС/ХСС потерял 22 депутатских места (4,6 процента), столь низких показателей (44,2 процента голосов) обе партии не имели с 1949 года. Более полутора миллионов сторонников ХДС/ХСС отвернулись от них, проголосовав за СДПГ, почти сохранившую свой прежний результат (37,3 процента) и за СвДП (9,1 процента).

Свободные демократы сумели при этом существенно укрепить позиции в правительстве и будут теперь располагать значительно большим числом мандатов, а возможно, и министерских постов.

Партия «зеленых», выдвинувшая на первое место в своей предвыборной программе проблемы экологии и разрядки, добилась, по словам их представительницы Ю. Дитфурт, «исторического успеха» (8,2 процента), в отдельных округах она набрала более 11 процентов.

Итак, христианские демократы не осуществили своей тайной цели — достижения абсолютного большинства. Несмотря на поддержку крупного капитала, выгодную экономическую конъюнктуру и усилия мощного пропагандистского аппарата, многие ее избиратели, видимо, не простили канцлеру опрометчивых демаршей, подрывавших восточную политику и ставивших под сомнение международный престиж ФРГ. Даже генеральный секретарь ХДС Х. Гайслер вынужден был признать: одна из главных причин неудачи заключается в том, что «некоторые правительственные политики поставили под вопрос продолжение политики разрядки».

Своеобразно реагировали на потерю очков в Баварии. Ф.-Й. Штраус, возглавляющий ХСС и усиленно толкавший всю коалицию вправо, недвусмысленно объявил, что во всем виноваты его старшие партнеры в Бонне, проводившие, по его мнению, «недостаточно жесткую» политику.

Социал-демократы не смогли дать Федеративной Республике нового канцлера Й. Рау, хотя он и боролся за этот пост с удивительным упорством и настойчивостью. Однако они выполнили другую важную задачу — добились консолидации партийного базиса после тяжелого поражения на земельных выборах в Гамбурге и совместно с «зелеными» остановили пропагандируемое «триумфальное шествие» ХДС/ХСС.

Е. БОВКУН.

POST-TEXT (using sentence structure):

1. In the first sentence of the article there is no "doer" in the nominative case because... (mark the correct answer):
    a. it is an *они–* construction.
    b. an impersonal construction.
    c. a "disguised" doer in the genitive.

2. Rewrite this sentence using direct word order. (see **Reading exercise 1, lesson 6.**)
3. Translate it into English.
4. In the first sentence of the next paragraph, find the word to which *пять* refers.
5. Rewrite this sentence using direct word order. (You can exclude the names of parties which follow the colon.)
6. Translate it into English.
7. Rewrite the second sentence of paragraph 6 using direct order.
8. Translate this sentence into English.
9. The first sentence of paragraph 7 has no "doer" in the nominative case because...(mark the correct answer):
    a. an impersonal construction is used.
    b. an *они–*construction is used.
    c. a "disguised" subject in the genitive case is used.

POST-TEXT (using context):

1. What is the English for *диспетчерская?*
2. Find the antonym for *минувший.*
3. Find the word *хозяева* in the text. What is the English equivalent for it in this context? Think of an antonym for it.
4. Make a list of word that you will need to talk about elections.

READING EXERCISE 4

PRE-TEXT:

Read the text with the following questions in mind:

1. What is the main idea of the article?
2. The elections in Austria were... (true or false for each):
    a. regular elections.
    b. early elections.
    c. elections to both chambers of Parliament.
    d. elections to one chamber of Parliament.

3. How many seats did the Socialists have before the elections?
4. Which other parties lost seats?

5.   The parties which improved their positions were...   (true or false
     for each):
     a.   the Austrian People's Party.
     b.   the Greens
     c.   the Austrian Freedom Party.
     d.   the Communist Party.
6.   Which party formed a coalition with the Socialist Party?.
7.   List the reasons for the decision to break up the previously existing
     coalition.   What was its name?
8.   Summarize paragraph 6.
9.   What could create the basis for "the Grand Coalition"?
10. Is it a new idea?

Что показали выборы

Социалисты сохранили большинство в парламенте Австрии

Итак, короткая и в то же время горячая пора избирательной кампании в Австрии позади. Расчеты руководства правящей социалистической партии, связанные с проведением досрочных выборов в национальный совет—одну из двух палат парламента страны, в какой-то мере оправдались. Хотя они и не принесли СПА успеха (партия потеряла десять мест и будет теперь располагать лишь 80 мандатами из 183), тем не менее социалисты сохранили относительное большинство, а значит, и право возглавить новое правительство.

Ощутимые потери на выборах понесла и другая крупнейшая партия — австрийская народная (АНП): консерваторы имеют теперь 77. Австрийская партия свободы (АПС) на 6 мест увеличила свое представительство в национальном совете и имеет теперь 18 мандатов. Впервые в парламент избраны 8 представителей движения «зеленых» — сторонников охраны окружающей среды, которое возглавляет Ф. Майснер-Блау, ранее состоявшая в СПА.

Определенного успеха добилась Коммунистическая партия Австрии, хотя она и была лишена возможности использовать в ходе предвыборной кампании радио и телевидение, которыми распоряжались по сути дела буржуазные партии. Тем не менее за кандидатов-коммунистов в целом по стране было отдано несколько больше голосов, чем на предыдущих выборах.

Как уже отмечалось, прошедшие выборы — досрочные. Решение об их проведении 23 ноября, а не в апреле будущего года, как положено по конституции, было принято после того, как руководство правящей соцпартии разорвало существовавшую с 1983 года коалицию с партией свободы. Основанием для принятия такого решения послужило резкое поправение руководства АПС. Председателем этой партии стал 36-летний мультимиллионер Й. Хайдер, потеснивший Н. Штегера, который занимал в «малой коалиции» пост вице-канцлера, а также федерального министра торговли, ремесел и промышленности. Объясняя решение о разрыве «малой коалиции», федеральный канцлер социалист Ф. Враницкий заявил, что новый председатель АПС «не может гарантировать преемственность федерального курса», который проводил его предшественник на посту лидера партии.

Однако, как считают здесь, изменение в руководстве АПС — младшего партнера по коалиции— стало лишь одной из причин для роспуска кабинета и назначения досрочных выборов. Перенесением выборов на 23 ноября соцпартия стремилась в какой-то мере сохранить свой авторитет среди избирателей, удержать хотя бы относительное большинство мест в парламенте. Ибо время работало против социалистов.

Как известно, социалистическая партия около 16 лет находится у руля правления. За это время внутриполитическая ситуация в стране обострилась. Резко подскочило число безработных, особенно среди молодежи и женщин. Из года в год увеличивается бюджетный дефицит. Растут цены на продукты питания, товары первой необходимости. Трудные времена переживает национализированный сектор промышленности. В поисках выхода правящая соцпартия предложила методы «оздоровления» экономики, и в частности национализированного сектора промышленности. Эти методы известны: сокращение занятости на государственных предприятиях, передача части из них в руки частного капитала, урезывание социальных завоеваний трудящихся. Иными словами, «оздоровление» предполагается провести целиком за счет трудящихся.

Естественно, принимать в одиночку столь непопулярное решение социалисты опасаются. Поэтому, идя на досрочные выборы, СПА рассчитывала (хотя об этом на первом этапе предвыборной кампании из тактических соображений вслух не говорилось) если не увеличить, то во всяком случае сохранить число мест в парламенте. Тем самым это создавало базу для сформирования правительства «большой коалиции» СПА — АНП.

Нет недостатков в прогнозах по поводу сформирования нового кабинета. «Я рад результатам выборов,— заявил федеральный канцлер Ф. Враницкий.— Социалистическая партия остается сильнейшей в стране». Отвечая на вопрос о составе будущего правительства, Ф. Враницкий подчеркнул, что «коалиция с Й. Хайдером исключается».

Остается единственное решение — это «большая коалиция», иными словами, правительство из представителей двух партий — СПА и АНП. Такая коалиция последний раз создавалась два десятилетия назад—с 1964 по 1966 год, когда представитель АНП Й. Клаус возглавлял правительство.

Но не будем торопиться с выводами. Пройдет несколько дней, и новое правительство Австрии будет сформировано и представлено на утверждение федеральному президенту.

Б. ДУБРОВИН.
(Соб. корр. «Правды»).
Вена, 25 ноября.

POST-TEXT (using sentence structure):

1. Explain the inverted word order in the first sentence of paragraph two.
2. Re-write sentences three and four of paragraph four using direct word order. (see **Reading exercise** 1, lesson 6)
3. Translate these sentences into English.
4. Paragraph 4 contains an... (Mark the correct answer):
   a. introduction of the problem described in paragraph 3.
   b. illustration of the problem described in paragraph 3.

5. Explain the absence of the "doer" in the nominative case in the last sentence of paragraph 4.
6. Re-write the first sentence of the fifth paragraph using direct word order.
7. Translate this sentence into English.
8. Sentence one of paragraph 6 has no subject because... (mark the correct answer):
   a. it contains an impersonal construction.
   b. it contains the *они*-construction.
   c. the doer is "disguised" in genitive clothing.

POST-TEXT (using context):

1. Find the Russian equivalent for *early elections.*
2. What case is used after the word *выборы?* Provide further illustrations of the use of this case in the text.
3. What is the meaning of *–ся* in *расчёты оправдались.*
4. Find the Russian equivalent for *to suffer losses.*
5. Give the English equivalent for *состоять в партии.* How can you say it differently?
6. Find the word *распоряжаться* in the text.
7. Spell out *36-летний.* Form some more expressions following the same pattern.
8. Find the Russian equivalent for *dismissal of the cabinet.*
9. What is the synonym for *у руля правления?*
10. Find the sentence beginning with *За годы правления.* What aspect is used in this sentence and the next one? Explain why.
11. What is the English for *предоставить на утверждение?*
12. Find all the uses of the instrumental case in the article.
13. Make a list of words that you will need to talk about elections.

INSTRUMENTAL CASE

USES:	PREPOSITIONS:	QUESTION:	VERBS:
Tool	English "by" "with"	Кем? Чем?	
Together with	С	С кем? С чем?	говори́ть познако́миться сове́товаться ви́деться
Location	НАД ПОД ЗА ПЕРЕД МЕЖДУ	Где? Над чем? За кем?	
A part of predicate		Кем? Чем?	быть (past, future, infinitive) явля́ться to be (no perf) станови́ться каза́ться счита́ть(ся) называ́ть(ся)
Other verbs		Кем? Чем?	занима́ться руководи́ть пра́вить интересова́ться торгова́ть облада́ть
The "doer" in a passive type construction		Кем? Чем? С кем?	

TIME-EXPRESSIONS:	USEFUL IDIOMS:

<table>
<tr><td>лéтом
зимóй
óсенью
веснóй</td><td>After:
поздрáвить с - to congratulate on
рабóтать над - to work on
послáть за - to send for</td></tr>
<tr><td>днём
ýтром
вéчером
нóчью</td><td>отвéтственность пéред
- responsibility before
рáзница мéжду - difference betw.
отношéния мéжду - relations betw.</td></tr>
<tr><td>порóй

часáми</td><td>богáтый нéфтью - rich in oil
        урáном - rich in uranium
бéдный ресýрсами - poor in
                resources</td></tr>
<tr><td>недéлями

месяцáми</td><td>довóльный плáном - satisfied with
соглáсный с плáном
соглáсен,-а,-о,-ы - in agreement
                with</td></tr>
<tr><td></td><td>какúм óбразом? - in what way?</td></tr>
<tr><td></td><td>путём рефóрм - by means of
                reforms
        нарáщивания вооружéний
        - arms build-up</td></tr>
<tr><td></td><td>пять с половúной - five and a half
пять с чéтвертью - five and
                a quarter</td></tr>
</table>

CIRCLE
TWO

CIRCLE TWO

LESSON ONE

AUDIO-COMPREHENSION EXERCISE

part 1

You will now hear a text about a government crisis. Review the key words
below. Then listen to the text with the following questions in mind.
Afterwards, listen to the text again and write down the answers.

1. What do you already know about the stability of post-war
   parliamentary governments in Italy? How do changes of government
   usually occur in that country?
2. How many cabinet members deserted the coalition government? What
   party did they represent?
3. What motivated their action? What specific measure were they
   protesting?
4. The party in question had supported some economic belt-tightening
   measures. What were they designed to do?
5. What specifically did the measures consist of?

Key words

при́нято реше́ние о вы́ходе из прави́тельства – a decision to resign is made
наста́ивать на безотлага́тельных рефо́рмах – to insist on urgent reforms
в ито́ге та́йного голосова́ния – as a result of secret ballot
провали́ть законопрое́кт – to block a bill
предусма́тривать введе́ние нало́гов – to provide for new taxes
одо́брены ме́ры «жёсткой эконо́мии» – measures of "austerity policy" are approved
увеличе́ние ря́да прямы́х и ко́свенных нало́гов – an increase of a number of
              direct and indirect taxes
расхо́ды на социа́льные ну́жды – expenses for social needs
рост цен на това́ры пе́рвой необходи́мости – growth of prices for first necessity
              goods

TEXT: Read the following text. Be able to translate it in written form.

Прави́тельственный кри́зис в Ита́лии   Часть 1

 Рим, 6 (ТАСС). В сообще́нии ТАСС говори́тся, что в Ита́лии начался́ но́вый
полити́ческий кри́зис. По́сле дли́тельного совеща́ния секретариа́та Италья́нской
социалисти́ческой па́ртии мину́вшей но́чью при́нято реше́ние о вы́ходе из
прави́тельства семи́ мини́стров-социали́стов, наста́ивавших на безотлага́тельных

реформах. Это произошло после того, как два дня назад в палате депутатов в итоге тайного голосования христианским демократам удалось провалить законопроект, предусматривающий введение дополнительных налогов на нефтяные компании.

Документ, разработанный социалистом, министром финансов Р. Формикой, представлял собой составную часть одобренных на днях правительством мер «жёсткой экономии», направленных на сокращение дефицита бюджета. Они предусматривают увеличение ряда прямых и косвенных налогов, уменьшение государственных расходов на социальные нужды, рост цен на товары первой необходимости. Р. Формика и ранее подчёркивал, что Италия нуждается в переменах.

Words and expressions to part 1

начался	политический	кризис
кончился	экономический	
продолжался	правительственный	

начинаться/начаться
    -ются начнутся
начатый
начало

кончаться/кончиться
    -ются   -атся
конченный
конец

продолжаться/продолжиться
     -ются   -атся
продолженный
продолжение

социалист
социал-демократ
коммунист
лейборист
республиканец
демократ
член социал-христианской партии
член партии труда

принимать/принять   решение о выходе из правительства - resignation from the
    -ют примут   government
                  меры   по новому законопроекту
                  шаги   в направлении урегулирования - to take steps
                                    towards the settlement
принимать участие   в голосовании - to participate in voting

при́нятый
приня́тие

пала́та депута́тов
      представи́телей
      о́бщин

кандида́т   в прави́тельство
баллоти́роваться   сена́т
    -уются   конгре́сс

                в президе́нты - a presidential candidate
                конгрессме́ны
                чле́ны политбюро́ - a candidate-member for the
                                Politbureau

кандида́т   на пост президе́нта
баллоти́роваться   сена́тора

пост (pl. посты́, посто́в)

наста́ивать/настоя́ть   на   вво́де войск
     -ют   -я́т   введе́нии но́вых нало́гов

в ито́ге та́йного голосова́ния - as a result of secret ballot
      встре́чи в верха́х

голосова́ть/проголосова́ть
   -у́ют   -у́ют
голосова́ние

прова́ливать/провали́ть   законопрое́кт - to kill the draft of the bill
     -ют прова́лят   кандида́та
                 назначе́ние
прова́ленный
прова́л

зако́н предусма́тривает введе́ние дополни́тельных нало́гов
     - a law providing for additional taxes
                    коменда́нтского ча́са
                    жёсткой эконо́мии

нало́ги на   компа́нии - corporate taxes
         и́мпорт
         э́кспорт
подохо́дный нало́г - income tax

<pre>
                              (где?)
вводи́ть/ввести́ рефо́рмы в о́бласти промы́шленности
   -ят введу́т   эконо́мики
                                      се́льского хозя́йства
                         в образова́нии
                            здравоохране́нии
                            социа́льном обслу́живании

                         (куда?)
              войска́   в Афганиста́н
                        на Ку́бу
введе́ние   рефо́рм
but:
ввод   войск

разраба́тывать/разрабо́тать   докуме́нт
       -ют   -ют   план отступле́ния
                                    наступле́ния
                                бюдже́т на сле́дующий фина́нсовый год
разрабо́танный
разрабо́тка

представля́ть/ собо́й   составну́ю часть мер по сокраще́нию бюдже́та
        -ют
предста́вить   агре́ссию
      -ят   наруше́ние прав челове́ка
предста́вленный

одобря́ть/   ме́ры
    -ют
одо́брить   увеличе́ние расхо́дов на   оборо́ну
    -ят   жили́щное строи́тельство - housing contruction
                                     нау́чные иссле́дования
одо́бренный
одобре́ние

шаги́, напра́вленные на увеличе́ние ря́да прямы́х и ко́свенных нало́гов
                        уменьше́ние госуда́рственных расхо́дов

рост цен   на   нефть
                това́ры пе́рвой необходи́мости - first necessity goods
                       широ́кого потребле́ния - consumer goods
                сырьё

направля́ть/ движе́ние за неприсоедине́ние - non-aligned movement
       -ют   замора́живание расхо́дов
напра́вить   мир - peace movement
    -ят   неиспо́льзование я́дерного ору́жия пе́рвыми
                      - to direct the No-First-Use Movement
</pre>

направля́ть движе́ние   про́тив испыта́ний хими́ческого ору́жия
напра́вленный
                         (в чём?)
нужда́ться (imperf.)   в сырье́ – to be in need of raw materials
                         подде́ржке – to be in need of support

VOCABULARY EXERCISES

Look through the vocabulary for part 1 of the text «*Прави́тельственный кри́зис в Ита́лии*». Do the following exercises.

A. Give the nominative and genitive plural for the following nouns. Mark the stress.

агре́ссия, челове́к, оборо́на, цена́, пра́во, эконо́мика, па́ртия, политбюро́, конгрессме́н, рефо́рма, и́мпорт, иссле́дование, ору́жие, сырьё, часть, э́кспорт, пост.

B. Paraphrase the italicized words.

уча́ствовать в движе́нии, *кандида́т в конгре́сс*, *реши́ть* вы́йти из сове́та, приня́ть *шаги́*, встре́ча *на вы́сшем у́ровне*, пала́та *представи́телей*, ввоз не́фти, движе́ние *против испо́льзования*, *оста́вить на пре́жнем у́ровне* расхо́ды на оборо́ну, *сокраще́ние бюдже́та*, *быть во главе́* движе́ния.

C. Give the opposite for the italicized words.

прямы́е нало́ги, война́ *начала́сь*, *откры́тое* голосова́ние, *вход* в прави́тельство, *и́мпорт*, *увеличе́ние* расхо́дов, план *отступле́ния*, *одо́брить* ме́ры, движе́ние за *присоедине́ние*, това́ры *широ́кого потребле́ния*, *уваже́ние* прав челове́ка.

D. Form verbs out of the following nouns. Make necessary changes.

нача́ло кри́зиса, продолже́ние голосова́ния, коне́ц инфля́ции, вы́ход из прави́тельства, вход в коали́цию, приня́тие реше́ния, прова́л законопрое́кта, голосова́ние по законопрое́кту, введе́ние нало́гов, ввод войск, одобре́ние пла́на.

E. Give Russian equivalents for the following English phrases.

  - prices for basic necessities
  - No-First-Use Movement

- human rights violations
- to be in need of social services
- to insist on export tariffs
- to direct the non-aligned movement
- to draft a document
- housing construction
- budget for the next fiscal year
- to kill a bill
- Austerity Policy
- congressional candidate (3 variants)
- to block somebody's candidacy
- decrease of federal expenditures
- corporate taxes
- to run for President
- as a result of secret ballot
- a Social-Christian

F. Write sentences to fill in the blanks in each of the groups below. Be able to translate your sentences.

(что?)

1.   Администра́ция начала́ _________________

____

продолжа́ла _________________

____

ко́нчила _________________

____

Change the sentences above using the same verbs with «СЯ».

2.   Он явля́ется кандида́том   (куда?)

____

____

(на каку́ю до́лжность?)

____

____

(на како́й пост?)

____

____

(на что?)

3.   Газе́ты писа́ли о нало́гах на_________________

____

____

4.   Опя́ть наблюда́ется рост цен на _________ (на что?)
    ____
    ____

5.   Расхо́ды на _________ снижа́ются. (на что?)
    ____

    _________ повыша́ются.
    ____

6.   Страна́ нужда́ется в _________ (в чём?)
    ____
    ____

7.   Конгре́сс наста́ивает на _________ (на чём?)
    ____
    ____

8.   Происхо́дит введе́ние _________ (чего?) _________ (где?)
    _________ _________

    ввод _________ (чего?) _________ (куда?)
    _________ _________

9.   _________ (кто? что?) представля́ет собо́й _________ (кого? что?)
    _________ _________
    _________ _________

10.   Обще́ственность выража́ет уве́ренность _________ (в чём?)
    ____
    ____

11.   Конгре́сс при́нял ме́ры, напра́вленные на _________ (на что?)
    ____
    ____

GRAMMAR: TIME EXPRESSIONS

At such-and-such a moment, minute, hour, day

в + accusative:
   в э́тот моме́нт, в э́ту мину́ту, в э́тот час, в э́тот день, в сре́ду

Note also: в э́то вре́мя – at that time, meanwhile
           в настоя́щее вре́мя – at present

Such-and-such a week

на + prepositional:
   на э́той неде́ле, на про́шлой неде́ле, на сле́дующей неде́ле

Such-and-such a month

в + prepositional:
   в э́том ме́сяце, в про́шлом ме́сяце, в сле́дующем ме́сяце, в а́вгусте
   семидеся́того го́да

Such-and-such a year, decade, century

в + prepositional:
   в э́том году́, в про́шлом году́, в бу́дущем году́, в девяно́сто второ́м году́,
   в про́шлом десятиле́тии, в двадца́том ве́ке

In such-and-such a decade (in the eighties)

в восьмидеся́тых года́х	In the 80's
в нача́ле / в конце́ восьмидеся́тых годо́в	In the early / late 80's

Calendar dates

Это случи́лось...	It happened...
пя́того ма́я двадца́того го́да.	on May 5, 1920. Genitive alone
в ма́е двадца́того го́да.	in May, 1920. Prepositional + genitive
в двадца́том году́.	in 1920. Prepositional

From ... to

exclusive – с + genitive + до + genitive:
   с пя́того ма́я до пе́рвого ию́ня

inclusive – с + genitive + по + accusative:
   с пя́того ма́я по пе́рвое ию́ня

In the morning, in winter

Instrumental with *no preposition:*

Memorize the expressions:
    у́тром, днём, ве́чером, но́чью; зимо́й, весно́й, ле́том, осенью.

Note that но́чью really means "early morning": from about midnight to four in
the morning.

O'clock a.m. and p.m.

genitive after an "o'clock" expression:
    де́вять часо́в утра́
    час дня
    шесть часо́в ве́чера
    два часа́ но́чи (*not* ве́чера! See the note in the category above.)

Note that for official schedules the 24-hour clock is used:
    6:00 pm = в восемна́дцать часо́в or even more officially,
восемна́дцать-ноль-ноль.

In the mornings, on Wednesdays

по + dative: Memorize по утра́м, по вечера́м, по ноча́м, as well
    as по plus dative plural of days or the week, e.g. по сре́дам.
But note that "in the afternoons" is днём. There is no "по" equivalent.

Every (day, week, month, summer, etc.)

Ка́ждый + accusative with no preposition:
    Ка́ждый день, ка́ждую неде́лю, ка́ждый ме́сяц, ка́ждое ле́то

A certain amount of time before or after an event

before: За + accusative time expression + до + genitive:

    Всё случи́лось за два дня   It all happened two days
    до конфе́ренции.   before the conference.

after: Че́рез + accusative time expression + по́сле + genitive:

    Всё случи́лось че́рез два   It all happened two days
    дня по́сле конфере́нции.   after the conference.

Note that while English uses no prepositions, Russian requires за...до *and*
через...по́сле.

By a certain time

к + dative:
    к двум часа́м – by two o'clock.

In an amount of time (After... amount of time)

че́рез + accusative or че́рез + number + genitive:

План бу́дет одо́брен че́рез неде́лю.	The plan will be passed after a week's time
Они́ отве́тят че́рез две мину́ты.	They will answer in two minute's time.

Note that че́рез literally means "after a certain amount of time," but it is usually used for "in a certain amount of time."

Within an amount of time, over a certain time

за + accusative or за + number + genitive:

План бу́дет одо́брен за неде́лю.	The plan will be approved within a week.
За после́дние два ме́сяца...	Over the last two months...

За + accusative is used only when "within" is heavily emphasized, and then almost always with perfective. In most situations use че́рез.

Duration: For an amount of time

Accusative without a preposition or number plus genitive:

Кри́зис продолжа́лся ме́сяц. В а́рмии слу́жат два го́да.	The crisis lasted for a month. People serve in the army for two years.

в тече́ние + genitive:

Кри́зис продолжа́лся в тече́ние двух неде́ль.	The crisis lasted for two weeks.

Planned events: For an amount of time

на + accusative or на + number + genitive:

Делега́ция отбыла́ на неде́лю.	The delegation left (now) for (a future period) of a week.

Note that English uses *for* in both durative (*worked for a week*) and planned-event (*will go for a week*) expressions. However durative time expressions can be replaced by constructions which omit the "for" (*worked for a week, spent a week working*). This is not true of expressions denoting planned events.

During

во вре́мя + genitive: во вре́мя войны́ – during the war

Under or during someone's rule

при + prepositional: при Ста́лине – under Stalin

Letter (newspaper, telegram) of such-and-such a date

от + genitive: газета от пятого мая

GRAMMAR EXERCISE: TIME EXPRESSIONS

Read the review of time expressions and do the following exercises. Fill in the blanks. Be able to translate these sentences into English.

1. _______________________________ отношения между Алжиром и Морокко
   (At the present moment)

   остаются напряжёнными.

2. Совет Безопасности принял эту резолюцию_______________.
   on Sept 7, 1987

3. Только _______________ возглавляемое им правительство установило
   (last spring)

   дипломатические отношения с КНР.

4. Война между Ираном и Ираком продолжается уже_______________.
   (for seven years)

5. _______________ Претория обещала перебросить в лагеря бандитов оружие
   (By February)

   и боеприпасы.

6. Ожидается, что конвой войдёт в Персидский залив_______________
   (the next day)

   _______________ по местному времени.
   (at noon)

7. Уборка урожая начинается_______________ и будет продолжаться
   (next week)

   _______________.
   (an entire fall)

8. На совести ди Карло и его сообщников убийство__________ шефа
    (in 1979)
    палермской полиции.

9. ________________________________ описанного инцидента Карачи стали
    (Several weeks prior to)

    ареной кровопролитных столкновений.

10. Встречи с матерями воинов, оказавшихся в плену, будут происходить
    ________________________________.
    (from May 30 through June 4)

11. ________________________ переговоров с муджахиддинами наши военнопленные
    (Three months after)

    станут возвращаться домой.

12. Партизаны совершали налеты только__________ под прикрытием темноты.
    (nights)

13. Следствие под кодовым названием «Оперейшн диванш» закончится
    ________________________.
    (in 6–7 months)

14. Два кувейтских танкера__________________________ под американскими
    (for the first time)

    флагами пересекут Ормузский пролив.

15. ________________________ произошёл полный распад старых колониальных
    (In the XX century)

    империй.

16. ________________________ город сбрасывал в реку свыше *200* тысяч кубометров
    (Every Wednesday)

    грязных вод.

17. Нации нашей планеты______________ израсходуют около триллиона
    (in the 80s)

    долларов на военные расходы.

18. В газетах сообщалось, что ________________________ цены на
(during the Winter Games)

билеты на городской железной дороге, в метро и автобусах будут

повышены.

19. Помощник мэра часто уезжала в командировки_____________________
(for an indefinite

_________________.

period of time)

20. __________________________ банда ворвалась в посёлок.
(on Monday)   (at five a.m)

21. В телеграмме____________________ говорилось о никогда не
(dated by April 1)

происходивших событиях.

22. ____________________ арестовали всех священнослужителей.
(Within two hours)

23. __________________________ началась разработка новой конституции?
(Under what General Secretary)

24. Кооператив «Нарын»____________________ полностью перестанет зависеть
(in the early 90s)

от госторговли.

GRAMMAR: VERBAL ASPECT

Imperfective aspect is used in the infinitive after:

1. начина́ться(ся), стать, продолжа́ть(ся), конча́ть(ся), привыка́ть/привы́кнуть, учи́ться/научи́ться or any other verb indicating beginning or ending.

> Утром на́чали прибыва́ть делега́ции.
> Delegations began to arrive in the morning.

> Они́ не привы́кли соблюда́ть зако́ны.
> They are not used to observing laws.

2.   нельзя, when it means "musn't" or "not allowed"

> Нельзя называть тему дискуссии.
> The topic of discussion is not to be announced!

3.   **Nearly all negated infinitives.**

> Кабинет решил не объявлять комендантский час.
> The Cabinet decided against a curfew.
> Власти просили население не выходить из домов.
> The authorities asked the population not to leave their homes.

4.   **не надо, не стоит, достаточно, хватит, вредно, зачем and избегать to express needlessness of action.**

> Не стоит обыскивать всех прибывающих пассажиров.
> It is not worth it to search all arriving passengers.

> Советский Союз избегает вводить войска в Румынию.
> The Soviet Union avoids bringing its troops into Rumania.

Perfective aspect is used in the infinitive after:

1.   **нельзя, when it means "impossible."**

> Нельзя будет обсудить проект.
> It will not be possible to discuss the project.

2.   **забыть, удаться, успеть.**

> Войскам удалось быстро оцепить район беспорядков.
> Troops succeeded quickly to cordon off the area of unrest.

GRAMMAR EXERCISES: VERBAL ASPECT

Review the use of verbal aspect as presented in Circle One, Lesson 1.   Then review the grammar presentation in this lesson and do the following exercises.

A.   Give perfective forms for the following verbs.   Conjugate both forms. Mark the stress.

принимать, баллотироваться, проваливать, начинать, кончать, продолжать, вводить, одобрять, направлять, настаивать.

B. Fill in the blanks. Explain your choice of aspect. Be able to translate these sentences into English.

1. К этому моменту стюарду-конголезцу удалось____________________________
                                    обезвреживать/обезвредить

    пирата.

2. Недавно закончили ________ _____________ крупный посёлок
                          строить/построить

    газодобытчиков.

3. Пассажиры в панике____________________ из самолёта по запасной
                        броса́ться/бро́ситься

    лестнице, а потом ______________________________________ прямо
                        начинать/начать   прыгать/прыгнуть

    на асфальт.

4. Советским судам нельзя___________________ в эти порты для дозаправки
                            заходить/зайти

    горючим и продовольствием.

5. В настоящее время эсминец находится в британском порту, куда уже

    ____________________ для его приёмки чилийский экипаж.
       прибывать/прибыть

6. Хотя переговоры___________________ полтора месяца, они ни к чему
                     проходить/пройти

    не _____________________.
         приводить/привести

7. За последние 5 лет на вооружение чилийских ВВС______________________
                                                    поступать/ поступить

    40 английских самолётов.

8. 30 лет назад Советский Союз первым______________________ устав
                                        одобрять/одобрить

    Международного агентства по атомной энергии (МАГАТЭ).

9. Без полной реконструкции ________________________ план полностью просто
    выполнять/выполнить

нельзя.

10. В условиях перестройки на заводах каждый день________________________
     совершаться/совершиться

настоящая научно-техническая революция.

11. Только за сутки им________________________ увидеть 17 космических
     приводиться/привестись

восходов и закатов.

12. Время от времени страны Латинской Америки________________________
     приобретать/приобрести

массу ненужных товаров.

13. Условлено, что стороны будут продолжать________________________
     искать/поискать

новые подходы для оздоровления обстановки в регионе.

14. Каждый год станки________________________ по 10–15 раз.
     ремонтировать/отремонтировать

15. М. Харрари успел ________________________ своего брата и двух арабов.
     освобождать/освободить

C. Translate the following.

1. Central American foreign ministers developed a new regional peace plan in two days of meetings here.
2. The Greens began to lead the movement against chemical weapons testing.
3. For two days they participated in an offensive.
4. It took the president two terms to give Americans a decent health care system.
5. On Wednesday the House approved an increase in housing construction expenditures.
6. Nicaraguan opposition leaders continued to make erroneous decisions about their participation in the plan.
7. According to Soviet law, religious organizations can now conduct charity (благотворительный) work.
8. They took a vote on corporate taxes and introduced a new legislation.

9.   It will be impossible to kill the new bill without strong resistance from the Democrats.

10.   By the end of the next fiscal year prices for basic necessities will increase.

11.   We advise you not to make a decision on this matter at this time. In fact, we can not make a decision without all the facts.

12.   People have become used to electing candidates whom they do not support.

13.   According to the minister's statement, it is not worth acquiring the latest technology in the 90s.

14.   The General Secretary will go to Washington for three days. There he will hold talks with the President and to meet with leading members of Congress.

SPEAKING EXERCISES

Transition words link ideas together by bridging sentences or paragraphs.
(They can mark the introduction of the story, its development, different
points of an argument, the conclusion etc.)

A. Расскажи́те часть 1 те́кста.   В своём расска́зе испо́льзуйте сле́дующие
слова́:

итáк; наприме́р; не то́лько..., но...; ведь; вот почему́.

B. Опиши́те прави́тельственный кри́зис в друго́й стране́.

C. Отве́тьте на сле́дующие вопро́сы:

1. Что привело́ к прави́тельственному кри́зису в Ита́лии?
2. Кака́я па́ртия реши́ла вы́йти из кабине́та?
3. Почему́ италья́нские социали́сты выступа́ли за дополни́тельные нало́ги?
4. Кака́я па́ртия возража́ла про́тив дополни́тельных нало́гов?
5. Как ча́сто происхо́дят прави́тельственные кри́зисы в Ита́лии?

D. Дополни́тельные вопро́сы: (optional)

1. Почему́ вопро́с о нало́гах приобрёл символи́ческое значе́ние в США?
2. Каки́е европе́йские па́ртии вы зна́ете?

AUDIO-COMPREHENSION EXERCISE

part 2

This part tells you what led to the crisis.   Listen to it with these questions in mind.

1. According to the report, how did many Roman pundits characterize the results of the vote?
2. What happened to the coalition after the opposition's walkout?
3. How many parties made up the coalition?
4. Who are Spadolini and Pertini? What have they pledged not to do?
5. What is the general opinion about their chances for success?

Key words

осуждáть часть законопроéкта – to condemn a part of the bill
провалúть законопроéкт – to block the bill
побéда нефтянóго лóбби и трéстов – a victory of oil lobby and trusts
потерáть необходúмое большинствó – to lose a necessary majority
сложúвшееся положéние – an existing situation
акцентúровать обы́чные разноглáсия – to emphasize usual differences
неизбéжность отстáвки – the inevitability of resignation
непримирúмые разноглáсия – irreconcilable differences (contradictions)

TEXT: Read the following text. Be able to translate it in written form.

Правúтельственный крúзис в Итáлии   Часть 2

Наканýне голосовáния в палáте депутáтов ряд представúтелей, входя́щих в правúтельство христиáнско-демократúческой пáртии, откры́то осуждáл ту часть законопроéкта, котóрая предусмáтривала увеличéние налóгов на нефтепромы́шленников. Пóсле провáла депутáтами э́того докумéнта в рúмских политúческих кругáх стáли откры́то говорúть о «побéде нефтянóго лóбби и трéстов».

Пóсле вы́хода из кабинéта социалúстов правúтельственная коалúция, в котóрую вхóдят пять пáртий, потеря́ла необходúмое большинствó в парлáменте. Сложúвшееся положéние бýдет обсуждáться сегóдня на э́кстренной встрéче председáтеля совéта минúстров Дж. Спадолúни и президéнта респýблики Пертúни, котóрые обещáли не акцентúровать свои́ обы́чные разноглáсия. Тем не мéнее мнóгие здесь выскáзывают увéренность в неизбéжности отстáвки кабинéта, учúтывая непримирúмые разноглáсия мéжду прáвящими пáртиями.

Words and expressions to part 2

накану́не голосова́ния по законопроéкту
        войны́
        вы́боров
война́ (pl. во́йны, во́йн)

входи́ть/войти́ в   коали́цию – to join the coalition
вхо́дят войду́т   си́лу – to come into effect
        употребле́ние – to come into use

вход

осужда́ть/осуди́ть   наруше́ния прав челове́ка
  -ют осу́дят   наруше́ние прекраще́ния огня́ – to condemn violation of
                            cease-fire
          зако́на
осуждённый
осужде́ние

выходи́ть/вы́йти из   употребле́ния – to go out of use
        прави́тельства
     с   террито́рии
        За́падного бе́рега – to withdraw from the West Bank
     в   отста́вку – to resign
вы́ход

в   полити́ческих   кругáх
   вое́нных
   прави́тельственных

побе́да нефтяно́го ло́бби (unchanged)
    изра́ильского

оде́рживать/одержа́ть побе́ду – to win the victory
   -ют оде́ржат

нести́/понести́ пораже́ние – to suffer defeat
несу́т понесу́т поте́ри – to suffer losses
        уще́рб – to suffer damage
понесённый

наноси́ть/нанести́   тяжёлые поте́ри – to inflict heavy losses
  -ят   -у́т   пораже́ние – to cause defeat
        пе́рвый уда́р – to deliver the first strike
нанесённый
лобби́ровать   в по́льзу иностра́нной держа́вы
  -уют   про́тив использования но́вых систе́м

теря́ть/потеря́ть необходи́мое большинство́ в парла́менте - to lose the necessary
   -ют   -ют   majority
поте́рянный
поте́ря - a loss
(pl. поте́ри - losses, поте́рь)

обсужда́ть/обсуди́ть ситуа́цию на чрезвыча́йной встре́че Сове́та Безопа́сности
    -ют обсу́дят кри́зис   э́кстренной встре́че Генера́льной Ассамбле́и ООН
              положе́ние
обсуждённый
обсужде́ние

отста́вка кабине́та   неизбе́жна
безрабо́тица
энергети́ческий кри́зис   неизбе́жен
вое́нное столкнове́ние   неизбе́жно - an armed clash is inevitable

                              (ме́жду кем?)   (из-за чего́?)
непримири́мые разногла́сия ме́жду партнёрами   из-за торго́вли
                           фи́рмами   ры́нков
                           сою́зниками

проявля́ются разногла́сия и́з-за строи́тельства газопрово́да
                       территориа́льных ди́спутов
проявля́ться/прояви́ться
     -ются проя́вятся
проя́вленный

проявле́ние   тре́ний и́з-за поли́тики
               раско́ла
тре́ние (pl. тре́ния, тре́ний) - frictions

                              (в чём?)
выска́зывать/вы́сказать уве́ренность в неизбе́жности войны́
      -ют   -жут   побе́де
                         необходи́мости рефо́рм
вы́сказанный

пра́вящая па́ртия
         коали́ция

пра́вить страно́й
  -ят   наро́дом

правле́ние

VOCABULARY EXERCISES

Look through the vocabulary for part 2 of the text «*Правительственный кризис в Италии*». Do the following exercises.

A. Give the nominative and genitive plural forms for the following nouns. Mark the stress.

война́, ло́бби, поте́ря, уще́рб, бе́рег, страна́, разногла́сие.

B. Paraphrase the italicized words.

па́ртия *у вла́сти, незадо́лго до* вы́боров, *победи́ть, руководи́ть* страно́й, зако́н *на́чал де́йствовать, ну́жное* большинство́, *вы́разить неодобре́ние, говори́ть о* кри́зисе, нанести́ уда́р *пе́рвым, специа́льно назна́ченная* встре́ча, *сро́чная* встре́ча, инфля́цию *невозмо́жно предотврати́ть, бой,* разногла́сия *стано́вятся я́вными.*

C. Give the opposite for the italicized words.

бе́лое меньшинство́, вы́йти из употребле́ния, побе́да, лобби́ровать в *по́льзу* басту́ющих, *войти́ на* За́падный бе́рег, *понести́* ущерб, *лёгкие* поте́ри, *пе́рвый* уда́р, *очередна́я* се́ссия, *получи́ть* большинство́.

D. Form verbs from the following nouns. Make necessary changes.

осужде́ние вы́хода в отста́вку, обсужде́ние положе́ния, правле́ние страно́й.

E. Give Russian equivalents for the following English phrases.

   – to become obsolete
   – to express confidence in the inevitability of his resignation
   – to win the victory
   – Security Council emergency session
   – violation of cease-fire
   – irreconcilable differences over markets
   – to suffer damage
   – to come into use
   – to inflict heavy losses
   – to lobby for a foreign government
   – signs of schism
   – to run the country

F. Write sentences to fill in the blanks in each of the groups below. Be able to translate your sentences.

(что?)

1)
_______________ неизбёжна
_______________ неизбёжен
_______________ неизбёжно
_______________ неизбёжны

Change the sentences above using «невозмо́жно предотврати́ть» (чему́? кому́?)

(что?)

2)
_______________ вы́шло из употребле́ния
_______________ вы́шла
_______________ вы́шел
_______________ вы́шли

Change the sentences above using «войти́ в употребле́ние».

(что?)

3)   Ги́тлер   понёс   _______________
     Сове́тская армия   понесла́ _______________
     Прави́тельство   понесло́ _______________

Change the sentences above using «нанести́».

(ме́жду кем?)   (из-за чего́?)

4)   Проявля́ются разногла́сия _______________   _______________
                              _______________   _______________
                              _______________   _______________

(в чём?)

5)   Горбачёв   выска́зывает уве́ренность в _______________
     Демокра́ты   выска́зывают
     Сена́тор Ке́ннеди выска́зывал   _______________

REVIEW: QUOTING SOURCES

ЛЮДИ

телекомментáтор
представйтель МИД СССР
главá опозйции
лйдер
помóщник минйстра
обозревáтель
совéтник по делáм...
замминйстра
госсекретáрь
etc

ГОВОРЯТ

говорйт,   что...
          о...
подчёркивает что...
заявйл, что...
объявйл о...
отмечáет, что...
сказáл в интервью
в передáче по рáдио
по телевйдению
считáет, что
вýступил с...за(прóтив)...
трéбует + gen.
чтобы + subj.
недовóлен + inst.

Printed or broadcast formats:

в телепрогрáмме «Новости»
в телепередáче
в статьé
в конститýции
в докумéнте
в договóре
в интервью́
в рéчи
в передовйце
в доклáде
в закóне
в выступлéнии
в прéссе

говорйтся, что...
            о...
говорйлось

сообщáется, что...
            о...
сообщáлось

отмечáется, что

отмечáлось

Media:

ПО рáдио
ПО телевйдению
ПО седьмóй прогрáмме

сообщáлось, что...
          о...
передавáлось, что...
           о...

According to:

ПО слова́м а́втора кни́ги
ПО мне́нию а́втора статьи́
ПО пра́вилам
ПО конститу́ции
ПО зако́ну

В соотве́тствии с   зако́ном
                        пра́вом
                        ре́чью
                        конститу́цией
                        заявле́нием
                        выступле́нием
                        да́нными
                        информа́цией
         со   статьёй
                        передови́цей
                        интервью́
                        исто́чниками Бе́лого до́ма
         со   слова́ми а́втора

In English sources can speak. In Russian ИСТО́ЧНИКИ can not ГОВОРИ́ТЬ.

ИЗ журнали́стских   ста́ло изве́стно, что...
ИЗ вое́нных   о
ИЗ секре́тных   исто́чников
ИЗ америка́нских

ИЗ исто́чников   Пентаго́на   ста́ло изве́стно, что...
                 Бе́лого до́ма   о....
                 ЦРУ

also:

ИЗ програ́ммы «Вре́мя»   ста́ло изве́стно, что
         интервью́   о...
         заявле́ния
         телепереда́чи
         радиосообще́ния

EXERCISES: QUOTING SOURCES

Review Quoting sources as presented in this lesson and do the following exercises.

A.   Translate the following expressions.

1.   according to a communique on armed clashes
2.   U.S. sources disclosed that...
3.   the Summit agreements emphasized that...
4.   a Channel 4 broadcast said that...
5.   the CIA sources said that...
6.   according to the strike leaders
7.   National Security Adviser remarked that...
8.   the White House spokesman appeared on TV with a statement
9.   according to some US Kremlinologists
10.   Defense Department sources said that...
11.   yesterday's editorial remarks that....
12.   according to the author of the Monroe Doctrine
13.   he made a new statement which emphasized...
14.   he appeared on TV with a proposal
15.   she made a speech before Congress which stressed the necessity
16.   the TV programm "Good Morning America" announced that...

B.   Write your own sentences with the above expressions.

GRAMMAR EXERCISES: VERBAL ASPECT (Continued)

A.   Give perfective forms for the following verbs.   Conjugate both forms. Mark the stress.

входи́ть, осужда́ть, оде́рживать, наноси́ть, проявля́ться, пра́вить, выска́зывать.

B.   Fill in the blanks.   Explain your choice of aspect.   Be able to translate these sentences into English.

1.   За период проведения этой гуманной политики ____________________________

возвраща́ться/возврати́ться

свыше 7.600 обманутых пропагандой афганцев.

2.   В задачу тральщиков входит_________________________ и
                        обнаруживать/обнаружить

_________________________ мины.
   обезвреживать/обезвредить

3.   Было объявлено, что сотрудникам советского посольства будет нельзя

_________________________ конференцию.
   посещать/посетить

4.   Это один из лучше всего сохранившихся античных театров в мире. Его

огромный амфитеатр_________________________ 15.000 зрителей.
                    вмещать/вместить

5.   Вашингтон_________________________ _________________________
              продолжать/продолжить осуществлять/осуществить

стационарное размещение передового командного пункта центрального

командования США (СЕТКОМ).

6.   Если не _________________________ эти вопросы к началу семестра, то
            решать/решить

завтра можно_________________________ в пиковом положении.
              оказываться/оказаться

7.   Нельзя столько времени_________________________ «советской угрозе».
                          уделять/уделить

8.   Только за последнюю неделю душманы трижды_________________________
                                              переходить/перейти

советскую границу.

9.   Ежегодно предприятия не успевают_________________________
                                    выполнять/выполнить

заключаемые договоры на ремонт и поставку техники.

10.   (Они) _________________________ (past) выпуск отечественных ЭВМ и
           планировать/запланировать

_________________________ _________________________ операторов для них.
   забывать/забыть   готовить/подготовить

11. Первый день конвой_____________________ (past) без сопровождения.
                           идти/пойти

12. Проект _____________________ (fut) на известной концепции
             основываться/основаться

«обычной стабильности».

13. Сумма недостач, невозмещённых убытков и порчи за последние годы не

_____________________ (present).
уменьшаться/уменьшится

C. Translate the following.

1. Within five years these nuclear missiles will become obsolete.
2. Most of the black mine workers in South Africa never counted on an increase in pay.
3. The Iranian Foreign Affairs Minister says that he cannot accept the U.N. Security Council resolution.
4. An Iraqi communique has reported that there there are signs of a schism in the Khoumeini regime.
5. For six months Iran's mines have been threatening any Iraqui ship.
6. In the forthcoming senatorial elections the Republicans will regain the necessary majority.
7. Within a week the strike will come to an end and the workers will resume full production.
8. According to the American Constitution, any new law comes into effect only after the President signs it.
9. The latest military reports said that our troops are suffering heavy losses.
10. The officers who launched last week's rebellion are now demanding their leader's resignation.
11. Do not forget to ask about the new export tariffs. Sulimov forgot to inform us when they will take effect.
12. In the opinion of the committee members it is not worth continuing these contacts.
13. The President has begged Congress not to raise taxes, but nearly all economists agree that without new taxes a financial crisis is unavoidable.
14. The new Christian Democratic government managed to receive the support of both the Socialists and the Greens.
15. Soviet public figures are now learning to use television effectively to state their points of view.

RENDERING

Render the following information. Do not translate it word for word. Instead convey as much of the information you can with Russian that you have learned so far.

Could there ever be a military takeover of the United States government? Political chaos resulting in the military occupation of cities, martial law? Novelists Fletcher Knebel and Charles Bailey gave the matter some serious thought several decades ago in their political thriller "Seven Days in May." An annotated version of the novel was used for a number of years as an English-language text in Soviet language institutes.

The novel, written in 1962, is set in the early 70's. A Democratic administration has been in power for about three years and has signed with the Soviets a general disarmament treaty, which the Senate has just ratified.

As of May 15, the charismatic General James Scott, in concert with the Joint Chiefs of Staff, is in the final stages of plotting the overthrow of the administration. A member of the general's staff, Colonel Casey, learns of the plot, and despite his own opposition to the treaty, follows the Constitutional callings of his conscience and informs the White House.

By the next morning, the President has assembled a crisis-management team, including his old friend and confidant the Democratic Senator from Georgia, his national security advisor and Colonel Casey.

Meanwhile, General Scott, in addition to completing plans for the overthrow, rallies the citizenry against the administration. The threat he represents is real. Over the last month the general has criss-crossed the country making speech after speech, accusing the President of outright lack of patriotism. Many, including members of both houses of Congress, are more than willing to support the general out of fear of the consequences of such a wide-ranging treaty with the Soviets. And it is precisely because of the general's popularity throughout the country that the President shies away from dismissing him outright.

Over the course of the next five days the President's men collect the evidence they need to confront Scott with his insubordination. The Senator from Georgia travels to a secret base in Texas, where troops are being readied for deployment in major

American cities. The President's chief of staff flies to Spain to wrangle a signed confession from a weak-kneed admiral. And Colonel Casey has the unenvious job of digging up dirt on Scott's love life.

On the eve of the planned operation, the President's men have confirmed everything that Colonel Casey first reported a week before.

The President calls General Scott in for the final confrontation. Scott claims that he has no intention of taking the Presidency by force. Nevertheless, the General says, all the polls show that no one supports the President on the matter of the treaty. Given that lack of support, General Scott continues, the President in is no position to ask for his resignation.

What Scott doesn't know is that the President has hard evidence that Scott has been leading a conspiracy against him. Confronted with signed confessions from other officers, Scott finds that he has no choice but to resign.

Words and expressions:

a military takeover – вое́нный переворо́т
martial law – чрезвыча́йное положе́ние
charismatic personality – вдохнове́нная ли́чность
Joint Chiefs of Staff – Объединённый комите́т нача́льников штабо́в
a crisis-management team – гру́ппа по управле́нию кри́зисом
insubordination – неповинове́ние

SPEAKING EXERCISES

A. **Расскажи́те часть 2 те́кста. В своём расска́зе испо́льзуйте сле́дующие слова́.**

как изве́стно; во-пе́рвых,... во-вторы́х; причём; поэ́тому.

B. **Расскажи́те исто́рию «Прави́тельственный кри́зис в Ита́лии» с то́чки зре́ния италья́нского социали́ста.**

C. **Отве́тьте на сле́дующие вопро́сы.**

1. В чём причи́на нестаби́льности италья́нского прави́тельства?
2. Кака́я па́ртия домини́рует в полити́ческой жи́зни Ита́лии по́сле войны́?
3. Почему́ в ри́мских полити́ческих круга́х ста́ли пря́мо говори́ть о «побе́де нефтяно́го ло́бби и тре́стов»?

D. **Дополни́тельные вопро́сы. (optional)**

1. В чём разли́чие ме́жду америка́нской и европе́йской полити́ческими систе́мами?
2. Что тако́е лобби́зм?
3. Есть ли у президе́нта США большинство́ в америка́нском конгре́ссе?

READING EXERCISE

Больше не глушим   Владимир Острогорский

PRE-TEXT: In May, 1986, the Soviet Union stopped jamming the BBC and the Voice of America. Shortly thereafter the jamming of Radio Free Europe and Radio Liberty also came to an end.   Read the questions below. See if you can guess some of the answers before reading the article. Then read the text to see if you were right. Answer the questions in written form in English.

1.   What event prompted the author to write this piece?

PARAGRAPHS 2, 3
2.   There are two different sets of reasons why foreign broadcasts were jammed. Name them.

PARAGRAPH 4
3.   According to the author, what made the jamming senseless?

PARAGRAPH 5
4.   Name the reasons why it made sense to cease jamming.

PARAGRAPH 6, 7, 8
5.   The author accuses the Soviet mass media of a lack of spontaneity. How does he illustrate this point?

PARAGRAPH 9
6.   Ostrogorsky makes an important distinction between Radio Liberty from other countries' stations. What is it?

PARAGRAPH 9, 10
7.   The author concludes that diversity in the modern world must lead to... (true or false for each item):
   a.   isolation.
   b.   mutual intellectual enrichment.
   c.   exchange of information on current events.
   d.   occasional misunderstandings.

POST-TEXT: (using context)

Transition markers are the words that link ideas together.   They bridge sentences or paragraphs.

Here is a list of some frequently used transition words:

итак	вот почему
во-первых, во-вторых	однако
с одной стороны, с другой стороны	наоборот
например	ведь
..., а...	разве
не только..., но и ...	как известно; общеизвестно
причём	следовательно
при этом	кстати
между тем	дело в том, что
	etc.

Do the following exercises:

1. Find some transition markers in the introduction.   What is the function of each?
2. *Голос* is used frequently throughout this text.   In what context?

PARAGRAPHS 2, 3
3. Mark the words which indicate...
    a.   beginning of the argument
    b.   development of the argument
    c.   conclusion of the topic

PARAGRAPH 4
4. Find the words which introduce the reasons for calling the cessation of jamming an *аванс.*

PARAGRAPH 5,6,7
5. What markers are used to contrast two ways of covering the earthquake in Armenia?
6. What is the synonym for *радио* **передаёт** in the article?   Find other forms of this word in the text.
7. Find the word *to jam* (a broadcast) in the text. What is the name of the machine that does *jamming?*

8. Find the meanings of the following word(s) in the text.

рассказывать басни a. ____ to relate a legend
         b. ____ to tell a false story
         c. ____ to tell a short story with animals.

аванс   a. ____ overtures
         b. ____ progress
         c. ____ payment beforehand

запретный   a. ____ quarantined fruit
         b. ____ prohibited activities

указания свыше   a. ____ words of God
         b. ____ directions from above
         c. ____ abovementioned

9. Find the Russian equivalents for:

- to go on the air
- to give up taboos
- to spread rumours

10. Find a synonym for *текущие события*.
11. Translate the title of the story.

ЗАМЕТКИ НАБЛЮДАТЕЛЯ

Недавно в СССР снято глушение радиопередач «Немецкой волны», «Голоса Израиля» и радиостанции «Свобода», вещающей из Мюнхена на американские деньги. Другие западные передачи на языках народов нашей страны перестали глушить еще раньше. Итак, воя глушилок в нашем эфире больше не слышно. Событие, которое на свой лад свидетельствует о прогрессе гласности.

БОЛЬШЕ НЕ ГЛУШИМ

«Голоса» подвергались — правда, с перерывами — глушению на протяжении нескольких десятилетий. Почему? По причине распространявшихся ими слухов, передержек, а подчас и прямого вранья в их передачах. Но иностранный «голос», рассказывающий басни, не очень опасен. Раньше ли или позже он утратит доверие аудитории. Зачем же его глушить?

Дело, однако, в том, что зарубежные вещатели не только лгали. Пользуясь царившей в нашем обществе безгласностью, они проталкивали в эфир свой идеологический товар в упаковке информации, на которую у нас существовал запрет. О беззаконии, творившемся сталинизмом. О нравственном разложении и сползании экономики к кризису в семидесятых — первой половине восьмидесятых годов. Об уровне благосостояния, науки и техники на Западе, о демократических институтах буржуазного общества, столь разительно отличавшихся от наших. Вот почему их искали в эфире. И выли на коротких волнах дорогостоящие глушилки.

Интерес к «голосам» стал падать, а глушение — терять смысл по мере того, как мы отказывались от многочисленных «табу» на актуальную информацию, от стремления рисовать мир двумя красками: розовой — для себя и «своих» и черной — для всех прочих.

И все же думаю, что отмена глушения — своеобразный аванс. Во-первых, советским радиослушателям, которым еще предстоит учиться критическому отношению к зарубежной информационной продукции. То есть тому, чему нельзя было научиться в обстановке искусственно создавшейся информационной стерильности, делавшей запретный плод сладким. А во-вторых, это аванс нашим средствам массовой информации, привыкшим по меньшей мере внутри страны работать вне подлинной конкуренции.

К чему ведет их неповоротливость, показала информационная обстановка, возникшая сразу же после трагической вести о землетрясении в Армении.

over

Та же «Свобода», отменив регулярные русскоязычные передачи, весьма оперативно вышла в эфир с большой программой на эту тему. В ее рамках были переданы выступления на армянском, азербайджанском и грузинском языках, обзоры откликов в разных странах мира и другие информационно насыщенные материалы. Кроме того, мюнхенская радиостанция предложила радиослушателям из пострадавших районов воспользоваться ее каналами для поиска родных и близких.

А чем в эти часы занималось наше радиовещание? На его волнах шли обычные, видимо, задолго до трагического события заверстанные в программу концерты и репортажи. Чего ждали? Указания свыше? Или специальные передачи пробирались к эфиру по длинной лесенке виз, обычных на нашем радио?

В отличие от прочих «голосов», мюнхенская «Свобода» претендует на роль голоса нашего собственного народа, по крайней мере тех наших соотечественников, которые оказались за рубежом, но считают нашу страну своей. Не стоит в этом контексте выяснять, насколько правомерна эта претензия и что за нею стоит. Но в данном случае на чужой волне действительно звучало то, что должно было прозвучать прежде всего на нашей.

С глушением покончено. Это хорошо. Это закономерный вывод из того факта, что различия в современном мире должны вести не к обособлению, а ко взаимному обогащению знаниями, опытом, культурой. А также информацией об актуальных событиях.

Но уж о том, что происходит в нашей стране, да еще в экстремальных ситуациях, мы все же хотели бы раньше и полнее узнавать не из зарубежных, а из национальных источников. И прежде всего из самого по природе своей оперативного — радио.

**Владимир ОСТРОГОРСКИЙ,
кандидат исторических наук.**

CIRCLE TWO

LESSON TWO

AUDIO-COMPREHENSION EXERCISE

part 1

You are about to hear a text about American aid to Israel. Review the key words below. Then listen to the text with the following questions in mind. Afterwards, listen to the text again and write down the answers.

1. Characterize the Soviet attitude towards Israel since the 1967 Six Day War. Based on that, how would you expect the Soviet press to treat Israel? Listen to the first few sentences and decide whether your conclusions were correct.
2. What was cited in the report as the backdrop for the official U.S. delegation arriving in Tel Aviv?
3. What was the delegation's mission in Israel? With whom did they speak and what did they see?
4. What did the Bush Administration say about the status of the delegation?
5. What did the *New York Post* say about the real purpose of the visit?

Key words

твори́ть геноци́д – to carry out genocide
ва́рварски расправля́ться – to crack down in a barbaric fashion
ми́рные жи́тели – civilian population
осмо́тр вое́нных пози́ций – a review of military positions
открести́ться от – to distance oneself from
полуторачасова́я встре́ча – an hour-and-a-half meeting
изра́ильская вое́нщина – the Israeli militarists
не утаи́ть са́мых мра́чных дета́лей – not to conceal the most gloomy details
сиони́стская организа́ция – a Zionist organization
отставны́е офице́ры – retired officers
стреми́ться узна́ть подро́бности – to seek to find out details
как прояви́ло себя́ ору́жие? – how did the weapon perform?

TEXT: Read the following text. Be able to translate it in written form.

Кто вооружа́ет уби́йц?   Часть 1

Нью-Йо́рк, 14. (Соб. корр. «Пра́вды»). В тот моме́нт, когда́ изра́ильские вла́сти, продолжа́ющие отка́зывать палести́нцам в пра́ве на самоопределе́ние, ва́рварски расправля́ются с ми́рными жи́телями, в Иерусали́ме побыва́ла делега́ция представителей военных кругов США.   Она совершила осмотр военных позиций израильтян, имела полуторачасовую встречу с И. Рабином. Как сообщает печать, израильская военщина не утаила от своих гостей из-за океана даже самых мрачных деталей геноцида.

Администрация Буша сразу же попыталась откреститься от этих вояжёров, заявив, что эта поездка, организованная одной из сионистских организаций, носит, якобы, неофициальный характер, а члены делегации - лишь отставные офицеры и генералы.   Однако трудно сомневаться в истиных намерениях участников группы.   Как стало известно газете «Нью-Йорк пост», подобным образом делегация бывших амерканских военных стремится узнать подробности того, как «проявило» и «проявляет» себя американское оружие в руках Иерусалима, которому Пентагон ни в чём не отказывает.

Words and expressions to part 1

соб.кор. - собственный корреспондент
спец.кор.- специальный корреспондент

варварски расправляться/   (с кем?)
                -ются   с мирными жителями
                             с военнопленными
           расправиться   с гражданским населением - to crack down on
                -ятся   civilians in a barbaric fashion

гражданин (pl. граждане, граждан, гражданами)

быть   (где?) в плену
попадать/попасть   (куда?) в плен - to be taken prisoner
     -ет попадут
(past tense: попал)

брать/взять   в плен (куда?) - to take prisoner
берут возьмут
взятый

представители восставших - spokesmen for the rebels

восстание

подавлять/подавить восстание - to supress the rebellion
     -ют подавят
подавленный

совершать/совершить   осмотр   войск - to review the troops
     -ют   -ат   военной техники
                             военных позиций
                             военных объектов

совершённый

войска́ (pl.)

соверши́ть ата́ку   на войска́ проти́вника
        нападе́ние
        преступле́ние (про́тив)

име́ть часову́ю встре́чу
       получасову́ю встре́чу
       полуторачасову́ю встре́чу

вое́нные, гражда́нские (adj. noun)
вое́нщина

ута́ивать/утаи́ть секре́тные дета́ли
    -ют   -я́т
та́йна
та́йный

                    (от чего́?)
откре́щиваться/ от де́йствий партнёров из-за океа́на
      -ются   уча́стия в агре́ссии
откости́ться   раси́стской пра́ктики - to divorce oneself from....practice
      -я́тся

ра́са, ра́совый, раси́стский

заявля́ть/заяви́ть, что ...   - to declare (state) that...
    -ют зая́вят
зая́вленный
заявле́ние

объявля́ть/объяви́ть о налёте - to announce a raid
    -ют объя́вят
объя́вленный
объявле́ние

я́кобы - allegedly
            (в чём?)
сомнева́ться в и́стинных наме́рениях
        эффекти́вности ору́жия
        партнёрах - to doubt your partners

отставны́е офице́ры

подо́бным о́бразом
ничего́ подо́бного - nothing of the kind
каки́м о́бразом?

	(как?)	(где?)
оружие	проявило себя отлично	в бою
сухопутные войска	проявили себя отлично	в обороне

- land forces performed well in defense

зенитные орудия	плохо	при испытаниях

- anti-aircraft guns performed poorly in testing

	(как?)
он проявил себя	как отличный офицер
	отличным офицером

бой (pl. бои, боёв)

проявлять/проявить
    -ют проявят
проявленный

	(кому?)	(в чём?)
отказывать/отказать	союзникам	в поддержке
-ют откажут	населению	первой помощи

VOCABULARY EXERCISES

**Look through the vocabulary for part 1 of the text «Кто вооружает убийц?».
Do the following exercises.**

**A.   Give the nominative and genitive plural for the following nouns. Mark the
stress.**

гражданин, плен, житель, военнопленный

**B.   Give perfective forms for the following verbs; conjugate both forms. Mark
the stress.**

брать, открещиваться, утаивать, совершать, подавлять, попадать.

C.   Paraphrase the italicized words.

истреблять мирных жителей, тайные детали, иметь *будто (бы)* неофициальный
характер, *аккредитованный* корреспондент, он *показал* себя трусом, *держать в
секрете* детали, он *стал военнопленным, жестоко* уничтожить движение,
провести атаку на войска, *заявить, отказываться* от действий партнёров.

D.   Give the opposite for the italicized words.

сою́зные войска́, *бежа́ть из пле́на*, *вое́нные*, изве́стная пра́ктика, *дру́жеский* хара́ктер, офице́р *на действи́тельной слу́жбе*.

E.   Form verbs from the following nouns.   Make necessary changes.

объявле́ние о вы́борах, уничтоже́ние военнопле́нных.

F.   Give Russian equivalents for the following English phrases.

- to take somebody prisoner
- to suppress a rebellion
- to launch an offensive
- to inspect military installations
- a 30-minute meeting
- to be of a businesslike nature
- to perform perfectly in battle
- allegedly
- in a similar fashion
- to distance oneself from racist practices
- during weapons testing
- to deny first aid
- doubts about one's true intentions

G.   Write sentences to fill in the blanks in each of the groups below. Be able to translate your sentences.

      (кто? что?)

1.   ____________ попа́л   в плен
    ____________ попа́ли
    ____________ попа́ла
    ____________ попа́ло

Change the sentences above using "взять в плен".   (they took so-and-so prisoner)

        adj.   noun

2.   я́кобы   ____________   ____________
         ____________   ____________
         ____________   ____________

        (что?)   (на что?)

3.   Авиа́ция соверша́ет   __________   __________
    Пехо́та   __________   __________
    Артилле́рия   __________   __________

(кто? что?)

4. ____________ подави́л восста́ние
____________ подави́ли
____________ подави́ло
____________ подави́ла

(о чём?)

5. По ра́дио объяви́ли о____________
____
____

(в чём?)

6. Изра́иль   открести́лся от уча́стия   ____________
Администра́ция открести́лась   ____________
Террори́сты   открести́лись   ____________

(в чём?)

7. Америка́нский наро́д сомнева́ется   ____________
В Бе́лом до́ме   сомнева́ются   ____________
Президе́нт   сомнева́лся   ____________

(кто? что?)

8. Этот офице́р   прояви́л себя́ как ____________
Но́вое ору́жие   прояви́ло   ____________
Эти га́убицы   прояви́ли   ____________

(кому?)   (в чём?)

9. Вла́сти   отка́зывают____________ ____________
Раси́сты   ____________ ____________
Сандини́сты   ____________ ____________

GRAMMAR EXERCISES: REVIEW OF CASES

Review the use of cases as presented in Circle One.   Do the following exercises.

A. Determine the use of case in the sentences below.   Fill in the blanks. Be able to translate the sentences into English.

1. При (советский ядерный взрыв) _____________ на (остров) _____________ Новая Земля произошел радиоактивный выброс, зарегестрированный за (пределы советской территории) _____________.

2. Хотя с (1939 год) _________ прошло без (малое) _________ полвека, вновь встаёт вопрос: неужели нельзя было избежать (война) ______?

3. (Какой свой шаг) _________ президент Эйзенхауэр впоследствии назвал («самое непрятное дело) _____________ за (все 8 лет) _________ пребывания в Белом доме»?

4. Политбюро видело (задача) _________ в том, чтобы показать (народ) _______ (историческое значение Октября) _________.

5. «Бриджтон» наскочил на (мина) _________ и получил (пробоина) _________ в (нижняя часть корпуса) _________.

6. В центре внимания делегатов находилось (положение) _________ на (Ближний Восток) _________.

7. (Решение верховного суда) _________ объявлялось (противоречащее) _____________ конституции, (разрушающее) _____________ «дружеские отношения» между (белые и черные расы) и (играющее) _________ на руку мировому коммунизму.

8. В те июньские дни (1941 года) _____________ советская сторона была одна и ждать ей (помощь) _________ было неоткуда.

9. Капризная практика (американские власти) _____________ в отношении советских представителей противоречит (те отношения) _____________ , которые устанавливаются в (настоящее время) _____________ между США и СССР.

10. В (1944 год) _________ при (отступление фашистских войск) _____________ _____________ он бежал на (запад) _____________ и обосновался в (Великобритания) _____________.

B. Translate the following sentences.

1. Officers insisted on an immediate attack against enemy troops.
2. Normal relations with Communist China were established by Richard Nixon.
3. The United States does not have a clear policy vis-a-vis the Soviet Union.
4. According to the Foreign Ministry's spokesman, recent decisions on agriculture do not interfere with perestroika.
5. The public became acquainted with the limits established by the treaty two hours after its signing.
6. Developing countries need more foreign currency for their economies.
7. Former Secretary of Defense McNamara supports the No-First-Use movement both in the U.S. and abroad.
8. There are three dangers for Moscow in the Middle East.
9. Submarines succeeded in approaching Soviet warships.
10. International terrorism is becoming a real force in the twentieth century.
11. The Gulf of Mexico is bigger than the Persian Gulf.
12. On the eve of the meeting Soviet diplomats did not respond to Reagan's invitation to Gorbachev to visit the U.S.
13. Western European countries demanded US protection against a possible Soviet missile threat.
14. If he agrees to democratic changes next November, he will lose a necessary majority in Parliament.
15. The other day at a session of congress the white-majority leader openly denied blacks equal rights.
16. The next day the entire population will have a chance to vote for the candidates of the National Liberation Front.

GRAMMAR EXERCISE: REVIEW OF ACTIVE PARTICIPLES

Review Active participles as presented in Circle One, Lesson 3. Do the following exercise.

Determine the type of participle in the sentences below. Translate these sentences into English.

1. Вся ответственность за совершённое преступление возлагается на вашингтонскую администрацию, вооружающую и финансирующую сомосовских наёмников.
2. Посольство СССР в Вашингтоне вручило государственному департаменту заявление, привлекавшее серьёзное внимание к нарушению США договора 1974 года об ограничении мощности ядерных взрывов.
3. Бундесвер тщательно проводил подготовку к проведению совместных западногерманско-французских манёвров, проходящих в настоящее время во Франции.

4. В официальном Токио предпочитают полагаться на слово Вашингтона, осуществляющего опасное наращивание ядерных арсеналов в регионе.
5. Мы – реалисты и учитываем сотрудничество, сложившееся между США и ФРГ во многих областях.
6. Это будут первые подобные крупные манёвры с участием воинских подразделений ФРГ и Франции, не являющейся членом военной организации блока НАТО.
7. Об этом сообщается здесь сегодня в заявлении фракции «зелёных», уже ранее выступившей с аналогичным требованием.
8. К пирсу подъехало несколько специальных грузовиков с громкоговорителями, начавшими извергать потоки антисоветской брани.
9. На днях стало известно о новых материалах, подтверждающих факт секретной договорённости между Вашингтоном и Токио о ввозе в Японию американского ядерного оружия.
10. Министр иностранных дел пообещал парламентариям расследовать вопросы, возникающие в связи с публикацией документов Пентагона.

GRAMMAR: SINGULAR AND PLURAL OF COGNATES

Many cognates have to do with professions and the people in them. As a rule, the professions themselves are feminine singular (never plural: экономика = *economics*), while the people are masculine. Note the list below:

КТО	ЧТО	КАКОЙ
физик	физика	физический
математик	математика	математический
политик	политика	политический
генетик	генетика	генетический
химик	химия (!)	химический

-ologist: (note stress)

социолог	социология	социологический
психолог	психология	психологический

And finally some exceptions:

экономист	экономика	экономический
юрист	право	юридический
технолог	технология	технологический

Applies to "technological planning"

техник	техника	технический

Use this for "technological"

милиционер	милиция	милицейский
полицейский (adj.)	полиция	полицейский

There are other confusing cognates as well. The chart below indicates problems with gender and number:

English	Masculine or Neuter	Feminine	Plural allowed?

Ending in -m:

English	Masculine or Neuter	Feminine	Plural allowed?
form		фо́рма	
platform		платфо́рма	
problem		пробле́ма (1 м)	
program		програ́мма (мм)	
sum		су́мма (мм)	
system		систе́ма (м)	
telegram		телегра́мма (мм)	
blockade		блока́да	

Ending in -y or silent -e:

English	Masculine or Neuter	Feminine	Plural allowed?
alternative		альтернати́ва	
catastrophe		катастро́фа	
critique, -s (criticism, -s)		кри́тика	NO
decade		дека́да	
discipline		дисципли́на	NO
economy, -ies		эконо́мика	NO
initiative		инициати́ва	
note		но́та	
phase		фа́за	
phrase		фра́за	
perspective		перспекти́ва	
policy, -ies		поли́тика	NO
sphere		сфе́ра	
zone		зо́на	

Ending in -ic or -ics:

English	Masculine or Neuter	Feminine	Plural allowed?
economics		эконо́мика	NO
mathematics		матема́тика	NO
physics		фи́зика	NO
etc.		etc.	NO
polemic, polemics		поле́мика	NO
politics, policy, -ies		поли́тика	NO
republic		респу́блика	
rhetoric		рито́рика	NO
but:			
narcotic	нарко́тик		

English	Masculine or Neuter	Feminine	Plural allowed?
Consonant ending:			
attack		атáка	
group		грýппа	
missile, rocket		ракéта	
model		модéль	
press, –es (media)		прéсса	NO
Consonant ending:			
control	контрóль		NO
export, –s	экспорт		NO
import, –s	ймпорт		NO
risk	риск		NO
Miscellaneous:			
embargo, –es	эмбáрго		NO
militia, –s		милйция	NO
myth	миф		
police		полйция	NO
technology, –ies		тéхника	NO
Non–cognates with no plural:			
damage, –es	ущéрб		NO
lie, –s		лóжь	NO
weapons	орýжие		NO

   but note that **вооружéния** 'armaments' is usually plural.

English	Masculine or Neuter	Feminine	Plural allowed?
shortage, –s		нехвáтка	NO

GRAMMAR EXCERCISES: SINGULAR AND PLURAL OF COGNATES

Review the commonly used cognates above, then do the following exercises.

A. Make up sentences according to the model.

Example: physics:
> —→ A *phycisist* does *physics* in the *physics* division.
> —→ *Физик* занимается *физикой* на *физическом* отделении.

1. mathematics:
2. politics:
3. economics (Careful: –ист!)
4. genetics:
5. biophysics:
6. sociology:
7. psychology:
8. biology:
9. anthropology:
10. law:

B. Give the nominative and genitive plural of all the words in the cognate list.

C. Fill in the blanks.

1. Употребление *(narcotics)* ______________ является характерной чертой некоторых *(sects)* ________________.

2. *(The rocket)* ______________ была запущена на орбиту в 11 часов *(22 minutes, 32 seconds)* ___________________.

3. *(The press)* ______________ подвергла предлагаемую *(program)* ____________ поощрения *(of initiative)* __________ резкой *(criticisms)* ____________.

4. Несмотря на *(attack)* ___________справа, демократы не включили в свою *(platform)* ____________ вопрос о развёртывании новых *(systems)* ____________ вооружений.

5. Очевидно, что некоторые из советских *(republics)* ______________ выходят из *(sphere)* ___________влияния Москвы. В этой связи многие считают, что Эстония может стать *(model)* __________ для других *(republics)* ____________.

6. После (*blockade*) ___________ началась новая (*phase*) ___________ войны. Генералы приняли (*tactic*) _____________ выжженной земли, но это только привело к (*panic*) ___________ среди населения.

7. К сожалению, (*these policies*) ________________ не гарантирует окончания (*of shortages*) _______________ (*of new technologies*) ___________________, поскольку подготовка нового поколения (*of mathematicians and physicists*) _______________________ не предусмотрена. Одним словом, претворение в жизнь (*of these programs*) ______________ непременно нанесёт (*damage*) _____________ дальнейшему развитию (*physics*) ___________ и (*mathematics*) _____________.

8. Дипломатическая (*note*) ____________содержала очень (*strange phrase*),___________________________, написанную в довольно (*old style*) ______________________.

9. К сожалению, у нас не существует (*controls*) ___________ ни над (*imports*) ___________, ни над (*exports*) ___________.

10. (*The militia arrested*)______________________ пять человек за нелегальное хранение (*of illegal weapons*) ____________________.

11. (*This form of polemics*) ___________________ не оставляет для нас (*any alternatives*)________________: если мы хотим избежать (*panic and disaster*) _____________ _____________, надо будет вызвать дополнительные подразделения (*of the police*) ___________.

12. Войдя в (*zone*)___________беспорядков, мы не могли не отметить высокий уровень (*of discipline*) ______________ среди работников (*of the militia*)_____________.

SPEAKING EXERCISES

A.   Расскажи́те пе́рвую часть те́кста. В своём расска́зе испо́льзуйте сле́дующие слова́.

В то вре́мя, как...; ме́жду тем, одна́ко, подо́бным о́бразом.

B.   Расскажи́те ту́ же исто́рию с то́чки зре́ния жи́теля се́верного Изра́иля, постоя́нно подверга́емого опа́сности налёта террори́стов.

C.   Отве́тьте на сле́дующие вопро́сы.

1.   Что де́лала делега́ция америка́нских отставны́х вое́нных в Изра́иле?
2.   Чьим ору́жием была́ вооружена́ изра́ильская а́рмия во вре́мя опера́ции на оккупи́рованных террито́риях?
3.   Осве́домлены ли США о хара́ктере изра́ильских репре́ссий про́тив палести́нцев?
4.   В како́м то́не напи́сана э́та статья́? Найди́те слова́, подтвержда́ющие ва́шу то́чку зре́ния.

D.   Дополни́тельные вопро́сы. (optional)

1.   При каки́х обстоя́тельствах произошло́ созда́ние госуда́рства Изра́иль?
2.   Почему́ США предоставля́ют по́мощь Изра́илю?
3.   Что тако́е геноци́д?

AUDIO-COMPREHENSION EXERCISE

part 2

In this part some information from *Time* magazine was cited. Listen to the tape to find out:

1. How much aid has the U.S. provided Israel since its founding?
2. To what degree is the Israeli military dependent on U.S. technology: how much of the air force is made up of American planes. What kind and how many U.S. tanks do the Israelis have? What about armored personnel carriers? Name three types of American artillery in the Israeli arsenal. What percent of Israeli artillery does this American equipment comprise?
3. What military aid does Congress intend to give Israel in the coming fiscal year?
4. What did the U.N. Security Council resolution call for?

Key words

военно-воздушные силы - air force
в распоряжении - at one's disposal
бронетранспортёр - armored personnel carrier
пушка - artillery gun (cannon)
гаубица - howitzer
вести убийственный огонь по - to fire mercilessly at
отвергнуть резолюцию - to turn down a resolution
прекратить военную поддержку - to stop military support
полагаться на содействие Пентагона - to rely on the assistance of the Pentagon

TEXT: Read the following text. Be able to translate it written form.

Кто вооружает убийц?   Часть 2

Вот такие данные приводит в своём последнем номере журнал «Тайм». С момента образования государства Израиль США предоставили ему помощь на сумму в 14,9 миллиарда долларов. На вооружении военно-воздушных сил Тель-Авива находится 85 процентов американских самолётов. В распоряжении у израильской армии —— 1400 танков «М-60» и «М-48», 4 тысячи бронетранспортёров, закупленных в США. 90 процентов артиллерии —— и в первую очередь 175-миллиметровые пушки, 155- и 203-миллиметровые гаубицы, из которых вёлся убийственный огонь кассетными снарядами по Западному Бейруту, —— также из арсеналов Пентагона.

Несмотря на то, что Израиль осуществил кровавую агрессию против ливанского и палестинского народов, Конгресс США намеревается в следующем финансовом году выделить Тель-Авиву рекордную военную помощь в 1,7 миллиарда долларов.

Отвергнув резолюцию Совета Безопасности, призвавшую все страны прекратить военную поддержку тель-авивским ястребам, Вашингтон ясно дал понять, что Израиль может полагаться на его содействие. Он и дальше намерен присылать сюда военную технику, чтобы Израиль «обкатывал» её в боях против арабских соседей.

Words and expressions to part 2

приводить/привести данные
приводят приведут информацию
                     факты
                     статистику
приведённые данные – cited data

последний номер   журнала
                    газеты

образование   государства
               коалиции
               блока

образовывать/образовать
        -ют образуют
образованный
                                (в каком количестве?)
помощь   на сумму (acc.)   в 12 миллиардов долларов
избрание   на срок (acc.)   в 4 года
город   на расстоянии (acc.) в 9 километров от границы

(где?)
на вооружении ВВС находятся   новые самолёты – the Air Force has new
                                                  planes in its arsenal

           ВМФ (Navy)   подлодки
           армии   танки
                                бронетранспортёры
                                гаубицы
                                175-миллиметровые пушки

             (куда?)
принимать/принять на вооружение – to take into its inventory
      -ют примут   (acc)
принятый

Палести́на, палести́нцы, палести́нские бе́женцы - refugees
                    (по чему́?)   (чем?)
вести́ огóнь   по террито́рии   снаря́дами - to shell the territory
ведýт   побере́жью
                городáм   авиáцией
- to bombard cities

                                         кассéтными снаря́дами
                                         (cluster bombs)
                                         боеголóвками
гóрод (pl. городá, городóв)

отправля́ть/отпрáвить в Изра́иль   вое́нную тéхнику
    -ют   -ят   боевýю
                                    ракéтные устанóвки
отпрáвленный
отпрáвка

ООН, Совéт Безопáсности ООН, Генерáльная Ассамблéя ООН, Генерáльный Секретáрь
    ООН
чрезвычáйные си́лы ООН - UN special forces
представи́тель ООН, наблюдáтель ООН

отвергáть/отвéргнуть   резолю́цию
    -ют   -ут   пóмощь - to turn down assistance
                         торгóвые отношéния с СССР
                         ми́рное разрешéние конфли́кта
отвéргнутый

                                             (сдéлать что?)
призывáть/ все стрáны   прекрати́ть вое́нную пóмощь + dat.
    -ют   воюющие стóроны   прекрати́ть огóнь - to cease fire
призвáть   члéнов Совéта Безопáсности
призовýт
            населéние   (к чему́?)
            избирáтелей   к   акти́вному голосовáнию
при́званный
при́зыв

давáть/дáть я́сно поня́ть , что...
дают   дадýт

                                                (где?)
испы́тывать/испытáть вое́нную тéхнику   в атмосфéре
    -ют   -ют   орýжие   вóздухе
                    нóвые систéмы   океáне
                    нейтрóнную бóмбу   под водóй
                    бактериологи́ческое орýжие   землёй
                                             в кóсмосе

испытáние

испы́танный ме́тод – a tested method
        сою́зник – a tried and true ally
        аппара́т
  -ое   сре́дство

                    (на что?)
полага́ться/положи́ться на   артилле́рию – to rely on artillery
  -ются поло́жатся   кандида́тов

VOCABULARY EXERCISES

Look through the vocabulary for part 2 of the text «*Кто вооружа́ет уби́йц?*»,
then do the following exercises.

A. **Give the nominative and genitive plural forms for the following nouns.
Mark the stress.**

коали́ция, информа́ция, но́мер, стати́стика, бе́женец, побере́жье, по́мощь,
го́род, палести́нец, те́хника, секрета́рь, наблюда́тель, населе́ние, сре́дство.

B. **Give perfective forms for the following verbs. Conjugate both forms. Mark
the stress.**

дава́ть, отверга́ть (past form), призыва́ть, отправля́ть, образо́вывать,
предоставля́ть, принима́ть, полага́ться.

C. **Paraphrase the italicized words.**

прове́ренный спо́соб, *сформирова́ть* блок, *биологи́ческое* ору́жие, испыта́ния в
атмосфе́ре, испыта́ние в океа́не, *жи́тели, посыла́ть* те́хнику, *сде́лать я́сным,*
цити́ровать да́нные, стреля́ть по города́м, взять на вооруже́ние.

D. **Give the opposite for the italicized words.**

нача́ть ого́нь, *ненадёжное* сре́дство, *пасси́вное* уча́стие, разреше́ние конфли́кта
с примене́нием си́лы, приня́ть резолю́цию, *опа́сность, пе́рвый* но́мер.

E. **Form nouns out of the following verbs. Make necessary changes.**

образо́вывать госуда́рство, предоставля́ть по́мощь, отправля́ть те́хнику,
призыва́ть к прекраще́нию огня́, испы́тывать ору́жие.

F.   Give Russian equivalents for the following English phrases.

- assistance in the amount of $5,000
- to shell the territory
- APCs are in the army's inventory
- to send missile launchers to Nicaragua
- refugee camps
- a tried and true ally
- to turn down trade relations with Iran
- to take a nuclear sub into the arsenal
- to call upon the fighting parties for a cease-fire
- to make clear to somebody that...
- to test a neutron bomb underground
- to rely on U.N. special forces

G.   Write sentences to fill in the blanks in each of the groups below. Be able to translate your sentences.

                   (чего?)   (что?)

1.   На вооружéние _______ приняли _______
                  _______   _______
                  _______   _______

Change the sentences above using **находúться на вооружéнии.**

                      (кого?) (к чему?)

2.   Пáртия призывáет   _______ _______
     Совéт Безопáсности призывáет _______ _______
     Либерáлы призывáют   _______ _______

Change the sentences above, if possible, using **призывáть + *infinitive.***

                 (кому?) (что?)

3.   США предоставляют   _______ _______
                   _______ _______
                   _______ _______

                 (что?) (где?)

4.   Пентагóн испытывает _______ _______
     Изрáиль   _______ _______
     ВВС   испытывают _______ _______

                          (на что? на кого?)

5.   Нáши партнёры по НАТО полагáются на _______________
     Трéтий мир   полагáется на _______________
     Избирáтели   полагáются на _______________

GRAMMAR: "THE MEASURED"

Review the Table 4 "The Measured" as presented in Circle One, Lesson 2. Then study the following.

"The measured" – compound adjectives with numerals as their first part.

Example: двадцатимиллио́нный бюдже́т
            1   2
            Twenty million [dollar, etc., according to context] budget

Numeral in genitive case:	Adjective:	Noun:
A. пяти...................	ты́сячный	жи́тель
девяти................	ме́сячное	чрезвыча́йное положе́ние
трёх....................	миллио́нный	избира́тель
восьми.................	миллиа́рдный	дефици́т
шести.................	веково́й	гнёт
сорокадвух.............	ле́тний	офице́р
одиннадцати............	дне́вный	переры́в
полу́тора...............	часова́я	програ́мма
пятидесяти.............	метро́вое	расстоя́ние
четырнадцати...........	сантиметро́вое	окно́
двухсот................	километро́вая	грани́ца
четырёхсотшестидесяти...	то́нный	урожа́й
семисоттридцати........	килограммо́вый	снаря́д
тридцатипяти...........	гра́дусный	моро́з
семи...................	ле́тний	план
восьми.................	неде́льное	прекраще́ние огня́

BUT:

Numerals 100 and 90 in nominative case.

стопятидесяти...........	миллиметро́вая	га́убица
девяносточетырёх........	ле́тний	стари́к
B. шести́ с полови́ной	ты́сячное	коли́чество мест
полу́тора...............	часова́я	програ́мма
полу...................	часова́я	речь

GRAMMAR EXERCISES: "THE MEASURED"

A. Translate the following phrases using the В + accusative construction and, whenever possible, use as an alternative a compound numeral adjective phrase.

1.   a ten-item plan of retreat
2.   a four-ship convoy
3.   a 12-member group of analysts
4.   a 46,000-ton supertanker
5.   a half-million-man army
6.   a five per cent rate of growth
7.   an 11-hour flight
8.   a 203-millimeter howitzer
9.   a 40,000 kilimeter range missile
10. an $18 billion volume of trade
11. a $5 per barrel increase in the price of oil
12. an eight-week cease-fire
13. at a distance of 12 miles from the capital
14. a 26-million dollar credit
15. a 12-month state of emergency
16. a seven-vote majority
17. a two-day conference
18. a five-year plan
19. a half-hour break
20. a 3,000-year history
21. a 1,600-exhibit show
22. a nine-year "tanker" war
23. an hour-and-a-half intermission
24. a 30-minute speech

B. Write your own sentences with some of the above expressions.

GRAMMAR EXERCISES: REVIEW OF ACTIVE PARTICIPLES (Continued)

A. Determine the type of participle in the sentences below. Replace them with relative clauses. Be able to translate them into English.

Example: Он выступил на *состоявшейся* сегодня в посольстве СССР в Италии пресс-конференции советских ученых.

    ⟶ Он выступил на пресс-конференции советских учёных, *которая состоялась* сегодня в посольстве СССР в Италии.

1. В обстановке гласности можно добиться положительных результатов, *способствующих* дальнейшему прогрессу человечества.
2. В экспозиции более 1600 экспонатов, *знакомящих* американцев с жизнью советских людей.
3. Декларацию подписали ученые, *принявшие* участие в седьмом международном симпозиуме.
4. *Прошедшая* в Риге конференция представляет собой существенный шаг к созданию сектора науки, свободного от секретов.
5. Советские рыбаки, *рассчитывавшие* после нескольких месяцев промысла получить двухнедельную передышку, встретили недружественный приём.
6. К подобному курсу, не *отвечающему* принципам добрососедства, относится также травля японских компаний, *поддерживающих* взаимовыгодные отношения с СССР.
7. Эти совместные предприятия смогут избавиться от *отнимающих* время безрезультатных переговоров.
8. США используют аргументы, не *имеющие* никакого отношения к политике и *ведущие* к росту нестабильности.
9. Остановлено движение по важным железнодорожным магистралям, *связывающим* восточные и западные районы страны.

B.   Translate the following.

1. A delegation of U.S. congressmen who had inspected a secret Soviet radar in Siberia appeared on TV yesterday.
2. The heads of five states had a three-hour meeting which was of a friendly and businesslike character.
3. What is the name of the Filipino officer who suppressed the army rebellion?
4. The President nominated a man who never distanced himself from the Nixon Administration.
5. Some of the US soldiers taken prisoner in Vietnam in the 60s were barbarically murdered.
6. The Washington Post correspondent had a conversation with Congressman Brown (D-Conn) who is running for the Senate in the forthcoming elections.
7. The rebels in Nicaragua are requesting Stinger type rockets (ракеты типа Стингер) which were holding up so well in the hands of the Afghan Mujahedins.
8. A group of activists leading a growing pro-Palestinian movement released a report about arrests of Arab children on the West Bank.
9. The body which makes laws in Great Britain is called the House of Commons.
10. It is difficult to trust a government which constantly conceals the most fundamental facts from its people.

GRAMMAR: WORD ORDER IN RUSSIAN

Students of Russian often are told that thanks to the Russian case system word order is free. If that were only totally true! While freer than that of English, Russian word order adheres to some fairly strict rules, especially in a more formal style (such as the kind of Russian you are expected to understand, read, write, and speak). The following rules therefore apply to standard "neutral" prose:

1.   Old or non-essential information first; new or main information last.

2.   Interrogative words come first.

In the examples below, the new or main information is in boldface.

a.   Где состоялось **совещание?**   **Совещание** is "main"
     Совещание состоялось **в Ри́ге.**   Now совещание is "old";
                                             the new information is **в Ри́ге.**

b.   Кто встреча́л делега́цию?   Interrogative **кто** starts the question.
     Делега́цию встра́чал **Рыжко́в.**   **Рыжков** is important because his name
                                             answers the question.

A few corollaries:

1.   The concept of old versus new information often corresponds to English *the*
     (old) and *a* (new):

     Появи́лось **реше́ние.**   *A* solution appeared.
     Реше́ние **появи́лось.**   *The* solution appeared.

2.   If old (or secondary) information consists of a verb and something else
     (an object, time, place, or circumstance), the verb does *not* come first.
     Verbs occupy initial position in a sentence only as a last resort:

     a.   Здесь живёт **Смирно́в.**   **Smirnov** lives here. (Both *lives* and
                                             here are old information, but the verb
                                             "tries" not to come first.)

     b.   Говори́т **Москва́.**   This is **Moscow** speaking. (Moscow is
                                             the main information, and that leaves
                                             no choice but to put the verb first.)

3.   Subject pronouns usually are placed at the beginning of the sentence
     regardless of how new the information is:

     – Кто говори́т?   – Он говори́т.

4. In "A=B" type sentences involving instrumental case, the noun in instrumental is the "less permament" member of the equation, which may be either old or new information:

Муга́бе был **пе́рвым президе́нтом Зимба́бве.**	Mugabe was **Zimbabwe's first president.**

(Mugabe was "Mugabe" longer than he was president.)

Пе́рвым президе́нтом Зимба́бве был **Муга́бе.**	The first president of Zimbabwe was **Mugabe.**

GRAMMAR EXERCISES: WORD ORDER IN RUSSIAN

Review the material on *Word Order*, then do the exercises below.

A. Look at the English sentences and pick the correct Russian word order.

1. A new program has begun.
   a. Началась новая программа.
   b. Новая программа началась.

2. The General Secretary works in *the Kremlin.*
   a. Генеральный секретарь работает в Кремле.
   b. В Кремле работает Генеральный секретарь.

3. *The General Secretary* lives on Kutuzovsky Prospekt.
   a. Генеральный секретарь живёт на Кутузовском проспекте.
   b. На Кутузовском проспекте живёт Генеральный секретарь.

4. The director has *a plan.*
   a. У директора есть план.
   b. План у директора.

5. *The director* has *the* plan.
   a. У директора есть план.
   b. План у директора.

6. – Over the past ten months *inflation* has appeared.
   a. За последние 10 месяцев появилась инфляция.
   b. За последние 10 месяцев инфляция появилась.

7. – No, I don't agree. Prices have *fallen.*
   Нет, я не согласен...
   a. Снизились цены.
   b. Цены снизились.

8. – *Information exchange* was on the agenda.
   a.   На повестке дня стоял обмен информацией.
   b.   Обмен информацией стоял на повестке дня.

9. – Yes, information exchange is an important topic.
   a.   Да, обмен информацией – важная тема.
   b.   Да, важная тема – обмен информацией.

10. – Computer technology will also be discussed.
   a.   Также будет обсуждена вычислительная техника.
   b.   Вычислительная техника также будет обсуждена.

11. The reason for the rise in prices was a bad harvest.
   a.   Плохой урожай был причиной повышения цен.
   б.   Причиной повышения цен был плохой урожай.

12. *Yuri Gagarin* was the first man in space.
   a.   Юрий Гагарин был первым человеком в космосе.
   b.   Первым человеком в космосе был Юрий Гагарин.

13. It is Gorbachev's policies that form the basis for perestroika.
   a.   Политика Горбачёва является основой для перестройки.
   b.   Основой для перестройки является политика Горбачёва.

B. Answer the questions in full sentences with any answer that fits. Make sure that new information comes last.

1. Кто выступал на Генеральной Ассамблее ООН?
2. Когда началась Первая мировая война?
3. Какое известное событие имело место в 1968 году?
4. Какие виды оружия были включены в условия договора ОСВ-I?
5. Какие советские города названы «городами-героями»?
6. Кто возглавлял временное правительство до Октябрьской революции?
7. Какая страна занимала первое место по производству стали до Второй мировой войны?
8. Кто был Генеральным секретарём ООН после Вальдхайма?
9. Какая страна первая запустила на орбиту искусственный спутник земли?
10. Чья политика привела к Карибскому кризису 1962 года?

C.   The word order in many of the sentences below is incorrect.   Unscramble and rewrite the following two paragraphs so that the word order becomes neutral.

35219 случаев заболевания СПИД — синдром приобретённого иммунодефицита — было зарегистрировано с июня 1981 года в США. Смертельным исходом завершились 58 процентов из них, национальный центр по контролю над заболеваниями сообщил в четверг. Мужчины составляли две трети больных СПИД. Употребляли наркотики 17 процентов.

На днях о создании комиссии для выработки рекомендаций по борьбе со СПИД президент США, провозгласивший болезнь «врагом здоровья нации номер один», объявил. 766 миллионов долларов уже выделено на эти цели в текущем году из федерального бюджета.

RENDERING

From the desk of I. M. Lissnin, Senior Analyst:

We believe that a military coup in the Republic of San Marco is likely in the course of the next six to eighteen months. Our conclusions are based on the following evidence:

1.   The current civilian government of liberal President Juan Martinez Salgada is a weak coalition of disorganized liberal and moderate splinter parties, which does not include the Popular Front, which has strong backing among peasants especially in the outlying provinces.

2.   San Marco's generals feel threatened by the Martinez administration. The fear is justifiable: Martinez has promised to reduce military spending overall. He has just canceled a $50-million shipment of American light artillery, and is eyeing cuts in the general staff. The necks of at least 10 officers are on the block. Forcibly retired officers are disgruntled officers.

3.   Martinez's military cuts may be designed to win applause among the civilian population, but so far no one is clapping. Peasants, especially those in the outlying provinces, fear that the money saved on military procurement will find its way into bureaucrats' pockets. Despite Martinez's intentions, corruption is rampant, and there is no tradition of serious social spending.

4.   The military, with a reputation for discipline and efficiency, actually enjoys some popularity among the peasants, especially in the northern regions. Some local commanders act virtually independently of the civilian government, often helping local farmers to avoid red tape and taxes emanating from the capital.
*   However, there is the dark side of military brutality. Indian peasants along the southern coast are sure to lend support to the civilian administration under attack. Coastal Indians have bitter memories of the part played by the army in "pacification" programs carried out under military rule five years before Martinez's ascendancy to the presidency. By all objective accounts "pacification" often resulted in the*

annihilation of clusters of villages.   And current members of the Martinez government have openly referred to the army's past actions as genocide.

5.   Business leaders unanimously pledge support to the principles of democracy and civilian rule, but most believe that the business community would privately welcome an end to the current administration, no matter what the means.

6.   An attack on the capital is military child's play. Marco City is surrounded by three well armed military garrisons, whose commander's loyalty to civilian rule is dubious. The infantry's loyalty to the officer staff, however, is not.

7.   On-site intelligence suggests that the top brass already has a secret plan to take effect once a successful attack is mounted. The picture that comes through is not one of a benign coup with the usual escape of some of the civilian opposition to Mexico City. A successful insurgency would doubtless be a bloody affair with the execution of many members of the cabinet, including the president, the placement into detention camps of the leading Liberal Party MPs, and repressive measures, bordering on genocide, against the civilian coastal population.

8.   It is our conclusion that President Martinez is unaware of the magnitude of the threat posed by his military men, the depth of their disloyalty, the softness of support for the civilian government outside the capital (fueled by disdain for the country's lethargic and corrupt bureaucracy), or of the imminence of the personal danger he and those around him face.

9.   Civil war between the army and the Popular Front would be sure to ensue, virtually wrecking the fragile Marconian economy.

SPEAKING EXERCISES

A. Расскажи́те втору́ю часть те́кста. В своём расска́зе испо́льзуйте сле́дующие выраже́ния.

вот каки́е да́нные ста́ли изве́стны..; при э́том; несмотря́ на то́, что...; сле́довательно.

B. Расскажи́те весь текст с то́чки зре́ния:
- чле́на изра́ильской па́ртии труда́
- чле́на консервати́вной па́ртии Лику́д

C. Отве́тьте на сле́дующие вопро́сы.

1. Как повлия́ла изра́ильская опера́ция в Лива́не на америка́нскую по́мощь Тель-Ави́ву?
2. Каки́е ти́пы ору́жия получи́л Изра́иль от США?
3. Каковы́ масшта́бы америка́нской по́мощи Изра́илю?
4. К чему́ призыва́ла резолю́ция Сове́та Безопа́сности ООН?

D. Дополни́тельные вопро́сы. (optional)

1. В чём состоя́т разногла́сия СССР и США по вопро́су ара́бо-изра́ильского конфли́кта?
2. Кого́ подде́рживает Сове́тский Сою́з на Бли́жнем Восто́ке?
3. Каку́ю пози́цию занима́ет большинство́ чле́нов ООН по вопро́су конфли́кта Изра́иля и ара́бских госуда́рств?

READING EXERCISE

Не только «Старк», но и «Либерти».   А. Николаев

PRE–TEXT: This article is typical of the ubiquitous фельетонный стиль, characterized by an overlay of somewhat smirky sarcasm.   Read the text with the following exercises in mind.

1.   Skim the article for the main idea.   Then look at the questions below.   Try to predict the answers in advance.   Then re–read the article to see if you were correct.   Answer the questions in written form.

PARAGRAPH 1
2.   According to the author, Washington is ready to sacrifice the life of its citizens...(mark the correct answer):
   a.   when national security is at stake.
   b.   to meet its selfish ends.
   c.   during a military intervention.

3.   What is the point of mentioning Grenada?

PARAGRAPH 2
4.   Why was the USS Liberty on patrol in that region?
5.   The Israelis decided to interfere with the mission of the Liberty... (mark the correct answer):
   a.   to alert the US to a forthcoming Syrian attack.
   b.   to obtain electronic data for rapid analysis.
   c.   to prevent the US from learning about the impending seizure of the Golan Heights.

PARAGRAPH 3
6.   A US ex–intelligence officer leaked details of the Israeli decision to the press.   Where did he get this information?

PARAGRAPH 4
7.   Why should the Israelis have known that it was an American boat?
8.   How long did the air raid last?
9.   There were four stages of the operation.   Name at least three.
10.   How many planes shot at the USS Liberty?

PARAGRAPH 5
11.   Upon the USS Liberty's signal planes of the 6th Fleet immediately took off...(mark the correct answer):
   a.   to pick up wounded American sailors.
   b.   but were recalled after take–off.
   c.   and escorted the ship to Malta.
   d.   and engaged the Israelis.

12.   When did the rescue helicopters arrive?

PARAGRAPH 6
13.   Two explanations of the raid are cited in the article. What were they?

PARAGRAPH 7
14.   Why was the "real story" classified?

PARAGRAPH 8
15.   What aroused the indignation of the Liberty veterans?

POST-TEXT (using context):

1.   The article starts with...(mark the correct answer):
     a.   a statement followed by illustrations.
     b.   a list of examples concluded by a statement.

PARAGRAPH 1
2.   What word signals the contrast contained in paragraph 1?

PARAGRAPH 2
3.   Review Word Order in Russian as presented in the grammatical section of this lesson.   Explain the word order used in the first and second sentences.
4.   Which word in the second sentence indicates the answer why the USS Libery patrolled the region?
5.   Find the word in the third sentence which introduces the motives for the Israeli intervening with the Liberty's mission.
6.   Translate the second paragraph into English.

PARAGRAPH 3
7.   To which word(s) does Об этом решении... refer to?

PARAGRAPH 4 and 5
8.   These two paragraphs contain the illustaration of the point made by the author.   Make a list of time-expressions used to describe the sequence of events.
9.   In sentence two of paragraph 4, underline the subject. Explain its position in the sentence.
10.   There is an abundance of military vocabulary in paragraphs 4 and 5. Make a list of military terms.
11.   The author has two very expressive phrases for the intensity of fire. Find them in the text.   Think of an equally striking way of saying them in English.

PARAGRAPH 6
12.   Explain the word order in the first sentence.
13.   Which word signals that the two interpretations of the attack are different?

PARAGRAPH 7

14. Find the word used by the author to introduce the reasons for making
     this story classified.

15. The paragraph contains some financial metaphors: list them.   Explain
     the meaning of each in the given context.

16. Pick the correct meaning of the following words below:

пойти на
  a. to move towards
  b. to resort to

ра́ди
  a. for the sake of
  b. to be glad

предло́г
  a. a preposition
  b. a pretext

разга́р
  a. erosion
  b. the heat, height

достове́рный
  a. reliable
  b. faithful

истека́ть
  a. to expire
  b. to bleed profusely

отозва́ть
  a. to recall
  b. to answer

16. Find the Russian for:

  - killed
  - wounded
  - double standard
  - golden rule

17. The tone of the article is...(mark the correct answer):
     a. neutral
     b. approving
     c. ironic
     d. sarcastic

18. Make a list of words which support you answer to # 17.

Не только «Старк», но и «Либерти»

Развитие событий после инцидента с фрегатом «Старк» в Персидском заливе вновь напомнило всему миру о том, что Вашингтон готов пойти на умышленную гибель своих граждан ради достижения корыстных целей, хотя, когда нужно, Пентагон быстро готов под предлогом «угрозы безопасности соотечественников» предпринять самые бесцеремонные меры вплоть до интервенции (вспомним Гренаду!).

...8 июня 1967 года — в самый разгар «шестидневной войны» на Ближнем Востоке — разведывательный корабль ВМС США «Либерти» патрулировал в международных водах Средиземного моря вблизи района конфликта. Политическому и военному руководству Соединенных Штатов необходимы были достоверные сведения о быстро менявшейся ситуации в регионе, поэтому в задачу корабля входил электронный перехват и передача добытых данных в Вашингтон для анализа. Израильское командование решило помешать этому, т. к. не хотело, чтобы США преждевременно узнали о планах предстоявшего на следующий день захвата сирийских Голанских высот.

Об этом решении стало известно совсем недавно агентству Рейтер от отставного офицера американской разведки, в свое время осуществлявшего контакт со спецслужбами Израиля.

После того как «Либерти» подвергся неоднократному облету израильскими самолетами-разведчиками, на которых не могли не заметить поднятый над кораблем американский флаг, на «Либерти» обрушилось море огня. Вслед за ракетным залпом двух «миражей» еще двумя израильскими самолетами были сброшены напалмовые бомбы. Заполыхали не только надстройки, но и расположенные ниже палубы отсеки. Продолжавшуюся час с четвертью атаку завершили военные катера, поливая «Либерти» свинцом из пулеметов. Корпус корабля был поражен торпедой, спасательные средства уничтожены. 34 американца были убиты, 171 — ранен.

Успевшие взлететь по переданному с «Либерти» сигналу о нападении самолеты шестого флота США были быстро отозваны назад по причине, которую до сих пор никто из официальных представителей Пентагона даже не попытался объяснить. Истекавшие кровью американские моряки дождались спасательных вертолетов лишь спустя несколько долгих часов. Корабль, чудом удержавшийся на плаву, был доставлен на Мальту.

В Ваш[...] ление с[...] гибель и[...] Никто и[...] США до[...] нием Те[...] шло нед[...] дескать,[...] ским ко[...] по убеж[...] риканско[...] торый пр[...] свое имя,[...] ренной акц[...]

Огласка э[...] труднить ока[...] Штатам военн[...] лю, курс акци[...] захвата новых а[...] рий еще более п[...] шингтонской пол[...] же. Поэтому свед[...] дии «Либерти» во[...] ведомством США б[...] чены.

После того как Рейган недавно причи[...] паж фрегата «Старк» [...] нальным героям», воз[...] ветераны «Либерти». О[...] них, рассказавший недавн[...] ставителям печати подроб[...] устроенной 8 июня 1967 [...] бойни, заявил: «Это позор! И[...] годня конгресс предоставл[...] Израилю все, что он запросит.

Как видим, двойная мораль [...] прежде была золотым правилом творцов американской внешней политики.

А. НИКОЛАЕВ.

CIRCLE TWO

LESSON THREE

AUDIO-COMPREHENSION EXERCISE

part 1

You are about to hear a text about South Africa under President Botha. Review the key words below. Then listen to the text with the following questions in mind. Afterwards, listen to the text again and write down the answers.

1. What kind of reports would you expect to hear in the Soviet press about South Africa? Would they differ significantly from Western reports?
2. What did President Botha announce in his television speech?
3. What happened eighteen hours before the speech?
4. What does Reuter report about the situation at the Johannesburg airport?
5. What measures did the police take against motorists?
6. What groups of people were arrested the night before?
7. What is the goal of the United Democratic Front?
8. What powers have the police been given?
9. How many people did UPI report arrested? How many of those were clergy members?

Key words

трансли́ровать по телеви́дению – to broadcast on T.V.
введе́ние чрезвыча́йного положе́ния – an introduction of the state of emergency
беспрецеде́нтная кара́тельно-полице́йская опера́ция – an unprecedented police operation
оцепи́ть гéтто – to cordon off the ghettos
нача́ть óбыски – to begin searches
пóдступы к аэропóрту – approaches to the airport
обы́скивать автомаши́ны – to search cars
лиша́ть води́тельских прав – to revoke a driver's licence
подозрева́емые в подрывнóй де́ятельности – those suspected of subversive activity
хвата́ть профсою́зных де́ятелей – to arrest trade union activists
свяще́нники – clergy
боро́ться с апартейдом – to fight against apartheid
равнопра́вие рас – equality of races
неограни́ченные полномóчия – unlimited authorities

TEXT: Read the following text. Be able to translate it in written form.

Чрезвычайное положение   Часть 1

Президент ЮАР П. Бота в речи, которая транслировалась по телевидению, объявил в четверг на заседании парламента в Кейптауне о введении по всей стране чрезвычайного положения.

Однако за 18 часов до этого в 00.01 минуту 12 июня по его приказу началась беспрецедентная даже по меркам расистского государства карательно-полицейская операция. Вооружённые до зубов отряды «сил безопасности» вместе с белыми резервистами, оцепив африканские гетто, начали повальные обыски и погромы в пригородах Йоханнесбурга, Кейптауна, Дурбана, Порт-Элизабета. Согласно сообщению агенства Рейтер, моторизованная полиция патрулирует подступы к международному аэропорту имени Яна Смэтса в Йоханнесбурге. Она обыскивает автомашины и лишает водительских прав подозреваемых в подрывной деятельности.

По заранее составленным спискам в минувшую ночь хватали профсоюзных деятелей, священников, учащихся и других активистов Объединённого демократического фронта -- массовой организации, борющейся против апартеида и стремящейся к равноправию рас. В телеграмме корреспондента агенства ЮПИ говорится, что уже арестовано свыше 1200 человек, среди них 200 церковнослужителей.

В соответствии с опубликованным в четверг декретом полиция получает неограниченные полномочия вводить комендантский час и оцеплять районы «беспорядков», а также расправляться с инакомыслящими.

Words and expressions to part 1

речь   транслировалась по телевидению
выступление   транслировалось по радио

транслироваться (no perf)
        -уются
трансляция
                                         (как?)
карательно-полицейская операция кончилась успешно - a police operation was a
                                                                success
военная   провалом - a military operation was
                                                                a failure

операция по высадке - a landing operation
        переброске - an air-lift operation
        захвату заложников - an operation to take hostages

отряды сил безопасности - security forces
        милиции
        специального назначения - special forces
        партизан
        резерва

запа́с
быть в запа́се
офице́р запа́са

де́йствующие си́лы – active forces
офице́р де́йствующих сил

оцепля́ть/оцепи́ть   ге́тто (unchanged)
   –ют оце́пят   при́городы – to cordon off the suburbs
       войска́   проти́вника
оце́пленный
оцепле́ние

патрули́ровать (no perf) по́дступы к го́роду
   –уют   к междунаро́дному аэропо́рту
– to patrol approaches to the international airport
        у́лицы
        вое́нный ла́герь
патрули́рование
патру́ль (masc. pl. патрули́, патруле́й)

ла́герь (pl. лагеря́)

моторизо́ванная поли́ция (no plur)
моторизо́ванные пехо́тные ча́сти

обы́скивать/обыска́ть   гра́ждан – to search citizens
   –ют обы́щут   населе́ние
       маши́ны
       приезжа́ющих
       инакомы́слящих
обы́сканный
о́быск
пова́льные о́быски – mass searches

граждани́н (pl. гра́ждане, гра́ждан)

       (чего́?)
лиша́ть/лиши́ть   свобо́ды – to deprive of freedom
  –ют –а́т   води́тельских прав – to revoke a driver's licence
       докуме́нтов
лишённый
лише́ния – privations

       (в чём?)
подозрева́ть (no perf)   в подрывно́й де́ятельности
   –ют   шпиона́же
       изме́не

приходи́ть/прийти́ с о́быском – to come with a search
прихо́дят приду́т

о́рдер на о́быск
(pl. ордера́, ордеро́в)

по спи́ску
    зара́нее соста́вленным спи́скам – according to previously composed lists

                        (куда́?)
попа́сть/попада́ть в чёрный спи́сок – to be blacklisted
попаду́т   -ют

ма́ссовая организа́ция – a large-scale organization
        демонстра́ция
ма́ссовый ми́тинг

боро́ться (no perf) про́тив дискримина́ции по при́нципу ра́сы
бо́рются   по́ла
                                              рели́гии

борьба́
            (к чему́)
стреми́ться   к равнопра́вию рас – to seek equality of races
    -я́тся   урегули́рованию
стремле́ние   к ми́ру
                                    (де́лать что?)
получа́ть неограни́ченные полномо́чия   вводи́ть   коменда́нтский час
    -ют/   отменя́ть са́нкции
– to receive full authority to lift the curfew
получи́ть   подавля́ть бунт
полу́чат   стреля́ть по толпе́
                                    оцепля́ть райо́ны
                                    обы́скивать маши́ны

полу́ченный
получе́ние

толпа́ (pl. то́лпы, толп)

            (к чему́?)
перехо́д   к репре́ссиям
                терра́ктам
                наси́лию

в масшта́бе всей страны́ – nation-wide
        всего́ контине́нта
        всего́ ми́ра

                    (от чего́?)
избавля́ться/изба́виться от борцо́в за гражда́нские права́
    -ются   -ятся   конкуре́нтов
                            безрабо́тицы

изба́вленный

разоблачáть себя как полицéйский режúм   фашúстского тóлка
      -ют   тоталитáрную систéму коммунистúческого тóлка
разоблачúть   расúстского тóлка
      -ат
разоблачённый
разоблачение

        (на чём?)
игрáть на предрассýдках – to exploit prejudicies
        расúзме
        антисемитúзме

шýмно привéтствовать эту áкцию
          -уют   кампáнию в прéссе
    (no perf.)   кандидáта в президéнты

сочýвствовать полúтике правúтельства
      -уют   тоталитáрным мéтодам
(no perf)   инакомы́слящим
              бóрющимся за свобóду слóва
сочýвствие

свобóда слóва – freedom of speech
        собрáний – freedom of assembly
        сóвести – freedom of religion

годовщúна расстрéла
        революции
                            (комý?)
бросáть/брóсить вы́зов всей мировóй общéственности
   -ют   -ят   реáкции
брóшенный

рассмáтривать/рассмотрéть   ситуáцию
        -ют рассмóтрят   положéние
to examine the situation
рассмóтренный
рассмотрéние

VOCABULARY EXERCISES

Look through the vocabulary for part 1 of the text «*Чрезвычáйное положéние*». Do the following exercises.

A. Give the plural forms, where they exist, for the following nouns. Mark the stress.

лáгерь, трансляция, рáдио, час, странá, гéтто, гражданúн, полúция, óбыск, óрдер, пехóта, спúсок, инакомы́слящий, рáса.

B. **Give perfective forms for the following verbs. Conjugate both forms and mark the stress.**

получа́ть, обы́скивать, патрули́ровать, объявля́ть, боро́ться, стреми́ться.

C. **Paraphrase the italicized words.**

по́лное право, *беспоря́дки*, *жи́тели*, по ра́дио *передава́лся* конце́рт, *окружи́ть* войска́.

D. **Give the opposite for the italicized words.**

вы́ступить *про́тив* апартейда, *введе́ние* коменда́нтского ча́са, *ввод* войск в страну́, офице́р *запа́са*, ко́нчиться *прова́лом*, *отъезжа́ющие* пассажи́ры

E. **Form verbs from the following nouns. Make necessary changes.**

оцепле́ние ге́тто, о́быск маши́н, борьба́ про́тив дискримина́ции, стремле́ние к равнопра́вию.

F. **Give Russian equivalents for the following English phrases.**

- to patrol approaches to the city
- to surround the suburbs
- martial law (state of emergency)
- a landing operation
- to revoke a driver's licence
- to be suspected of subversive activity
- to seek equality
- large scale searches
- a search warrant
- to suppress a riot
- to take reprisals against dissidents
- arriving passengers
- sex discrimination
- to be blacklisted
- reserve units

G. **Write sentences to fill in the blanks in the each of the groups below. Be able to translate your sentences.**

(что?)

1.   Отря́ды сил безопа́сности оцепи́ли ______________
     партиза́н   ______________
     сил резе́рва   ______________

(кака́я?)

2. __________ опера́ция по __________ ко́нчилась успе́шно
    __________   __________   прова́лом

(что?)

3. Моторизо́ванная поли́ция патрули́рует__________
                                         ____
                                         ____

(чего?)

4. Поли́ция лиша́ет инакомы́слящих __________
                     гра́ждан   __________
                     приезжа́ющих   __________

(в чём?)

5. Он подозрева́ется в __________
                        ____
                        ____

(чему́?)

6. АНК стреми́тся к__________
                   ____
                   ____

(чего́?)

7. Инакомы́слящие бо́рются против __________
                                  ____
                                  ____

GRAMMAR EXERCISES: REVIEW OF CASES

Review the use of cases as presented in Circle One. Do the following exercises.

A. Determine the use of case in the sentences below. Fill in the blanks. Be able to translate the sentences into English.

1. Поправка к конституции была поддержана (конгрессмены-расисты) ______________ в Арканзасе.

2. Товарищ Ельцин сказал, что перестройка противоречит (интересы трудящихся) ______________.

3. Испания пробилась в (Европейское экономическое сообщество) ______________.

4. Начальник отдела заработной платы Государственного отдела СССР по трудовым и социальным вопросам напомнил об (основной принцип, положенный) __________________ в (основа) _______ правительственного постановления.

5. Территориальные претензии (сионисты) _________ на Палестину не имеют под собой (почва) _________.

6. Эта статья провозглашает иностранной миссией (любая организация, занятая) ____________________ в США правительственной деятельностью от имени (зарубежные правительства) ______________.

7. Президент Рейган воспользуется (своё право) ______________ вето в случае принятия в конгрессе этого решения.

8. Перонисты взорвали (бомба) _________ за (дом) _______ судьи, который ведёт дела по (нарушения прав человека) _________.

9. Парламентская фракция СДПГ потребовала (созыв) _______ на (следующая неделя) __________ экстренного заседания Бундестага для (обсуждения) __________ позиции правительства ФРГ по вопросу о (72 ракеты) _________ Першинг-1А.

10. В (последнее время) ______________ они систематически подвергаются обстрелам из (реактивные ракетные установки) __________________.

B. Translate the following sentences.

1. What attitude do business circles in the U.S. have toward trade with the USSR?

2. Does society have a responsibility to the unemployed, the poor, and the sick?
3. The 71-year-old senator announced that his committee would rule on the issues of arms control and human rights.
4. A recent appeal to voters will lead to active participation in the forthcoming presidential elections.
5. Never before have there been any visible frictions within the communist bloc.
6. In the late 70s, during the Brezhnev era, the Soviet Union badly needed perestroika.
7. Apart from his usual tactics of intrigue (cognate), Stalin insisted on the direct use of force.
8. The administration called the recent accusations against its fiscal policy totally groundless.
9. In his youth Abu Nidal was suspected of organizing a terrorist group.
10. Developing countries have been relying on US economic aid over the last 35 years.
11. During an hour-and-a-half meeting the participants wanted to know how the new military technology held up in battle.
12. The United States ought to strive for a transition to a new stage in its participation in the Middle East peace process.
13. The House subcommittee (подкомитет) on taxation has drafted measures designed to decrease direct corporate taxes.
14. When the troops approached the refugee camps, they were met by crowds of people.
15. The civilian industries were deprived of vast resources due to large investments in the defense industry.
16. In 1981 the Italians started to have some doubts about the intentions of their NATO partners.
17. According to today's editorial we do expect another era of detente.
18. The members of the party were not pleased with the nomination of Comrade Petrov.

GRAMMAR EXERCISES: REVIEW OF PASSIVE PARTICIPLES AND PASSIVE REFLEXIVES

Review passive participles as presented in Circle One, Lesson 4. Do the following exercises.

A. Determine the type of participle in the sentences below. Replace them with relative clauses. Be able to translate them into English.

Example: Вот интервью, *опубликованное* на страницах «Правды».
      ⟶ Вот интервью, *которое опубликовали* на страницах «Правды».

1. Советские консульские работники встречаются с представителями соответствующих израильских учреждений для решения технических вопросов, *связанных* с пребыванием советских граждан в Израиле.

2. Хорошо *продуманные* меры контроля всех фаз разоружения должны стать фактором создания взаимного доверия.

3. В заявлении привлекается внимание к *зафиксированному* 13 августа советскими сейсмическими средствами ядерному испытанию в Неваде.

4. СССР всегда выполнял договоры, *заключённые* с иностранными фирмами.

5. Достижению этих благородных целей способствует *рождённый* в нашей стране процесс нового политического мышления.

6. Перестройка нацелена на создание полностью *сбалансированной* экономической системы.

7. Рекомендации, *выработанные* специальной комиссией ЦК, остались на бумаге.

8. Заместитель начальника ЦСУ подчеркнул, что *принятые* июльским Пленумом ЦК КПСС документы расчищают путь полному хозрасчёту.

9. Опрос, *проведённый* ЮСИА в прошлом месяце, показал, что 63 процента европейцев считают, что инициативы г-на Горбачёва открывают путь к прогрессу.

B. **Determine the type of participle in the sentences below. Rephrase them avoiding the use of passive constructions. If you do not see a logical "doer" of the action, use the «ОНИ» construction.**

Example: Эта клубника *выращена* в зоне Чернобыля.
$\longrightarrow$ Эту клубнику *вырастили* в зоне Чернобыля.

1. Его интервью *было опубликовано* в очередном номере еженедельника «Новое время».

2. Более того, контроль над частичным сокращением вооружений всегда при желании может *быть объявлен* недостаточным.

3. Вера в беспредельное совершенство техники существенно *подорвана* гибелью космического корабля «Челленджер».

4. Гость *был ознакомлен* с задачами, которые поставил перед собой Пленум ЦК БКП.

5. С болгарской стороны вновь *была выражена* поддержка борьбы народов Африки против империализма.

6. Заявление фракции *будет распространено* перед заседанием Бундестага представителем «зелёных».

7. Особое внимание *уделено* дозиметрическому контролю при разведении овощей в зоне аварии.

8. Отдельный раздел выставки *будет посвящён* истории русско-американских и советско-американских отношений.

9. Командующему американскими вооружёнными силами в регионе *поручено* выработать эффективные планы «контроля» над такими инцидентами.

C.   Review Table 8 in Lesson 4, Circle One.   Determine the type of participle in the sentences below. Rephrase these sentences using relative clauses with a «СЯ» verb instead of a participle.

Example: Советская консульская группа, *возглавляемая* заместителем
начальника консультативного отдела МИД СССР, прибыла в Тель-Авив.
      ⟶ Советская консульская группа, *которая возглавляется*
начальником консульского отдела отдела МИД СССР, прибыла в Тель-Авив.

1.   Академик М. Марков в статье, *публикуемой* на страницах «Правды», убедительно показывает иллюзорность доктрины «ядерного сдерживания».
2.   Автор делает вывод о необходимости запрограммированного, этапами *осуществляемого* всеобщего и полного разоружения.
3.   Подобные действия идут вразрез с коллективными усилиями, *предпринимаемыми* сейчас постоянными членами Совета Безопасности.
4.   Документ отражает тревогу определённых кругов, *вызываемую* у них утратой США лидирующих позиций.
5.   *Проводимые* радиобиологической лабораторией практические испытания помогут возродить землю вокруг Чернобыля.
6.   Директор Института экономики АН СССР коснулся широко *дискутируемой* проблемы рынка.
7.   Давайте обсудим вопрос, *рассматриваемый* в статье «Две политики – две доктрины».
8.   *Провозглашаемая* Японией безъядерная политика допускает ввоз или транзит через японскую территорию американского ядерного оружия в случае чрезвычайных обстоятельств.

D.   Translation.

1.   All citizens suspected of breaking the law fear searches.
2.   According to an AP story translated into Russian and published in *Pravda*, reports on anti-government protests in Estonia last week were broadcast only over local television.
3.   The current administration wants to do away with the death penalty, which was instituted after the military came to power.
4.   The question of racial equality was raised at a working session of the Committee for Human Rights.
5.   Martial law was declared, and reserve troops were deployed in the capital.
6.   The Government suspects the Citizens' Committee, which fights for human rights, of subversive activity.   Many committee members actively participating in mass meetings have been blacklisted.
7.   The government got unlimited curfew powers, as well as the right to cordon off rebellious areas of the city.
8.   The authorities now search all those arriving in the capital.
9.   Infantry troops on active duty now partol all neighborhoods in order to put down the rebellion.
10.   According to recent polls conducted this week the repressive measures adopted by the government will end in failure.

SPEAKING EXERCISES

A. Расскажи́те пе́рвую часть те́кста. В своём расска́зе испо́льзуйте сле́дующие слова́.

как ста́ло изве́стно; одна́ко; согла́сно сообще́нию; не то́лько..., но и....

B. Сумми́руйте пе́рвую часть в двух-трёх предложе́ниях.

C. Отве́тьте на сле́дующие вопро́сы.

1. Кто объяви́л о введе́нии чрезвыча́йного положе́ния в ЮАР?
2. Каки́е си́лы бы́ли испо́льзованы для введе́ния чрезвыча́йного положе́ния?
3. Про́тив кого́ бы́ли напра́влены но́вые репресси́вные ме́ры?
4. К чему́ стремя́тся активи́сты Объединённого демократи́ческого фро́нта?
5. Каки́е полномо́чия получа́ет поли́ция?

D. Дополни́тельные вопро́сы. (optional)

1. Что тако́е «чрезвыча́йное положе́ние»?
2. Почему́ обостри́лись ра́совые отноше́ния в ЮАР?
3. Почему́ южноафрика́нское прави́тельство подверга́ется кри́тике со стороны́ консервати́вных элеме́нтов в свое́й стране́?
4. Наско́лько далеко́ иду́т рефо́рмы, принима́емые президе́нтом Де Кле́рком?

AUDIO-COMPREHENSION EXERCISE

part 2

Listen to the tape with following questions in mind:

1. What activities have been banned in South Africa?
2. What penalties have been introduced for violations of the new laws?
3. Who welcomed Botha's actions?
4. The report notes that the imposition of the state of emergency comes at a particularly delicate time. In what sense?
5. What did a group of African nations ask the U.N. to do?
6. What was the White House's comment?
7. What did the ANC spokesman say?
8. What was in the statement issued by the United Democratic Front?

Key words

отсе́чь от вне́шнего ми́ра – to cut off from the outside world
запреща́ется фотографи́ровать – taking pictures is prohibited
райо́ны волне́ний – areas of unrest
сообща́ть в печа́ти имена́ – to publish names in the press
за наруше́ние пра́вил полага́ется заключе́ние; штраф – violation of rules is
                                    punishable by an imprisonment; a fine
разоблачи́ть себя́ как... – to expose oneself as...
приве́тствовать а́кции прави́тельства – to welcome the actions of government
годовщи́на расстре́ла – an anniversary of an execution
вы́зов мирово́й обще́ственности – an affront to the entire world opinion
созва́ть Сове́т Безопа́сности – to convene the Security Council
прозвуча́ли голоса́ сожале́ния – voices of regret were heard
введе́ние экономи́ческих са́нкций – introduction of economic sanctions
взять под защи́ту своего́ партнёра – to take one's partner under its protection
«конструкти́вное сотру́дничество» – "constructive engagement"
усугуби́ть вну́тренний кри́зис – to aggravate the domestic crisis
реши́мость наро́да не сломи́ть! – the determination of the people is not to be
                                    broken!

TEXT: Read the following text. Be able to translate it in written form.

Чрезвыча́йное положе́ние   Часть 2

Что́бы отсе́чь ЮАР от вне́шнего ми́ра и опусти́ть «желе́зный занавес», вла́сти ввели́ драко́новскую цензу́ру. Запреща́ется фотографи́ровать райо́ны волне́ний, сообща́ть в печа́ти имена́ аресто́ванных, цити́ровать их выска́зывания. За наруше́ние дли́нного сво́да полице́йских пра́вил полага́ется до 10 лет заключе́ния и штраф в 20 ты́сяч ра́ндов (о́коло 8 ты́сяч до́лларов).

Ита́к, режи́м перешёл к откры́тым террористи́ческим де́йствиям в масшта́бах всей страны́, что́бы изба́виться от борцо́в за гражда́нские права́ и свобо́ды. Тем са́мым э́тот режи́м разоблачи́л себя́ как режи́м расистско-полице́йской диктату́ры меньшинства́, кото́рый отбра́сывает деко́рум буржуа́зного парламентари́зма и испо́льзует тотали́та́рные ме́тоды фаши́стского то́лка, игра́я на ра́совых предрассу́дках. Неда́ром а́кцию Бо́ты шу́мно приве́тствовали неонаци́сты из консервати́вной па́ртии и «Африка́нского движе́ния сопротивле́ния», сочу́вствующие поли́тике прави́тельства.

Введе́ние чрезвыча́йного положе́ния в кану́н деся́той годовщи́ны расстре́ла демонстра́ции в Соуэ́то -- вы́зов всей мирово́й обще́ственности, небезразли́чной к положе́нию в ЮАР.

Гру́ппа африка́нских стран обрати́лась к Генера́льному секретарю́ ООН сро́чно созва́ть Сове́т Безопа́сности. В о́бщем хо́ре проте́стов прозвуча́ли и голоса́ «сожале́ния» со стороны́ прави́тельств США и Англии. При э́том представи́тель Бе́лого до́ма поспеши́л заяви́ть, что США не собира́ются рассма́тривать вопро́с о введе́нии в отноше́нии ЮАР экономи́ческих са́нкций. Таки́м о́бразом, Вашингто́н вновь взял под защи́ту своего́ партнёра по «конструкти́вному сотру́дничеству».

Де́йствия власте́й ЮАР лишь усугубя́т вну́тренний кри́зис, сопротивле́ние на́шего наро́да бу́дет нараста́ть, заяви́л в Луса́ке представи́тель Африка́нского национа́льного конгре́сса. Ста́ло изве́стным заявле́ние Объединённого демократи́ческого фро́нта. В нём говори́тся: реши́мость наро́да поко́нчить со злом систе́мы апарте́йда не сломи́ть никаки́ми репре́ссиями.

ПРЕСС-СЛУЖБА «ИЗВЕСТИЙ»

Word and expressions to part 2

опуска́ть/опусти́ть желе́зный за́навес
    -ют опу́стят
опу́щенный

поднима́ть/подня́ть
    -ют подни́мут
по́днятый

вводи́ть/ввести́ драко́новскую цензу́ру
вво́дят введу́т экономи́ческие са́нкции про́тив ЮАР
                        (чего́?)   (кому́)
        эмба́рго на прода́жу зерна́ По́льше
                        (чего́?)   (у кого́?)
        поку́пку зерна́ у По́льши
- to introduce embargo on purchases of grain from Poland

отменя́ть/отмени́ть са́нкции - to lift sanctions
    -ют отме́нят эмба́рго

отменённый
отме́на

                      (де́лать что?)
запреща́ется   фотографи́ровать райо́ны волне́ний
                      сообща́ть имена́... в печа́ти
                      цити́ровать выска́зывания
запреща́ть/запрети́ть
        -ют   -ят
запрещённый
запреще́ние

(за что?)
за наруше́ние пра́вил полага́ется   срок   в 10 лет
                       поря́дка   заключе́ние   до 14 су́ток
                       зако́на   штраф   в 50 до́лларов
                                                  пожи́зненное заключе́ние
                                                  сме́ртная казнь – violation of rules is
                                                          punishable with death penalty
                      (за что?)
штрафова́ть/оштрафова́ть за   цити́рование... – to fine for quoting...
        -у́ют   -у́ют   фотографи́рование
оштрафо́ванный

                 (к чему́?)   (про́тив кого́? чего́?)
переходи́ть   к откры́тым де́йствиям про́тив   борцо́в
перехо́дят/   отделе́ния от СССР
перейти́   присоедине́ния к США
перейду́т   (за что?)
                                            за   незави́симость
                                                    гражданские права

рассма́тривать ситуа́цию, как наруше́ние (acc) – to see the situation as a
(no perf)   violation
But: счита́ть ситуа́цию наруше́нием (inst) – to consider the situation to be
                                                          a violation

                     (к чему́?)
(не)безразли́чный   к   страда́ниям люде́й
                          судьбе́ зало́жников
                          погро́мам
                          несправедли́вости – indifferent to injustice
безразли́чие

брать/взять   под защи́ту своего́ партнёра по   бло́ку
беру́т возьму́т   па́ртии
                                            «конструкти́вному сотру́дничеству»
                          зало́жников
                          военноплённых
                          ра́неных – to take the wounded under its protection
взя́тый

```
                (с чем?)
покончить  со    злом
    -ат           отсталостью
(no imperf)       зависимостью
                  задолженностью
```

решймость народа не сломить! – our people's determination is no to be broken!
нашу волю к победе не сломить!
наш народ не победить!

VOCABULARY EXERCISES

Look through the vocabulary for part 2 of the text «*Чрезвычайное положение*».
Do the following exercises.

A. Give the plural forms, where they exist, for the following nouns. Mark
the stress.

занавес, насилие, мир (peace), эмбарго, пресса, раненный, зло,
военнопленный, задолженость, блок.

B. Give perfective forms for the following verbs; conjugate both forms and
mark the stress.

приветствовать, опускать, поднимать, вводить, запрещать, переходить,
сочувствовать, бросать, избавляться, рассматривать.

C. Paraphrase the italicized words.

санкции *в отношении* Польши; *жёсткая* цензура; *показать* себя как..., режим
антисемитского *характера*; в *мировом* масштабе; *запрещается снимать*;
индифферентный к страданиям; *защищать* гражданское население; *призвать*
ООН рассмотреть ситуацию; *считать* терракт вызовом; *расплатиться* с
задолженностью; наш народ *невозможно* победить.

D. Give the opposite for the italicized words.

в *районном масштабе*, *тайные действия*, *присоединение* к России, *соблюдение*
правил, *разрешается*, *опустить* занавес, *попасть* в зависимость,
безразличный.

E. Form verbs from the following nouns. Make necessary changes.

отмéна сáнкций, сочýвствие полúтике, рассмотрéние ситуáции, перехóд к насúлию, запрещéние фотографúровать.

F. Give Russian equivalents for the following English phrases.

- to challenge the entire world opinion
- on a national scale
- to lift sanctions against Poland
- to give a strong ovation to Gorbachev's release of prisoners
- to expose oneself as a racist
- an anniversary of the revolution
- to introduce draconian censorship
- to publish names in the press
- to put an end to evil
- to view the situation as a violation
- to pay off the debt
- to take one's partner in the bloc under one's protection.
- indifferent to politics

G. Write sentences to fill in the blanks in each of groups below. Be able to translate your sentences.

                                                  (чегó?)   (комý?)

1. Кáртер ввёл эмбáрго на продáжу ________ ________
                                                 ________ ________
                                                 ________ ________

Change the sentences above using «эмбáрго на покýпку» (embargo on puchase of so-and-so from so-and so)

                                               (что?)

2. За нарушéние порядка полагáлось   ________
                      закóна   ________
                      конститýции   ________

                      (к чемý?)

3. Произошёл перехóд ________ в масштáбах всей страны́.
                         ________   всегó райóна
                         ________ мировóм масштáбе.

    (кто?)

4. ________ игрáл(-а,-о,-и) на предрассýдках
      ________   расúстских настроéниях
                      антисемúтских настроéниях

(кто?)

5. ________ сочу́вствовал (–а,–о,–и)   инакомы́слящим
                                          тоталита́рным ме́тодам
                                          ма́ссовым репре́ссиям

		(кого́? что?)		(кого́? что?)
6.	ООН	рассма́тривает	_________ как	_________
	Республика́нцы	рассма́тривают	_________	_________
	Обще́ственость	рассма́тривает	_________	_________

Change the sentences above using «счита́ть»

(с чем?)

7. Необходи́мо, чтобы но́вая администра́ция поко́нчила с _________
____
____

(к чему́?)

8. Во вре́мя войны́ мир был безразли́чен к _________
                погро́мов   _________
                депре́ссии   _________

9. Партиза́ны взя́ли под защи́ту _________
США   _________
войска́   _________

GRAMMAR EXERCISES: REVIEW OF PASSIVE PARTICIPLES (Continued)

Review Passive participles as presented in Circle One, Lesson 4.   Do the following exercises.

A.   **Look at the sentences below and determine what form the   italicized verbs are in.   Rephrase each sentence replacing the verb with a passive participle. Make necessary changes.   Be able to translate these sentences into English.**

Examples: Этот документ *положили* в основу мифа о Советском Союзе – «враге ислама».

 —→ Этот документ *был положен* в основу мифа о Советском Союзе – «враге ислама».

 Резервы, которые *используют* в экономической системе, недостаточны для увеличения объёма производства.

 —→ *Резервы, используемые* в экономической системе, недостаточны для увеличения объёма производства.

1.   В национальном архиве в Дели имеется секретный меморандум бывшего вице-короля Индии, который он *направил* английскому правительству 17 декабря 1921 года.

2.   Советский Союз сегодня объявил о пусках   ракет–носителей, которые *проводятся* в районах акватории Тихого океана.

3.   Иранское правительство *аннулировало* навязанное Англией Тегерану в 1919 году унизительное соглашение.

4.   *Освободят* ли людей, которых заключили в   тюрьму   за   критику политической установки компартии Китая?

5.   В частности, будет обсуждаться программа изучения и освоения Марса, которую *предложил* СССР.

6.   Миф о Советском Союзе – «враге ислама», который   *распространяется* как на Западе, так и на Востоке, широко используют наши враги.

7.   ТАСС *уполномочили* заявить, что правительство СССР   просит правительства других государств не заходить в эти районы.

8.   Мусульмане не могут забыть чувство доброты и симпатии, которое *проявляли* большевики к каждому мусульманскому государству, оказавшемуся в беде.

9.   Как крупный успех советской космонавтики охарактеризовала телекомпания Би–би–си новый рекорд продолжительного пребывания человека в космосе, который *установил* советский космонавт Ю. Романенко.

10.   Провозглашение Фиджи республикой на этом драматическом фоне подчёркивает противоположности характера трансформации, которую *переживает* страна.

11.   На военный объект Шиханы *пригласили* представителей всех государств-участников и всех государств-наблюдателей женевских переговоров по химическому оружию.

12. Эта практика противоречит тем отношениям, которые *устанавливаются* в настоящее время между СССР и США.

13. Венская консульская конвенция предусматривает право консульских должностных лиц свободно встречаться с гражданами, государства которых они *представляют*.

14. Как мне известно, за подобные вещи у нас никого не *арестовали* и не *посадили* в тюрьму.

15. В ходе беседы *обсудят* вопросы перспектив урегулирования арабо-израильского конфликта.

16. Он дал интервью корреспонденту ТАСС в связи с Международным днём врачей, который *отмечается* сегодня.

17. Сегодня здесь, на брифинге, было привлечено внимание к факту попрания прав человека в отношении советской гражданки, которую на днях зверски *избили* в Канаде.

18. На Фиджи военные, которыми *предводительствует* полковник Рабука, еще в мае сбросили правительство лейбористов.

B. Translate the following.

1. The Citizens' Council declared that it views the prohibition of open demonstrations as a deprivation of basic human rights.

2. An agreement was signed, repressive measures halted, and sanctions lifted.

3. Photography in the riot zone is strictly prohibited. Violations will lead to large fines and even imprisonment.

4. Human rights groups have called upon the Justice Ministry to put an end to capital punishment.

5. According to the U.S. Constitution police may not conduct searches or arrest citizens without a warrant. Nevertheless, violations of these rights sometimes occur.

6. The press exposed a plan worked out by the nation's bankers to get rid of foreign debt.

7. The hostages were freed in a complicated landing operation.

8. The development plan for the so-called new economic zones has been introduced on a national scale.

9. The political agenda presented by the National Union Party plays on the prejudices of the middle class.

10. The question of racial discrimination is always raised at these meetings.

GRAMMAR: "SOME-," "ANY-" AND "NO-" CONSTRUCTIONS

Look at the following sentences and there translations:

Львóва когó-нибýдь знáет?	Does Lvova know somebody? Does Lvova know anybody?
Львóва что-то знáет.	Lvova knows something.
Львóва ничегó не знáет .	Lvova doesn't know anything. Lvova knows nothing.

"As you can see, "something," "anything," and "nothing" are rendered by **-то**, **-нибýдь**, and **ни-...не** constructions, although *there is no direct one-to-one correspondence between the English words and their Russian counterparts.*

Note these **-то, -нибýдь,** and **ни-...не** forms:

что-то	что-нибудь	ничегó не	*something*
кто-то	кто-нибудь	никтó не	*someone*
когдá-то	когдá-нибудь	никогдá не	*at some time*
где-то	где-нибудь	нигдé не	*somewhere*
кудá-то	кудá-нибудь	никудá не	*to somewhere*
как-то	как-нибудь	никáк не	*somehow*

The following rules govern the use of -то, -нибýдь, **and** ни-...не:

1. Use **ни-...не constructions** in *all* negative sentences:

    Мы никáк не кóнчим проéкт.

    In genitive sentences indicating absence use **ни-...нет, ни-...нé было,** or **ни-... не бýдет:** Здесь нет никогó. Здесь нé было никогó.

2. **Use -нибýдь:**

    a. Future tense or idea: Мы что-нибудь сдéлаем! Нáдо что-нибудь дéлать.
    b. Questions: Онá что-нибудь читáла?
    c. Commands: Сдéлайте что-нибудь!
    d. With adverbs indicating habitual action: Онá всегдá что-нибудь дéлает.
    e. With adverbs of probability: навéрно, мóжет быть, etc.
        Онá, навéрно, когó-нибудь знáет.

    Do NOT use -нибýдь **in negative constructions. Use** ни...не **constructions instead.**

3. **Use -то** in most other situations:

    Она что-то говорит. Он где-то был.

Note also:

a. words with **что** and **кто** decline: чему́-то, чему́-нибудь, ничему́ не;
    кого́-то, кого́-нибудь, никого́ не, etc.

b. When a **ни-...не** construction includes a preposition, the preposition
    breaks up the **ни-** word:

Вы кого́-нибудь ви́дели?	Нет, мы никого́ не ви́дели.

but:

Вы о ком-нибудь говори́ли?	Нет, мы ни о ком не говори́ли.
Вы с кем-нибудь бы́ли?	Нет, мы ни с кем не говори́ли.
Вы кому́-нибудь сообщи́ли?	Нет, мы ни кому́ не сообщи́ли.

"SOME-," "ANY-" AND "NO-" CONSTRUCTIONS WITH ADJECTIVES: "SOMETHING INTERESTING"

Forms such as **кто-то, кто-нибудь,** and **никто́...не,** as well as **что-то,
что-нибудь,** and **ничего́...не** take long form declinable adjectives as in the
following examples:

кто-то интере́сный (always masculine!)	*someone interesting*
кому́-нибудь интере́сному	*to someone interesting*
что-нибудь интере́сное (always neuter!)	*something interesting*
ни о чём интере́сном	*about nothing interesting*

"SOME SORT OF": КАКОЙ-ТО, КАКОЙ-НИБУДЬ, AND НИКАКОЙ НЕ

Note the following examples:

Сообща́ли о каки́х-то волне́ниях.	Some sort of riots were reported.
Сообща́ли о каки́х-нибудь волне́ниях?	Were some sort of riots reported?
Ни о каки́х волне́ниях не сообща́ли.	No riots were reported.
Никаки́х волне́ний не было.	There were no riots.

Note that **какой-нибудь** is an adjective. It may not stand alone!

GRAMMAR EXERCISES: "SOME-", "ANY-", "NO-" CONSTRUCTIONS

Read through the explanation on "some," "any," and "no-" constructions.

A. Choose the correct word.

1. Мы бои́мся, что (no one will) помо́жет нашим борца́м за свобо́ду.
    (кто-то не, кто-нибудь не, никто не)

2.   Меры, принятые сегодня, действительно (not anyone) помогут. (кому-то не, кому-нибудь не, никому не)

3.   Надо будет готовить (some sort of) подходящий ответ. (какой-то, какой-нибудь, никакого нет)

4.   (There aren't any) расистских высказываний в выступлении лидера партии. (нет каких-то, нет каких-нибудь, нет никаких)

5.   – Вы (with someone) обсуждали изменения нашей политики? (с кем-то, с кем-нибудь, ни с кем не)

6.   Будет ли на повестке дня (any) пункт, касающийся введения черезвычайного положения в стране? (какой-то, какой- нибудь, никакой не)

7.   (Not for anything) отдадим наше право голоса! (за что-то не, за что-нибудь не, ни за что не)

8.   Вы думаете, что вы (somewhere) найдёте идеальное решение? Нет, вы идеального решения (not anywhere) найдёте. (где-то, где-нибудь, нигде не)

9.   В нашей стране (there have been no) репрессий. (каких-то, каких-нибудь, не было никаких)

10.   В Советском Союзе (at one time) запрещалась неофициальная литература. (когда-то, когда-нибудь, никогда не)

B.   Use -то and ни-...не constructions to answer the questions according to the model.

Example: Кто-нибудь выступал?
        ⟶ Да, *кто-то* выступал.
        ⟶ Нет, *никто не* выступал.

1.   Куда-нибудь высылают этих инакомыслящих?
2.   Как-нибудь справятся с кризисом?
3.   Кто-нибудь интересовался нашим вопросом?
4.   Что-нибудь решили по этой проблеме?
5.   Где-нибудь строят новые церкви?
6.   Когда-нибудь аннулировали конституцию?
6.   Ваши люди с кем-нибудь говорили по этому поводу?
7.   Пресса о чём-нибудь сообщила?
8.   В стране были какие-нибудь репрессии?
9.   «ЛГ» когда-нибудь писала о лагерях?
10.   У нашего комитета есть какое-нибудь полномочие?
11.   Вы обращались к каким-нибудь руководителям партии?
12.   Они сотрудничали с какими-нибудь фашистами?
13.   Вам сообщили о каком-нибудь плане?
14.   Ассамблея ввела какие-нибудь санкции?
15.   Наша фирма продавала СССР какую-нибудь технологию?

C.   Translate the phrases.   Follow the models.

Examples: about somebody?   ⟶ *о ком-нибудь?*
            of something [was]   ⟶ *чего-то*
            not with anyone   ⟶ *ни с кем не*

1.   anywhere?
2.   somehow?
3.   to no one
4.   someone [was]
5.   something [will]
6.   not about anything
7.   nowhere
8.   in front of someone [was]
9.   behind no one
10.   not for anyone
11.   some sort of measures [are]
12.   about any sorts of measures?
13.   there were no measures
14.   about no measures
15.   something interesting [is]
16.   about something bad?
17.   with anyone interesting?
18.   nothing good
19.   of something good?
20.   to something bad?

D.   Translate the word under the blank with forms of -то, -нибудь **or** ни-...не

1.   ______________ из представителей сказал, что он боится, что не будет
      Someone
     принято ___________ мер.
               no

2.   ______________ задавал вопросы на брифинге?
      Someone

3.   Состоялись ____________________ антигосударственные демонстрации, но
                    some kind of
     местная полиция ____________ арестовала.
                        no one

4.   Говорят, что __________________ волнений, но я лично ___________
                    there were no   *no one*
     верю.

5.   - Освободили _____________ из политзаключённых?
                        anyone

     - Нет, пока __________ освободили. Мы надеемся, что _____________
                  no one   *someone*
     будет освобождён накануне годовщины Революции.

6.   К сожалению, мы _________________ не можем согласиться.
                      not with anyone

7.   _________________ террористы захватили самолёт и приказали полететь
     Some sort of
     в __________ исламскую страну.
       some

8.   _________________ политическое положение в Никарагуа было лучше, но
     At one time
     оно __________ обещало особенно светлого будущего для народа.
          never

9.   Мы ____________ переубедим наших соперников, хотя у нас
        somehow
     _______________ представления, как мы это сделаем.
      no sort of

10. Предложите _______________!
                 something

E. Translate the following sentences.

1.   We thought that someone from South Africa had participated in the session, but then it turned out that no one from Africa was there.
2.   Do the people in this region have any rights?   No, they have no rights.
3.   Someone said that there was some sort of announcement about some new policy on discrimination, but no one heard it.
4.   Our government will not suspend this law for anyone.
5.   At one time Zimbabwe was a white-ruled state.
6.   The government suspected the protesters of some sort of terrorist acts, but the authorities couldn't prove anything.
7.   Do something! Make some sort of decision!
8.   Do you have any other proposals for us? So far we have seen nothing constructive.
9.   We demanded a new session, and then something interesting happened: the other side made some sort of concrete proposal.
10. Do we have any policy on terrorism?

RENDERING

Render the following information into Russian.

The African country of Karpusu Lasi has been dependent on U.S. aid for the last twenty years. However, lately it has become abundantly clear that the country's ailing (and senile) president Kwanda Mbuto is on the outs.

Quite plainly, Mbuto, once viewed in Washington as a left-leaning but non-communist, forward-looking leader, has lost control. A quick look at the evidence will show why:

→ While surrounded by countries where human rights are treated more like a doormat than an icon, Mbuto has maintained a semblance of civilization. That no longer is the case. Mbuto is old and tired. The army has been given nearly total control. Warrentless searches and arrests, arbitrary repression of dissidents, as well as summary executions have become the norm. Entire villages where dissident activity is suspected have been put off limits to travelers.

→ The economy, never strong, is in a total shambles. With the private sector almost totally broke, the army soaked up most of the younger unemployed. If you want to get something done quickly, you had better be in good with someone in uniform. Mbuto knows that if he wants to stay in power (or, for that matter, alive), it's best to feed the brass.

→ If Mbuto is tired of active rule, so the people are tired of Mbuto. Nearly everyone in the country once viewed Mbuto as a transitional leader from the chaos of independence to an orderly democracy. The transition part is still there. What is absent is the democracy. Either way, the military wins: if Mbuto dies soon, the army is sure to declare martial law and take over "for a transitional period"; if not, the military is sure to persuade Mbuto to step down before he is too... incapacitated to run a government.

The question at hand is, what should happen to U.S. aid and trade. Karpusu Lasi has been one place on the continent where America's stock in trade has traditionally been high, but the slow degeneration of the Mbuto government has been accompanied by a crash in American prestige. Perhaps it's time to cut our losses early on?

SPEAKING EXERCISES

A.   Расскажи́те втору́ю часть те́кста.

B.   Расскажи́те ту же исто́рию с то́чки зре́ния чле́на консервати́вной па́ртии.

C.   Сумми́руйте пе́рвую и втору́ю ча́сти э́того те́кста. В своём расска́зе испо́льзуйте сле́дующие выраже́ния.

ита́к; с одно́й стороны́,... с друго́й стороны́..; ра́зве...? ме́жду тем; и́менно поэ́тому.

D.   Отве́тьте на сле́дующие вопро́сы.

1.   Каки́е шаги́ предпринима́ли вла́сти ЮАР, чтобы не допусти́ть голосо́в проте́ста?
2.   Как впи́сывались полице́йские ме́ры Прето́рии в традицио́нные демократи́ческие но́рмы?
3.   Как реаги́ровали на поли́тику прави́тельства Бо́ты други́е африка́нские госуда́рства?
4.   Каки́е стра́ны выступа́ют про́тив са́нкций в отноше́нии Ю́жной Африки?
5.   Сломи́ли ли официа́льные репре́ссии во́лю к сопротивле́нию со стороны́ Африка́нского конгре́сса и его́ сою́зников?

E.   Дополни́тельные вопро́сы. (optional)

1.   Назови́те изве́стные вам гражда́нские свобо́ды. Объясни́те ка́ждую.
2.   Что тако́е поли́тика апартеи́да?
3.   В чём суть америка́нской поли́тики «констру́кти́вного сотру́дничества»?
4.   Наско́лько эффекти́вными оказа́лись са́нкции про́тив ЮАР?

READING EXERCISE

Америка в общеевропейском доме.   Сергей Караганов

PRE-TEXT: This is an article written by a prominent political observer who is a frequent contributor to the weekly *Moscow News.* Read the text with the following questions in mind.   Then look at the questions below.   Try to predict the answers in advance.   Then re-read the article to see if you were correct and answer the questions in written form.

1.   What is the main idea of the text?

PARAGRAPH 1
2.   Opponents of the Common European Home call it unrealistic because...
(Mark the correct answer):
   a.   they view it as economically hazardous.
   b.   they do not want to give up the Cold War.
   c.   they see no future for it.

PARAGRAPHS 2, 3, 4
3.   Karaganov cities a number of objections based on past Soviet actions.
What is his comment?
4.   There are reasons why Western Europe fears pushing America out of the European system of security.   Name them.

PARAGRAPHS 4
5.   Why are these fears ungrounded?

PARAGRAPHS 5, 6
6.   There are reasons why some circles in the U.S. fear this idea.   Name three.

PARAGRAPHS 7, 8, 9
7.   What are the connections between the U.S. and Western Europe, according to the author?

PARAGRAPH 10
8.   Before the concept of the Common European Home can be realized it is necessary to... (Mark the correct answer):
   a.   withdraw all US troops from Europe.
   b.   withdraw the troops of both superpowers.
   c.   exclude the US from the European security system.
   d.   reduce both US and Soviet presence to a minimum.

PARAGRAPH 11
9.   The author mentions Washington's having considered the use of nuclear weapons in Korea, Vietnam and in the Straits of Taiwan.   What is his point?

PARAGRAPH 12
10.   What does the author say about Moscow's first steps towards the Common European Home?

POST–TEXT   (using context):

Literary **Redundancy** through use of synonymous phrases is one of the main stylistic devices of expository prose.   Writers use redundancy to hold a paragraph or series of paragraphs together.   This allows the reader to follow the direction of a writer's line of argument.   Note the following example:

Мы **поражались** происходящему **массовому** строительству бомбоубежищ.
Нас **удивлял масштаб** этого строительства.

Неслыханным образом война **ускорила социальное развитие**.
Она **подтолкнула историю**.

In this lesson and the ones to follow you will often be asked to find instances of stylistic redundancy.

Do the following exercises:

1.   The article proceeds from... (Mark the correct answer):
    a.   examples to statement.
    b.   statement to illustrations.

PARAGRAPH 1
2.   The use of a dash after *И не без дальнего прицела...* indicates... (Mark the correct answer):
    a.   shifting to another point.
    b.   explanation of the main point.

PARAGRAPHS 2, 3, 4
3.   These paragraphs describe fears regarding the idea of the Common European Home in Western Europe itself.   Find the phrase which confirms your assumption that the author means Western Europe.
4.   In both paragraphs 2 and 4 Karaganov indicates a certain degree of scepticism about commonly held fears about the European Common Home. What word signals that scepticism?

PARAGRAPH 3
5.   Name the markers that signal enumeration of reasons to fear the idea. Do you see any use of redundancy here?
6.   Which phrase shows the author's thinking on the earlier Soviet attitute towards the U.S. in Europe?
7.   Explain the composition of the word *небезосновательный*.
8.   Give the opposite of *второй план*.
9.   Find the paragraphs which describe US fears regarding the idea.
10.   Explain the composition of the word *подсознание*.

PARAGRAPHS 7, 8, 9

11. These paragraphs contain the Soviet attitude to the US–Western Europe connection. Find the words which mark the enumeration of the author's points.

PARAGRAPH 9

12. Which sentence uses a metaphor to describe the military interdependence of the West?

PARAGRAPH 10

13. *Однако* here marks... (Mark the correct answer):
    a. support of the previous statement.
    b. contradiction of the previous statement.

14. Find the opposite for *противодействовать.*
15. Find the words which twice emphasize that the point of view expressed here belongs to the other side.

PARAGRAPH 11

16. *Достаточно вспомнить* signals... (Mark the correct answer):
    a. support
    b. contradiction

17. Pick the correct meanings for each of the words below:

| прицел | a. | sight |
| | b. | aim |

| наследие | a. | legacy |
| | b. | inheritance |

| благотворный | a. | charitable |
| | b. | positive |

| при этом | a. | while doing so |
| | b. | in the vicinity |

18. Find the Russian for:

   - to sow doubts regarding so-and-so
   - to drive a wedge between so-and-so
   - to insist on the opposite
   - a cautious approach

СТРАНИЦА ТРЕХ АВТОРОВ

МИР НА МОЕМ ДИСПЛЕЕ

Америка в общеевропейском доме

Сергей КАРАГАНОВ

КОНЦЕПЦИЯ общеевропейского дома встречает в мире не только поддержку. Немало и критики. Многие на Западе пытаются представить ее нереалистичной. И не без дальнего прицела — эти круги не хотят назревших изменений нынешней, унаследованной от «холодной войны» системы безопасности в Европе.

Нередко претензии оппонентов идеи общеевропейского дома сводятся к тому, что эта концепция подразумевает якобы «выталкивание» Америки из Европы, из европейской системы безопасности.

Для таких заявлений есть немало предлогов. Есть семантические: словосочетание «общеевропейский дом» вызывает образ чего-то замкнутого, ограниченного одним континентом. Есть и небеззосновательные подозрения, основанные на историческом опыте: Советский Союз и социалистические страны, к сожалению, пытались на дальних подступах к Хельсинки 1975 года исключить США и Канаду из будущего общеевропейского процесса.

К счастью, мы относительно недолго настаивали на такой нереалистической, да и, прямо скажем, вредной позиции. Но шлейф подозрений не рассеялся.

С опаской к идее общеевропейского дома в Западной Европе подходят и по другой причине: шаги к ее осуществлению якобы подтолкнут Соединенные Штаты еще больше уделять внимание азиатско-тихоокеанскому региону и отодвинут американские интересы на старом континенте на второй план. Страхи эти, думаю, необоснованные. США, несмотря на все утверждения о концентрации их внимания к странам тихоокеанского бассейна, отнюдь не собираются «уходить» из Европы и лишаться влияния на континенте, который остается первостепенным средоточием экономической, политической, военной и идейной мощи.

В Соединенных Штатах оппозиция идее общеевропейского дома зиждется на опасениях, порождаемых ростом самостоятельности европейских держав и падением популярности Америки в Европе.

Страхи и смутные подозрения — это скорее из сферы

подсознания. Ну а в реальности за заявлениями, что Советский Союз пытается «вытолкнуть» Америку из Европы, стоят вполне определенные интересы. Главный — стремление посеять сомнения в отношении советской европейской политики, ослабить ее притягательность. Заявления на Западе о попытках Советского Союза вбить «клин» в отношениях между Америкой и Западной Европой делаются все чаще по мере того, как советские руководители последовательно утверждают обратное — о том, что СССР не собирается раскалывать западный союз, вытеснять США, поскольку считает это ненужным и нереальным.

В Советском Союзе хорошо осознают, что Соединенные Штаты в историческом, религиозном, духовном и, главное, в политическом отношении — часть Европы.

Тесно привязаны к Западной Европе Соединенные Штаты и в экономической сфере, и оторваться от нее или быть оторванными США не могут.

Теснейшим образом Соединенные Штаты привязаны к Европе и в сфере безопасности. Развитие современных вооружений и вооруженных сил сузили Атлантический океан до ширины пролива. Теперь США в военном плане так же близки к континенту, как Англия в начале этого века.

Естественно, напрашивается вывод, что участие Соединенных Штатов в будущей системе европейской безопасности, в строительстве «общеевропейского дома» и закономерно, и необходимо. Однако, с нашей точки зрения, это отнюдь не означает, что военное присутствие Соединенных Штатов на континенте должно оставаться на сегодняшнем столь высоком уровне. Полагаем, что необходимо сокращение этого, равно как и советского, военного присутствия до минимального уровня. С дальнейшим укреплением и стабилизацией европейской системы безопасности логично и избавление от этого обременительного наследия «холодной войны». Однако это отнюдь не предполагает исключения США из системы общеевропейской безопасности и после того, как большинство иностранных солдат (или все) уйдут из других государств.

Участие Соединенных Штатов в европейской системе безопасности позволит сохранить и воздействие — по большей части благотворное — европейских держав на политику и военную стратегию США. Опыт учит, что влияние европейских союзников, опасения потерять их поддержку наряду с другими факторами не раз содействовали сдерживанию Вашингтона от начала или продолжения авантюристических действий. Достаточно вспомнить влияние позиции западноевропейцев, когда в Корее, Вьетнаме, в Тайваньском проливе Вашингтон подумывал о возможности применения ядерного оружия.

Концепция общеевропейского дома — идея новая. На пути ее реализации делаются только первые шаги. К ним можно отнести в первую очередь оживленный политический диалог Москвы с западноевропейскими столицами. При этом в советской столице неоднозначно заявляют, что двусторонние контакты, с нашей точки зрения, никак не ущемляют интересы третьих стран. Это в полной мере относится и к Соединенным Штатам, приглашение которым участвовать в строительстве общеевропейского дома остается в силе.

CIRCLE TWO

LESSON FOUR

AUDIO–COMPREHENSION EXERCISE

part 1

You are about to hear a text about democratization in the Soviet Union. Review the key words below. Then listen to the text for the following information. Afterwards, listen to the text again and write down the answers.

1. After a few years of Gorbachev the Soviet press began to subject the country to much critical introspection. What was suggested in the press during that period? What reforms were discussed? With those questions in mind answer the questions below.
2. According to the report, what sort of discussion has now begun in the Soviet Union?
3. What is cited as a characteristic of Soviet society today?
4. What is seen as a prerequisite for the continuance of perestroika?
5. What is given as a cause for the woes of the system as it exists today?
6. What problems are seen as having plagued the Soviets of People's Deputies up until now?
7. What does Article 94 of the proposed legislation say about the Soviet of People's Deputies?
8. What is said about the make-up of the Congress of People's Deputies?
9. What role will the Committee on Constitutional Review play?

Key words

всенаро́дное обсужде́ние – public discussion
изменéния и дополнéния (к) Конститу́ции – changes and amendments to
             the Constitution
вы́йти из состоя́ния апа́тии – to become active
сде́лать необрати́мым – to make irreversible
оказа́ться безвла́стными – to prove to be powerless
управлéнческая пра́ктика – managerial practice
слéдовать свое́й ло́гике – to follow one's own logic
администрати́вный произво́л – administrative lawlessness
исключа́ться из полити́ческой систéмы – to be excluded from the political system
отлича́ться от перио́да засто́я – to be different from the period of stagnation
территориа́льный о́круг с ра́вной чи́сленностью избира́телей – territorial district
             with an equal amount of voters
избира́тельный о́круг – electoral district
общесою́зная организа́ция – all-union organization
обеспéчивать контро́ль за соотвéтствием зако́нов Конститу́ции – to provide
      control of correlation of laws and the Constitution

TEXT: Read the following text. Be able to translate it in written form.

Демократизáция нáшей жи́зни   Часть 1

Началóсь всенарóдное обсуждéние проéктов Закóнов об изменéниях и дополнéниях Конститýции (Основнóго закóна) СССР и о вы́борах нарóдных депутáтов СССР.

Cáмая характéрная чертá, котóрая отличáет сегóдняшний этáп обновлéния нáшего óбщества, состои́т в том, что миллиóны совéтских людéй вы́шли из состоя́ния апáтии и станóвятся на акти́вные граждáнские пози́ции. Важнéйшим рычагóм дальнéйшего подъёма э́той акти́вности нарóда, направлéния её в еди́ное созидáтельное рýсло должнá стáть рефóрма полити́ческой систéмы.

Почемý стал вопрóс об изменéниях и дополнéниях Конститýции? Зачéм понáдобился нóвый Закóн о вы́борáх нарóдных депутáтов СССР? Они при́званы сдéлать необрати́мым революциóнный процéсс перестрóйки. Дéло в том, что, в цéлом акти́вно рабóтая на социали́зм, нáши закóны не сумéли, как покáзывает óпыт, сопротивля́ться ря́ду серьёзнейших негати́вных явлéний, в котóрых мы справедли́во усмáтриваем коренны́е причи́ны переживáемых сегóдня óбществом трýдностей.

Ны́не существýющая полити́ческая систéма десятилéтиями приспосáбливалась не к организáции общéственной жи́зни на демократи́ческих началах, а прéжде всего к выполнéнию администрати́вных указáний. Для неё бы́ло характéрным всё бóльшее сосредотóчение управлéния в рукáх партийно-полити́ческого руковóдства и исполни́тельного аппарáта. Оказáлись безвлáстными Совéты нарóдных депутáтов. За недостáтком реáльных полномóчий рéзко ослáбла рабóта правоохрани́тельных óрганов. Сложи́лась пародоксáльная ситуáция, когдá и конститýция, и нáши закóны жи́ли как бы сáми по себé, а управлéнческая прáктика слéдовала своей лóгике администрати́вного произвóла.

И глáвное -- мы привы́кли к тому, что человéк исключáется из полити́ческой систéмы как основнóе дéйствующее лицó. Трибýнные заклинáния о народовлáстии, волюнтари́зм и субъективи́зм на прáктике, говори́льня о демократи́ческих институ́тах и реáльное попрáние норм социалисти́ческого óбраза жи́зни -- всё это были не едини́чные слýчаи в систéме руковóдства.

Дополнéния и изменéния Конститýции СССР, нóвый закóн о вы́борах обши́рны. Речь идёт по существý о полновлáстии нарóда. Дéятельность Совéтов нарóдных депутáтов, говори́тся в статьé 94 проéкта нóвого Закóна, бýдет отличáться от пери́ода застóя. Она бýдет стрóится на оснóве коллекти́вного, свобóдного, деловóго обсуждéния и решéния вопрóсов, глáсности, регуля́рной отчётности исполни́тельных и распоряди́тельных óрганов перед ни́ми и населéнием, широ́кого привлечéния к учáстию в их рабóте. Эта статья́, как, впрóчем, и други́е, значи́тельно расши́рена по сравнéнию с Конститýцией, при́нятой в 1977 годý.

Вы́сшим óрганом госудáрственной влáсти стáнет съезд нарóдных депутáтов СССР в состáве 2250 депутáтов: 750 депутáтов от территориáльных округóв с рáвной чи́сленностью избирáтелей, 750 депутáтов -- от национáльно-территориáльных избирáтельных округóв и 750 депутáтов -- от общесоюзных общéственных организáций. Съезд Совéтов будет собирáться для решéния важнéйших задáч ежегóдно. Други́ми бýдут структýра и фýнкции Верхóвного Совéта. Он стáнет

постоя́нно де́йствующим законода́тельным, распоряди́тельным и контро́льным о́рганом
госуда́рственной вла́сти СССР.

Возгла́вит рабо́ту Верхо́вного Сове́та и формиру́емого им Президиума Председа́тель Верхо́вного Сове́та СССР. Исключи́тельно ва́жное ме́сто в систе́ме вы́сших о́рганов вла́сти отво́дится Комите́ту конституцио́нного надзо́ра, кото́рый бу́дет избира́ться Съе́здом наро́дных депута́тов и обеспе́чивать контро́ль за соотве́тствием издава́емых зако́нов и постановле́ний прави́тельства, норма́тивных а́ктов други́х госуда́рственных о́рганов и обще́ственных организа́ций Конститу́ции.

Words and expressions to part 1

прое́кт зако́на об измене́ниях конститу́ции
                о   дополне́ниях (к) конститу́ции
                о   вы́борах наро́дных депута́тов
     попра́вки к конститу́ции - a draft of an amendment to the constitution

                (на что?)
станови́ться/стать   на акти́вные гражда́нские пози́ции
стано́вятся   ста́нут   ревизиони́стские
                   троцки́стские

                (чем?)
                важне́йшим рычаго́м перестро́йки - to become the engine of
                                       perestroika
                   регули́рования эконо́мики
                   контро́ля

при́зван,-а,-о,-ы   сде́лать необрати́мым - designed to make irreversible
                 рабо́тать на социали́зм
                 сле́довать демократи́ческим но́рмам

                (чему́?)
сопротивля́ться (no perf.)   негати́вным явле́ниям
      -ются   пережива́емым тру́дностям
                 парти́йному аппара́ту
сопротивле́ние
               (чему́?)
сле́довать (no perf.)   маркси́стским до́гмам
  -уют   указа́ниям све́рху
               тео́рии относи́тельности
               администрати́вным указа́ниям - to observe administrative
                                  prerogatives
                   (к чему́?)
приспоса́бливаться/приспосо́биться к выполне́нию указа́ний - to get adjusted to
       -ются   -ятся   directions from above
                  к произво́лу - to conform to lawlessness
приспосо́бленный
приспособле́ние

ока́зываться/оказа́ться   безвла́стным
     -ются ока́жутся   исключённым из полити́ческой систе́мы

                         (чего́?)
за недоста́тком   реа́льных полномо́чий
 (for lack of)   демокра́тии
                  полити́ческого контро́ля

                         (к чему́?)
приводи́ть/привести́   к попра́нию норм – to result in disregard of norms
приво́дят   приведу́т   засто́ю
                          регуля́рной отчётности (accountability)

приведённый
                         (от чего́?)
отлича́ться (no perf)   от исполни́тельных о́рганов – executive branches
     -ются   распоряди́тельных о́рганов – managerial branches
                            правоохрани́тельных о́рганов – law-enforcement agencies

отли́чие
                         (к чему́?)
привыка́ть/привы́кнуть   к бе́дности
     -ют   -ут   тру́дным усло́виям
                          наси́лию
                          говори́льне – to get used to hoopla
(past tense: привы́к, привы́кла,о,и)

на пра́ктике
                              (пе́ред кем?)
отчи́тываться/отчита́ться пе́ред   населе́нием
     -ются   -ются   па́ртией
                                  избира́телями
– to report back to the electorate

съезд   собира́ется   ежего́дно
пле́нум   ежеме́сячно
                           еженеде́льно

собира́ться/собра́ться
     -ются   -у́тся

ва́жное ме́сто отво́дится конституцио́нному надзо́ру – constitutional oversight is
                                                given an important place
                   избира́тельным округа́м – electoral districts are ...
                   Сове́там наро́дных депута́тов

о́круг (pl. округа́, округо́в)

отводи́ть/отвести́
отво́дят   отведу́т
отведённый

VOCABULARY EXERCISES

Look through the vocabulary for part 1 of the text «*Демократизация нашей жизни*». **Do the following exercises.**

A. **Give the nominative and genitive plural for the following nouns. Mark the stress.**

отчётность, дополнéние, конститýция, трýдность, óкруг, полномóчие, произвóл.

B. **Give perfective forms for the following verbs. Conjugate both forms and mark the stress.**

становúться, собирáться, приспосáбливаться, сопротивлáться.

C. **Paraphrase the italicized words.**

противостоáть трýдностям, *из-зá отсýтствия нýжного колúчества дéнег, в реáльной жúзни, отвечáть* перед нарóдом, *съезд встречáется раз в год, соблюдáть* нóрмы поведéния, *нарушéние* конститýции.

D. **Give the opposite for the italicized words.**

в теóрии, нарушáть демократúческие нóрмы, *подчинáться* сúле, *полновлáстный, прогрéсс.*

E. **Form verbs from the following nouns.**

приспособлéние к реáльности, сопротивлéние бюрокрáтии.

F. **Give Russian equivalents for the following English phrases.**

  - an important place is given to managerial bodies
  - to conform to lawlessness
  - resistance to bureaucracy
  - to work for socialism
  - amendments to the constitution
  - to convene annually
  - for lack of true authority
  - law enforcement agencies
  - flagrant disregard for norms of behavior
  - regular accountability of executive branches to councils

- to prove to be powerless
- a draft of legislation
- to assume an active role in electoral districts
- to observe administrative prerogatives
- to be different from stagnation

G. **Write sentences to fill in the blanks in each of the groups below. Be able to translate your sentences.**

                                                  (на какие позиции?)

1. Предыдущая администрация   встала на ______________________
    Активисты 60-х годов   встали   ______________________
    Третий мир   встал   ______________________

                        (к чему?)

2. Мир привык   ______________________
    Американцы не привыкли   ______________________
    Советские граждане привыкли   ______________________

                             (от чего?)

3. Политика разрядки отличается ______________________
    Соблюдение законов   ______________________
    Плановая система хозяйства   ______________________

                      (чему?)

4. Важно сопротивляться   ______________________
    Нельзя   ______________________
    Невозможно   ______________________

                             (сделало что?)

5. За недостатком средств   правительство ______________________
                энергии   ______________________
                власти   ______________________

                        (к чему?)

6. При Сталине   люди приспосабливались ______________________
    Во время войны   ______________________
           депрессии   ______________________

GRAMMAR EXERCISES: REVIEW OF CASES

Review the use of cases as presented in Circle One. Do the following exercises.

A. Determine the use of case in the sentences below. Fill in the blanks. Be able to translate the sentences into English.

1. Главная из (причины) _________ - ослепляющий антикоммунизм, из-за (который) _________ многие (страны) _________ не оказали (отпор) _________ фашизму.

2. За (первое полугодие) _________ новая система введена уже более чем в (четыре тысячи объединений и организаций) с общей численностью в (три миллиона человек) ________________.

3. Коммунисты выступают за (медицинское обслуживание и пенсии, доступные трудящемуся населению) ________________.

4. (Пребывание) _________ в лагерях он «искупил» свою вину перед (общество) _________.

5. Политический авантюризм тов. Ельцина имел целью противопоставить (московская партийная организация) ________________ (Центральный комитет КПСС) ______________.

6. Большое место в (дискуссия) _________ занял (вопрос) _________ о (созыв) _________ международной конференции под (эгида) _________ ООН.

7. Поощряемые (власти) _________ расисты бесчинствовали по (весь штат) _________.

8. (Идентичное обвинение) ____________ предъявлено (все аккредитованные в США советские корреспонденты) __________________.

9. США необходимо при (выработка политики) ____________ учитывать привлекательность для (западноевропейские союзники) _____________ советских предложений.

10. На афганской территории вдоль (граница) _________ с (Пакистан) _________ расположены пункты по приёму репатриантов.

B. Translate the following sentences.

1. The outspoken opponents of the reforms resisted the unavoidable weakening of political controls in the country.
2. The destruction of the Pershing-2 missiles is considered to be our international obligation.

3. In his television address yesterday the candidate stated that he will have to rely on financial support from the business sector in order to run for president in 2000.
4. The Kremlin is avoiding the policy of support for the Sandinista government.
5. A racist government plays on the prejudices of one race against another.
6. The convoy of ships was sailing slowly along the coastline of Kuwait.
7. The treaty provides for bilateral, on-site inspections.
8. At the emergency session of the U.N. Security Council not for the first time frictions among Council members emerged.
9. Before the Soviet Foreign Minister's trip to Latin America the Soviet Union had almost no relations with countries of that part of the world.
10. This action is similar to all previous incidents of interference by the Soviet Union in the internal affairs of Finland.
11. The Soviet Union celebrates the anniversary of the Revolution of 1917 on November 7.
12. The correspondent was wrong in his prediction of the outcome of the elections.

GRAMMAR EXERCISES: REVIEW OF IMPERFECTIVE VERBAL ADVERBS

Review the use of imperfective verbal adverbs as presented in Circle One, Lesson 5. Do the following exercises.

A. **Combine the following sentences by forming imperfective verbal adverbs from the italicized verbs.   Be able to translate your sentences into English.**

Example: Официальный Вашингтон *разглагольствует* на тему «борьбы с терроризмом».   Однако он ничего при этом не предпринимает.
 ⟶ *Разглагольствуя* на тему «борьбы с терроризмом», официальный Вашингтон ничего не предпринимает.

1. Пэт Робертсон *стремился* избавиться от представления о себе как о сугубо религиозном деятеле, и поэтому за день до выдвижения своей кандидатуры он сложил с себя сан баптистского священника.
2. Когда председатель государственного Комитета по использованию атомной энергии *отвечал* на вопросы журналистов, он подчеркнул серьёзность изучения последствий аварии на Чернобыльской АЭС.
3. В то время как парижский корреспондент «Правды» Вл. Большаков *анализирует* реакцию во Франции на советско-американскую договорённость по РСД, он делает следующий вывод.

4. Запад *пытался* помешать сближению Советской России и мусульманского Востока. Он развернул мощную пропагандистскую кампанию. Тем самым он *искажал* сущность советской политики по отношению к народам Востока.

5. США должны сознавать, что это долгосрочная политика, и *не выдвигать* при этом никаких нереалистических экономических надежд.

6. Так как ракета «Ланс» *является* оружием «двойного назначения», наряду с обычной она может быть оснащена ядерной боеголовкой.

7. Представитель Пентагона сообщил, что в ближайшее время *будет* задействована ещё одна плавучая база. При этом он *не называл* своего имени.

8. Поскольку участники семинара *не планируют* показать методику токсикологической оценки параметров этих химикатов, они осложняют заключение конвенции.

B. Translate the following sentences.

1. By adopting laws concerning changes and amendments to the constitution, Gorbachev hopes to make the perestroika process irreversible.

2. The government is trying to achieve more efficiency by giving an important place to managerial bodies.

3. While working for socialism, they failed to resist some serious negative phenomena.

4. Law enforcement agencies can prove effective without violating the rights of the people.

5. The party can once again assume an active role in society by convening plenums often.

6. When people submit to administrative prerogatives, they gradually stop playing an active role in the political system.

7. By presiding over the work of the Supreme Soviet, the Committee for Constitutional Oversight will assure compliance of executive branch with the constitution.

8. Nikita Khrushchev threatened the nomenclatura by refusing to protect its interests.

9. Hitler attacked the Soviet Union without a declaration of war.

10. The government is trying to achieve true reconciliation by appealing to the population to compromise.

SPEAKING EXERCISES

A.   Расскажи́те пе́рвую часть те́кста. В своём расска́зе испо́льзуйте сле́дующие
слова́.

итáк; важне́йшим фáктором явля́ется...; почему́ же...? дéло в том, что...; и
глáвное; таки́м óбразом, напримéр.

B.   Расскажи́те ту же часть с тóчки зрéния убеждённого сталини́ста.

C.   Отвéтьте на сле́дующие вопрóсы.

    1.   Почему́ потрéбовалась рефóрма полити́ческой системы в СССР?
    2.   Почему́ Совéты нарóдных депутáтов в прóшлом не игрáли реáльной
          рóли?
    3.   В чём бýдут состоя́ть фýнкции съéзда нарóдных депутáтов СССР?
    4.   Чем бýдет занимáться комитéт конституциóнного надзóра?
    5.   Кто бýдет возглавля́ть рабóту Верхóвного Совéта?

D.   Дополни́тельные вопрóсы. (optional)

    1.   Зачéм провóдится перестрóйка в СССР?
    2.   В чём смысл всенарóдного обсуждéния проéктов закóнов?
    3.   Оъясни́те значéние слóва «говори́льня» в дáнном контéксте.
    4.   Что такóе «волюнтари́зм» и «субъективи́зм»?

AUDIO-COMPREHENSION EXERCISE

part 2

Listen to the tape with the following questions in mind:

1. How are the Soviets (councils) being reorganized?
2. How will the system ensure that elected deputies will respond to the voters' needs?
3. What organizations will provide a third of the deputies to be elected?
4. What concrete measures are being adopted as the basis for the formation of a legally constituted socialist state?

Key words

возраста́ет роль – the role is growing
устраня́ть пара́дность – to eliminate "showing off"
спосо́бный проводи́ть в жизнь – capable of implementing
на осно́ве всео́бщего, ра́вного избира́тельного пра́ва при та́йном голосова́нии –
    based on universal, equal and direct suffrage with secret ballot
поднима́ть авторите́т суда́ – to increase the authority of the court

TEXT: Read the following text. Be able to translate it in written form.

Демократиза́ция на́шей жи́зни   Часть 2

В ко́рне меня́ется сама́ организа́ция рабо́ты Сове́тов всех ступене́й. Возраста́ет роль се́ссий, постоя́нных коми́ссий, депута́тов.   Устраня́ются пара́дность, параллели́зм в рабо́те, показно́е единогла́сие. Как говори́тся, вре́мя, когда́ в Сове́тах голосова́ли все «за» и сто́я, пусть оста́нется для пери́ода засто́я.   Недопусти́мо бо́льше терпе́ть, что́бы аппара́т, исполко́м подменя́ли представи́тельный о́рган, каки́м явля́ется Сове́т.
Рабо́та Сове́тов во мно́гом бу́дет зави́сеть от депута́тского ко́рпуса. В о́рганы вла́сти должны́ быть и́збраны лу́чшие представи́тели на́шего о́бщества, спосо́бные выража́ть и проводи́ть в жизнь интере́сы избира́телей.   Осуществи́ть это на де́ле помо́жет но́вый Зако́н о вы́борах наро́дных депута́тов СССР.   Они прово́дятся по одноманда́тным избира́тельным округа́м на осно́ве всео́бщего, ра́вного и прямо́го избира́тельного пра́ва при та́йном голосова́нии -- так гласи́т статья́ пе́рвая законопрое́кта.   Кро́ме того́, по но́рмам, устано́вленным Конститу́цией СССР, одна́ треть наро́дных депута́тов бу́дет избира́ться от общесою́зных обще́ственных организа́ций -- Коммунисти́ческой па́ртии Сове́тского Сою́за, профессиона́льных сою́зов, коoperatíвных организа́ций, Всесою́зного Ле́нинского Коммунисти́ческого Сою́за Молодёжи, объедине́ний же́нщин, ветера́нов войны́ и труда́, науч́ных рабо́тников, тво́рческих сою́зов и други́х со́зданных в устано́вленном зако́ном поря́дке обще́ственных организа́ций и объедине́ний гра́ждан СССР.

В опубликóванных законопроéктах определены́ конкрéтные меры по формировáнию социалисти́ческого правовóго госудáрства, перестрóйки рабóты правоохрани́тельных óрганов.   Поднимáется авторитéт судá, обеспéчивается незави́симость судéй и подчинéние их тóлько закóну.   Судьи всех судóв избирáются на срóк в дéсять, а нарóдные заседáтели в пять лет.   Они отвéтственны перед избирáтелями или избрáвшими их Совéтами нарóдных депутáтов, отчи́тываются пéред ни́ми и мóгут быть отóзваны в устанóвленном закóном порядке.

Words and expressions to part 2

устраня́ть/устрани́ть в кóрне показнóе единоглáсие - to root out phony
   -ют   -ят   unanimity
                              говори́льню - hoopla
устранённый   незави́симость судéй
устранéние   правовóе госудáрство
                          - legal state, a state based on the rule of law

проводи́ть/провести́ решéния пáртконферéнции в жизнь - to implement decisions
провóдят проведу́т пятилéтний план
                   предвы́борные обещáния

проведённый
проведéние

избирáть/избрáть
   -ют изберу́т
и́збранный
избрáние

на оснóве всеóбщего, рáвного и прямóго избирáтельного прáва

при тáйном голосовáнии - by secret ballot

в устанóвленном закóном   порядке - in the order established by law
                 Верхóвным судóм
                 конгрéссом

суд
судья́ (pl. су́дьи, судéй, су́дьям)
                     (чему́)
подчиня́ться/подчини́ться си́ле - to give in to force
   -ются   -ятся авторитéту

подчинённый
подчинéние   закóну

отзывáть/отозвáть судью́ - to remove from office
   -ют отзову́т

отзыва́ть/отозва́ть посла́ – to recall
ото́званный
отзы́в

VOCABULARY EXERCISES

Look through the vocabulary for part 2 of the text «*Демократиза́ция на́шей жи́зни*». **Do the following exercises.**

A. Give the nominative and genitive plural for the following nouns. Mark the stress.

суд, жизнь, реше́ние, судья́, посо́л, единогла́сие.

B. Give perfective forms for the following verbs. Conjugate both forms and mark the stress.

устраня́ть, подчиня́ться, избира́ть.

C. Paraphrase the italicized words.

уничто́жить незави́симость суде́й; *ненастоя́щее* единогла́сие; *осуществи́ть* реше́ния съе́зда па́ртии; план в 5 *лет*; обеща́ния, *сде́ланные пе́ред вы́борами*; в *усло́виях* та́йного голосова́ния, *верну́ть* посла́.

D. Give the opposite for the italicized words.

сла́бость; *разногла́сие*; госуда́рство *беспра́вия*.

E. Form verbs from the following nouns.

устране́ние говори́льни, подчине́ние авторите́ту, отзы́в судьи́.

F. Give Russian equivalents for the following English phrases.

  - a recalled ambassador
  - to eliminate false unanimity
  - by secret ballot
  - in a manner established by law
  - a state based on the rule of law
  - to remove a judge from office

- based on universal, equal, and direct suffrage
- subordination to law

G.   Write sentences to fill in the blanks in each of the groups below.   Be able to translate your sentences.

(что?)

1.   В правовóм госудáрстве в кóрне устраняются ___________
     При диктатýре пролетариáта   устраняется ___________
     ____

(чему?)

2.   Граждани́ну нýжно подчиня́ться ___________
     Не слéдует   ___________
     ____

(когó?)

3.   Пóсле разры́ва дипломати́ческих отношений   отзывáют ___________
     За неподчинéние закóну   отозвáли ___________
     ____

GRAMMAR EXERCISES: REVIEW OF PERFECTIVE VERBAL ADVERBS

Review the use of perfective verbal adverbs as presented in Circle One, Lesson 5. Do the following exercises.

A. Combine the following sentences by forming perfective verbal adverbs from the italicized verbs. Make necessary adjustments. Be able to translate your sentences into English.

> Example: Самолёты ВВС Ирака *поразили* «крупную морскую цель» у побережья Ирана и возвратились на свои базы.
>
>   —→ *Поразив* «крупную морскую цель» у побережья Ирана, самолёты ВВС Ирака вернулись на свои базы.

1. США *сконцентрировали* в районе Персидского залива крупнейшую со времён второй мировой войны военно-морскую группировку. Тем самым они обеспечили боевые операции американских вооружённых сил на международных морских коммуникациях.
2. Советский Союз *предложил* создание всемирной космической организации (ВКО). Тем самым он реализует конкретную программу сотрудничества.
3. Мусульманские народы *сбросили* с себя вековую спячку. Они приветствовали подъём большевизма.
4. Если *проинспектировать* один из американских кораблей, то можно установить, нарушают ли США один из трёх безъядерных принципов.
5. После того как Чжао Цзыян *коснулся* вопроса советско-китайских отношений, он сказал, что эти отношения в некоторой степени улучшились.
6. Сначала США *развернули* эти ракеты на территории Бельгии и Великобритании, а затем они приступили к размещению их на территории ФРГ, Италии и Нидерландов.
7. «Силы самообороны» сражались упорно. Они *потеряли* в боях 40 процентов личного состава.
8. Президент США *встретился* с вернувшимися из СССР государственным секретарём и помощником президента по национальной безопасности. В ходе совещания они обсудили итоги состоявшихся в Москве переговоров.

B. Translate the following sentences.

1. After recalling our ambassador, the Department of State warned Iran about the possible consequences.
2. The reform will fundamentally change the effectiveness of the Soviets by eliminating false unanimity and "hoopla".
3. After electing their own representatives into the Soviets, voters can expect a certain improvement in their standard of living.
4. By signing a peace treaty with Israel, President Anwar Sadat put Egypt in an almost ten-year isolation within the Arab world.

5. The president could not have come to power without supporting the military-industrial complex.
6. The parliament brought about a cabinet shake-up (перестановка) without declaring a war on the oil companies.
7. President Bush prevented a hostile takeover in Panama by sending troops there.
8. The government wants to enact new social programs without raising taxes.
9. The Kremlin leadership wants to boost the national income without introducing full privatization.

GRAMMAR EXERCISES: REVIEW OF SUBJUNCTIVE

Review the use of subjunctive as presented in Circle One, Lesson 6. Do the following exercises.

A. Analyze the following sentences and translate them into English.

1. Нужно ограничить размеры ежегодных платежей стран-должников так, чтобы это не причиняло ущерба интересам их социально-экономического развития.
2. Необходимо, чтобы общественность начала борьбу с протекционизмом.
3. СССР просит правительства других государств, чтобы морские и воздушные суда не заходили в эти районы и воздушное пространство над ними ежедневно с 6 до 19 часов по местному времени.
4. Пора, чтобы у нашей партии были и устав, и программа, которую её члены должны соблюдать.
5. Мы требуем от писателя как члена партии, чтобы он соблюдал её программу и устав.
6. Конгресс принял этот закон, чтобы все американские ведомства могли расширить борьбу против наркотиков.
7. Новое руководство хочет, чтобы китайско-американские отношения получили здоровое развитие.
8. В этом аспекте мы также желаем, чтобы США продолжали усилия во имя ещё более значительного развития экономического, торгового и технического сотрудничества между Китаем и США.
9. Желательно, чтобы США и СССР совместно способствовали смягчению международной обстановки.
10. Важно, чтобы договор по ракетам средней и меньшей дальности стал хорошей прелюдией к решению более крупной задачи.
11. Мы настаиваем на том, чтобы широкие массы американцев узнали «настоящую правду о Советском Союзе».
12. Сенатор Джексон ввёл свою поправку, чтобы разрядка в международных отношениях пришла к концу.

B. Substitute the infinitive after the verb «*хотеть*» with a subjunctive clause. Use the word in parentheses as the subject of your subordinate clause. Be able to translate both sentences into English.

Example: Он хочет восстановить американцев против СССР. (пресса)
      ⟶ Он *хочет, чтобы пресса восстановила* американцев против СССР.

1. Министр не хочет выступать в роли миротворца. (посол)
2. Члены парламента хотят установить хорошие отношения с Польшей. (министрество иностранных дел)
3. Военно-промышленный комплекс хочет проводить форсированную разработку СОИ. (Пентагон)
4. Войска противника хотят подорвать нашу ракетную установку. (партизаны)
5. Пресса не хочет манипулировать общественным мнением. (кандидаты)
6. Горбачёв хочет сделать необратимым процесс перестройки. (закон)

C. Substitute direct speech after the verb «*требовать*» with a subjunctive clause. Make necessary changes and be able to translate your sentences into English.

Example: Чёткий голос потребовал: «Оружие остается на виду!»
      ⟶ Чёткий голос *потребовал, чтобы оружие осталось* на виду.

1. Общественность требует: «Нужно изменить саму организацию работы Советов!»
2. Закон требует: «Выборы должны проводиться при тайном голосовании.»
3. Новая практика требует: «Судьи отзываются только в установленном законом порядке.»
4. Жизнь требует: «Человек не должен исключаться из политической системы как основное действующее лицо.»
5. Представители «Солидарности» требуют: «Нужно расширить полномочия профсоюзов.»

D. Substitute the infinitive of purpose in the sentences below with a subjunctive clause. Make necessary changes.

Example: Советский Союз делает все усилия, чтобы продвигать вперёд переговоры по ядерным и космическим вооружениям.
      ⟶ Советский Союз делает все усилия, *чтобы переговоры* по ядерным и космическим вооружениям *продвигались* вперёд.

1. Стороны встретились, чтобы достигнуть договорённости о глобальной ликвидации РСД и ОТР.
2. Западные державы посылают оружие в Афганистан, чтобы еще более накалить обстановку в этом районе.

3. Вашингтонские пропагандисты хитроумно манипулируют сознанием американцев, чтобы удерживать свое население на пути неверия в искренность Советского Союза.

4. Пентагон рассылает по всему миру свои войска, чтобы повсеместно осуществлять имперский курс США.

5. США гонится за военным превосходством над Советским Союзом, чтобы утвердить диктат и силу в международных отношениях.

6. Важно проявлять высокую революционную бдительность, чтобы отражать «психологические» атаки американских «крестоносцев» на советское общество.

7. Делегация СССР предпринимает усилия с тем, чтобы сделать единый текст из двух проектов.

E. Translate the following sentences.

1. It is desirable that both superpowers assume a more active role in arms control.

2. President Nixon wanted the U.S. to establish diplomatic relations with Communist China.

3. The new censorship prohibits printing the names of the accused so that the world will not know about new arrests.

4. Many developing countries want the industrialized world to provide the technical and economic assistance they need.

5. It is high time that the U.S. introduced an embargo on trade with South Africa.

6. The world public demands that the UN send its peace-keeping forces to the area of conflict.

7. The commander ordered the special forces to break the enemy's resistance within five hours.

8. The Deputy Minister asked that the American ambassador be present at the conference on arms reduction.

9. The Communist Party has rendered its support to the Social Democrats during the recent elections so that the communists would have seats in the new cabinet.

10. We want our newspapers to expose this regime as one with a fascist orientation.

GRAMMAR: ASPECT IN IMPERATIVES

A rule of thumb for the use of aspect in imperatives is as follows:

1. **Use perfective for affirmative commands:**

    Сообщи́те об э́том Козло́ву!

    Exceptions: Obviously, if the imperative refers to repeated action, or a process verb, use imperfective: Пиши́те ка́ждый день! Рабо́тайте! (process verb).

2. **Use imperfective for...**

    a.   Negative commands: Не расска́зывайте глу́постей!
              Exceptions: Не упади́те! Не забу́дьте!
    b.   Invitations: Пожа́луйста, заходи́те!

    Note that **не на́до** + imperfective infinitive is often used instead of a negative imperative: **не на́до расска́зывать!**

FIRST PERSON IMPERATIVES: "LET'S..."

    First person imperatives are formed by the construction:
Дава́йте + future of **мы:**
        Дава́йте посмо́трим.
        Дава́йте не бу́дем смотре́ть.

As you can see, both perfective and imperfective forms can be used.

    Russians often omit **бу́дем** in **дава́йте** constructions:
        Дава́йте не смотре́ть всё это сейча́с.

    The rules given for imperatives above apply to Дава́йте + future (let's) constructions, as shown in the examples above.

THIRD PERSON IMPERATIVES: "LET HIM, LET HER, LET THEM..."

    Third person imperatives are formed with **пусть** + third person verb of either aspect: Пусть Козло́в сообщи́т. Пусть Козло́в не сообща́ет.

    Again, the examples above show that the aspectual rules for imperative apply here.

GRAMMAR EXERCISES: ASPECT IN IMPERATIVES

Read through the explanation of aspect and imperative and then do the following exercises.

A. Negate the following commands, using direct imperative and не надо forms.

Example: Покажите ваш план! ⟶ *Не показывайте вашего плана!*
⟶ *Не надо показывать вашего плана!*

1. Спросите об этом!
2. Задайте свой вопрос!
3. Обратитесь к специалисту!
4. Подумайте об этом!
5. Решите этот вопрос сегодня же!
6. Рассмотрите это дело сейчас!
7. Отдайте их территорию!
8. Вернитесь на родину!
9. Объявите войну!
10. Помогите!

B. Now change the negative commands into affirmative ones.

1. Не передавайте этой информации!
2. Не оказывайте никакого сопротивления!
3. Не пользуйтесь своим правом голоса!
4. Не сообщайте о последних событиях!
5. Не делайте заявления!
6. Не начинайте бесед!
7. Не обсуждайте таких вопросов!
8. Не принимайте такого решения!
9. Не отвечайте на их вопрос!
10. Не возвращайте этих документов!

C. Make the sentences given in Exercises A and B above into affirmative "Let's" suggestions and negative "Let's" suggestions according to the model.

Example: Покажите ваш план! ⟶ *Давайте покажем наш план!*
⟶ *Давайте не будем показывать нашего плана!*

D. Make the sentences given in Exercises A and B above into affirmative "Let them" suggestions and negative "Let them" suggestions according to the model.

Example: Покажите ваш план! ⟶ *Пусть покажут наш план!*
⟶ *Пусть не показывают нашего плана!*

RENDERING

Explain the Bill of Rights, reproduced below, to a Soviet delegation. Included are the first ten amendments, as well as Amendment 13, which ended slavery, and the first sections of Amendments 14 and 15, which extended the guarantees of the Bill of Rights from the realm of the federal government to that of the individual states and also guaranteed voting rights.

Keep in mind that now, more than in any previous rendering exercise, you will have to circumlocate your way around difficulties.   Do not translate. Convey as much as you can, not what you can't.   You may want to add your own examples and commentary, depending on your personal interpretation of the U.S. Constitution:

Amendment 1. Congress shall make no law respecting an establishment of religion, or prohibiting the free exercise thereof; or abridging the freedom of speech, or of the press; or the right of the people peaceably to assemble, and to petition the government for a redress of grievances.

Amendment 2. A well-regulated militia, being necessary to the security of a free State, the right of the people to keep and bear arms, shall not be infringed.

Amendment 3. No soldier shall, in time of peace be quartered in any house, without the consent of the owner, nor in time of war, but in a manner to be prescribed by law.

Amendment 4. The right of the people to be secure in their persons, houses, papers, and effects, against unreasonable searches and seizures, shall not be violated, and no warrants shall issue but upon probable cause, supported by oath or affirmation, and particularly describing the place to be searched, and the persons or things to be seized.

Amendment 5. No person shall be held to answer for a capital, or otherwise infamous crime, unless on the presentment or indictment of a grand jury, except in cases arising in the land or naval forces, or the militia, when in actual service in time of war or public danger; nor shall any person be subject for the same offense to be twice put in jeopardy of life or limb; nor shall be compelled in any criminal case to be a witness against himself, nor be deprived of life, liberty, or property, without due process of law; nor shall private property be taken for public use, without just compensation.

Amendment 6. In all criminal prosecutions, the accused shall enjoy the right to a speedy and public trial by an impartial jury of the State and district wherein the crime shall have been committed, which districts shall have been previously ascertained by law, and to be informed of the nature and cause of the accusation; to be confronted with witnesses against him; to have compulsory process for obtaining witnesses in his favor, and to have the assistance of counsel for his defense.

Amendment 7. In suits at common law, where the value in controversy shall exceed twenty dollars, the right of trial by jury shall be preserved, and no fact tried by a jury, shall be otherwise re-examined in any court of the United States than according to the rules of common law.

Amendment 8. Excessive bail shall not be required, nor excessive fines imposed, nor cruel and unusual punishments inflicted.

Amendment 9. The enumeration in the Constitution of certain rights shall not be construed to deny or disparage others retained by the people.

Amendment 10. The powers not delegated to the United States by the Constitution, nor prohibited by it to the States, are reserved to the States respectively, or to the people.

Amendment 13. Neither slavery nor involuntary servitude, except as a punishment for crime whereof the party shall have been duly convicted, shall exist within the United States, or any place subject to their jurisdiction.

Amendment 14. Section 1. All persons born or naturalized in the United States and subject to the jurisdiction thereof, are citizens of the United States and of the State wherein they reside. No State shall make or enforce any law which shall abridge the privileges or immunities of citizens of the United States; nor shall any State deny any person of life, liberty, or property, without due process of law; nor deny any person within its jurisdiction the equal protection of the laws.

Amendment 15.   Section 1.   The right of citizens of the United States to vote shall not be denied or abridged by the United States or any state on account of race, color, or previous condition of servitude.

Words you may need:

bail – де́ньги на поручи́тельство
give testimony; be a witness – дава́ть показа́ние
grand jury – "большо́е жюри́".   But most Russians don't know what that is.   Be
    prepared to explain.
jury (members) – прися́жные заседа́тели.   (Note that with the exception of the
    specialized term «большо́е жюри́» given above, «жюри» usually refers to a
    judging panel in a competition.)
suit at common law = civil suit – гражда́нский иск
trial by jury – суд прися́жных заседа́телей
witness – свиде́тель
    call witnesses – вызыва́ть / вы́звать (вы́зовут) свиде́телей

SPEAKING EXERCISES

A.   Расскажи́те втору́ю часть те́кста. В своём расска́зе испо́льзуйте сле́дующие выраже́ния.

...в ко́рне меня́ется; вре́мя, когда́..., ко́нчилось; во-пе́рвых,...во вторы́х... кро́ме того́; таки́м о́бразом.

B.   Расскажи́те весь текст с то́чки зре́ния сторо́нника бо́лее радика́льных рефо́рм.

C.   Отве́тьте на сле́дующие вопро́сы.

1.   Каки́е о́рганы узурпи́ровали власть, кото́рая должна́ была́ принадлежа́ть Сове́там?
2.   Как бу́дут избира́ться наро́дные депута́ты?
3.   В чём суть конце́пции социалисти́ческого правово́го госуда́рства?

D.   Дополни́тельные вопро́сы. (optional)

1.   Прокомменти́руйте фра́зу: «голосу́ют все «за» и сто́я».
2.   Наско́лько незави́сим сове́тский суд?
3.   Опиши́те отноше́ния ме́жду исполни́тельной, законода́тельной и суде́бной вла́стью в СССР.
4.   Опиши́те отноше́ния ме́жду э́тими властя́ми в США.

READING EXERCISE

Ни опровергнуть, ни подтвердить...   Николай Португалов

PRE-TEXT: The author is a prominent Soviet political observer who is a frequent contributor to the weekly *Moscow News*. This article deals with the issue of defense spending in the Soviet Union. Read the text with the following questions in mind. Compare your expectations with the answers you find in the text. Answer the questions in written form.

1.   What is the main idea of the article?

PARAGRAPH 1

2.   The West German Defense Minister made an observation that...(mark the correct answer):
   a.   there are serious discrepancies between the Soviet political posture and its actual behavior in the world arena.
   b.   there exist serious discrepancies between Soviet political posture and its military might.

3.   How did the West German minister substantiate this observation?
4.   The West German Minister made this observation... (true or false for each item):
   a.   on T.V.
   b.   in the German press.
   c.   in a speech.
   d.   in the Soviet press.

PARAGRAPH 2

5.   What is suggested as the source of this information?

PARAGRAPH 3

6.   Soviet observers did not refute this claim because... (mark the correct answer):
   a.   it was an obvious misrepresentation.
   b.   this subject was taboo for open discussion.
   c.   Soviet military observers have no access to this information.

7.   The Soviet Union is prepared to disclose such information...(check the correct answer):
   a.   in the West.
   b.   in the Soviet press.
   c.   at the Warsaw Pact meeting.
   d.   at the negotiating table.

PARAGRAPH 4

8.   According to Kohl's colleagues, what can affect the final decision about the modernization of the NATO countries' tactical nuclear forces?

PARAGRAPH 6
9. What is said to be an obvious difference between the Soviet military-industrial complex and that of the West?
10. There are reasons why the Soviet generals and defense producers can be called an interest group. Name three.

PARAGRAPGS 7,8
11. Compare the process of control over the military-industrial complex in today's Soviet Union with that in Western democracies.

PARAGRAPH 9
12. The author wants to be able to discuss publicly...(true or false for each item):
   a. design specifications of new systems.
   b. numbers of new weapons.
   c. defense budget.
   d. strategical planning.

13. How did the Soviet side know about the defense capabilities and defense budget of the West during the Cold War?

PARAGRAPH 10
14. What does the author of the article expect from Soviet parliamentary reform?

POST-TEXT (using context):

PARAGRAPH 1
1. This paragraph proceeds from...(mark the correct answer):
   a. statement to illustration;
   b. examples to statement.

2. What is the English for подкрепи́ть утвержде́ние приме́ром?

PARAGRAPH 2
3. To what do the words Это изве́стный те́зис... refer?
4. Explain the composition of the word разведда́нные. What does the first part of the word stand for?

PARAGRAPH 3
5. The tone of this paragraph is...(mark the correct answer):
   a. humorous
   b. upbeat
   c. dramatic
   d. neutral

Find the word(s) which confirm your point.

6. Find the antonym for опроверга́ть. Form a noun from it.

PARAGRAPH 4

7. Which marker(s) signal(s) that this paragraph is contrasted to paragraph 3?

PARAGRAPH 5

8. What does ВПК stand for?

PARAGRAPH 6

9. This paragraph...(mark the correct answer):
    a. is a shift to another topic
    b. supports the previous point

10. Find the English equivalents for:

    - гру́ппы влия́ния
    - положа́ ру́ку на се́рдце

PARAGRAPH 7

11. This paragraph...(mark the correct answer):
    a. indicates a shift to another subject
    b. is a support of the previous point.

    Find the word(s) which confirm your answer.

PARAGRAPH 8,9

12. Find the markers which indicate the author's frustration with the absence of public control over the Soviet defense budget.
13. Does the expression гла́сность теря́ет го́лос have a literal meaning or is it a figure of speech? Are the words гла́сность and го́лос related?
14. Find a synonym for «ежего́дно».

PARAGRAPH 9

15. The author argues that public discussion of matters of defense spending is safe. Which two examples does he use?
16. The overall tone of the entire article is...(mark the correct answer):
    a. reserved
    b. optimistic
    c. bitter
    d. neutral

17. Find Russian equivalents for:

    - design specifications
    - combat characteristics

18. Make a list of military terminology which is new to you. Find English equivalents for each expression.

19. Find the meaning of the words below in the text:

из за́падных уст

   a. from Western regulations
   b. from Western lips
   c. from Western sources

оглаша́ть секре́ты

   a. to mute secrets
   b. to make secrets public.

Ни опровергнуть, ни подтвердить...

Николай ПОРТУГАЛОВ

НЕДАВНО на страницах «МН» министр обороны ФРГ Р. Шольц писал: «В СССР... существуют серьезные расхождения между заявлениями о политических намерениях и развитием военной мощи». В своей речи в Академии бронетанковых войск в Москве в дни визита в СССР канцлера ФРГ Коля министр повторил, что нынешняя советская политика вооружений вызывает озабоченность, и подкрепил это утверждение конкретным примером, заявив, что в СССР с 1984 по 1986 год ежегодно вводилось в строй около 1600 танков, то есть за три года почти столько же новых танков, сколько их имеет на вооружении ФРГ.

Это известный тезис, повторяемый с вариациями ведущими западными политиками. Западные средства массовой информации, публикуя подобные данные, ссылаются на разведданные Пентагона, на анализы институтов стратегических исследований...

В выступлениях Р. Шольца было немало других положений, вызывавших у нас обоснованные возражения. Но вот данные о выпуске наших танков советские наблюдатели нигде не опровергали.

И немудрено — они не в состоянии ни опровергнуть, ни подтвердить их, как, впрочем, и любые приводимые Западом данные о масштабах нашего военного производства и военных расходах. Никому из них эти данные неизвестны и получить их они не могут. Остается лишь говорить, что данные Пентагона сомнительны, а институты могут и ошибаться. «Так-то оно так,— ответствуют западные оппоненты, — но приведите свои данные сами». «Нет, не можем!» Это государственная тайна, известная лишь крайне узкому кругу наших военных и оборонно-промышленных руководителей. Обменяться данными о вооружениях на переговорах — к этому мы готовы, но огласить сведения о количестве выпускаемых боевых систем и затраченных на них миллиардах — ни боже мой.

Между тем в те же дни пребывания Коля в Москве видные эксперты из его сопровождения говорили, что окончательное решение вопроса о модернизации тактического ядерного оружия в европейских странах НАТО будет зависеть от прогресса на предстоящих переговорах о сокращении войск и вооружений в Европе и в не меньшей степени — от готовности СССР ограничить производство наступательных систем, в частности танков. «Как вы уладите это дело с вашим военно-промышленным комплексом — ваша проблема»,— заметил один из моих собеседников из ФРГ.

«Ваш ВПК»... Полно, да существует ли он? Вопрос — закономерный, даже если и советские эксперты нет-нет да и произносят эти слова: «...наш ВПК».

over

Сразу же напрашивается весьма веское возражение: наши генералы и руководители оборонной промышленности прибылей от продажи оружия государству не получают. Различие тут с Западом радикальное. Но, положа руку на сердце — разве влияние на внутреннюю и внешнюю политику, на весь экономический процесс и, что, пожалуй, самое главное — возможность беспрепятственно расходовать астрономические суммы не достаточно прочный цемент, способный спаять влиятельную «группу давления» с ее специфическими интересами, в чем-то отличными от интересов экономики в целом?

Тема эта широка, и хотелось бы поставить лишь один вопрос — об ограниченности возможностей общества контролировать расходование средств на военные цели под покровом абсолютной тайны. В самом деле, военные расходы на Западе находятся под контролем парламентов. Данные о запланированных боевых системах и о расходах на них — предмет открытых обсуждений в выборных органах и в прессе. Конечно, западные ВПК в борьбе за ассигнования умудряются объегоривать парламенты. Но им и в голову не придет поставить под вопрос право законодателей публично контролировать военные расходы страны.

А у нас? Гласность сразу же теряет голос, когда речь заходит о военных расходах и военном производстве. В бюджете они стабильно определяются почти традиционной суммой в 20,2 млрд. рублей в год — против примерно 300 млрд. долларов в США. Правда, мы уже признали, что это лишь часть расходов на «обеспечение обороноспособности».

А, быть может, стоит, все же сейчас назвать хотя бы примерную цифру реальных военных расходов? Но это о бюджете. А что же говорить о количестве планируемых систем оружия, тех же танков, например. «Сгинь, нечистая сила!» — скажут, поди, некоторые. Это же военная тайна! Но разве при этом оглашаются действительные военные секреты: конструкционные особенности и боевые характеристики наших систем? И почему даже в период «холодной войны» наши потенциальные противники и не думали урезать контрольные права своих парламентов? И нам из западных уст было известно, сколько тех или иных боевых систем намеревались выпустить на Западе и во сколько это обойдется налогоплательщикам.

Представляется, что открытый контроль законодателей за военными расходами и масштабами военного производства является неотъемлемой чертой народовластия в социалистическом правовом государстве и что это найдет свое выражение в ходе проходящей у нас грандиозной парламентской реформы.

AUDIO-COMPREHENSION EXERCISE

part 1

You will now hear a text about French elections. Review the key words below. Then listen to the text with the following questions in mind. Afterwards, listen to the text again, and write down the answers.

1. What do you already know about French politics? Does France have a parliamentary or congressional system of government? How is the president selected? What about the prime-minister? Where is Francois Mitterand on the political spectrum? What party does he represent? Who is Le Pen?
2. When did the French elections take place?
3. What positions were up for grabs?
4. Who won? How many seats did the losers take?
5. Do the results represent a change from the status quo?
6. How many seats make up the national legislature?
7. What do Mitterand and the right-wing parties have to agree on?
8. According to the report, was the victory of now-majority coalition absolute?
9. Name three representatives of the winning coalition.
10. How many seats did the winning coalition take? Was that a wide margin of victory?
11. Which party has the largest single block of seats? How many?
12. How many seats do the Communists control? What about the centrist parties?
13. How many seats does Le Pen control? Why is that significant?

Key words

Национа́льное собра́ние – National Assembly
региона́льные сове́ты – regional councils
принести́ успе́х – to bring success
взя́ться за по́иск согласо́ванного реше́ния – to begin the search for a balanced
decision
соста́в прави́тельства – composition of government
отража́ть сдвиг впра́во – to reflect a shift to the right

TEXT: Read the text below. Be able to translate it in written form.

Фра́нция по́сле вы́боров   Часть 1

Пари́ж, 17. (Соб. корр. «Пра́вды»). Состоя́вшиеся 16 ма́рта во Фра́нции вы́боры в Национа́льное собра́ние и региона́льные сове́ты принесли́ успе́х пра́вым си́лам. Они́ завоева́ли большинство́ парла́ментских мест и посто́в сове́тников, убеди́в избира́телей в свое́й спосо́бности попра́вить экономи́ческое положе́ние в стране́. Пра́вящая социалисти́ческая па́ртия, кото́рая с 1981 го́да облада́ла абсолю́тным большинство́м в Национа́льном собра́нии, на э́тот раз смогла́ провести́ вме́сте с ле́выми группиро́вками в вы́сший законода́тельный о́рган (состоя́щий из 577 депута́тов) 216 свои́х кандида́тов. Этому в значи́тельной сте́пени способ́ствовала но́вая вы́годная для социали́стов избира́тельная систе́ма.

До второ́го апре́ля, когда́ состои́тся пе́рвое заседа́ние Национа́льного собра́ния но́вого соста́ва, президе́нту респу́блики Ф. Миттера́ну и руководи́телям пра́вых па́ртий парла́ментского большинства́ предстои́т взя́ться за непросто́й по́иск согласо́ванного реше́ния относи́тельно кандидату́ры премье́р-мини́стра, а возмо́жно, и самого́ соста́ва бу́дущего прави́тельства.

Сложи́вшаяся в центра́льном прави́тельстве и на места́х расстано́вка сил, хотя́ и отража́ет о́бщий сдвиг впра́во, тем не ме́нее остаётся насто́лько сло́жной, что да́же ли́деры одержа́вших побе́ду па́ртий избега́ют дава́ть ей однозна́чную оце́нку.

Коали́ция пра́вых оппозицио́нных сил, в кото́рую входи́ли Объедине́ние в подде́ржку респу́блики (Ж. Шира́к) и Сою́з за францу́зскую демокра́тию (Жиска́р д'Эсте́н и Р. Барр), а та́кже кандида́ты, избира́вшиеся по спи́ску «разли́чные пра́вые», получи́ла 291 манда́т, то есть на два бо́льше, чем необходи́мо для абсолю́тного большинства́.

Среди́ парла́ментских групп социалисти́ческая па́ртия сохраня́ет пе́рвое ме́сто, а коммунисти́ческая с её 35 депута́тами идёт сле́дом за ОПР и СФД. Профаши́стский «национа́льный фронт» Ле Пе́на, вполне́ проби́вшийся в вы́сший законода́тельный о́рган, получи́л 34 ме́ста.

Words and expressions to part 1

		(куда́?)
всео́бщие вы́боры		в Национа́льное собра́ние
состоя́вшиеся		региона́льные сове́ты
неда́вние		о́рганы ме́стного самоуправле́ния
		– local government

		(кому́?)
вы́боры принесли́	успе́х	пра́вым си́лам – elections brought success to the right
	побе́ду	це́нтру
	пораже́ние	ле́вым группиро́вкам
		агра́рной па́ртии

приноси́ть/принести́
прино́сят   принесу́т
принесённый

завоёвывать/ большинство   парла́ментских мест при голосова́нии
      -ют   посто́в сове́тников
завоева́ть   голосо́в
завою́ют   манда́тов
завоёванный

го́лос (pl. голоса́, голосо́в)

ме́сто (pl. места́, ме́ст, места́ми)
                                    (в   чём?)
убежда́ть/убеди́ть   в   свое́й спосо́бности
    -ют   -ят   невино́вности – to convince of one's innocence
                                  необходи́мости програ́ммы СОИ

убеждённый
              (чем?)
облада́ть   абсолю́тным большинство́м
    -ют
(no perf)
облада́ние
              (чему́?)
благодаря́   но́вой избира́тельной систе́ме
               расстано́вке сил на места́х – local balance of power
               вы́годной сде́лке
               нало́говому послабле́нию – owing to tax leniency

                                       (куда́?)
проводи́ть/провести́ свои́х   кандида́тов   в сена́т
прово́дят   проведу́т   сторо́нников
                             ста́вленников в ЦК
                                           в ме́стные комите́ты

проведённый
                          (чему́?)
спосо́бствовать (no perf)   успе́ху на вы́борах
    -уют   реше́нию пробле́мы

состоя́лось пе́рвое заседа́ние но́вого прави́тельства
                           Сове́та национа́льной безопа́сности но́вого соста́ва

(кому́?)   (что?)
президе́нту   предстои́т   по́иск согласо́ванного решения
    – the president will have to find a balanced decision
руково́дству   реше́ние пробле́мы до́лга

                                 (сде́лать что?)
секретарю́ райко́ма   найти́ согласо́ванное реше́ние
па́ртии   реши́ть пробле́му госуда́рственного до́лга

		(за что?)
бра́ться/	за	непросто́й по́иск
беру́тся		перестро́йку – to undertake a perestroika
взя́ться		
возьму́тся		

сложи́вшаяся   расстано́вка сил   отража́ет о́бщий сдвиг впра́во
   – the current situation reflects a general move to the right
настоя́щая   ситуа́ция в стране́   вле́во
существу́ющая   недово́льство – discontent
                                             но́вую тенде́нцию

отража́ть/отрази́ть
    –ют   –я́т
отражённый
отраже́ние

	(де́лать что?)
избега́ть/избежа́ть	дава́ть однозна́чную оце́нку – to avoid a simple evaluation
–ют избегу́т	уча́ствовать в вы́борах

          (чего́?)
          неоднозна́чной оце́нки
          уча́стия в вы́борах

	(как?)
избира́ть(ся)	по спи́ску... – to be elected on the slate of...
–ются	единоду́шно
	большинство́м в 3 го́лоса
и́збранный	25 про́тив 24

сохраня́ть/сохрани́ть	пе́рвое ме́сто
–ют –я́т	второ́е
сохранённый	

получа́ть/получи́ть	20 мест
–ют полу́чат	10 манда́тов
полу́ченный	

	(куда́?)
выходи́ть/вы́йти	на пе́рвое ме́сто – to come in first
	после́днее

	(за ке́м?)
идти́ сле́дом за	неофаши́стами – to follow behind neo-fascists
	лейбори́стами

	(куда́?)
пробива́ться/проби́ться	в вы́сший законода́тельный о́рган
–ются пробью́тся	госаппара́т – to make it to government
	Бе́лый дом

пробива́ться/проби́ться   (к чему́?)
                                      к вла́сти – to make it to power
                                         деньга́м – to become rich
                                         вхо́ду – to elbow one's way to the entrance

VOCABULARY EXERCISES

Look through the vocabulary for part 1 of the text «*Фра́нция по́сле вы́боров*».
Do the following exercises.

A.   **Give the nominative and genitive plural for the following nouns. Mark the
stress.**

пост, го́лос, прави́тельство, сде́лка, заседа́ние, ме́сто, спи́сок.

B.   **Give perfective forms for the following verbs. Conjugate both forms and
mark the stress.**

пробива́ться, отража́ть, облада́ть, завоёвывать, бра́ться.

C.   **Paraphrase the italicized words.**

настоя́щая расстановка сил, *победи́ть* на вы́борах, *избра́ть* в *секретари́*
райко́ма, *во вре́мя* голосова́ния, *получи́ть* 200 манда́тов, *име́ть* абсолю́тное
большинство́, *помо́чь пройти́* свои́м кандида́там, ситуа́ция *пока́зывает* о́бщий
сдвиг впра́во, *единогла́сно*, *пройти́* в сена́т.

D.   **Give the opposite for the italicized words.**

принести́ *успе́х*, *предстоя́щие* вы́боры, *законода́тельный* о́рган, *побе́да*,
многозна́чный, избира́ться *индивидуа́льно*.

E.   **Form verbs out of the following nouns. Make necessary changes.**

облада́ние большинство́м голосо́в, отраже́ние расстано́вки сил.

F.   **Give Russian equivalents for the following English phrases.**

   – to run on the slate
   – balanced decision
   – recent elections

- current situation
- tax relief
- secretary of the regional party committee
- owing to regional balance of power
- elections for the office of president
- to enjoy absolute majority
- to avoid simple evaluations
- to win the majority of seats
- new NSC
- to come in first
- to make it to the Supreme Court

G. **Write sentences to fill in the blanks in each of the groups below. Be able to translate your sentences.**

                          (куда́?)   (кому́?)

1.   Всео́бщие   выборы __________ принесли́ успе́х ___________

       Неда́вние   __________   ___________

       Состоя́вшиеся   __________   ___________

                                                    (в чём?)

2.   Кандида́ты всегда убежда́ют избира́телей   ___________

       Президе́нт Ни́ксон убеждал общественность   ___________

       Пентаго́н убеждал Конгресс   ___________

                          (чем?)

3.   Избира́тели   облада́ют _____________

       Неофаши́сты   _____________

       Глава́ па́ртии облада́ет _____________

                                            (благодаря́ чему́?)

4.   Консерва́торы завоева́ли большинство́ мест _____________

                                          ____

                                          ____

                              (чему́?)

5.   Высо́кие учётные ста́вки спосо́бствуют ___________

       Инфля́ция спосо́бствует   ___________

       Высо́кий у́ровень жи́зни спосо́бствует   ___________

                            (чего́?)

6.   Состоя́лось пе́рвое заседа́ние   __________ но́вого соста́ва

                                     ____

                                     ____

(что?)

7. Безрабо́тица   отража́ет ____________
    Пораже́ние в войне́   ____________
    Перестро́йка в СССР   ____________

(чего?)

8. Администра́ция избега́ет ____________

                             ____

                             ____

Change the sentences above using: избега́ть **+ imperfective infinitive**

(кому́?)

9. ____________________ предстои́т перестро́ить систе́му руково́дства.
    ____________________   реши́ть пробле́му бездо́мных.
    ____________________   провести́ нало́говую рефо́рму.
    ____________________   вы́ступить пе́ред наро́дом.

Change the sentences above using: предстоя́ть **+ noun**

(куда́?)

10. Но́вый   президе́нт провёл свои́х сторо́нников ____________
             премье́р   ____________
             генера́льный секрета́рь   ____________

(куда́?)

11. Неофаши́сты проби́лись ____________
     Коммуни́сты   ____________
     «Зелёные»   ____________

H. Translation.

1. Due to the regional balance of power, the Labor Party received an extra 30 seats.
2. The candidate won a majority of votes by pursuing the interests of his constituency.
3. The new composition of Parliament threatens the effectiveness of minor parties.
4. Inasmuch as he enjoys an absolute majority in the South, it will be easy for him to bring in his candidates.
5. A large group left the coalition of right-wing forces, which reflected a general shift to the left.
6. What is the attitude of the specialists to the new plan to reduce the national debt?
7. The Democrats have to be well prepared for the forthcoming elections.

GRAMMAR EXERCISES: REVIEW OF CASES

Review the use of cases as presented in Circle One.   Do the following exercises.

A.   Determine the use of case in the sentences below.   Fill in the blanks. Be able to translate the sentences into English.

1.   Они передумали и отказываются встречаться с (советский представитель) ______________.

2.   Запущенная с (надводный корабль) ______________ ракета пролетела свыше (800 километров) ______________ до (заданный район) ______________.

3.   Новое политическое мышление могло бы способствовать (окончательная выработка) ______________ текста конвенции.

4.   Силы второго эшелона передвинулись под (прикрытие) ______________ артиллерии.

5.   Он отказался говорить про (аппаратура) ______________ американского и японского происхождения, (находящаяся) ______________ за (фанерная перегородка) ______________.

6.   Только (усиление) ________ гарантий прав граждан мы сможем углубить нашу демократию.

7.   Несколько (направляющиеся) ______________ на родину (беженцы) ________ было задержано.

8.   Они навязывают (советские журналисты) ______________________ ультимативно (самые дорогие транспортные билеты) ______________.

9.   Специалисты из Пентагона стоят за (срочная «модификация») ______________ устаревших радаров на (Британские острова) ________.

10.   В (ход) ________ нынешнего процесса представители компаний упорно твердят, что им ничего не известно про (шпионское оборудование) ______________.

B.   Translate the following sentences.

1.   Developing countries are rarely grateful to the U.S. for its economic assistance to them.
2.   For the first time since the coup d'etat the authorities ordered the police to fire upon a peaceful demonstration.
3.   Frictions within the Warsaw Pact did not exist.

4. The surprise defeat convinced the leadership of the need to buy new Soviet anti-aircraft systems.
5. Russia today, as in previous centuries, still trades in raw materials.
6. Brazil was denied a $5 billion credit.
7. Islamic fundamentalists believe in Western technology but they do not believe in Western ideas.
8. During the war they got accustomed to poverty.
9. Journalists are not allowed to write about morning cabinets meetings.
10. This machine is radically different from the Soviet planes of the 70s.

GRAMMAR EXERCISE: REVIEW OF CONDITIONAL CLAUSES

Review the use of Conditional clauses as presented in Circle One, Lesson 6. Do the following exercise.

Translate the following real condition clauses into English. Change them into clauses of unreal condition. Translate them into English.

Examples: *Если* зарплата трудящихся значительно *возрастёт*, то многие *захотят* выкупить свои государственные квартиры.
→ *If* the salaries *increase* dramatically, many people *will want* to purchase their state-owned apartments.

Если бы зарплата значительно *возросла*, то многие *захотели бы* выкупить свои государственные квартиры.
→ *Were* the salaries *to increase* dramatically, many *would like* to purchase their state-owened apartments.

1. *Если* представитель в КОКОМ *примет* строгие меры против «технобандитов», то западные компании, которые порываются торговать с СССР, *не смогут* этого делать.
2. *Если* в ряде западноевропейских стран *не возьмёт* верх здравый смысл в отношении поставок оборудования Советскому Союзу, то они *потеряют* на этом много денег.
3. Против западногерманских фирм *будут приняты* «жёсткие меры», *если* они всё ещё *намереваются* воспротивиться американскому нажиму.
4. Наследие «холодной войны» *будет* искусственно *сохраняться*, *если* Пентагон *расширит* список запрещённых к экспорту товаров.
5. *Если* Советский Союз *будет продолжать* имперскую политику по отношению к своим соседям, то дискриминационные препятствия в торговле западных стран с социалистическими странами ещё более *усилятся*.
6. Мы *получим* данные о распределении жилья, *если будет проведена* жилищная перепись.
7. *Если останется* табу на политические реформы, то это *погубит* все попытки экономических преобразований.

8. Наше общество *начнёт* приходить в движение, *если* в душе каждого *исчезнет* страх.

9. *Если будет существовать* серьёзная общественная критика крупных проектов, то *не будет* безнравственного отношения к природным богатствам.

10. *Если* учёные и инженеры *поверят* в свою силу, то они *увидят* возможность победы в борьбе за свои убеждения.

SPEAKING EXERCISES

A.   Расскажи́те пе́рвую часть те́кста. В ва́шем расска́зе испо́льзуйте сле́дующие выраже́ния.

итáк; при э́том; вот почему́; возмо́жно, что...;

B.   Расскажи́те э́ту часть те́кста от лица́ представи́теля Объедине́ния в подде́ржку респу́блики.

C.   Сумми́руйте часть 1 в двух-трёх предложе́ниях.

D.   Отве́тьте на сле́дующие вопро́сы.

1.   Каки́е вы́боры состоя́лись во Фра́нции?
2.   Кому́ они́ принесли́ успе́х?
3.   Ско́лько депута́тов смогла́ провести́ пра́вящая па́ртия?
4.   Почему́ президе́нту предстои́т непроста́я зада́ча?
5.   Каки́е па́ртии вхо́дят в коали́цию пра́вых сил?
6.   Ско́лько необходи́мо получи́ть манда́тов для абсолю́тного большинства́?
7.   Кака́я па́ртия сохраня́ет пе́рвое ме́сто среди́ парла́ментских групп?
8.   На како́м ме́сте коммунисти́ческая па́ртия?
9.   Кака́я па́ртия получи́ла 34 ме́ста?

E.   Дополни́тельные вопро́сы. (optional)

1.   Объясни́те ра́зницу ме́жду Национа́льным собра́нием и региона́льными сове́тами.
2.   Как результа́ты вы́боров мо́гут отража́ть сдви́ги впра́во (вле́во)?
3.   Что зна́чит избира́ться по спи́ску «разли́чные пра́вые»?

AUDIO–COMPREHENSION EXERCISE

part 2

Listen to the tape with following in mind:

1. The report says that many French voters failed to go to the polls. A number of reasons for such apathy were cited. Name at least two.
2. How did the French Communist Party explain the election results?
3. What did *Humanité* hint about the strategy of the French socialists?
4. What course of action did the Communists call for?

Key words

обострившийся кризис – an aggravated crisis
ответственность за неуспéх ложится на – responsibility for failure lies with
отстранить коммунистов от политической жизни – to remove the communists from
political life
борьбá в защиту своих прав – struggle in defense of one's rights

TEXT: Read the following text. Be able to translate it in written form.

Фрáнция пóсле вы́боров.   Часть 2

Обострившийся экономический кризис, в пéрвую óчередь рост мáссовой безрабóтицы, снижéние жи́зненного у́ровня, обострéние социáльных противорéчий в хóде реализáции правительством политики «жёсткой эконóмии» и други́х усту́пок кру́пному капитáлу и прáвым си́лам, факти́ческое налáживание за послéдние гóды «сосуществовáния» мéжду социалисти́ческой и прáвыми буржуáзными пáртиями в антирабóчих и други́х áкциях привели́ к тому́, что миллиóны францу́зов отказáлись учáствовать в ны́нешних вы́борах.   Други́е отдáли голосá поднимáющим гóлову ультрапрáвым си́лам. Оши́блись в свои́х прогнóзах те, кто говори́л, что францу́зы не бу́дут голосовáть за прáвых экстреми́стов.

В заявлéнии Политбюрó Францу́зской коммунисти́ческой пáртии отмечáется, что ответственность за неуспéх лéвых сил ложи́тся в пéрвую óчередь на социалисти́ческую пáртию. Вмéсте с тем, укáзывает газéта «Юманитé», éсли бы не провали́лись плáны отстрани́ть коммунистов от полити́ческой жи́зни, то это бы́ло бы плóхо не тóлько для просты́х францу́зских семéй, но и в цéлом для Фрáнции.

Итáк, говори́тся в заявлéнии Политбюрó ФКП, прáвые одержáли верх. ФКП призвалá коммунистов, трудя́щихся, все прогресси́вные си́лы страны́ продолжáть борьбу́ в зашиту свои́х прав и национáльных интерéсов, за нóвое объединéние большинствá.

Words and expressions to part 2

экономи́ческий кри́зис   обостри́лся
полити́ческий
напряжённость (tension)   обостри́лась
борьба́
социа́льные противоре́чия   обостри́лись
          (contradictions, tensions)
обостря́ться/обостри́ться
      -ются   -я́ться
обострённый
обостре́ние

рост ма́ссовой безрабо́тицы   1) rate; 2) increase
     цен
     жи́зненного у́ровня

сниже́ние у́ровня произво́дства
          у́ровня жи́зни
                         (чему́?)
идти́ / пойти́ на усту́пки   кру́пному капита́лу
-ду́т   -ду́т   тре́бованиям рабо́чих - to make concession to
                                            workers' demands

                    (между кем? между чем?)
сосуществова́ние   ме́жду разли́чными па́ртиями
                     разли́чными социа́льно-экономи́ческими систе́мами
тео́рия ми́рного сосуществова́ния

антирабо́чие   а́кции
антиправи́тельственные
антисове́тские

ультрапра́вые   си́лы поднима́ют го́лову - the ultra-right are on the rise
неофаши́стские
шовивини́стские

голова́ (pl. го́ловы, голо́в)

поднима́ть/подня́ть
      -ют   -и́мут
по́днятый
                    (в чём?)
ошиба́ться/ошиби́ться в   свои́х прогно́зах - to be wrong in one's prognoses
    -ются   -у́тся   партнёрах по бло́ку
(past. ошибся, -лась)   пра́вильности реше́ния
оши́бка

       (за что?)   (на кого́)

ответственность за неуспе́х   ложи́тся на социали́стов

   – responsibility for defeat lies with the socialists

               поражéние   администрáцию

               переворóт   ультрапрáвых

               дефици́т   воéнные расхóды

               сниже́ние у́ровня жи́зни

ложи́ться/лечь

  –áтся   ля́гут

                          (за что?)   (на кого́?)

возлагáть/возложи́ть ответственность за уще́рб   на США

    –ют возлóжат   авáрию   СССР

                             жéртвы   Изрáиль

– to place responsibility for victims on Israel

возлóженный

плáны провали́лись

                         (от чего́?)

отстраня́ть/   коммуни́стов   от   полити́ческой жи́зни

    –ют   неофаши́стов   руковóдства

отстрани́ть   прави́тельство   регули́рования экономи́ки

    –ят   сторóнников   влáсти

               рефóрмы

   – to remove supporters of reform from power

отстранённый

отстранéние

                     (над кем?)

одéрживать/одержáть верх   над   проти́вником – to defeat the enemy

    –ют одéржат   побéду   врагóм

одéржанный

врáг (pl. враги́, врагóв)

                     (к чему́?)

призывáть трудя́щихся   к борьбе́ в защи́ту свои́х прав

        прогресси́вные си́лы   профсою́зов

                         за мир

                         поддéржку ФКП

– to call upon progressive forces to fight in support of...

VOCABULARY EXERCISES

Look through the vocabulary for part 2 of the text *«Фра́нция по́сле вы́боров».*
Do the following exercises.

**A. Give the nominative and genitive plural for the following nouns. Mark the
stress.**

цена́, у́ровень, голова́, тео́рия, противоре́чие, прогно́з, вра́г, социали́ст,
а́кция, рабо́чий.

**B. Give perfective forms for the following verbs. Conjugate both forms and
mark the stress.**

обостря́ться, поднима́ть, ошиба́ться, ложи́ться.

C. Paraphrase the italicized words.

принима́ть уча́стие в вы́борах, *обраща́ться к* трудя́щимся, шовини́сты
активизи́руются, кри́зис *уси́лился, повыше́ние* у́ровня жи́зни, *одержа́ть верх* над
враго́м, пла́ны *потерпе́ли неуда́чу,* агресси́вные *де́йствия.*

D. Give the opposite for the italicized words.

повыше́ние цен, пла́ны *бы́ли реализо́ваны,* борьба́ *осла́билась, сторо́нник,*
проправи́тельственный, привести́ к *согла́сию.*

E. Form verbs from out of the following nouns.

обостре́ние кри́зиса, оши́бка в прогно́зах, отстране́ние от вла́сти.

F. Give Russian equivalents for the following English phrases.

   - to result in mass unemployment
   - tension has grown
   - responsibility for a huge deficit lies with this leadership
   - to follow the democrats
   - to come into money
   - to keep the state out of economic control
   - to make concessions to reactionaries
   - a drop in the standard of living
   - to rear one's (ugly) head (to be on the rise)
   - socialists are to blame for the defeat in the war
   - the struggle in defense of trade unions

G.   Write sentences to fill in the blanks in each of the groups below. Be able to translate your sentences.

(на кого? на что?)

1.   Отве́тственность за ава́рию ложи́тся ____________________
         кри́зис ____________________
         пораже́ние ____________________

(что?)

2.   ____________________ обостри́лся
     ____________________ обостри́лась
     ____________________ обостри́лось
     ____________________ обостри́лись

(каки́е си́лы?)

3.   ____________________ в СССР поднима́ют го́лову.
     ____________________ в ФРГ
     ____________________ в Изра́иле.

(кого́?)   (от чего́?)

4.   Пла́ны отсрани́ть ____________ ____________ провали́лись
                       ____________ ____________
                       ____________ ____________

(кому́?)

5.   Профсою́з пошёл на усту́пки ____________________
     Администра́ция пошла́ ____________________
     Террори́сты пошли́ ____________________

(в ком? в чём?)

6.   Ва́жно не ошиба́ться ____________________
     Ста́лин оши́бся ____________________
     Пра́вые оши́блись ____________________

(к чему́)

7.   Рост цен приведёт ____________
     Антиправи́тельственные демонстра́ции приведу́т ____________
     Пораже́ние в войне́ привело́ ____________

H.   Translation.

1.   It was essential for the Republicans to solve the problems of 7% unemployment and 10% inflation.
2.   Supporters of economic reforms managed to come in first in the final round of elections.
3.   Having made it to power, he seeks an alliance with big capital.
4.   It is high time for different left factions to get used to the idea of a united front.

5. At that time it was necessary for Gorbachev to make at least insignificant concessions to the party apparatus.
6. Economic stagnation brought the country to a serious drop in the standard of living.
7. Owing to the Austerity program, the administration has won the respect of the population for its program.

GRAMMAR: SEQUENCE OF TENSE

Russian sequence of tense is not like that of English. Note these examples:

Она́ сказа́ла, что совеща́ние **бу́дет** здесь.	She said the session **would be** here.
Она́ сказа́ла, что совеща́ние здесь.	She said the session **was** here.

Note that the action in the second clause takes place *concurrently* with the action of the first clause.

Она́ сказа́ла, что совеща́ние **бы́ло** здесь.	She said the session **had been** here.

Note that the action of the second clause *preceeds* the action of the first clause.

Remember that **бы** is used for *would* only in truly conditional sentences (If A were true then B *would* be true). If you don't have an *if...then* situation, you probably are dealing with sequence of tense and should use the forms given above.

Note also the following examples for **если** and **когда** clauses:

Если ООП **пойдёт** на компроми́сс, перегово́ры **даду́т** конкре́тные результа́ты.	If the PLO **agrees** to compromise, the negotiations **will produce** concrete results.
Когда́ ООП **пойдёт** на компроми́сс, перегово́ры **даду́т** конкре́тные результа́ты.	When the PLO **agrees** to compromise, the negotiations **will produce** concrete results.

As you can see, if the main clause is in the future tense, the **е́сли** or **когда́** clause is also in the future tense.

GRAMMAR EXERCISES: SEQUENCE OF TENSE

Review the use of sequence of tense at the beginning of this lesson. Then do the following exercises.

A. Choose the correct form of the verb in parentheses.

1. Уровень безработицы снизится, только когда администрация серьёзно (занимается, займётся) этим вопросом.

2. Если Мишкин (объявляет, объявит) о своей кандидатуре, он непременно будет избран.
3. Каждый раз, когда (предлагают, предложат) ввести новый налог на бензин, возникают громкие протесты.
4. Если конгресс (принимает, примет) программу президента, военный бюджет будет резко сокращён.
5. Когда (происходит, произойдёт) какая-нибудь трагедия, корреспонденты спешат на место происшествия.
6. Если программа правого правительства (проваливается, провалится), мы, наверно, увидим сдвиг влево.
7. Никто не знал, что (произошло бы, произойдёт), когда Горбачёв пришёл к власти.
8. Если бы Брежнев умер раньше, Горбачёв не (пришёл бы, придёт) к власти.
9. Если бы разрешено было экспортировать новейшую технику в Советский Союз, американские фирмы (расширили бы, расширят) контакты с СССР.
10. Сенатор заявил, что он не (стал бы, станет) кандидатом в президенты.
11. Премьер думал, что президент США не (отказался бы, откажется) от предложения.
12. Многие выражают мнение, что если бы было возможно иметь свободу выбора, многие республики (вышли бы, выйдут) из состава Советского Союза.

B. **Pick the correct verb. Base your decision on whether the action in the second clause is concurrent or previous to the action in the first clause. If both verbs are possible, explain why.**

1. I didn't know that U.S. representatives were elected every other year. Я не знал, что американские конгрессмены (избирались, избираются) раз в два года.
2. We were told that up until the beginning of the nineteenth century, the loser in a presidential election used to become vice president. Нам сказали, что до начала девятнадцатого века, проигравший кандидат в президенты (становится, становился) вице-президентом.
3. By the middle of the eighties it became clear that Gorbachev was proposing major changes. К середине восьмидесятых годов стало ясно, что Горбачёв (предлагал, предлагает) крупные перемены.
4. Upon leaving office Reagan said that Gorbachev was his friend. По выходе в отставку Рейган сказал, что Горбачёв (был, Ø) его друг.
5. The president said yesterday that the world was no longer as dangerous as it once was. Президент сказал, что мир сейчас (был, Ø) менее опасен, чем раньше.
6. The economists agreed that prices had fallen by 10 percent and that they were still falling. Экономисты согласились, что цены (снижаются, снизились) на 10 процентов и (продолжили, продолжают) снижаться.

7. The State Department spokesman said that the parties reached agreement without particular difficulty. Представитель Госдепартамента сказал, что стороны (достигли, достигают) договорённости без особого труда.
8. Everyone knew that the vice president was sick. Все знали, что вице-президент (болел, болеет).
9. No one would tell the prime-minister that he was in danger. Никто не сказал премьер-министру, что он (находился, находится) в опасности.
10. If you said that the earth was round, he would say it was flat. Если бы ты сказал, что земля (была, Ø) круглая, он бы ответил, что она (была, Ø) плоская.

C. Fill in the blanks.

1. Генеральный секретарь выразил уверенность, что он

   _______________________ народ в необходимости реформ.
   would convince

2. Все опросы общественного мнения показывали, что президент страны

   _________________________.
   would be re-elected

3. Если бы президент высказался против абортов, он _____________________.
   would be re-elected

4. Стало известно, что социалисты ___________ из правительства.
   would leave

5. Никто не мог предсказать, что банки _____________.
   would close

6. Наша фирма ___________ больше контрактов с советскими
   would sign

   предприятиями, если бы рубль был конвертируемым.

7. Кеннеди не верил, что война во Вьетнаме значительно

   _____________________.
   would become wider

8. Если бы социалисты имели абсолютное большинство, тогда парламент

   _______________________ меры относительно бездомных.
   would take measures

9. В 1960 году никто не подозревал, что Р. Рейган _________________________.

would run for president

10. Политический курс страны существенно изменится, когда

_________________ новое правительство.

comes to power

11. Если партия не __________ своим кандидатам, они потерпят

help

сокрушительное поражение.

12. Договор обречён на гибель, если его не __________ лидеры обеих

support

палат Конгресса.

13. Положение станет яснее, когда президент __________ по телевидению.

appears

14. Коалиция не будет нужна, только когда партия ____________

receives

абсолютное большинство в парламенте.

15. Вооружённые силы можно будет вывести только тогда, когда

__________ война.

ends

**D. Translate the following clauses of unreal condition into English. Change
them into clauses of real condition. Translate them again into English.**

Examples: *Если бы отменили лимит на подписку, то тираж «Московских
новостей» удвоился бы.*

⟶ *If* they *stopped* limiting subscription, the circulation of
"Moscow News" *would double.*

*Если отменят лимит на подписку, то тираж «Московских
новостей» удвоится.*

⟶ *If* they *stop* limiting subscription, the circulation of
"Moscow News" *will double.*

1. *Если бы была созвана* международная конференция по политическому
урегулированию на Ближнем Востоке, то она *должна была бы* включить все
заинтересованные стороны.

2. Израильские власти не *ввели бы* круглосуточный комендантский час, *если
бы не продолжались* демонстрации против израильской оккупации на
Западном берегу и в секторе Газа.

3.   Израильский адвокат Лангер *не потребовала бы* возбуждения уголовного дела против израильской военной администрации, *если бы* палестинцы *не подвергались* пыткам и издевательствам в израильских тюрьмах.
4.   *Если бы не было* провозглашения политического национального примирения, то шесть руководителей крупных групп душманов, приговорённых к смертной казни, *не были бы помилованы*.
5.   Запуск космического корабля многоразового пользования *не был бы перенесён, если бы не обнаружили* новые неполадки, показанные ультразвуковым «просвечиванием».

E.   Translate the following sentences.

1.   You would be wrong if you held communists responsible for all regional conflicts.
2.   If the new right had won, they would have brought their people into the White House.
3.   What would happen if neofascists became active?
4.   If the U.S. closed down the Lybian mission to the U.N., the press would accuse Washington of violating its international commitments. (международные обязательства)
5.   If the Administration had not sent arms to Iran, there would be fewer new hostages.
6.   The authorities will have to suppress the rebellion if they lift the curfew.
7.   Should the tensions in the international arena continue to grow, it might become necessary to hold a special meeting of the UN Security Council.
8.   If the company makes concessions to the workers at this point, it will have to lower its rate of production in the future.
9.   Had Great Britain recognized this white minority regime, it would have betrayed its former colonies, who are now Commonwealth members. (Британское содружество наций)

RENDERING

Below is an explanation of the preliminary description of the Soviet Union's first "elected" legislative body, as enacted into law in 1988 and put to the first electoral test the following year. After you have rendered the information, give your view of the effectiveness of this first step.

The new Soviet legislature, called the Congress of People's Deputies, was to consist of 2250 members chosen by voters in multi-candidate elections in which non-party members were eligible to run. Nevertheless, the laws governing the election were complicated, so much so that it would be safe to say that despite all the media hoopla few Soviet citizens understood the process fully.

Most analysts would agree that the Party did everything it could to stack the odds in its favor. One hundred of the seats were reserved for candidates nominated directly by the party leadership.

A third of the seats were assigned to "social" organizations. These ranged from the Communist Party itself to the Academy of Sciences to stamp collectors. The Party automatically reserved 100 of the seats for its own candidates. And the Soviet press has reported that non-party candidates had been forced to observe the letter of the election law, while officially supported candidates breezed through pre-election meetings designed to pare down the choice of candidates. The meetings, which some have tried to compare to American pre-election caucuses, were often boisterous affairs. Things were made more difficult by a rule providing that candidates be approved not by the majority of those attending the meeting, but by a majority of all eligible to vote.

Another third of the seats were apportioned geographically by population with about one deputy for every 300,000 voters. The Party fielded a candidate in each location. Again, pre-election meetings were held to eliminate candidates. Finally, the last third of the seats go in equal sized blocs to each of the national republics (35 apiece) and autonomous regions (15 apiece).

Despite the barriers a number of well-known dissidents ran, including Andrei Sakharov.

The final election held after all the eliminating rounds did not actually produce a true parliament, but rather a kind of national electoral college, which in turn elected an executive 422-member parliament.

SPEAKING EXERCISES

A. Расскажи́те втору́ю часть те́кста для чте́ния. В своём расска́зе испо́льзуйте сле́дующие выраже́ния.

между тем, поэ́тому, вместе с тем, ита́к.

B. Расскажи́те весь текст с то́чки зре́ния францу́зского консерва́тора.

C. Сумми́руйте весь текст в двух-трёх предложе́ниях.

D. Отве́тьте на сле́дующие вопро́сы.

1. Каки́е фа́кторы привели́ к тому́, что миллио́ны францу́зов отказа́лись уча́ствовать в вы́борах?
2. На каку́ю па́ртию политбюро́ ФКП возлага́ет отве́тственность за неуспе́х ле́вых сил?
3. Что бы произошло́, е́сли бы удало́сь отстрани́ть коммуни́стов от полити́ческой жи́зни?
4. К чему́ ФКП призвала́ коммуни́стов, трудя́щихся и все прогресси́вные си́лы?

E. Дополни́тельные вопро́сы. (optional)

1. Каки́е фа́кторы обы́чно влия́ют на избира́телей?
2. Почему́ упа́ло влия́ние францу́зских коммуни́стов?
3. Как реаги́руют западноевропе́йские коммуни́сты на переме́ны в СССР?
4. Есть ли разногла́сия ме́жду францу́зскими социали́стами и пра́выми си́лами по вопро́сам вне́шней поли́тики?
5. Как мо́жно объясни́ть, что в демократи́ческих стра́нах За́падной Евро́пы пра́вым экстреми́стам удаётся получи́ть подде́ржку значи́тельной ча́сти населе́ния?

READING EXERCISE

Моя национальность – моё дело   **Виктор Козлов**

PRE-TEXT: Read the text with the following questions in mind:

1.   What is the article about?

PARAGRAPH (1)
2.   The internal passport system   (pick the correct answer)
       a.   existed before the 30s
       b.   was introduced only in the early 30s
       c.   was abandoned in the early 30s
       d.   never existed before the 30s

3.   Why is an internal passport important? Name two reasons.

PARAGRAPH (2)
4.   According to the author, how should the question about one's
       nationality in the passport be approached?

PARAGRAPH (3)
5.   This question is (pick the correct answer):
       a.   as important as the question about socio-political affiliation.
       b.   more important than one's socio-political affiliation.
       c.   less important than one's socio-political affiliation.
       d.   also represented in an internal passport.

PARAGRAPII (4)
6.   Why was "affirmative action" in hiring policy introduced?

PARAGRAPH (5)
7.   The author maintains that in some ways the Soviet nationalities have
       not changed in the past decades and in some ways change has occurred.
       Illustrate this statement.

PARAGRAPH (6)
8.   What would real national equality mean, according to the author?

PARAGRAPH (7)
9.   Why can this question in the passport be considered harmful?

PARAGRAPH (8)
10.   How did national origin become equated with race or blood type?
11.   How does the population census prove that this policy lacks logic?

PARAGRAPH (10)
12.   In what circumstances would the question about nationality make
       sense, according to the Institute of Ethnology?

PARAGRAPH (11)
13.   What question should replace it in personnel forms?
14.   In what other ways can one demonstrate his or her nationality?

PARAGRAPH (12)
15.   What would freedom of choice of nationality accomplish?

POST–TEXT: using context

PARAGRAPH (1)
1.   Which word marks the "punchline" here?   It
       a.   brings in a new dimension to the first sentence.
       b.   contradicts it.

PARAGRAPH (2,3)
2.   Find the marker(s) which introduce(s) the challenge to the statement
       above.

PARAGRAPH (4)
3.   The expression «Было время....» serves as (mark the correct answer)
       a.   a flashback/illustration
       b.   a solution of the problem

4.   Find the word which is a key to the question about the necessity of
       "affirmative action".

PARAGRAPH (5)
5.   Find the word which sums up the argument of the paragraph.

PARAGRAPH (7)
6.   Find the words which   a) mark the introduction of the argument;   b)
       develop it; and   c) conclude it.

PARAGRAPH (8)
7.   Which word supports the statement that national origin became a
       synonym of race?

PARAGRAPH (11)
8.   Find the conclusion. How did you identify it?

PARAGRAPH (12)
9.   The final paragraph...(mark the correct answer):
       a.   introduces the new argument.
       b.   concludes the old one.

10. What can you infer about the author's attitude on this subject? Prove your point.   His feelings about it are (pick the correct answer)
    a.   well controlled
    b.   obvious

11. Make a list of vocabulary useful for a discussion about ethnic groups and civil rights.

12. Find the opposite for «разобраться в чём-то на уровне эмоций» in the text.

13. Find the Russian for "nothing bad comes of".

14. What is the English for «с учётом деловых качеств»? Form a verb from the noun «учёт».   Find a phrase with this verb in the article.

15. Interpret the meaning of the following expressions in the given text.

никто не сомневался	a)	nobody had any doubts
	b)	anybody would have doubts
сложилась практика	a)	the practice was discontinued
	b)	the practice was established
смешанные семьи	a)	funny families
	b)	mixed families
целинные земли	a)	virgin lands
	b)	entire land
служебные анкеты	a)	auxilliary forms
	b)	personnel files
умалить роль	a)	to beg for a role
	b)	to diminish the role

Моя национальность — мое дело

Виктор КОЗЛОВ

Почти все мои молодые собеседники, с кем приходилось вести разговоры о паспорте, очень удивлялись, услышав, что паспортная система в СССР введена лишь в начале 30-х годов. Впрочем, никто не сомневался: без паспорта у нас жить трудно, о полезности его спорить не приходится. За датой рождения, скажем, стоят правовые элементы: право участвовать в выборах, получить пенсию по возрасту и т. п.

Но нужна ли в паспорте отметка о национальности?

Это вопрос, о котором сейчас начали и говорить, и писать. Но попробуем разобраться в нем не на уровне эмоций, а на уровне фактов и доводов.

Сторонники этой графы полагают, что она необходима, потому что отражает национальные чувства гражданина. Давайте подумаем: социально-классовая принадлежность в общественно-политическом отношении важнее национальной, но в паспорте она никак не отражается — и ничего плохого от этого не происходит.

Было время, когда различ-

ные национальности СССР были фактически неравными в социально-экономическом и культурном отношениях и требовались меры для сглаживания этого неравенства. Именно поэтому создавались условия, при которых те или иные национальности, ранее отсталые, получали более благоприятные возможности для развития отчасти за счет дотаций из центрального бюджета. С этой целью проводилась и «коренизация» управленческого аппарата, когда на административные посты выдвигались люди с учетом прежде всего их национальности, а затем уже деловых качеств. А для создания национальной интеллигенции тысячи юношей и девушек из национальных республик и областей направлялись для внеконкурсного поступления в центральные вузы.

За прошедшие десятилетия ситуация сильно изменилась. Конечно, народы СССР не могли стать одинаковыми: они продолжают различаться по численности и природным условиям обитания, по языку и культуре, по способу ведения хозяйства... Но это уже совсем другие отличия — разительная социально-экономическая и образовательная разница устранена. В ряде случаев возникли даже новые различия: грузины, например, превосходившие в 1926 году по степени урбанизации белорусов, к 1979 году уступили им в этом отношении, но зато значительно превзошли их по доле научных работников. Неожиданно высокой оказалась доля научных работников у бурят. Словом, в новых условиях оказалось, что прежние нормативы по тем или иным национальностям надо периодически пересматривать...

Впрочем, стоит ли этим вообще заниматься? Может быть, настало время ввести во всех сферах действительное национальное равноправие — учитывать в первую очередь способности и деловые качества, а не национальную принадлежность?

У отметки в паспорте есть и, прямо скажем, вредный оттенок. Ведь национальные общности людей являются образованиями **социальными.** И подобно тому, как человек, родившийся в крестьянской семье, может со временем стать рабочим или служащим, изменив свою социально-классовую принадлежность, так и человек, родившийся в белорусской или, скажем, узбекской семье, может, оказавшись в инонациональной среде, со временем относить себя к другой национальности. А между тем в паспорте национальность незыблема.

Такая практика сложилась не сразу. В первые годы после введения паспортов национальность записывалась по желанию самого гражданина, по его собственному самосознанию. Но потом по неизвестным для общественности причинам — вопрос открыто не обсуждался — было принято решение, по которому национальность определялась только национальностью родителей (а в смешанных семьях по отцу или матери) и сохранялась в течение всей жизни. Тем самым национальная принадлежность стала приравнена к группе крови или расе — то есть по существу биологизирована! Логики здесь мало — и характерно, что во время переписей сохраняется верный принцип: допускается, чтобы ответ о национальности не совпадал с отметкой в паспорте.

На пороге 80-х годов в СССР было почти 10 миллионов этнически смешанных семей. Чувашский юноша, переселившийся на целинные земли Казахстана, мог жениться там на украинской девушке; дети их, очевидно, воспринимали русский язык, как основной язык межнационального общения. Но наступало время получать паспорт — и они вынуждены были выбирать между чувашской и украинской национальностями...

Институт этнографии Академии наук СССР, где я работаю, получает множество писем от людей, оказавшихся в похожем положении. Они просят нас сделать так, чтобы им «присвоили» именно ту национальность, какую они хотят. И мы иногда обращаемся в органы внутренних дел, поддерживая такие просьбы. Указываем, что в прошлом существенным признаком была, например, та или другая религия, а какое отношение имеет Аллах или Иегова к паспорту человека неверующего?

Убежден: пришло время для утверждения принципа свободного выбора национальности или даже ликвидации этой отметки в паспорте (в служебных анкетах вместо нее правильнее давать, наверное, сведения о знании языка коренной национальности республики и русского). Все это не умалит роли национального фактора. Тот, кому хочется показать, скажем, что он русский или украинец, грузин или таджик, может сделать это другими способами: речью, поведением, одеждой или как-то еще.

Свобода выбора национальности при получении паспорта уменьшила бы формализацию национальных чувств, еще и сегодня питающую местный национализм.

CIRCLE TWO

LESSON SIX

AUDIO-COMPREHENSION EXERCISE

Part 1

You are about to hear a text about the Soviet economy in the year 1989, just as great changes had begun throughout Eastern Europe. The Soviet Union itself was ailing. With the Baltics demanding independence, the southern republics on the verge of civil war, and the economy in tatters, few could predict anything but a bleak future. Listen to this piece for both the facts presented, as well as its tone, in order to find out the information requested below. Review both the questions and the key words before listening.

1. The author starts out saying that the audience would rather hear a different kind of report on the economy. What kind does he have in mind: (a) the old style -- a glowing report about the people's economic achievements, (b) a more truthful report about the *true* state of the economy, or (c) a report promising a brighter future?
2. What is the current state of the economy? Give at least two supporting examples of this conclusion.
3. Is the country apathetic about the economy? What leads you to your conclusion?
4. Where was the economy most hotly debated? What action was taken? What, according to the commentator, is the most important step to be taken now?

Key words

экономика на перевале – economy in transition
патриотические песни вперемёжку с (чем) – patriotic songs mixed with
трудовы́е сверше́ния – labor achievements
бы́стро та́ют на прила́вках това́ры – goods are growing scarce on the shelves
расстро́ены фина́нсы – finances are in disarray
де́нежное обраще́ние – monetary circulation
хозрасчёт, аре́нда, самофинанси́рование – self-accounting, lease, self-financing
нет недоста́тка в обсужде́нии альтернати́вных вариа́нтов – there is no lack of
discussion of alternatives

вы́сказаться ... ро́зовыми реча́ми – to express oneself in rosy speeches
програ́мма поэта́пного обновле́ния эконо́мики – program of economic recovery by
stages

перейти́ от конце́пции к пра́ктике – to move from theory to practice

TEXT: Read the following text; be able to translate it into English in written form.

Экономика на перевале   Часть 1

Ах, как хотелось бы всем нам услышать сегодня по радио патриотические песни вперемежку с бойкими сообщениями о великих трудовых свершениях в стиле, предшествовавшем периоду перестройки! Но не слышно бравурных маршей. И это, конечно, далеко не случайно. Экономика страны переживает глубокий кризис. Быстро тают на прилавках товары. Покупатель не обеспечивается самым необходимым. Никто даже не вспоминает о некогда казавшейся грандиозной Продовольственной программе. Впрочем, и вспомнить-то нечего, хотя пришёл срок её завершения. Директивные «цветочки» не стали полновесными плодами. Хозяйство не встало на ноги. Расстроены финансы, денежное обращение. Производителю сегодня ближе к сердцу такие понятия, как хозрасчёт, аренда, самофинансирование...

Право же, нет недостатка в обсуждении разных, подчас альтернативных вариантов нашего развития, свободного от жёсткого регулирования. Высказались и рабочие, и учёные, и политики. Разумеется, высказались по-своему: то забастовками, то розовыми речами. Но особенно жаркие дебаты о намеченных правительством мерах разгорелись на втором Съезде народных депутатов СССР. Несмотря на беспощадную критику, программа поэтапного оздоровления экономики принята. Но критика не противоречит хорошим намерениям, и сейчас важно перейти от концепции - к практике, подкрепить слова делами.

Но чем же отличаются показатели минувшего 1989 года от предыдущего? Хотя статистика не любит прогнозов, мы всё же попросили работников Госкомстата СССР заранее поделиться с нашими читателями некоторыми предварительными оценками.

Words and expressions to part 1

	(чему?)
предшествовать	периоду перестройки
-уют	оздоровлению экономики
	завершению программы
	намеченным мерам

это далеко не случайно - this is no accident

экономика	переживает	глубокий кризис
хозяйство	(imperfective)	поэтапное оздоровление
автомобильная промышленность		расширение производства
		- expansion of production
частные предприятия	переживают	проникновение иностранного
		капитала

- private enterprises are experiencing an infiltration of foreign capital

наро́д пережи́л   войну́
      (perfective)   лише́ния
                       го́лод
пережива́ть/пережи́ть – to live through, to survive
      -ют переживу́т

това́ры на прила́вках – goods on the shelves

                              (кого́?)   (чем?)
обеспе́чивать/обеспе́чить   покупа́теля   са́мым необходи́мым
      -ют   -ат   – to provide the customer with the essentials
                              компа́нию   обору́дованием
обеспе́ченный
социа́льное обеспече́ние

не́когда грандио́зная програ́мма
        здоро́вая эконо́мика
        свобо́дный от госуда́рственного регули́рования – at one time free from
                                                      state control

освобожда́ть/освободи́ть
        -ют   -я́т
                        (чего́?)
пришёл срок   заверше́ния програ́ммы

                        (сде́лать что?)
                        уви́деть полновесные плоды́
                        ввести́ хозрасчёт – the time has come to introduce
                                        self-accounting

                              (на что?)
встава́ть/встать   на́ ноги – to get back on one's feet
встаю́т   -нут   на коле́ни – to go down on one's knees
                              на путь свобо́дного предпринима́тельства
                                       рефо́рм
                        (где?)
стоя́ть   на пути́
                        на нога́х – to stand on one's two feet; to stand tall
                        на коле́нях – to be kneeling; to be humbled
нога́ (pl. но́ги, ног)
путь (pl. пути́, путе́й)

расстро́ены   фина́нсы – finances are in disarray
расстро́ено   де́нежное обраще́ние
расстро́ен   темп ро́ста валово́го национа́льного проду́кта (ВНП) – the GNP

(кому́?)   (что?)
производи́телю   бли́же к се́рдцу   самофинанси́рование
покупа́телю   аре́нда

		(чем?)
рабо́чие	вы́сказались	забасто́вками
учёные	– to express themselves by..	жа́ркими деба́тами
слу́жащие		беспоща́дной кри́тикой
поли́тики		ро́зовыми реча́ми
рабо́тники комите́та стати́стики		прогно́зами

выска́зываться/вы́сказаться
      –ются   –жутся
вы́сказанный
выска́зывание

разгоре́лись деба́ты – discussions flared up
деба́ты (no sing.)

противоре́чить (no perf.)

(чему?)
хоро́шим наме́рениям
предвари́тельным оце́нкам – preliminary estimations
официа́льным да́нным по у́ровню (чего?)
      безрабо́тицы
      валю́тного ку́рса
      – rate of exchange
      рожда́емости
      – birthrate
      сме́ртности
      – mortality

отлича́ться (no perf.)
    –ются

(от чего?)
от ста́рых показа́телей
от но́вых да́нных (no sing.) – new data
от заплани́рованной производи́тельности труда́

VOCABULARY EXERCISES

Look through the vocabulary for part 1 of the text «Эконо́мика на перева́ле», then do the following exercises.

A. Give the nominative and the genitive plural for the following nouns. Mark the stress.

ме́ра, оздоровле́ние, лише́ние, капита́л, хозя́йство, нога́, путь, учёный, поли́тик, показа́тель, стати́стика, промы́шленность.

B. Give perfective forms for the following verbs. Conjugate both forms and mark the stress.

отлича́ться, противоре́чить, предше́ствовать, встава́ть, обеспе́чивать, освобожда́ть.

C. Paraphrase the italicized words.

инфильтра́ция иностра́нного капита́ла, *пройти́ че́рез лише́ния*, *происходи́ть до* кри́зиса, *предоста́вить* покупа́телю са́мое необходи́мое, *постепе́нное оздоровле́ние*, това́ры в *магази́нах*, увидеть *результа́ты* своего́ труда́, *горя́чая диску́ссия*, *и́ндекс*, но́вая *информа́ция*, *жесто́кая кри́тика*, *предсказа́ние*, *пришло́ вре́мя*.

D. Give the opposite for the words in italics.

сокраще́ние произво́дства, *ни́зкая сме́ртность*, *сла́бая* эконо́мика, *госуда́рственные* предприя́тия, *отмени́ть* хозрасчёт, стоя́ть на *коле́нях*.

E. Give Russian equivalents for the following English phrases.

- to experience expansion of production
- data on the rate of unemployment
- rate of exchange
- this is no accident
- an at one time sound economy
- automobile industry is going through a deep crisis
- finances are in disarray
- the time has come to see the results
- labor productivity
- money circulation
- to go down on one's knees
- low mortality

F. Write sentences to fill in the blanks in each of the groups below. Be able to translate your sentences.

<table>
<tr><td></td><td></td><td></td><td>(от чего́?)</td></tr>
<tr><td>1.</td><td>эконо́мика</td><td>свобо́дная</td><td>____________</td></tr>
<tr><td></td><td>о́бщество</td><td>свобо́дное</td><td>____________</td></tr>
<tr><td></td><td>предпринима́тели</td><td>свобо́дные</td><td>____________</td></tr>
<tr><td></td><td></td><td></td><td>(что?)</td></tr>
<tr><td>2.</td><td>предприя́тия</td><td>пережива́ют</td><td>____________</td></tr>
<tr><td></td><td>перестро́йка</td><td>пережива́ет</td><td>____________</td></tr>
<tr><td></td><td>промы́шленность</td><td>пережива́ет</td><td>____________</td></tr>
<tr><td></td><td></td><td></td><td>(что?)</td></tr>
<tr><td></td><td>сове́тский наро́д</td><td>пережи́л</td><td>____________</td></tr>
<tr><td></td><td>гражда́нское населе́ние</td><td>пережи́ло</td><td>____________</td></tr>
<tr><td></td><td>вся страна́</td><td>пережила́</td><td>____________</td></tr>
</table>

<table>
<tr><td></td><td></td><td></td><td>(на что?)</td></tr>
<tr><td>3.</td><td>По́льша</td><td>вста́ла</td><td>_________</td></tr>
<tr><td></td><td>эконо́мика</td><td></td><td>_________</td></tr>
<tr><td></td><td>рабо́чие</td><td>вста́ли</td><td>_________</td></tr>
</table>

Change the same sentences using «стоя́ть». (so-and-so is standing on its feet)

<table>
<tr><td></td><td></td><td></td><td>(чему́?)</td></tr>
<tr><td>4.</td><td>эти фа́кты</td><td>противоре́чат</td><td>_________</td></tr>
<tr><td></td><td>поли́тика президе́нта</td><td>противоре́чит</td><td>_________</td></tr>
<tr><td></td><td>де́йствия комите́та</td><td>противоре́чат</td><td>_________</td></tr>
</table>

<table>
<tr><td></td><td></td><td></td><td>(чему́?)</td></tr>
<tr><td>5.</td><td>экономи́ческий подъём</td><td>предше́ствовал</td><td>_________</td></tr>
<tr><td></td><td>забасто́вки</td><td>предше́ствовали</td><td>_________</td></tr>
<tr><td></td><td>рост ВНП</td><td>предше́ствовал</td><td>_________</td></tr>
</table>

<table>
<tr><td></td><td></td><td></td><td></td><td>(чем?)</td></tr>
<tr><td>6.</td><td>свобо́дная эконо́мика</td><td>обеспе́чивает</td><td>покупа́теля</td><td>_________</td></tr>
<tr><td></td><td>госуда́рство</td><td>обеспе́чивает</td><td>гра́ждан</td><td>_________</td></tr>
<tr><td></td><td>фе́рмеры</td><td>обеспе́чивают</td><td>населе́ние</td><td>_________</td></tr>
</table>

<table>
<tr><td></td><td></td><td></td><td>(от чего?)</td></tr>
<tr><td>7.</td><td>но́вые показа́тели</td><td>отлича́ются</td><td>_________</td></tr>
<tr><td></td><td>ва́ши да́нные</td><td>отлича́ются</td><td>_________</td></tr>
<tr><td></td><td>темп роста ВНП в 1989</td><td>отлича́ется</td><td>_________</td></tr>
</table>

GRAMMAR EXERCISE: REVIEW OF CASES

Review the use of cases as presented in Circle One. Do the following exercise.

Determine the use of case in the sentences below. Fill in the blanks. Be able to translate the sentences into English.

1. Советский Союз придаёт (чрезвычайное значение) _______________ (международное сотрудничество) ____________ в космических исследованиях.

2. Отвечая на (брифинг) _____________ на (вопрос) ____________ японского корреспондента, заместитель министра иностранных дел упомянул договорённость о (проведение) ____________ регулярных встреч министров иностранных дел СССР и Японии.

3. На рассвете (1 сентября) _________ Вермахт обрушился на (Польша) ________.

4. На (борт) _______ корабля срочно доставили продовольствие и питьевую воду.

5. Генерал, командующий (войска) ____________, призвал к себе (репортёры, фотографы и кинооператоры) ________________.

6. Участники направили (приветственная телеграмма) _______________ в адрес (Генеральный секретарь ЦК КПСС) ____________.

7. Итальянская полиция предупредила о (радиосигналы, посылаемые) ____________ за (пределы) _______ страны.

8. Специалисты выступят с (серия докладов) ____________ о (советская система) ____________ химического оружия.

9. У (афганские мятежники) ____________ стало больше (деньги и зенитные ракеты) ____________.

10. Сквозь (густой дым) ________ стали видны очертания (приближающиеся самолёты) __________________.

SPEAKING EXERCISES

A. Расскажи́те пе́рвую часть те́кста. В своём расска́зе испо́льзуйте сле́дующие выраже́ния.

в соотве́тствии с...; наприме́р; одна́ко; и́менно за э́то...; ведь.

B. Сумми́руйте часть 2 в не́скольких предложе́ниях.

C. Отве́тьте на сле́дующие вопро́сы.

1. В чём проявля́ется кри́зис сове́тской эконо́мики?
2. Какова́ судьба́ Продово́льственной програ́ммы, провозглашённой ещё при Бре́жневе?
3. Где разверну́лись спо́ры об альтернати́вных вариа́нтах разви́тия сове́тсткой эконо́мики?

D. Дополни́тельные вопро́сы. (optional)

1. Сравни́те экономи́ческие тру́дности в СССР и в США.
2. Расскажи́те, дала́ ли пла́новая эконо́мика положи́тельные результа́ты в каких-ли́бо стра́нах.

AUDIO-COMPREHENSION EXERCISE

Part 2

1.   A government commission provided some statistics on poor performance over the past year.   Listen to the tape and fill in the blanks with the information requested.   In some cases you will be given the category and asked for the numbers.   In others you will be supplied the statistic and asked for the category:

Category   **Figure**

a.   Targeted increase in labor productivity, 1989:   _______________%

b.   ________________________________ :   2.5%

c.   Production goals met by December, 1989:   _______________%

d.   Number of debt-ridden enterprises: _______________%

e.   ________________________________ :   over 9 billion rubles

f.   National internal debt: _______________rubles

g.   ________________________________ :   312 billion rubles

2.   There were some positive indicators. They were:

a.   ________________________________ :   seven-fold

b.   State budget deficit (to begin with):   _______________rubles

c.   Current deficit: _______________rubles

d.   ________________________________ :   22 billion rubles

e.   ________________________________ :   240 rubles

f.   For *kolkhoz* workers: _______________rubles

3.   Listen to Part 2 once again, and answer the questions based on the conclusions drawn by the commentator using the statistics you have just heard:
   a.   What is the significance of the figures in 2a, above, for production of consumer goods versus that of heavy industry. Which is referred to as Sector A and which as Sector B?
   b.   What hope (if any) does the commentator see for fuller shelves in the future?
   c.   How was the improvement indicated by the figures of 2b and 2c, above, achieved?

    d.   What do the flickers of prospective economic improvement signify for government coffers as indicated by the figure in 2d?

    e.   What mars the improvement indicated in 2e and 2f?

    f.   What measures may help to control inflation?

4.   What best summarizes the commentator's conclusions?

    a.   The ministries are slowly working out new ways for more efficient production, but the process is arduous.

    b.   The dialectical theory of how a superstructure is created is in desperate need of revision.

    c.   With regards to production methods, Sector A has much to borrow from Sector B, especially in return on investment.

    d.   The entire country must work together to improve the economy, rather than wait for directives from the top.

Key words

государственный внутренний долг – national internal debt
эмиссия – issuing of money
безработица пока не грозит – so far there is no threat of unemployment
позитивные перемены – positive changes
темпы прироста производства – production growth rate
группа «А», группа «Б» – Sector A, Sector B
опережать – to be ahead, to be higher
...станут заметнее и весомее – they will become more noticeable and important
пусть не сегодня, не сразу, но... – it doesn't have to be today, but...
удалось сократить... – they succeeded in reducing
увеличить и сократить расходы – to increase and to decrease expenditures
сверхплановые поступления налогов – extra tax revenues
эта добавка в кошелёк государства – additional money into government coffers
средняя зарплата рабочих и служащих возросла до... – average wages of blue-
                                             collar and white-collar workers increased to
кто у кого в долгу? – who owes whom?
исчисление цен – pricing

TEXT: Read the following text; be able to translate it into English in written form.

Экономика на перевале   Часть 2

    По словам работников Госкомстата СССР, многие плановые задания не выполнены. Производительность общественного труда возросла не на 4,5 процента, как намечалось, а лишь на два с половиной. Обязательства по поставкам промышленной продукции к декабрю были выполнены на 98,7 процента. Каждое четвёртое объединение и предприятие остаются пока должниками. Долг этот превысил девять миллиардов рублей. Возрастает государственный внутренний долг. К концу года он достиг, по предварительной оценке, 400 миллиардов рублей. Увеличилась и эмиссия. Кому как, а рабочим фабрик Гознака безработица пока не грозит.

Но не всё столь гру́стно. Есть и други́е но́вости, отча́сти отрази́вшие позити́вные переме́ны. Характе́рны они́ и́менно для ны́нешнего, а тем бо́лее для за́втрашнего эта́па разви́тия эконо́мики. Взят курс на её социа́льную переориента́цию. Ска́жем, те́мпы приро́ста произво́дства промы́шленной проду́кции гру́ппы «Б» в семь раз опережа́ют показа́тели гру́ппы «А» – тяжёлой промы́шленности. Таки́х измене́ний мы ра́ньше не зна́ли, а в бу́дущем они ста́нут ещё заме́тнее и весо́мее. Вро́де бы лёд тро́нулся. Есть наде́жда, что на́ши магази́ны пусть не сего́дня, не сра́зу, но изме́нят свой по́длинный «интерье́р» и на́ше настрое́ние.

Есть и така́я но́вость: удало́сь-таки сократи́ть дефици́т госуда́рственного бюдже́та. Вме́сто 120 миллиа́рдов рубле́й по первонача́льному пла́ну он соста́вит о́коло 92 миллиа́рдов. Как удало́сь? В основно́м за счёт мер, при́нятых прави́тельством по фина́нсовому оздоровле́нию эконо́мики. Это и помогло́ увели́чить дохо́ды и снача́ла заморо́зить, а пото́м сократи́ть расхо́ды на 2 миллиа́рда рубле́й. Ожида́ются сверхпла́новые поступле́ния нало́гов с оборо́та дохо́дов от внешнеэкономи́ческой де́ятельности.

Это доба́вка в кошелёк госуда́рства. А како́й она́ бу́дет в кошелька́х совреме́нников? Как мы бу́дем плати́ть за труд? К нача́лу декабря́ сре́дняя зарпла́та рабо́чих и служащих возросла́ до 240, колхо́зников – до 170 рубле́й. Вро́де хорошо́. Да опя́ть же не о́чень: ведь производи́тельность труда́ растёт намно́го ме́дленнее, чем зарпла́та. И потому́ непро́сто сказа́ть: кто у кого́ в долгу́? Пора́ найти́ отве́т на э́тот вопро́с. И э́то помо́жет сде́лать но́вая систе́ма исчисле́ния и́ндекса цен и инфля́ции.

Перестро́йка в пути́. Она́ мости́т доро́гу в бу́дущее. Коне́чно, неизбе́жны и разочарова́ния, но нельзя́ останови́ть вре́мя. Оно́ необрати́мо, как мирова́я исто́рия. Как бы поучи́тельны её уро́ки ни бы́ли, мы времена́ми наде́емся на то, что мо́жно подчини́ть эконо́мику директи́вам, сде́лать па́дчерицей надстро́йки. А ведь диале́ктика э́тих отноше́ний не столь проста́, как ко́е-кому́ ка́жется...

Что́бы «потреби́тельская корзи́нка» ста́ла полне́е, на э́ти це́ли, да́же при о́бщем вре́менном сниже́нии инвести́ций, дополни́тельно напра́влены мно́гие миллиа́рды рубле́й. И ещё ста́рые (к сожале́нию), и уже́ но́вые, в основно́м – но́вые ме́тоды хозя́йствования нужно́ испо́льзовать с максима́льной отда́чей, что́бы взять рубежи́ 1990 го́да. Ва́жно всем сохрани́ть чу́вство ло́ктя. Рабо́тать плечо́м к плечу́ и респу́бликам, и областя́м, и предприя́тиям. Если центр ещё чего́-нибу́дь не дорабо́тал, помоги́те ему́, поддержи́те свои́м дру́жным, тво́рческим трудо́м.

Алекса́ндр Ники́тин,
замести́тель реда́ктора «Пра́вды»
по отде́лу экономи́ческой поли́тики

Words and expressions to part 2

пла́новые зада́ния	ещё не вы́полнены
обяза́тельства по поста́вкам промы́шленной проду́кции	уже́ вы́полнены
первонача́льный план	перевы́полнен

выполня́ть/вы́полнить

    -ют   -ят

вы́полненный
выполне́ние

                                                              (на ско́лько?)
госуда́рственный вну́тренний долг   возро́с   на 4,5 проце́нта
эми́ссия   возросла́   на 2 миллио́на
дефици́т госуда́рственного бюдже́та   возро́с   в 3 ра́за
долг (pl. долги́, долго́в) – debt
должни́к (pl. должники́) – debtor

возраста́ть/возрасти́
возраста́ют возрасту́т
            (perfective past: возро́с, возросла́, возросло́, возросли́)
возро́сший
рост

ка́ждое четвёртое   предприя́тие – every fourth enterprise
                     объедине́ние
ка́ждый четвёртый   жи́тель

по предвари́тельной оце́нке – according to a preliminary estimate

те́мпы приро́ста произво́дства промы́шленной проду́кции гру́ппы «Б»
                                              тяжёлой промы́шленности
                                              лёгкой промы́шленности
                        превыша́ют   9 миллио́нов рубле́й
                                        все ожида́ния
– rates of growth in production exceed all expectations

превыша́ть/превы́сить
        –ют   –ят
превы́шенный
превыше́ние
                              (на что?)
брать/взять курс на   социа́льную переориента́цию эконо́мики
беру́т возьму́т   увеличе́ние дохо́дов колхо́зников   (от чего?)
                                                               прода́жи проду́ктов
                          сокраще́ние нало́гов (на что?)
                                        на оборо́т
                              – corporate tax revenues (capitalist)
                              – a turnover tax (socialist economy)
                          замора́живание расхо́дов   (на что?)
                                        на оборо́ну
взя́тый
взя́тка – a bribe
взя́точник – bribe-taker

        (чего́?)
за счёт мер по замора́живанию нало́га на потребле́ние не́фти – oil consumption
                                                                    tax
            увеличе́ния дохо́дов от внешнеэкономи́ческой де́ятельности
            – external economic activity
            сверхпла́новых поступле́ний нало́гов с оборо́та – through, by, due to
                                              extra turnover tax revenues

за счёт   социа́льного обеспече́ния – at the expense of social security
          бе́дных
          образова́ния –at the expense of education

замора́живать/заморо́зить
          –ют   –ят
заморо́женный

сокраща́ть/сократи́ть
     –ют   –я́т
сокращённый

доба́вка в кошелёк   госуда́рства – additional money into government coffers
                     гра́ждан – addition money into citizens' pockets

                              (за что?)
плати́ть/заплати́ть   за труд
пла́тят   запла́тят   за медици́нское обслу́живание
                              иску́сственное замора́живание креди́тных ста́вок
запла́ченный
за́работная пла́та, зарпла́та (no plur.) – salary, wages

кто у кого́ в долгу́? – who owes whom?

но́вая систе́ма   исчисле́ния   и́ндекса цен – new system of pricing
                                   инфля́ции
                    плани́рования
                    хозя́йствования
                    пла́ты за труд

                    (в чём?)
разочарова́ние   в результа́тах рефо́рм
                    в перестро́йке

                    (чем?)
                    результа́тами вы́боров
                    систе́мой образова́ния

разочаро́вывать(ся)/разочарова́ть(ся)
          –ют(ся) разочару́ют(ся)
разочаро́ванный
разочарова́ние

уро́ки исто́рии поучи́тельны – the lessons of history are instructive

                    (на что?)
надея́ться   на вре́менное сниже́ние инвести́ций
    –ются   – to rely on a temporary drop in investments
                    на но́вую валю́тно-фина́нсовую поли́тику – monetary policy
                    на экономи́ческую автоно́мию
наде́жда

при   о́бщем повыше́нии инвести́ций – at an overall increase in investments
           настоя́щих темпах приро́ста – at present rates of growth

с максима́льной отда́чей – with maximum output
рабо́тать плечо́м к плечу́ – to work side by side, to work as a team

VOCABULARY EXERCISES

Look through the vocabulary of part 2 of the text «*Эконо́мика на перева́ле*», then do the following exercises.

A.   Give the nominative and the genitive plural for the following nouns. Mark the stress.

разочарова́ние, инфля́ция, поступле́ние, взя́тка, долг, поста́вка, жи́тель, ожида́ние.

B.   Give perfective forms for the following verbs. Conjugate both forms and mark the stress.

возраста́ть, плати́ть, разочаро́вывать.

C.   Paraphrase the italicized words.

эми́ссия *увели́чилась*, по предвари́тельному *подсчёту*, тяжёлая *индустри́я*, превы́сить все *наде́жды*, *путём* сниже́ния нало́гов, уро́ки исто́рии *поле́зны*, *существу́ющие* темпы приро́ста, рабо́тать *сообща́*.

D.   Give the opposite for the words in italics.

вну́тренный долг *сократи́лся*, *лёгкая* промы́шленость, *дохо́ды от* внешнеэкономи́ческой де́ятельности, *постоя́нное* сниже́ние инвести́ций, *минима́льная* отда́ча.

E.   Form verbs for the following nouns.

наде́жда на экономи́ческую автоно́мию, *разочарова́ние* в перестро́йке, *пла́та* за образова́ние, *замора́живание* подохо́дного нало́га.

F.   Give Russian equivalents for the following phrases.

  - maximum output
  - average wages of blue-collar workers
  - new system of pricing

- monetary policy
- to remain a debter
- due to extra corporate tax revenues
- every third enterprise
- expenses exceed revenues
- to work as a team
- at a general increase in investments
- there is no threat of inflation
- extra money into the state's pocket
- social reorientation of the economy

G. **Write sentences to fill in the blanks in each of the groups below. Be able to translate your sentences.**

	(что?)			(чего?)
1.	__________	вы́полнена	за счёт	__________
	__________	перевы́полнены		__________
	__________	ужé вы́полнен		__________

	(что?)			(кого?)
	__________	сокращенó	за счёт	__________
	__________	вы́полнен		__________
	__________	заморóжен		__________

		(что?)
2.	возрóс	__________
	возрослá	__________
	возраста́ют	__________

			(на что?)
3.	экономи́сты	надéются	__________
	рабóчие и слу́жащие		__________
	колхóзники		__________

	(чего? кого?)		(на какóй процéнт?)
4.	числó __________	возрослó	__________
	у́ровень __________	сократи́лся	__________
	коли́чество __________	сократи́лось	__________

			(на скóлько миллиóнов?)
	числó __________	возрослó	__________
	у́ровень __________	сократи́лся	__________
	коли́чество __________	сократи́лось	__________

	(во скóлько раз?)
	__________
	__________
	__________

			(чём?)
5.	наблюда́ется разочарова́ние		_________
			_________
			_________

			(на что?)
6.	но́вое руково́дство	заморо́зило расхо́ды	_________
	демокра́ты	заморо́зили	_________
	республика́нцы		_________

			(на что?)
7.	администра́ция сократи́ла	нало́ги	_________
			_________
			_________

				(от чего́?)
8.	корпора́ции	получа́ют	дохо́ды	_________
	совме́стные предприя́тия		при́были	_________
	госуда́рство	получа́ет		_________

			(за что?)
9.	гра́ждане	должны́ плати́ть	_________
	компа́нии		_________
			_________

			(на что?)
10.	при Ру́звельте	США взя́ли курс	_________
	Ста́лине	СССР взял курс	_________
	Горбачёве		_________

H. Translate the following sentences using vocabulary from parts 1 and 2.

1. It is necessary that the consumer is provided at least with the essentials.
2. It is time that the government free trade unions from state control.
3. The data on the present level of labor productivity was published by all the leading newspapers.
4. Communists call large scale infiltration of foreign capital into the economy of a developing country "neocolonialism."
5. It is vital that the rate of mortality in the Third World drop.
6. Enterprises prefer that the state not increase corporate taxes.
7. The government altered the official data so that it will not reflect a new pricing system.
8. At the present rate of increase in investments we hope to see a maximum output by the end of the year.
9. Due to a freeze in corporate tax revenues the Federal Government will have to rely more heavily on income taxes.
10. The Secretary of the Treasury expressed his disappointment with the proposed pricing system.

GRAMMAR: MORE USES OF SUBJUNCTIVE

A. Emphatic constructions:

Где бы он **ни был**, все хотят говорить с ним.	No matter where he is, everybody wants to talk to him.

Subjunctive is used only in the subordinate clause of the construction. Note the absense of subjunctive in English.

Since such constructions by nature express regularity of action, the imperfective aspect is mostly found in them.

Куда бы он **ни шёл**, его узнают.	Wherever he goes, he is recognized.
Кто бы ни приходил, его реакция была всегда бурной.	Whoever arrives, his reaction was always loud.
С кем бы он **ни говорил**, он приводит одни и те же аргументы.	No matter with whom he talks, he uses the same argumentation.

Note the use of emphatic "НИ" before the verb.

B. After the verbs «бояться» and «опасаться».

Они **опасаются, как бы** СССР **не ввёл** войска в страну.	They are concerned lest the USSR should invade the country.

Note the use of the negative "НЕ" before the verb.

It is possible to use the indicative mood after these verbs as well.

Они боятся, что СССР введёт войска.	They are afraid the Soviet Union will invade the country.

GRAMMAR EXERCISES: MORE USES OF SUBJUNCTIVE

Read through the explanation of subjunctive above and then do the following exercises.

A. Analyze the following sentences and translate them into English:

1.   Горбачёв боится, как бы общественность не поддержала противников его реформ.
2.   Сколько бы ни продолжался полёт, горючего хватит.

3.   Кого бы ни назначили на этот пост, положение не улучшить!
4.   Иностранные вкладчики опасаются, как бы революционное правительство не начало ориентироваться на Советский Союз.
5.   Западная Европа боится, как бы страны ОПЕК значительно не повысили цены на нефть.
6.   В какой бы час дня или ночи самолёты ни приземлялись, воздушные диспетчеры ведут наблюдение за безопасностью посадки.
7.   Демократы опасаются, как бы экономический спад не кончился накануне выборов.
8.   Что бы вы ни говорили в своё оправдание, вам не поверят!
9.   Сталин боялся, как бы Бухарин не получил большинство в политбюро.
10.   Где бы ни проходили обыски, полиция повсюду находила наркотики.

B.   Translate the following.

1.   No matter how hard the pilot tried, he could not avoid the hostile plane.
2.   Whenever officials from oil-producing countries meet, they inevitably disagree.
3.   Whoever frees the people from the tyrant will become president.
4.   The public becomes disappointed in the administration whenever taxes go up.
5.   No matter how convincing he may be, he failed to pursuade our partners to reduce their allocations for space development.

GRAMMAR: VERBAL ASPECT OF MODALS

So far you have seen very strict rules about aspect, such as *Verbs that mean "beginning" or "ending" are always followed by imperfective infinitives.* However, deciding which aspect to use for infinitives which follow **modals** can be tricky. **Modals** are expressions that take infinitives and express volition, possibility, or obligation. They include words such as **надо, должен, хотéть, мочь, мóжно, невозмóжно,** and **нельзя.** The following rules govern infinitives that follow modals, but they are less rules than they are tendencies. Furthermore, they do not cover every syntactic eventuality, but they will guide you through most speech situations. Review the explanations on aspectual choice in the infinitive from Lesson One, Circle Two and then read the explanation below.

Look at the aspect of infinitives following modals category by category.

"Neutral" affirmative sentences:

Use a perfective infinitive, unless there are "imperfectivizing" circumstances. Look at the examples below:

Мы должны́ посла́ть телегра́мму.	*We should send the telegram.*
На́до верну́ться в посо́льство.	*We must return to the embassy.*
Мо́жно получи́ть докуме́нты здесь.	*You can get the papers here.*
Мо́гут дать вам всю информа́цию.	*They can give you all the information.*

"Imperfectivized" affirmative sentences (repetition):

If repetition is expressed explicity, use an imperfective infinitive:

Мо́жно получа́ть биле́т ка́ждый день.	*You can get a ticket daily.*
Всегда́ ну́жно дава́ть информа́цию.	*It is always necessary to give out information.*

But where **мочь** or **мо́жно** mean *might* or *can* in the sense that the possibility might exist, always use perfective, even if words such as **всегда́** are present: Всегда́ мо́жно переду́мать. *One can (might) always reconsider.*

Negative sentences: не на́до, не до́лжен, нельзя́ (in the meaning of "musn't"). Use imperfective: Не на́до задава́ть э́тот вопро́с. *That question need not (or: should not) be asked.*

Negative sentences: невозмо́жно, не мочь, нельзя́ (in the meaning of "impossible"). Use perfective: Мы не мо́жем отве́тить на ваш вопро́с. *We can't answer your question.*

Пора́. When **пора́** is indicates time to do something that is ordinarily done, use imperfective: Пора́ отвеча́ть на вопро́сы слу́шателей. *It's time to answer our listeners' questions.*

Note that when **на́до** is used as a synonym for this meaning of **пора́**, it too takes imperfective: На́до проверя́ть маши́ну. *It's time to check the car.*

When **пора́** means "It's high time something be done," use perfective: Пора́ отве́тить на вопро́сы слу́шателей. *It's high time we got around to answering our listeners' questions.*

	на́до до́лжен	не на́до не до́лжен	мо́жно, могу́ "can", "may"	мо́жно, могу́ "might"
"Neutral"	сде́лать		сде́лать	
Stated repetition	де́лать			

	не могу́ нельзя́ невоз- мо́жно	нельзя́ "musn't"	пора́ "scheduled"	пора́ "high time to"
"Neutral" Stated repetition	сде́лать	де́лать		сде́лать

GRAMMAR EXERCISES: VERBAL ASPECT OF MODALS

Review the explanation of aspect with modals and do the exercises below.

A.   Choose the correct verb.

1.   Стало ясно, что необходимо (сокращать, сократить) бюджет на 10 процентов.
2.   Установлено место переговоров. Пора (решать, решить) повестку дня.
3.   Не волнуйтесь: план всегда можно (восстанавливать, восстановить), если он понадобится.
4.   Есть опасение, что нельзя будет (завершать, завершить) работу над договором к концу года.
5.   Вы правы: мы не должны (вести, провести) переговоры с расистским правительством.
6.   К сожалению, более 40 процентов трудоспособного населения не может (находить, найти) работу.
7.   Из-за таких экологических ошибок может (гибнуть, погибнуть) тысяча человек.
8.   Я советую не (встречаться, встретиться) с прессой. На неконтролируемой пресс-конференции вы можете (говорить, сказать) что-нибудь не то.
9.   Не надо (делать, сделать) одностронних уступок. Другая сторона может это (принимать, принять) как знак слабости.
10. Надо всегда хорошо (продумывать, продумать) свою позицию, иначе можно (допускать, допустить) роковую ошибку.

B. **Translate the following short sentences. Compare the use of aspect.**

a. *сдаваться / сдаться*
1. We have to give up.
2. We should give up.
3. We musn't give up.
4. We can't give up.
5. It's about time we gave up.
6. We advise you to give up.
7. We advise you not to give up.

b. *вставать / встать*
1. We have to get up (it's 7:00 am).
2. It's impossible to get up.
3. We shouldn't get up.
4. It's best not to get up.

c. *забывать / забыть*
1. They must forget the past.
2. They can't (seem to) forget the past.
3. They can't (musn't) forget the past.
4. They might forget the past.
5. It's high time they forgot the past.
6. They promised not to forget the past.

d. *повышать / повысить*
1. It's impossible to raise taxes.
2. We can always raise taxes.
3. We'd better not raise taxes.
4. We musn't raise taxes.
5. We should raise taxes.
6. They asked us not to raise taxes
7. We want to raise taxes.

e. *начинать / начать*
1. He might start a war.
2. He shouldn't start a war.
3. He can start a war.
4. We warned him not to start a war

f. *избирать / избрать*
1. Time to elect a new president.
2. It's about time we elected a new president.
3. We are not allowed to elect a new president.
4. It's impossible to elect a new president.
5. We want to elect a new president

RENDERING

Give your own personal formula for fixing the Soviet economy. You may use any plan you wish. Pick and choose from some of the fixes below, or make up your own. But if your plan contains any of the following solutions, be prepared how you will deal (or not deal) with the possible consequences:

A convertible ruble

Convertible currency would allow Soviet citizens access to foreign goods and attract foreign investment by guaranteeing that profits could be taken out of the country. But with convertibility comes ruble devaluation and inflation. Foreign goods, such as Italian detergent, previously rationed, would now rise in price to levels that only the rich can afford.

Privatization of enterprises

Entrepreneurs might rush to get their hands the means of production. Free to invest, set prices, hire, and fire as they saw fit, the new managers would be sure to get enterprises on the road to efficiency. But cutting fat at overstaffed factories would add millions of resentful workers to unemployment rolls. Prices would rise to their natural market levels making efficiently produced goods generally available — but only to those who could now afford them. Those who remain on the government payroll or on fixed pension income are sure to see very hard times.

Privatization of agriculture

Agricultural reform along the lines of the Chinese program of the late 1970s and early 80s would almost certainly allow the country to feed itself, but again at the risk of unemployment (many former inefficient kolkhozniki with nothing to do, given that an efficient agriculture on the scale of a country as large as the USSR needs at most between two and ten percent of its people in the fields, not thirty or forty) and inflation (rising food prices: in 1990 a loaf of state-produced bread was drastically underpriced at the hard currency equivalent of two or three cents).

Limits on subsidized housing

Curtailing subsidized housing would encourage new home construction and put pressure on the government to do away with residence permits (пропиcка). But with real-market housing prices comes even more inflation, forcing low wage earners either into unemployment in the countryside (where agricultural work would be scarce - see above) or into slums. In short, housing reforms or an end to enforced residence permits could stimulate housing starts, or it could turn big cities into poverty-ridden carbon copies of Mexico City or S,o Paolo.

Privatization with a social safety net

Cutbacks in state spending to cover basic social needs on the level of, say, Scandinavian welfare states would guarantee education, medicine, and housing. After all, there are few, if any, homeless illiterates in Sweden. But Sweden's social welfare net is based on a large tax base built on an economic structure well in place. In short, a country can't share wealth that it does not yet have.

Creation of a meritocracy

Many argue that what is needed is not capitalism *per se*, but rather any system that leads to an order whereby merit is rewarded. Indeed, up until now inefficient foremen lived more or less the same as talented artists. But if in the future good work is rewarded at the expense of bad work, a great many bad workers will be out for blood.

SPEAKING EXERCISES

A.   Расскажи́те втору́ю часть те́кста. В своём расска́зе испо́льзуйте сле́дующие выраже́ния.

вот почему́...; при э́том; не то́лько..., но и...; кро́ме того́; неудиви́тельно.

B.   Расскажи́те весь текст с то́чки зре́ния за́падного экономи́ста.

C.   Сумми́руйте весь текст в не́скольких предложе́ниях.

D.   Отве́тьте на сле́дующие вопро́сы.

1.   Каки́е пла́новые зада́ния сове́тской эконо́мике не удало́сь вы́полнить?
2.   В чём суть позити́вных переме́н, говоря́щих, что перестро́йка ещё не обречена́?
3.   Что происхо́дит с дефици́том госуда́рственного бюдже́та СССР?
4.   Какова́ ситуа́ция с жи́зненным у́ровнем населе́ния?
5.   Отдаёт ли сове́тская эконо́мика предпочте́ние инвести́циям или потребле́нию?

E.   Дополни́тельные вопро́сы. (optional)

1.   Расскажи́те о том, как дефици́т госуда́рственного бюдже́та влия́ет на америка́нскую и сове́тскую эконо́мику.
2.   Объясни́те, почему́ сове́тские лю́ди не удовлетворены́ свои́м положе́нием, несмотря́ на значи́тельный рост дохо́дов.
3.   Ду́маете ли вы, что Горбачёв и его́ колле́ги отве́тственны за ны́нешние тру́дности в сове́тской эконо́мике?

READING EXERCISE

Ядерная война и политика.   Александр Бовин

PRE-TEXT: The author is a well known political commentator, who, even during the Brezhnev years, was viewed as more "liberal" than some in the official Soviet press. Read the text with the following questions in mind. Try to predict the answers in advance. Then re-read the article to see if you were correct and answer the questions in written form.

1. What is the main idea of the article?

PARAGRAPH1
2. What is Karl Clausewitz's definition of a war?
3. How has this formula been interpreted in the last several decades?

PARAGRAPH 2
4. Marxists considered this precept as... (Mark the correct answer):
  a.   a basis for understanding of each particular war.
  b.   a foundation for "a just war."

PARAGRAPH 3
5. Bovin quotes three points of Clausewitz's definition. Name them.

PARAGRAPH 4
6. Why is Clausewitz's formula valid for nuclear war?

PARAGRAPH 5
7. What determines the choice between diplomacy and fighting to attain one's goals?

PARAGRAPH 6
8. According to political thinking of the nuclear age... (Mark the correct answer):
  a.   there is no alternative to using nuclear weapons to achieve one's ends.
  b.   nuclear war will not jeopardize the human race.
  c.   under no circumstances can a nuclear war be viewed as a rational tool of policy.

PARAGRAPHS 8-14
9. Bovin indicates certain consequences of a nuclear war on political thinking. Name them.

PARAGRAPH 9
10. On the basis of the text, explain the notion of security through force and security instead of force.

PARAGRAPHS 11,12
11. Compare the rationality for waging war in pre-nuclear times and in the nuclear age.

PARAGRAPH 13

12. The issue of "a just war" in the nuclear age is a mere abstraction today because... (Mark the correct answer):
    a.   the concepts *just* and *unjust* are themselves abstract.
    b.   a nuclear war will last mere seconds.
    c.   without people to populate the Earth history stops.

13. What is the only reasonable, moral and politically justified attitude toward a nuclear war?

PARAGRAPH 14

14. Which Marxist thesis has to be adjusted vis-a-vis the justification for a nuclear war?
15. Lenin predicted in 1918 that... (Mark the correct answer):
    a.   the time would come when war becomes so destructive that it will not be worth fighting.
    b.   development of technology would speed up social stratification.
    c.   an abundance of military technology would force capitalists to use it.

PARAGRAPH 16

16. At what point do the interests of the capitalist and socialist worlds begin to coincide?

PARAGRAPH 17

17. What is the significance of the ratification of the INF Treaty?

POST-TEXT (using context):

PARAGRAPH 1

1. The introductory paragraph ... (Mark the correct answer):
    a.   makes a statement.
    b.   makes a statement and challenges it.

    Prove your point.

2. Paraphrase both words in the expression *другими способами.*

PARAGRAPH 2

3. Find the marker which signals the beginning of the analysis of the problem.
4. What derivatives of the word *труд* do you know?

PARAGRAPH 3

5. Find the synonym for **средство** поли́тики.
6. Find the opposite for на свое́й **ни́зшей** то́чке.
7. What is the opposite for **наси́льственными** сре́дствами?

PARAGRAPH 6

8. Find a synonym for *вы́йти из употребле́ния* in this paragraph.

PARAGRAPHS 8-12

9. Which markers indicate different consequences of a political thinking in the nuclear age?

PARAGRAPH 8

10. Find the use of redundancy here. What is its purpose?

PARAGRAPH 9

11. Find the opposite of **одностороннее** *сокращёние*.

PARAGRAPH 12,13

12. What question does *Поэтому* answer?
13. What uses of redundancy do you see in this paragraph?

PARAGRAPH 17

14. Find the use of redundancy in this paragraph.
15. Paraphrase **полностью** блокировать.
16. Can you infer why Bovin felt the need for his article?
17. Find paragraphs where the author's tone is:
　　a. playful
　　b. scholarly
　　c. positive
　　d. negative.

18. Pick the correct meaning for each of the words below:

　　1. иными срёдствами　　　　a. by foreign means
　　　　　　　　　　　　　　　b. in a different fashion

　　2. настáивать на обрáтном　a. to insist on returning
　　　　　　　　　　　　　　　b. to insist on the opposite

　　3. оценить　　　　　　　　a. to evaluate
　　　　　　　　　　　　　　　b. to appreciate

　　4. писáть нóты　　　　　　a. to make notes
　　　　　　　　　　　　　　　b. to write music

　　5. сменить перо на шпáгу　a. to exchange a feather for a sword
　　　　　　　　　　　　　　　b. to exchange a pen for a sword

　　6. труд «О войнé»　　　　a. the book "On Wars"
　　　　　　　　　　　　　　　b. labor concerning a war

　　7. любáя войнá　　　　　　a. a favorite war
　　　　　　　　　　　　　　　b. any war

　　8. неподвлáстный врéмени　a. always correct
　　　　　　　　　　　　　　　b. influenced by time

9. насилие есть повивальная
    бабка истории

   a. rape is the midwife of history
   b. violence is the midwife of history

10. приемлемая альтернатива

   a. an acceptable alternative
   b. an attractive alternative

11. род человеческий

   a. the human race
   b. human gender

12. шкала ценностей

   a. school of pricing
   b. scale of values

19. Find the Russian for:

- to attain one's ends
- suicidal consequences
- to go beyond the framework of...
- here our interests cross

ИЗВЕСТИЯ

Мнение политического обозревателя

ЯДЕРНАЯ ВОЙНА И ПОЛИТИКА

Уже НЕСКОЛЬКО десятилетий продолжались споры вокруг формулы известного немецкого военного теоретика начала XIX века Карла Клаузевица — война есть продолжение политики иными средствами. Применима ли эта формула в ядерный век? Точнее—к ядерной войне? Одни утверждали, что неприменима. Другие решительно настаивали на обратном. Однако, как мне представляется, реальная ситуация сложнее, чем жесткое, метафизическое противопоставление «да» и «нет».

Итак, обратимся к Клаузевицу. Вот его подлинные слова: «Война есть не что иное, как продолжение государственной политики иными средствами». В. И. Ленин, который внимательно изучал, конспектировал основной труд Клаузевица «О войне», так оценил его формулу: «Это знаменитое изречение принадлежит одному из самых глубоких писателей по военным вопросам, Клаузевицу. Марксисты справедливо считали всегда это положение теоретической основой взглядов на значение каждой данной войны».

Развивая свою мысль, немецкий теоретик отмечал: войну «мы должны мыслить при всех обстоятельствах не как **нечто самостоятельное**, а как орудие политики»; «военное искусство на своей высшей точке становится политикой, дающей сражение вместо того, чтобы писать ноты». И еще одно высказывание: «Ведение войны в его главных очертаниях есть сама политика, сменившая перо на шпагу...»

Итак, война есть орудие политики, продолжение политики. Думается, что этот тезис сохраняет свою силу применительно к любой войне, в том числе и ядерной. В самом деле. Ведь независимо от объективно неизбежных катастрофических, самоубийственных последствий такой войны те, кто захотел бы ее начать, будут продолжать свою политику, будут использовать войну именно как орудие политики, как средство достижения определенных политических целей. В этом отношении ядерная война не отличалась бы от войн доядерной эпохи. Здесь формула Клаузевица аксиоматична и неподвластна времени.

Но формула Клаузевица выходит за рамки указанной констатации. Она предполагает, что всегда существует возможность выбора: чтобы добиться поставленной цели, можно — в зависимости от конкретных обстоятельств — действовать либо мирными, либо «иными», насильственными, средствами. Все решает оценка соотношения сил. Оба варианта — перо и шпага, сражение и дипломатическая нота — в принципе полностью равноправны.

Здесь Клаузевиц устарел. У современного политика, имеющего в своем распоряжении ядерное оружие, такого выбора нет. Ибо нет и не может быть такой политической цели, ради достижения которой имело бы смысл начать ядерную войну, рисковать будущим человечества. Ни при каких обстоятельствах ядерная война не может рассматриваться как разумный выбор, как рациональное средство продолжения политики. Значит, мирному сосуществованию нет приемлемой для человечества альтернативы. Таков исходный постулат нового политического мышления, мышления ядерного века.

Из этого постулата можно извлечь любопытные и нетривиальные следствия. Укажу некоторые из них.

Качественно меняется назначение, смысл мирного сосуществования. Теперь это не только наиболее желательное, наиболее разумное состояние отношений между капиталистическими и социалистическими странами. Теперь это единственно возможное состояние. Теперь «сосуществование» немирное тождественно несуществованию, гибели рода человеческого.

Если раньше, в век доядерный, гарантией безопасности государства могло выступать накопление силы, оружия, то теперь односторонняя безопасность немыслима. Теперь гарантию безопасности могут дать только политические соглашения, предполагающие взаимное снижение военно-силовых потенциалов. Не безопасность как следствие силы, а безопасность вместо силы — так теперь стоит вопрос.

Пойдем дальше.

Почему воевали и воюют люди? Потому что — с точки зрения и тех, кто начинает войну, и тех, кто вынужден сопротивляться, — есть вещи, которые ценятся выше, чем мир. Для одних это — власть и богатство, для других — независимость и свобода. Для американцев в конце XVIII века и для вьетнамцев в середине XX века независимость была важнее мира. И они воевали. Они хотели победить и победили.

А если войну нельзя выиграть? Если тот, кто начинает первым, погибнет вторым? Тут прежняя шкала ценностей перестает действовать. Нет вещи важнее мира, если альтернативой миру служит ядерная катастрофа.

Абстрактно рассуждая, можно сказать, что ядерная война может быть справедливой — ответный ядерный удар, удар возмездия. Но это пустая, бессодержательная абстракция. Различение справедливого и несправедливого (если иметь в виду не субъективные ощущения воюющего, а объективный характер войны) получает смысл только для живых, только для истории, которая длится. Там же, где гибнет род людской, где история кончается, кончается и указанное различение. Поэтому применительно к ядерной войне ядерный пацифизм, то есть безусловное, если угодно, абсолютное отрицание правомерности такой войны, есть единственно разумная, единственно нравственная и политически оправданная позиция.

Подлежит, видимо, существенному ограничению и известный тезис марксизма: насилие есть повивальная бабка истории. В свое время В. И. Ленин имел все основания сказать о первой мировой войне, что она «неслыханным образом ускорила социальное развитие», что война «подтолкнула историю, и она летит теперь с быстротой локомотива». Это же можно сказать и о второй мировой войне. А о третьей? О войне ядерной? Как вспоминает Н. К. Крупская, еще в 1918 году, размышляя о характере войн, задумываясь над будущим, Ленин говорил, что «современная техника сейчас все более и более помогает разрушительному характеру войны. Но будет такое время, когда война станет настолько разрушительной, что она вообще станет невозможной».

Мы подошли к такому времени.

Насилие, которое таит в себе угрозу всемирной катастрофы, не может выступать в качестве ускорителя социального прогресса. Ядерное насилие несет смерть, а не обновление жизни. Применение ядерного оружия — это убийство и самоубийство. Здесь, в этой точке анализа перекрещиваются интересы и капиталистического, и социалистического миров, интересы всех участников мирового сообщества. И это вселяет надежду.

Предотвратить, наглухо блокировать ядерную войну — такова главная задача политики и политиков ядерного века. К ее решению ведет только один путь — ядерное разоружение. Ратификация Договора по РСД—РМД будет означать, что путь этот начат.

А. БОВИН.

AUDIO–COMPREHENSION EXERCISE

Part 1

You are about to hear a text about reductions in military outlays. Review the key words on the following page. Then listen to the text with the following questions in mind. Afterwards, listen to the text again, and write down the answers.

1. The beginning of the 1990s was buzzing with talk about the end of the Cold War and the possibility of massive cuts in military spending. Summarize what you already know about these developments.
2. What does the author say about the exchange of military information between the superpowers? What is said about the availability of this information to common citizens?
3. What is the goal of GON?
4. What did the Chief of the Soviet General Staff arrange for GON to do?
5. Who belongs to GON?
6. Supply the following statistical information:
    a. Cuts in military personnel: _______________________________.
    b. Number of officers retired: _______________________________.
    c. Number of warrant officers retired: _______________________.
7. List two military districts which were liquidated.
8. Name at least two other military units that were done away with.
9. Name three actions that were taken regarding the Soviet military presence in Mongolia.
10. Provide any statistics you can on the reduction of tanks, artillery, and aircraft in Europe.
11. What will be done with demobilized military personnel?

12.   Fill in any three items in the following table:

Group	Tanks	Equipment	Aircraft	Personnel
Western group				
Central Group				
Southern Group				
Mongolia				
TOTAL				

Key words

Генера́льный Штаб ВС СССР – General Staff of the Armed Forces of the USSR
ограниче́ние и сокраще́ние вооруже́ний – limitation and reduction of weapons
обме́н больши́м коли́чеством вое́нной информа́ции – exchange of a large amount of
defense information
Гру́ппа обще́ственного наблюде́ния – Public Oversight Group
проби́ть брешь в чрезме́рной секре́тности – to begin to reduce excessive secrecy
Каков́ же вы́вод...? – What is the conclusion?
брига́ды ПВО – Air Defense Force brigades
наступа́тельные возмо́жности вооружённых сил ОВД – offensive capabilities of
the Warsaw Pact armed forces
при́зрак «ру́сских казако́в, жела́ющих искупа́ть свои́ та́нки в Ла-Ма́нше» – the ghost
of "the Russian cossacks who want to wash their tanks in the English
Channel"

TEXT: Read the following text; be able to translate it into English in written form.

Пойду́т ли ру́сские к Ла-Ма́ншу?   Часть 1

При ны́нешних те́мпах сокраще́ния сове́тских войск э́та зада́ча ста́нет для них крайне риско́ванной, счита́ют америка́нские конгрессме́ны. Последняя сво́дка Генера́льного шта́ба ВС СССР подтвержда́ет сугу́бо оборони́тельный хара́ктер перестро́йки в на́шей а́рмии.
Гла́сность в вое́нной сфе́ре даётся нелегко́. Она́ отстаёт от остально́й перестро́йки. Да́же в после́дние го́ды, когда проце́сс перегово́ров об ограниче́нии

и сокращéнии вооружéний сдéлал нормáльным обмéн бóльшим колúчеством воéнной информáции мéжду Совéтским Сою́зом и Соединёнными Штáтами, э́та информáция, как прáвило, окáзывалась недостýпной широ́кой обще́ственности.   Создáние Грýппы обще́ственного наблюдéния (ГОН) за сокращéнием вооружённых сил и вооружéний в какóй-то мéре бы́ло при́звано пробúть брешь в чрезмéрной секрéтности, котóрая не шла на пóльзу отношéниям мéжду áрмией и óбществом.

Начáльник Генерáльного Штáба ВС СССР генерáл áрмии М. Моисéев помóг представúтелям ГОН – учёным, журналúстам, нарóдным депутáтам СССР – побывáть в совéтских грýппах войск и в Монгóльской Нарóдной Респýблике.   На минýвшей недéле, как ужé сообщáла «Прáвда», грýппа наблюдáла за вы́водом из боевóго состáва флóта подвóдной лóдки.

Какóв же вы́вод представúтелей «нарóдной дипломáтии»?   Совéтский Сою́з, считáет председáтель грýппы член-корреспондéнт АН СССР А. Кокóшин, осуществля́я при́нятые в одностороннем поря́дке решéния, демонстрúрует практúческую реализáцию при́нципа оборонúтельной достáточности.   И что осóбенно вáжно, э́тот процéсс мóгут воóчию наблюдáть представúтели обще́ственности.

Скóлько же вооружённых сил сокращенó?   На 1 ноября́, соглáсно полýченным в Генерáльном штáбе дáнным, чи́сленность Вооружённых Сил умéньшилась на 235,5 ты́сячи человéк.   Увóлено óколо 65 ты́сяч офицéров и бóлее 20 ты́сяч прáпорщиков. Упразднены́ два воéнных óкруга – Среднеазиáтский и Урáльский и управлéния четырёх армéйских кóрпусов.   Расформирóваны вы́веденные из состáва Зáпадной и Южной грýпп войск 13-ая, 25-ая и 32-ая гвардéйские тáнковые диви́зии и одúн авиациóнный полк.   Из МНР вы́ведены однá тáнковая диви́зия, три бригáды ПВО, а тáкже вы́ведены и расформирóваны авиациóнная диви́зия, авиациóнный полк и три отдéльных вертолётных отря́да.

Вот как вы́глядят на сегóдняшний день сокращéния Совéтских Вооружённых Сил за предéлами СССР:

Группы войск	Танки	Орудия	Самолеты	Личный состав
Западная группа	1 988	247	126	11 620
Центральная группа	192	22	20	1 500
Южная группа	447	176	76	10 800
Северная группа	87	16	88	3 500
Монгольская Народная Республика	404	307	41	22 900
ВСЕГО по группам войск и МНР	3 118	768	351	50 320

Всегó же в хóде проведённого сокращéния колúчество совéтских вооружéний в Еврóпе умéньшено на 7120 тáнков, 2964 артиллерúйские систéмы, 735 самолётов.

Каковы́ послéдствия э́тих сокращéний?   Да, наступáтельные возмóжности вооружённых сил ОВД в Центрáльной Еврóпе сократúлись.   В пéрвую óчередь речь идёт о так называ́емых оперативно-манёвренных грýппах, о котóрых произноси́лось мнóго речéй, пугáющих при́зраком «рýсских казакóв, желáющих искупáть свои́ тáнки в Ла-Мáнше».   Произошлó сокращéние воéнного противостоя́ния не тóлько в Центрáльной Еврóпе, но и на Дáльнем Востóке.   Существéнно повы́сились оборонúтельные возмóжности Совéтских Вооружённых Сил, осóбенно укрепи́лся потенциáл противотáнковой оборóны.   Вы́свободились и дополнúтельные ресýрсы рабóчей си́лы для нарóдного хозя́йства.

Words and expressions to part 1

	(чего?)
сокращёние	воённого противостоя́ния – military standoff
	коли́чества совётских вооруже́ний – reduction in the number of Soviet weapons
	чи́сленности вооружённых сил – reduction in the number of armed forces (personnel)
	наступа́тельных возмо́жностей

сокраща́ть/сократи́ть
      -ют   -я́т

сокращено́	коли́чество	та́нков
		артиллерийских систе́м
		самолётов – aircraft
сокращена́	чи́сленность	воённых округо́в
		операти́вно-манёвренных групп – operational-maneuver groups
		групп войск за преде́лами СССР – groups of forces outside the Soviet Union

обороми́тельный хара́ктер – defensive character
наступа́тельный хара́ктер – offensive character

отстава́ть/отста́ть   (от чего́?)
    -ют отста́нут   от остально́го ми́ра
                         от ра́звитых капиталисти́ческих стра́н
    – to fall behind the developed capitalist countries
отстава́ние

(не)досту́пный   (чему́?)
                        широ́кой обще́ственности
(in)accessible   рядовы́м гра́жданам – average citizens
                        гру́ппам обще́ственного наблюде́ния
                        – public oversight groups

при́зван(-а,-о,-ы)   сократи́ть чрезме́рную секре́тность
                        – to reduce excessive secrecy
                        увели́чить боеспосо́бность вооружённых сил

в односторо́ннем поря́дке   упраздни́ть два воённых о́круга
                                – to liquidate two military districts
                                расформирова́ть гру́ппу войск
                                – to disband a group of forces
                                вы́вести войска́ из Восто́чной Герма́нии
                                – withdraw troops from East Germany
                                уво́лить 65 ты́сяч офице́ров
                                – to retire 65 thousands officers

óкруг (pl. округá, округóв)

упразднять/упразднить
        -ют   -ят
упразднéние
упразднена́   Южная гру́ппа войск
упразднено́   управлéние четырёх армéйских кóрпусов
                       - command of four army corps

кóрпус (pl. корпуса́, корпусóв)

расформирóвывать/расформирова́ть
            -ют   -у́ют
расформирова́ние

расформирóвана   бригáда ПВО - Air Defense brigade
расформирóваны   гвардéйские та́нковые диви́зии - guards tank divisions

выводи́ть/вы́вести
вывóдят вы́ведут
вы́вод

вы́ведена   авиацио́нная диви́зия - air division
вы́веден   авиацио́нный полк - air regiment
вы́ведены   три вертолётных отря́да - three helicopter detachments
                из боевóго соста́ва - taken out of service

полк (pl. полки́, полкóв)

увольня́ть/увóлить
        -ют   -ят

увóлено   20 ты́сяч пра́порщиков - 20 thousand warrant officers
                      5 ты́сяч ста́рших офицéров - 5 thousand senior officers
                      23 ты́сячи ли́чного соста́ва - 23 thousand personnel

пониже́ние наступа́тельных возмо́жностей
повыше́ние оборони́тельных возмо́жностей - raising defensive capabilities
            потенциа́ла противота́нковой оборо́ны - raising the potential of
                                          anti-tank defense

VOCABULARY EXERCISES

Look through the vocabulary of part 1 of the text «*Пойдут ли русские к Ла-Маншу?*», **then do the following exercises.**

A. **Give the nominative and the genitive plural for the following nouns. Mark the stress.**

танк, система, группа, секретность, характер, сила, округ, дивизия, корпус, возможность, оборона, полк.

B. **Give perfective forms for the following verbs. Conjugate both forms and mark the stress.**

отставать, сокращать, расформировывать, увольнять.

C. **Paraphrase the italicized words.**

расформировать группу войск, *снижение* военного противостояния, *быть позади* остального мира.

D. **Give the opposite for the words in italics.**

наступательные возможности, *ввести* вертолётный отряд, *развивающиеся* страны, в *двустороннем* порядке, *повышение* потенциала.

E. **Form nouns from the following verbs.**

упразднить управление армейского корпуса, вывести авиационную дивизию, отставать от остального мира.

F. **Give Russian equivalents for the following English phrases.**

- reduction in number of U.S. Armed Forces
- reduction in the number of Soviet weapons
- falling behind capitalist countries
- to retire senior officers
- disbanding an Air Defense brigade
- lowering the potential of anti-tank defense
- designed to raise the combat ability of aircraft
- unilaterally
- withdrawal of 5 helicopter detachments

G. Write sentences to fill in the blanks in each of the groups below.
Be able to translate your sentences.

1. договор   призван   (сделать что?)
    сокращение сил   призвано   ____________
    расфомирование танковых   ____________
        дивизий   ____________

2. в одностороннем порядке   выведено   (что? сколько?)
                                                 сокращено   ____________
                                                 упразднено   ____________
                                                 уволено   ____________
                                                 расформировано   ____________

3. уровень   производства   (чего)   отстаёт   (от чего?)
               __________   __________
               сокращения
               __________   __________
               увольнений
               __________   __________

4. информация   доступна   (кому? чему?)
    эти данные   недоступны   ____________
    текст договора   недоступен   ____________
                                      ____

GRAMMAR EXERCISES: REVIEW OF CASES

Review the use of cases as presented in Circle One. Do the following exercises.

A. Determine the use of case in the sentences below. Fill in the blanks. Be able to translate the sentences into English.

1. Закон США об иностранных миссиях даёт (неограниченная власть) _____________ запретить (любая трансакция) _______________ (иностранные миссии) ________________.

2. Премьер-министр маневрирует, идёт на (уступки) _________, чтобы постепенно взять под (контроль) _____________ (оппозиция) _________.

3. Нынешнее панамское правительство похоже на (марионетка) ___________ в (руки) ________ Вашингтона.

4. Много (палестинцы) _________ покинуло родные места.

5. (Самые обиженные) __________ в результате уравнения в правах оказались наиболее (бедные и тёмные слои) _______________ белого населения.

6. Наши успехи при (социализм) _________ свидетельствуют о (правильность) __________ нашего выбора.

7. Генеральная Ассамблея требует (безопасный проход) _______________ гражданских судов через (Персидский залив) _________.

8. Некоторые (беженцы) _________ возращаются под конвоем в (лагеря) _________.

9. (Развитие атомной энергии) _________ принадлежит будущее.

10. После испытаний, через (которые) __________ прошёл наш народ, нам не могут показаться (страшные) __________ пустые угрозы.

B. Translate the following sentences.

1. Sociologists do not believe in the effectiveness of an alcohol consumption tax.
2. The co-authors of the bill thanked their advisers for the preparation of the "austerity policy" program.
3. After the signing procedure the Soviet delegation will tour the United States for a week.
4. International banks expect high interest rates as a result of the new US monetary policy.

5. Arms control became a must for the normalization of US–Soviet relations.
6. The Pentagon sources disclosed that American POWs in Vietnam were denied the right to correspond with their families.
7. Lybia blamed the United States for the air raid last week.
8. The information concerning a new Soviet submarine contradicts a secret CIA report.
9. Who preceded the general now presiding over the council?
10. Large budget cuts should contribute to the deficit reductions by at least $23 billion.

GRAMMAR: QUANTITIES IN OBLIQUE CASES

Look at the following sentences:

Nominative and accusative (when like nominative)	All other cases (oblique)
Мы прослу́шали мно́го рече́й.	Мы ду́мали о мно́гих реча́х.
Мы ви́дели два за́ла.	Мы бы́ли в двух за́лах.
Мы прослу́шали две ре́чи.	Мы ду́мали о двух реча́х.
Он всте́тил пять делега́тов.	Он поговори́л с пятью́ делега́тами.

As you can see, quantities, including numbers, decline except for a) in the nominative, and b) in the accusative (which looks like the nominative).

If a number or quantity is declined and the form changes (e.g. мно́го --> мно́гими), *the following noun does not automatically go into genitive.* Instead the case of the quantified noun is "normalized." In other words, the case corresponds to sentence position as if no number or quantity were present: **две кни́ги,** but о **двух кни́гах.**

In cardinal numbers ("1, 2, 3," not "first, second, third") *each digit* declines: от 123 челове́к = от ста двадцати́ трёх челове́к.

Mass quantities (**ско́лько, мно́го, не́сколько, не́которые**) are declined in *plural* with nouns that can be counted, which is the case in most situations.

Fortunately, except in the most formal of writing, multidigit numbers are not used in places where they would have to be declined. This especially applies to the English expression "between X and Y amount of something." Note that Russian avoids a ме́жду construction: "Between five and ten delegates were there" is **Там бы́ло пять – де́сять делега́тов.**

GRAMMAR EXERCISES: QUANTITIES IN OBLIQUE CASES

Review Quantities in Oblique Cases.   Then do the exercises below.

A.   Decline the following words.

	два	три	четыре	двести пятьдесят девять
чего	_______	_______	_________	_________________________
чему	_______	_______	_________	_________________________
чем	_______	_______	_________	_________________________
о чём	_______	_______	_________	_________________________

	много	сколько	несколько	некоторые	мало
	(G i v e p l u r a l f o r m s o n l y)				
чего	_________	_________	_________	_________	_________
чему	_________	_________	_________	_________	_________
чем	_________	_________	_________	_________	_________
о чём	_________	_________	_________	_________	_________

B.   Fill in the blanks with the correct form.   Write out all numbers.

1.   На съезд приехали делегаты из (*many cities*) _____________.

2.   В Европейской конференции участвует более (*35 nations*) _____________.

3.   Со (*many*) _____________ из предложений я не могу согласиться.

4.   По этому вопросу просто не может быть (*two points of view*) _____________.

5.   Мы познакомились с (*three delegates*) _____________– участниками конференции.

6.   Согласно компьютерным моделям, выработаннным (*by many scientists*) _____________, в результате одного атомного взрыва погибнет около (*two and a half million people*) _____________.

7.   Новая система распределения ресурсов планируется в (*four cities*) _____________.

8.   (*In several instances*) _____________ было арестовано более (*150 demonstrators*) _____________.

9.   Новое устройство сразу обеспечивает автоматическое дистанционное управление (*of three machines*) _____________.

10. Наш   отдел   сейчас   завершает   работу   над   *(several   projects)*
_________________ более чем в *(five areas)* _________________.

11. *(In how many countries)* _________________ есть настоящие гарантии
прав человека?

12. Данная техника позволяет перевод информации со скоростью до *(2400)*
_________________ бит в секунду.

SPEAKING EXERCISES

A. **Расскажи́те пе́рвую часть те́кста. В своём расска́зе испо́льзуйте сле́дующие выраже́ния.**

итáк; с э́той це́лью; с одно́й стороны́..., с друго́й стороны́...; в результа́те; тем бо́лее, что...; одна́ко; ведь.

B. **Сумми́руйте пе́рвую часть в не́скольких предложе́ниях.**

C. **Отве́тьте на сле́дующие вопро́сы.**

1. Как отрази́лась секре́тность на отноше́ниях ме́жду а́рмией и о́бществом в СССР?
2. В чём суть сокраще́ния вооружённых сил СССР?
3. Каковы́ после́дствия э́тих сокраще́ний?
4. Как отрази́лось сокраще́ние вооружённых сил СССР на сове́тской обороноспосо́бности?

D. **Дополни́тельные вопро́сы. (optional)**

1. Сравни́те отноше́ние к секре́тности в СССР и в США.
2. Объясни́те, как отража́ется односторо́ннее сокраще́ние сове́тских вооружённых сил на перегово́рах об ограниче́нии вооруже́ний.
3. Объясни́те, почему́ Сове́тский Сою́з полага́ет, что односторо́ннее сокраще́ние вооруже́ний не подверга́ет его́ опа́сности.

AUDIO-COMPREHENSION EXERCISE

part 2

Listen to the tape with the following questions in mind:

1. What military contacts took place in August?
2. What did a member of the American delegation say about Gorbachev's proposed cuts in the Warsaw Pact's military presence?
3. According to a member of the USA and Canada Institute, how did NATO react to the proposed cuts?
4. Name at least four actions taken by the U.S. that the Soviets find reassuring.
5. Why is the tone of this piece optimistic towards West Germany?
6. What is said about Canada?
7. In view of the developments cited, does the commentator believe that the arms race is a thing of the past?

Key words

по вопро́сам оборо́ны и госуда́рственной безопа́сности – on questions of
defense and national security
пала́та представи́телей Конгре́сса США – House of Representatives of
the US Congress
чи́сленность сил передово́го бази́рования Варша́вского Догово́ра – the number of
Warsaw Treaty forward-based forces
недопусти́мо риско́ванный – unacceptably risky
пе́рвые при́знаки практи́ческой реа́кции – first signs of a practical reaction
односторо́нние сокраще́ния – unilateral reductions
при́нято реше́ние не развёртывать... – a decision is made not to deploy...
на два го́да ра́ньше сро́ка – two years ahead of schedule
списа́ние ... устаре́вших эсми́нцев... – the retiring of obsolete destroyers
уда́рно-тра́нспортный самолёт – assault transport plane
ко́рпус морско́й пехо́ты – Marine Corps
отменены́ пла́ны оснаще́ния часте́й, обслу́живавших ра́нее раке́ты сре́дней да́льности
– plans to support units formerly servicing medium-range missiles
are canceled

Key verbs

приня́ть: При́нято реше́ние...– decision is made
ускóрить: Ускóрено списа́ние... – writing off is accelerated
сократи́ть: Сокращены́ закýпки ... – purchases are reduced
аннули́ровать: Аннули́рована програ́мма... – program is annulled
отмени́ть: Отменены́ пла́ны... – plans are cancelled
отложи́ть: Отло́жено реше́ние...– decision is postponed

TEXT: Read the following text; be able to translate it into English in written form.

Пойду́т ли ру́сские к Ла-Ма́ншу?   Часть 2

Побыва́вшая в а́вгусте э́того го́да по приглаше́нию Комите́та по вопро́сам оборо́ны и госуда́рственной безопа́сности Верхо́вного Сове́та СССР делега́ция коми́ссии по дела́м вооружённых сил пала́ты представи́телей Конгре́сса США во главе́ с Ле́сом Эспином констати́ровала в докла́де, пре́данном гла́сности две неде́ли наза́д, что америка́нская сторона́ не име́ет сомне́ний в серьёзности наме́рений сове́тского прави́тельства и что «сокраще́ния, предло́женные Горбачёвым, значи́тельно сократя́т чи́сленность сил передово́го бази́рования Варша́вского Догово́ра и сде́лают нападе́ние недопусти́мо риско́ванным с то́чки зре́ния Сове́тского Сою́за».

- Появи́лись и пе́рвые при́знаки, свиде́тельствующие о практи́ческой реа́кции стран НАТО на сове́тские односторо́нние сокраще́ния, - счита́ет заве́дующий отде́лом военно-полити́ческих иссле́дований Институ́та США и Кана́ды АН СССР до́ктор истори́ческих нау́к С. Ро́гов. - В Соединённых Шта́тах в 1990 - 1991 фина́нсовых года́х плани́руется сократи́ть чи́сленность вооружённых сил на три́дцать ты́сяч челове́к. При́нято реше́ние не развёртывать 15-ю авиано́сную гру́ппу и на два го́да ра́ньше наме́ченного сро́ка вы́веден из боево́го соста́ва авиано́сец «Ко́рал си» (по́сле вступле́ния в строй но́вого авиано́сца). Уско́рено списа́ние 14 устаре́вших эсми́нцев. Сокращены́ заку́пки самолётов F-14 и F/A-18 для ВМС. Аннули́рована програ́мма созда́ния уда́рно-тра́нспортного самолёта «V-22 Osprey» («Рыболо́в») для ко́рпуса морско́й пехо́ты сто́имостью в 27 миллиа́рдов до́лларов. Отменены́ пла́ны оснаще́ния часте́й, обслу́живающих ра́нее раке́ты сре́дней да́льности «Пе́ршинг-2», самохо́дными 155-мм га́убицами и́ли раке́тными систе́мами за́лпового огня́. Отло́жено реше́ние о развёртывании но́вых бомбардиро́вщиков B-2.

При́нято реше́ние о сокраще́нии вооружённых сил ФРГ на 33 ты́сячи челове́к, с 48 до 42 сокраща́ется число́ брига́д бундесве́ра, из кото́рых бу́дет изъя́то восемьсо́т та́нков ста́рых образцо́в. И Кана́да отказа́лась от пла́на строи́тельства фло́та их десяти́ - двена́дцати многоцелевы́х а́томных подво́дных ло́док о́бщей сто́имостью в 8 миллиа́рдов до́лларов. Это знак того́, что сою́зники США по НАТО то́же доверя́ют сове́тскому но́вому мышле́нию в вое́нных вопро́сах.

Пра́вда, счита́ет учёный, речь идёт скоре́е о замедле́нии те́мпов го́нки вооруже́ний, но не о её прекраще́нии. Пока́ США и стра́ны-чле́ны НАТО не хотя́т поступи́ться свои́ми основны́ми вое́нными програ́ммами, кото́рых, ви́димо, не хвата́ет для обеспече́ния национа́льной безопа́сности этих стра́н.

Н. Са́утин

Words and expressions to part 2

коми́ссия по дела́м вооружённых сил   пала́ты представи́телей
                                      сена́та
    – Armed Services Committee
коми́ссия по   иностра́нным дела́м   пала́ты представи́телей
    – House Committee on Foreign Affairs
                                        сена́та
    – Senate Foreign Relations Committee

                          (чему́?)
предава́ть/преда́ть гла́сности   результа́ты пое́здки
    –ют   –ду́т   ито́ги встре́чи в верха́х
пре́данный
                    (в чём?)
име́ть сомне́ния   в серьёзности сове́тских наме́рений
                    сокраще́нии ко́рпуса морско́й пехо́ты

                        (о чём?)
свиде́тельствовать   об односторо́ннем сокраще́нии
         –уют   о сокраще́нии сил передово́го бази́рования
– to testify to the reduction of forward-based forces
                  (чем?)
заве́дующий   отде́лом – Department chairman (research institutions)
             се́ктором – Section chaiman
             ка́федрой – Department chairman (educational institutions)

принима́ть/приня́ть реше́ние
    –ют при́мут
при́нятый
                    (perfective infinitive)
при́нято реше́ние   сократи́ть заку́пки истреби́телей в сле́дующем фина́нсовом году́
    – decision is made to reduce purchases of fighters in the next fiscal year
                   развернуть авиано́сные гру́ппы – to deploy aircraft-carrier
                                          groups
                   списа́ть 14 устаре́вших эсми́нцев – to retire 14 outmoded
                                          destroyers
                   аннули́ровать програ́мму созда́ния уда́рно-тра́нспортного самолёта
                     – to cancel the program to build an assault-transport plane

развора́чивать/разверну́ть
        –ют   –у́т
разве́рнуты   но́вые бомбардиро́вщики B-2
             си́лы передово́го бази́рования

спи́сывать/списа́ть
    –ют спи́шут
спи́сано   устаре́вшее обору́дование – obsolete equipment
спи́саны   пусковы́е устано́вки 70-х годо́в – launchers from the 70s

аннули́рована	програ́мма строи́тельства многоцелево́й а́томной подво́дной ло́дки
	– multi-purpose nuclear-powered submarine
аннули́ровано	обслу́живание раке́т сре́дней да́льности
	часте́й специа́льного назначе́ния

                   (imperfective infinitive)

при́нято реше́ние не отменя́ть пла́ны замедле́ния го́нки вооруже́ний

                  не выводи́ть из боево́го соста́ва э́тот авиано́сец

                  – not to take this aircraft carrier out of service

                  не вводи́ть в строй э́тот авиано́сец

                  – not to make this aircraft operational

                         (чем?)

оснаща́ть/оснасти́ть части   самохо́дными га́убицами

    –ют   –ят   раке́тными систе́мами за́лпового огня́

– to support units with MLRS (Multiple Launcher Rocket System)

                      та́нками ста́рых образцо́в

                       (чем?)

поступи́ться   вое́нным превосхо́дством в во́здухе

посту́пятся

– to sacrifice one's air superiority

                  основны́ми вое́нными програ́ммами

                     (чего́?)

(не) хвата́ет   но́вых вое́нных програ́мм

                   ли́чного соста́ва

нехва́тка (no pl.)   самолётов

                   артилле́рии

VOCABULARY EXERCISES

Look through the vocabulary for part 2 of the text «*Пойду́т ли ру́сские к Ла-Ма́ншу?*»**, and then do the following exercises.**

A. **Give the nominative and the genitive plural for the following nouns. Mark the stress.**

    заве́дующий, нехва́тка, представи́тель, пехо́та, ко́рпус.

B. **Give perfective forms for the following verbs. Conjugate both forms and mark the stress.**

    развора́чивать, спи́сывать, оснаща́ть.

C. Paraphrase the italicized words.

оглашáть результáты поéздки, *сомневáться в* серьёзности, *докáзывать* серьёзность намéрений, *главá* отдéла, *размещáть* сúлы передовóго базúрования, *брать на вооружéние, снабжáть* части самохóдными гáубицами, *откáзываться от* основнúх прогрáмм, *недостáток* артиллéрии.

D. Give the opposite for the words in italics.

вводúть в строй нóвую систéму, *держáть в секрéте* итóги встрéчи, *одноцелевóй.*

E. Give Russian equivalents for the following phrases.

- shortage of personnel
- decision was made not to retire the launchers
- to support the unit with self-propelled howitzers
- House Committee on Foreign Affairs
- forward-based forces are deployed
- doubts concerning possible reduction of marine corps
- department chairman (university)
- obsolete destroyers are retired
- servicing of special forces' units is cancelled

F. Write sentences to fill in the blanks in each of the groups below. Be able to translate your sentences.

        (о чём?)

1. сокращéние совéтских вооружéний свидéтельствует __________
    развёртывание нóвых систéм __________
    нехвáтка продýктов питáния __________

        (чего?)

2. в развивáющихся стрáнах не хватáет __________
    в Совéтском Союзе __________
    в войскáх __________

        (в чём?)

3. сенáторы   имéют сомнéния __________
    завéдующий сéктором   имéет __________
    комáндование áрмии __________

        (не дéлать чегó?)

4. главнокомáндующий   прúнял решéние __________
    ____
    ____

		(сделáть что?)
генерáльный штаб	прйнял решéние	____________
		____________
		____________

5. комйссия по делáм вооружённых сил предалá глáсности

(что?)

____

____

____

(чем?)

6. военнопромы́шленный кóмплекс не желáет поступйться
вы́сший офицéрский состáв
совéтское руковóдство

____

____

____

(чем?)

7. отмены́ плáны оснащáть чáсти

____

____

____

G. Translate the following sentences using vocabulary from parts 1 and 2.

1. The Air Force will never decide to sacrifice U.S. air superiority.
2. The Armed Services Committee made public its decision not to cancel the program for the development of a multi-purpose nuclear-powered submarine.
3. If we stop supporting troops with short range missiles, it will reduce our combat readiness.
4. Conservatives have doubts about Soviet intentions to retire thirty percent of their army personnel in Eastern Europe.
5. New purchases of F/A-18 fighters do not testify to a lack of financial support for defense programs on the Hill.
6. Unilaterally the Soviet Union has disbanded three groups of forces outside its territory.
7. A huge reduction in the number of Soviet weapons is intended to make the offensive character of the Soviet forces a defensive one.
8. The current retirement of thousands of personnel may lead to unemployment in the civilian branches of industry.
9. Public oversight groups make public information which is not accessible to the average citizen.
10. The number of operational-maneuver groups on Soviet territory exceeds the number of such groups overseas.

GRAMMAR EXERCISE: REVIEW OF CASES

Review the use of cases as presented in Circle One.   Do the following exercise.

Determine the use of case in the sentences below. Fill in the blanks. Be able to translate these sentences into English.

1. (Противоречивость) _______________ агрессивных (действия) _______________ США противостоит неуклонная политика мира СССР.

2. (Все) _______________ давно стало ясно, что план разработки СОИ лишён (любая человеческая логика) _______________.

3. (Ракеты) _______________ можно управлять с помощью (простейшая система дистанционного управления) ____________.

4. Беспорядки и манифестации послужили (повод) ____________ для (новая волна) _______________ массовых репрессий.

5. Стасов оказался (неспособный) _______________ командовать (целая дивизия) _______________.

6. В некоторых областях зравоохранение США отстаёт от (развитые капиталистические страны) _______________.

7. Стороны согласились на (обмен) ____________ (информация) ____________ относительно (потеря) _______________ озона в стратосфере.

8. Никарагуанский подход к вопросу подвергся (острая критика) _______________.

9. Экономический спад нанёс ущерб (целый ряд) _______________ (отрасли промышленности) _______________, в том числе и (электроника) _______________.

10. Многие считают (необходимое) _______________ рассчитывать на (ядерный арсенал) _______________ США для (полная безопасность) _______________ страны.

11. Организация «Международная амнистия» рассматривает гарантию прав человека как (одна из главных обязанностей) ____________ любого государства.

GRAMMAR: VERBS OF MOTION, CARRYING AND LEADING IN IDIOMATIC USAGE

A list of idioms with verbs of motion and their derivatives:

Verbs of going:

граница идёт на се́вер – the border runs north
о чём идёт речь? – what is being discussed?

это усло́вие вхо́дит в соглаше́ние – to enter into an agreement
он вхо́дит в комите́т по... – he is a member of the committee on...
зако́н вхо́дит в си́лу – the law goes into effect
вхожде́ние зако́на в си́лу – coming of law into effect
вход – entrance
входно́й биле́т – admission ticket

выходи́ть из комите́та по... – to leave a committee
выходи́ть в отста́вку – to retire, to resign
ничего́ из э́того не вы́шло – nothing came of it
вы́ход – exit
безвы́ходное положе́ние – a hopeless situation
выходно́й день – day off

дойти́ до примене́ния я́дерного ору́жия – to end up using nuclear weapons
дохо́д – income
подохо́дный нало́г – income tax

находи́ть вы́ход из положе́ния – to find a way out of a situation
находи́ться – to be located

переходи́ть в наступле́ние – to take the offensive
переходи́ть грани́цу – to cross a frontier, border
переходи́ть из рук в ру́ки – to change hands
переходи́ть в друго́е гражда́нство – to change one's citizenship
перехо́д – transition

приходи́ть к вы́воду – to come to a conclusion
приходи́ть к концу́ – to come to an end

подходи́ть к пробле́ме – to approach a problem
подхо́д – approach

проходи́ть исто́рию – to study history
прохо́д – passage
про́шлое – the past
проше́дшее вре́мя – past tense

сходи́ть с ума́ – to go mad, crazy
сумасше́ствие – madness
сумасше́дший – madman

Verbs of carrying:

вноси́ть предложе́ние – to submit a proposal
вноси́ть попра́вку – to introduce an amendment
вноси́ть в спи́сок – to enter on a list

выноси́ть пригово́р – to render a verdict
вынесе́ние пригово́ра – rendering of a verdict
выноси́ть страда́ния – to endure suffering
выно́сливость – endurance
выно́сливый – enduring
невыноси́мый – unbearable

наноси́ть пораже́ние – to inflict a defeat
нанесе́ние пораже́нения – inflicting of a defeat

понести́ пораже́ние – to suffer a defeat

относи́ться к пробле́ме с безразли́чием – to treat a problem with indifference
отноше́ния – relations
относи́тельный – relative *(adj.)*

произноси́ть речь – to make a speech
произноше́ние – pronounciation
ему́ везёт – he is lucky
везе́ние – luck

Verbs of leading:

вести́ перегово́ры – to conduct negotiations
веде́ние перегово́ров – conducting negotiations

вводи́ть рефо́рмы – to introduce reforms
вводи́ть зако́н в си́лу – to put a law into effect
введе́ние – introduction

вводи́ть войска́ – to bring in troops, to invade
ввод войск – bringing in troops
выводи́ть из тупика́ – to resolve a deadlock
выводи́ть войска́ – to withdraw troops
вы́вод войск – troop withdrawal

доводи́ть до све́дения – to bring to one's knowledge
до́вод – reasoning (in an argument)

заводи́ть в тупи́к – to deadlock
заводи́ть но́вые поря́дки – to establish new ways

наводи́ть раке́ты на города́ – to sight (aim) missiles at a city
наведе́ние раке́т – sighting (aiming) of missiles

приводи́ть к войне́ – to result in a war
приводи́ть в доказа́тельство – to produce evidence
приводи́ть в исполне́ние – to carry out, to execute
приводи́ть в удивле́ние – to surprise

перево́д – translation

поведе́ние – behavior

GRAMMAR EXERCISE: VERBS OF MOTION, CARRYING AND LEADING
IN IDIOMATIC USAGE

Use verbs of motion, carrying and leading to translate the sentences below:

1. Our Western and Eastern frontiers run along the ocean.
2. New legislation was adopted last March and will go into effect in January, 1988.
3. The discussion concerns new credits to regimes which do not respect the elementary rights of their citizens.
4. Nothing resulted from the new economic policy of economic austerity.
5. Which items of the agenda have become parts of the agreement?
6. Our negotiating team has walked out on the committee as a protest against the latest Sino-Soviet clashes.
7. Having lost in the presidential campaign, Stevenson retired after thirty years in active politics.
8. Do we have a progressive income tax in the United States?
9. –Do you see a way out?
   –No, I am afraid the situation is pretty hopeless.
10. During most of his days off he works on a project for a new system of tariffs.
11. It is possible that the continuous arms race will end in the actual use of nuclear weapons by one or more sides.
12. Where are the launching silos for the old Titan and Minuteman systems situated?
13. This piece of territory has changed hands at least five times in the last ten years.
14. After a prolonged defense, the army launched an attack.

15. We arrived at the conclusion that the Administration's policy of force jeopardizes stability in the hemisphere.
16. The ten-century rule of the dynasty has finally come to an end.
17. Although he has changed his country of residence, he has not changed his citizenship.
18. Last semester we covered the History of Soviet International Relations until the Second World War.
19. –What was going on in Afganistan in the eighties?
    –It turned into the Soviet version of Vietnam.
20. Nuclear war will be the last insanity of mankind.

RENDERING

The superpowers conclude a comprehensive agreement on general and complete disarmament. Nuclear, chemical, and biological weapons are to be scrapped totally. Research, development, and deployment of spaced-based weapons is banned. Troop strength is to be cut to less than 300,000. Each country is to be limited to no more than ten tank divisions. Military spending is to be slashed to no more than ten percent of GNP, with major cutbacks in research and development of new systems, as well as in the deliveries of existing systems. No new offensive aircraft systems are allowed. New missile systems are put on hold.

The billions of dollars saved are to be reinvested into domestic needs. This "peace dividend" makes the world a better place in which to live. Right?

Maybe. The world becomes a much safer place to live, or at least seems to be. But what does the peace dividend do for the economy of each country?

In the United States, a great many defense contractors are faced with either retooling for non-defense industry ("Now you can hunt rabbits with heat-seeking shotguns from your own Cessna"?) or laying off thousands. Local economies that depend on the Pentagon suffer. What would happen to the one set of government agencies, the Armed Forces, which have a good record as a anti-discriminatory employer to an upwardly mobile work force? Would Congress replace this with an equally massive jobs program? More likely Congress would seize the opportunity to turn military cuts into budget cuts.

The Soviet Union might face even greater problems. How would the Kremlin deal with its bloated officer corps? How would it handle the thousands of majors, colonels, and generals stripped of power and privilege? As one observer close to Gorbachev remarked at the beginning of the 1990s, "It is easier to retire a tank than a general. There is neither housing nor jobs for all the generals that we are supposed to bring home. We are moving into a very difficult moment that will be unpredictable."

Would a significant drop in military outlays not lead to rising expectations that could not be met? What would come of the much ballyhooed conversion of military resources to peaceful use, in which thousands of somewhat efficient defense industrial facilities are turned over to achingly inefficient civilian ministries whose main raison d'etre is turf protection? Privatization may provide a solution for those in the apparat brave enough to try it. But such efforts face formidable obstacles: a lack of know-how and start-up capital, as well as a lingering urge on the part of the military to keep what was classified classified.

One possible all-encompassing measure that might make kicking the military industrial habit easier all around would be a second Marshall Plan, this one for the Soviet Union. The promoters of a second Marshall plan see it as the logical extension of general disarmament. Don't run to cut the budget quite yet, they argue. Send would-be defense contractors to the Soviet Union thelp them with their economy while both countries get used to the idea of shrinking what was once a large section of of both countries' GNP.

SPEAKING EXERCISES

A. Расскажи́те часть 2 те́кста.

B. Расскажи́те ту же часть с то́чки зре́ния америка́нского вое́нного. В своём расска́зе испо́льзуйте сле́дующие выраже́ния.

причём; на са́мом де́ле; одна́ко; несомне́нно; неслуча́йно; вот почему́.

C. Сумми́руйте весь текст в не́скольких предложе́ниях.

D. Отве́тьте на сле́дующие вопро́сы.

1. Как сове́тские сокраще́ния рассма́триваются на За́паде?
2. Отвеча́ют ли США и их сою́зники по НАТО на сове́тские шаги́ по сокраще́нию сове́тских арсена́лов?

E. Дополни́тельные вопро́сы. (optional)

1. Счита́ете ли вы, что измене́ния в сове́тской вое́нной поли́тике позво́лят США дополни́тельно напра́вить кру́пные ассигнова́ния на ми́рные це́ли?
2. Полага́ете ли вы, что распа́д ОВД автомати́чески означа́ет зака́т НАТО?

READING EXERCISE

Бороться со сталинизмом.   Эльдар Рязанов

PRE-TEXT: Eldar Ryazanov is one of the Soviet Union's leading film-makers. His work includes some of the wittiest comedies to grace the Soviet screen. Read the text with the following questions in mind:

1.   What is the article about?

PARAGRAPH 2
2.   This paragraph emphasizes that... (Mark the correct answer):
   a.   it is only human nature to seek change.
   b.   people tend to cling to the past because their whole existence depends on it.

3.   What might the recognition of the past lead to?

PARAGRAPH 3
4.   Stalinist ideology... (Check the correct answer):
   a.   does not take a lot of brain power.
   b.   cannot be understood by the average person.

5.   According to the author, why were the best and the brightest annihilated?

PARAGRAPHS 4, 5, 6
6.   The author believes that at some point a basic change in fundamental concepts took place. Name three examples used to support this point of view.

PARAGRAPH 7
7.   What is said about many of today's textbooks? (Check the correct answer):
   a.   They teach critical thinking.
   b.   They give distorted information.
   c.   They contain well-formulated concepts.

PARAGRAPH 8
8.   Some have positive views of the past. How do they answer those who are more critical?

PARAGRAPH 9
9.   What is Ryazanov's comment on the rosy view of the past cited in paragraph 7?

PARAGRAPH 10
10.   The author believes that... (Check the correct answer):
      a.   there is no way out of such a deeply entrenched past.
      b.   positive change can be easily initiated from above.
      c.   it will take years of effort to break with the past.
      d.   no people can ever escape their own history.

POST-TEXT (using context):

1.   The idea in this story is developed...(check the correct answer):
      a.   from general to concrete.
      b.   by a list of examples leading to a general statement.

PARAGRAPH 2
2.   Find several uses of repetition or redundancy in this paragraph.

3.   Paraphrase the words *прошлое* and *по-моему*.

PARAGRAPH 3
4.   Find the sentence beginning with *потому-то и уничтожались
      смышлёные....*   To what statement does it refer?
5.   What is the opposite for *сложный*?

PARAGRAPH 4
6.   Paraphrase **произошло** *это*.

PARAGRAPHS 5, 6
7.   These paragraphs contain two definitions. Each one is followed by a
      question. These questions serve to... (Check the correct answer):
      a.   refute the definitions
      b.   support them

8.   Find uses of redundancy in this paragraph.

PARAGRAPH 7
9.   To what does *С этих* **позиций**... refer in the paragraph 6?
10.   Find the sentence beginning with *Чего же удивляться, что сталинщина
      пустила у нас глубокие корни?*. Is this a purely rhetorical question,
      or is an answer expected?

PARAGRAPHS 8, 9
11.   Does the statement in paragraph 9 contradict or illustrate the
      statement in paragraph 8 starting with words *Зато, – говорят эти
      некоторые, – были же в нашей истории Днепрогэс и Магнитка?*
12.   What derivatives for the word *чудовище* do you know?

PARAGRAPH 10
13.   Find uses of redundancy in this paragraph.

14. The tone of entire article is best characterized as a... (Mark the correct answer):
    a. sarcastic diatribe
    b. rose-colored sermon
    c. call to arms
    d. forecast of doom

15. Pick the correct meaning of the following words below:

ли́повый	a. lime-blossom b. phoney
впи́сываться в	a. to write in b. to blend in
досту́пный	a. accessible b. within reach
показу́шный	a. ostentatious b. for show
психу́шка	a. a madwoman b. a mental institution
смышлёный	a. sensible b. intelligent
вбива́ть зна́ния	a. to cram knowledge in b. to gain knowledge
пусти́ть ко́рни	a. to root b. to let someone settle down

16. Find the Russian for:

    - to be escorted
    - to breed and multiply
    - given a different turn of events
    - to report one's father to the authorities

Бороться со сталинизмом

Эльдар РЯЗАНОВ

Почему же у нас так много адептов сталинизма? На мой взгляд, существуют четыре причины, обеспечивающие его живучесть.

Во-первых, у нас немалое количество обычных, нормальных людей, которые идеализируют прошедшее, держатся за устаревшие взгляды, воинственно провозглашают умершие догмы. Происходит такое, с моей точки зрения, потому, что если признать ужас минувших лет, то придется во многом перечеркнуть свою жизнь. Придется отказаться от многих идеалов, которые оказались ложными. А ведь неоспоримо признать, что ты прожил под липовыми лозунгами, что не жалел своих сил и здоровья подчас ради обманных, показушных ценностей. И многие цепляются за сталинизм или за его разновидность, брежневщину.

Во-вторых, эта «идеология» удобна еще и потому, что не требует чрезмерных мозговых затрат. Она примитивна, четко сформулирована и поэтому доступна каждому. «Кто не с нами, тот против нас». «Если враг не сдается, его уничтожают». С таким упрощенным, практичным «марксизмом» командовать народом мог любой ефрейтор, неважно, был ли он в форме генералиссимуса или же в штатском. Потому-то и уничтожались смышленые, не вписывающиеся в казарменный социализм, талантливые, непокорные конкуренты. Тогда как безнравственные и послушные плодились и размножались...

В-третьих, у нас произошла подмена понятий. Случилось это еще в тридцатые годы. Скажем, слово «советский» означало практически слово «сталинский». К примеру, Советская, она же Сталинская, Конституция. Причем эта подмена жива и поныне и частенько ощущается в статьях разного рода.

Я много раз задавал себе вопрос, что означает такой термин, изобретенный в середине тридцатых, как «социалистический реализм». Что такое реализм вообще — известно. Реалистический — это жизненный, правдивый, взятый из жизни. А реализм социалистический? Что это — украшательский, лакировочный, льстивый, надувательский, угождающий власти, обманный? Кто-то из шутников сказал: «Соцреализм — это такой художественный метод, который рассказывает приятное начальникам в доступной им форме».

А что такое советский гуманизм? И чем он отличается от обычного? Нормальный, общепринятый гуманизм — это человечность, человеколюбие. А советский гуманизм вдохновлял Павлика Морозова доносить на отца. Советский гуманизм в сталинские времена отправлял на десять лет в лагеря тех, кто имел несчастье попасть в немецкий плен. Советский гуманизм в брежневские времена сажал в «пси-

хушки» или насильственно высылал из страны деятелей культуры за инакомыслие. Это наш, советский гуманизм придумал поистине иезуитскую формулировку: «Если тебя хвалит враг (т. е. империалисты), значит, ты льешь воду на мельницу врага, значит, ты — не наш человек...».

С этих позиций написаны сотни учебников по истории, литературе, юриспруденции, обществоведению, по всем гуманитарным наукам. По этим учебникам учились и учатся многие поколения, десятки миллионов. Людям с детства вбивали и продолжают вбивать мутные, искореженные, фальшивые знания. Чего же удивляться, что сталинщина пустила у нас глубокие корни? Уж очень питательна почва, благоприятна среда, удобен климат.

И, в-четвертых. Некоторым — и их немало — кажется, что, мол, хватит копаться в прошлом, «чернить» его, обнажать и вытаскивать всяческие мерзости из нашей истории. Им хочется комфортности души, они бронируют свою совесть, не желая знать

о чудовищном и кровавом. «Зато,— говорят эти некоторые,— были же в нашей истории Днепрогэс и Магнитка». Но, может, при другом повороте нашего развития у нас было бы десять Магниток и двадцать Днепрогэсов?

Кстати, помимо Магнитки и Днепрогэса, были еще и Беломорканал и канал имени Москвы, и Волго-Донской канал. И плывут сейчас по ним белоснежные корабли (и есть среди них те, что носят до сих пор имена Андрея Жданова и Михаила Суслова), над костями сотен тысяч несчастных, копавших эти каналы вручную под неусыпным конвоем ВОХРы...

Борьба со сталинизмом — это надолго. На многие годы. Она требует от каждого неустанных усилий. И наш долг — деятелей искусства — своими фильмами, книгами, картинами, спектаклями, статьями ежедневно разрушать, разбивать, разламывать это проклятое прошлое, которое сидит в каждом из нас.

APPENDIX

DECLENSION OF NOUNS

Masculine nouns

	-consonant	*-й*	*-ь*
Nom.	минйстр–	геро́ й	секрета́р ь
Gen.	минйстр а	геро́ я	секретар я́
Dat.	минйстр у	геро́ ю	секретар ю́
Acc.(1)*	минйстр а	геро́ я	секретар я́
(inanimate)	догово́р–	музе́ й	календа́р ь
Inst.(2)*	минйстр ом	геро́ ем	секретар ём
Prep.	минйстр е	геро́ е	секретар е́

	-consonant	*-й*	*-ь*
Nom.	минйстр ы	геро́ и	секретар й́
Gen.	минйстр ов	геро́ ев	секретар е́й
Dat.	минйстр ам	геро́ ям	секретар я́м
Acc.(1)*	минйстр ов	геро́ ев	секретар е́й
(inanimate)	догово́р ы	музе́ и	календар й́
Inst.	минйстр ами	музе́ ями	секретар я́ми
Prep.	минйстр ах	геро́ ях	секретар я́х

	-ий		*Fleeting o,e,ё*
Nom.	морато́ри й		америка́нец–
Gen.	морато́ри я		америка́нц а
Dat.	морато́ри ю		америка́нц у
Acc.(1)*	морато́ри й		америка́нц а
(animate)	пролета́ри й	*(inanimate)*	ве́тер–
Inst.(2)*	морато́ри ем		америка́нц ем
Prep.	морато́ри и		америка́нц е

	-ий		*Fleeting o,e,ё*
Nom.	морато́ри и		америка́нц ы
Gen.	морато́ри ев		америка́нц ев
Dat.	морато́ри ям		америка́нц ам
Acc.(1)*	морато́ри и		америка́нц ев
(animate)	пролета́ри ев	*(inanimate)*	ве́тры
Inst.	морато́ри ями		америка́нц ами
Prep.	морато́ри ях		америка́нц ах

---

1. The accusative case (singular and plural) of masculine animate nouns and the accusative *plural* of feminine animate nouns are the same as the genitive; the accusative of all other nouns is the same as nominative.

2. When stressed, *-ем* becomes *-ём* and *-ей* becomes *ёй*.

Feminine nouns

	- a	*- я*
Nom.	угро́з а	ассамбле́ я
Gen.	угро́з ы	ассамбле́ и
Dat.	угро́з е	ассамбле́ е
Acc.	угро́з у	ассамбле́ ю
Inst.(2)	угро́з ой	ассамбле́ ей
Prep.	угро́з е	ассамбле́ е

	- a	*- я*
Nom.	угро́з ы	ассамбле́ и
Gen.	угро́з-	ассамбле́ й
Acc.(1)*	угро́з ы	ассамбле́ и
(animate)	перево́дчиц-	тёт ей
Inst.	угро́з ами	ассамбле́ ями
Prep.	угро́з ах	ассамбле́ ях

	- ия	*- ь*
Nom.	делега́ци я	реч ь
Gen.	делега́ци и	ре́ч и
Dat.	делега́ци и	ре́ч и
Acc.	делега́ци ю	реч ь
Inst.(2)	делега́ци ей	ре́ч ью
Prep.	делега́ци и	ре́ч и

	- ия	*- ь*
Nom.	делега́ци и	ре́ч и
Gen.	делега́ци й	реч е́й
Dat.	делега́ци ям	реч а́м
Acc.(1)	делега́ци и	ре́ч и
Inst.	делега́ци ями	реч а́ми
Prep.	делега́ци ях	реч а́х

Neuter nouns

	- о	*- е*	*- ие*	*- мя*
Nom.	прави́тельств о	мо́р е	мне́ни е	вре́м я
Gen.	прави́тельств а	мо́р я	мне́ни я	вре́м ени
Dat.	прави́тельств у	мо́р ю	мне́ни ю	вре́м ени
Acc.	прави́тльств о	мо́р е	мне́ни е	вре́м я
Inst.	прави́тельств ом	мо́р ем	мне́ни ем	вре́м енем
Prep.	прави́тельств е	мо́р е	мне́ни и	вре́м ени

	- о	*- е*	*- ие*	*- мя*
Nom.	прави́тельств а	мор я́	мне́ни я	времен а́
Gen.	прави́тельств-	море́ й	мне́ни й	врем ён
Dat.	прави́тельств ам	мор я́м	мне́ни ям	врем ена́м
Acc.	прави́тельств а	мор я́	мне́ни я	времен а́
Inst.	прави́тельств ами	мор я́ми	мне́ни ями	времен а́ми
Prep.	прави́тельств ах	мор я́х	мне́ни ях	врем ена́х

The masculine noun *путь* has characteristics of both masculine and feminine declension patterns.

Nom.	пут ь
Gen.	пут й
Dat.	пут й
Acc.	пут ь
Inst.	пут ём
Prep.	пут й

Nouns with the ending – *анин/янин*

Nom.	англича́нин–
Gen.	англича́нин а
Dat.	ангича́нин у
Acc.	англича́нин а
Gen.	англича́нин ым
Prep.	англича́нин е

Nom.	англича́н е
Gen.	англича́н–
Dat.	англича́н ам
Acc.	англича́н–
Inst.	англича́н ами
Prep.	англича́н ах

DECLENSION OF PRONOUNS

Personal pronouns

Nom.	я	ты	он	она́	оно́
Gen.	меня́	тебя́	его́ (у него́)	её (у неё)	его (у него́)
Dat.	мне	тебе́	ему́ (к нему́)	ей (к ней)	ему́ (к нему́)
Acc.	меня́	тебя́	его́ (на него́)	её (на неё)	его (на него́)
Inst.	мной (мно́ю)	тобо́й (тобо́ю)	им (с ним)	ей, е́ю (с ней, с не́ю)	им (с ним)
Prep.	(обо) мне	(о) тебе́	(о) нём	(о) ней	(о) нём

Nom.	мы	вы	они́
Gen.	нас	вас	их (у них)
Dat.	нам	вам	им (к ним)
Acc.	нас	вас	их (на них)
Inst.	на́ми	ва́ми	и́ми (с ни́ми)
Prep.	(о) нас	(о) вас	(о) них

The reflexive pronoun *себя*

Nom.	–
Gen.	себя́
Dat.	себе́
Acc.	себя́
Inst.	собо́й
Prep.	себе́

Possessive pronouns/adjectives

Nom.	мо й	мо я́	мо ё	тво й	тво я	тво ё
Gen.	мо его́	мо ей	мо его́	тво его́	тво е́й	тво его́
Dat.	мо ему́	мо ей	мо ему́	тво ему́	тво ей	тво ему́
Acc.	мо его́	мо ей	мо ему́	тво его́	тво ю	тво ё
	мо й			тво й		
Inst.	мо и́м	мо ей	мо и́м	тво и́м	тво е́й	тво и́м
Prep.	(о) мо ём	(о) мо ей	(о) мо ём	(о) тво ём	(о) тво ей	(о) тво ей

Nom.	наш–	на́ш а	на́ш е	ваш–	ва́ш а	ва́ш е
Gen.	на́ш его	на́ш ей	на́ш его	ва́ш его	ва́ш ей	ва́ш его
Dat.	на́ш ему	на́ш ей	на́ш ему	ва́ш ему	ва́ш ей	ва́ш ему
Acc.	на́ш его	на́ш у	на́ш е	ва́ш его	ва́ш у	ва́ш е
	наш		ваш			
Inst.	на́ш им	на́ш ей	на́ш им	ва́ш им	ва́ш ей	ва́ш им
Prep.	(о) на́ш ем	(о) на́ш ей	(о) на́ш ем	(о) ва́ш ем	(о) ва́ш ей	(о) ва́ш ем

Nom.	мо й	тво й	на́ш и	ва́ш и
Gen.	мо и́х	тво и́х	на́ш их	ва́ш их
Dat.	мо и́м	тво и́м	на́ш им	ва́ш им
Acc.	мо и́х	тво и́х	на́ш их	ва́ш их
	мо й	тво й	на́ш и	ва́ш и
Inst.	мо и́ми	тво и́ми	на́ш ими	ва́ш ими
Prep.	(о) мо и́х	(о) тво и́х	(о) на́ш их	(о) ва́ш их

Interrogative pronouns

Nom.	кто?	что?
Gen.	кого́?	чего́?
Dat.	кому́?	чему́?
Acc.	кого́?	что?
Inst.	кем?	чем?
Prep.	(о) ком?	(о) чём?

Negative pronouns

Nom.	никто́		ничто́	
Gen.	никого́	(ни у кого́)	ничего́	(не для чего́)
Dat.	никому́	(ни к кому́)	ничему́	(не к чему́)
Acc.	никого́	(ни на кого́)	ничто́	(ни за что)
Inst.	нике́м	(ни с кем)	ниче́м	(ни с чем)
Prep.	ни о ко́м		ни о чём	

САМ, САМА, САМО, САМИ

Nom.	сам	сама́	само́	са́ми
Gen.	самого́	само́й	самого́	сами́х
Dat.	самому́	само́й	самому́	сами́м
Acc.	самого́	саму́ самое́	само́	сами́х
Inst.	сами́м	само́й	сами́м	сами́ми
Prep.	(о) сами́х	(о) само́й	(о) само́м	(о) сами́х

ВЕСЬ, ВСЯ, ВСЁ, ВСЕ

Nom.	весь	вся	всё	все
Gen.	всего́	всей	всего́	всех
Dat.	всему́	все́й	всему́	всем
Acc.	всего́ весь	всю	всё	всех все
Inst.	всем	всей	всем	все́ми
Prep.	(обо) всём	(обо) всей	(обо) всём	(обо) всех

ЧЕЙ, ЧЬЯ, ЧЬЁ, ЧЬИ

Nom.	чей	чья	чьё	чьи
Gen.	чьего́	чье́й	чьего́	чьих
Dat.	чьему́	чьей	чьему́	чьим
Acc.	чьего́ чей	чью	чьё	чьих чьи
Inst.	чьим	чьей	чьим	чьи́ми
Prep.	(о) чьём	(о) чьей	(о) чьём	(о) чьих

DECLENSION OF ADJECTIVES

Adjectives with stems ending in к, г, х, ж, ч, ш, щ take hard endings unless any of the following rules is violated:

1. After *к г х   ж ч ш щ,* ы is replaced by *и.*
    русский, большие

2. After   *ж ч ш щ,* unstressed *o* is replaced by *e.*
    хоро́шего but большо́го

Masculine adjectives

	H A R D		S O F T
	Regular	*Stressed Ending*	
Nom.	но́в ый	молод о́й	бли́жн ий
Gen.	но́во ого	молод о́го	бли́жн его
Dat.	но́в ому	молод о́му	бли́жн ему
Acc.	но́в ого	молод о́го	бли́жн его
	но́в ый	молод о́й	бли́жн ий
Inst.	но́в ым	молод ы́м	бли́жн им
Prep.(о)	но́в ом	(о) молод о́м	(о) бли́жн ем

Feminine adjectives

	H A R D		S O F T
	Regular	*Stressed Ending*	
Nom.	но́в ая	молод а́я	бли́жн яя
Gen.	но́в ой	молод о́й	бли́жн ей
Dat.	но́в ой	молод о́й	бли́жн ей
Acc.	но́в ую	молод у́ю	бли́жн юю
Inst.	но́в ой	молод о́й	бли́жн ей
Prep.(о)	но́в ой	(о) молод о́й	(о) бли́жн ей

Neuter adjectives

	H A R D		S O F T
	Regular	*Stressed Ending*	
Nom.	но́в ое	молод о́е	бли́жн ее
Gen.	но́в ого	молод о́го	бли́жн его
Dat.	но́в ому	молод о́му	бли́жн ему
Acc.	но́в ое	молод о́е	бли́жн ее
Inst.	но́в ым	молод ы́м	бли́жн им
Prep.(о)	но́в ом	(о) молод о́м	(о) бли́жн ем

Plural adjectives

	H A R D		S O F T
	Regular	*Sressed Ending*	
Nom.	нóв ые	молод ы́е	блúжн ие
Gen.	нóв ых	молод ы́х	блúжн их
Dat.	нóв ым	молод ы́м	блúжн им
Acc.	нóв ых	молод ы́х	блúжн их
	нóв ые	молод ы́е	блúжн ие
Inst.	нóв ыми	молод ы́ми	блúжн ими
Prep. (о)	нóв ых	(о) молод ы́х	(о) блúжн их

DECLENSION OF NUMERALS

ОДИН

	masc.	*neut.*	*fem.*	*plur.*
Nom.	одúн	однó	однá	однú
Gen.	одногó	однóй	однúх	однúх
Dat.	одномý	однóй	однúм	однúм
Acc.	одúн (*inanim*)	однó	однý	однú (*inanim*)
	одногó (*anim*)			однúх (*anim*)
Inst.	однúм		однóй (óю)	однúми
Prep.	(об) однóм	(об) однóй	(об) однúх	(об) однúх

	2	3	4	5 – 20,30
Nom.	два, две	три	четы́ре	пять
Gen.	двух	трёх	четырёх	пятú
Dat.	двум	трём	четырём	пятú
Acc.	два (*masc, neut*)	три (*masc, neut*).	четы́ре (*masc,neut*)	пять
	двух (*fem*)	трёх (*fem*)	четырёх (*fem*)	
Inst.	двумя́	тремя́	четырьмя́	пятью́
Prep.	(о) двух	(о) трёх	(о) четырёх	(о) пяти

	50 – 80	200 – 400	500 – 900
Nom.	пятьдеся́т	двéсти	пятьсóт
Gen.	пятúдесяти	двухсóт	пятисóт
Dat.	пятúдесяти	двумстáм	пятистáм
Acc.	пятьдеся́т	двéсти	пятьсóт
Inst.	пятью́десятью	двумястáми	пятьюстáми
Prep.	(о) пятúдесяти	(о) двухстáх	(о) пятистáх

	40,90,100	**1,5**
Nom. Acc.	со́рок, девяно́сто, сто	полтора́, полторы́
Gen. Dat. Inst. Prep.	сорока́, девяно́ста, ста	полу́тора

	498
Nom. Acc.	четы́реста девяно́сто во́семь
Gen.	четырёхсо́т девяно́ста восьми́
Dat.	четырёмста́м девяно́ста восьми́
Inst.	четырьмяста́ми девяно́ста восемью́
Prep.	(о) четырёхстах девяно́ста восьми́

VERBS

Note: The infinitive is not an accurate predicter of the present/perfective future conjugation. Students should learn the infinitive, as well as the third person plural (*они*) form of the present/future perfective conjugation.

PRESENT/FUTURE PERFECTIVE TENSE

A note on stress in the present/future perfective: There are three stress patterns:

1. Stem stress: *рабо́тать* with stress on the stem throughout.
2. Ending stress: *говори́ть* with stress on the endings throughout.
3. Mobile stress: *смотре́ть* – stress on the ending for infinitive, imperative, and first person singular (*я*): *смотре́ть, смотри́(те), смотрю́*; stress on the stem elsewhere: *смо́тришь, смо́трите, смо́трят.*

Conjugation I Verbs

Vowel stems:

Stem stress			*Ending stress (drop -ва-)*		
рабо́тать			встава́ть		
я	рабо́та	ю	я	вста	ю́
ты	рабо́та	ешь	ты	вста	ёшь
он	рабо́та	ет	он	вста	ёт
мы	рабо́та	ем	мы	вста	ём
вы	рабо́та	ете	вы	вста	ёте
они	рабо́та	ют	они	вста	ю́т

работа й(те)!   вста вай(те)!
Consonant stems:

Stem stress   *Ending stress*

встать   идти
я   встáн у   я   ид ý
ты   встáн ешь   ты   ид ёшь
он   встáн ет   он   ид ёт
мы   встáн ем   мы   ид ём
вы   встáн ете   вы   ид ёте
они   встáн ут   они   ид ýт

встáн ь(те)!   ид й(те)!

Conjugation II Verbs

Stem stress   *Ending stress*   *Mobile stress*

спóрить   говорúть   смотрéть
я   спóр ю   я   говор ю   я   смотр ю
ты   спóр ишь   ты   говор йшь   ты   смóтр ишь
он   спóр ит   он   говор йт   он   смóтр ит
мы   спóр им   мы   говор йм   мы   смóтр им
выи   спóр ите   вы   говор йте   вы   смóтр ите
они   спóр ят   они   говор ят   они смóтр ят

спóр ь(те)!   говор й(те)!   смотр й(те)

PAST TENSE

Stress in the past tense comes in one of three patterns: stem stress, ending
stress, and mobile stress. Past tense stress is often independent of
present/perfective future tense stress.

Stem stress   *Ending stress*   *Mobile stress*

Infinitives in *–ть:*

работать
он   работа л   он   бы л
она   работа ла   она   бы лá

оно рабо́та ло   оно бы́ ло
они рабо́та ли   они бы́ ли

Infinitives in *-сти:*

вести́
он   вё л
она ве ла́
оно ве ло́
они ве ли́

Infinitives in *-дти* **and vowel +** *ти:*

он   пришё л
она приш ла́
оно приш ло́
они приш ли́

Infinitives in *-зти* **and** *-чь:*

он   вё̄з,   мог,   тё̄к
она вез ла́,   мог ла́, тек ла́
оно вез ло́,   мог ло́, тек ло́
они вез ли́,   мог ли́, тек ли́

MAIN EXCEPTIONS

First Conjugation

1. Verbs   in   with   infinitives   ending   in   *-овать*   and   *-евать*   have
    present/perfective future stems ending in у-: *кома́ндовать: комна́ндую,*
    кома́ндуешь, кома́ндуют, комна́ндуй but past tense *кома́ндовал*

2. Verbs with infinitives ending in *-чь* have stems ending in *-г* or *-к* with
    mutations as follows:

    мочь: могу́, мо́жешь, мо́жет, мо́жем, мо́жете, мо́гут, мог, могла́, могло́, могли́
    течь: теку́, течёшь, течёт, течём, течёте, теку́т, тё̄к, текла́, текло́, текли́

3. Some first conjugation verbs undergo mutations *throughout the conjugation*
    according to the mutation chart below: *писа́ть: пишу́, пи́шешь, пи́шут,*
    пиши́(те), but *писа́л.*

Second Conjugation

1. Spelling rule:

    After к г х ц ж ч ш щ   ю and я are replaced by у and а:
    решйть: я решу́, они реша́т

2. Stem consonants in the first person singular mutate according to the table
    below:

    отве́тить: я отвечу, ты отве́тишь, они отве́тят
    возйть: я вожу́, ты во́зишь, они во́зят
    простить: я прощу́, ты прости́шь, они простя́т
    любить: я люблю́, ты лю́бишь, они лю́бят

Consonant mutation table

к, т ⟶ ч		пеку́, печёшь отве́тить, отве́чу
г, з ⟶ ж		могу́, мо́жешь возйть, вожу́
х, с ⟶ ш		маха́ть, машу́ писа́ть, пишу́
ст ⟶ щ and sometimes т ⟶ щ		прости́ть, прощу́ возврати́ть, возвращу́
в, ф, п, в, м ⟶ вл, фл, бл, пл, мл		лови́ть, ловлю́ люби́ть, люблю́ офо́рмить, офо́рмлю

GLOSSARY

А

авáрия – accident
авианóсец – aircraft-carrier
авиáция – aviation
авиациóнный – aviation *(adj.)*
авиациóнный полк – air regiment
автомобильный – automobile *(adj.)*
аграрный – agrarian *(adj.)*
администрáция – administration
амбиция – ambition
алмáз – diamond
аналогичный – analogous
антирабóчий – anti-labor *(adj.)*
антисемитизм – anti-semitism
аннулировать – to cancel
арéнда – leasing
áрмия – army
армéйский кóрпус – army corps
артиллéрия – artillery
артиллерийская систéма – artillery system
áтомная подвóдная лóдка – nuclear-powered submarine

Б

баллотироваться во что-то – to run for office
банкрóтство – bankruptcy
бéдность – poverty
бéдные – the poor *(adj.)*
бéженец, бéженцы – refugee
безвлáстный – powerless *(adj.)*
безопáсность – security
безрабóтица – unemployment
безрабóтные – the unemployed
безразличный к чемý-то – indifferent to something *(adj.)*
бесéды – talks
беспрецедéнтный – unprecedented *(adj.)*
беспощáдный – merciless
блáго – good, happiness
благодаря чемý-то – owing to something
боеголóвка – warhead
боевóй – combat *(adj.)*
боеприпáсы –ammunition
бóйкие сообщéния – peppy reports
бомбардирóвщик – bomber

боро́ться про́тив чего́-то – to struggle against something
борьба́ – struggle
бой – fight, battle
браву́рный марш – invigorating march
брать/взять в плен – to take prisoner
брать/взять под защи́ту – to take under protection
бра́ться/взя́ться за что-то – to undertake something
брать/взять курс на что-то – to take a course in the direction of
брига́да – brigade
бронетранспортёр – armored personnel carrier
броса́ть/бро́сить вы́зов кому́-то –1) to challenge somebody
                                  2) to be an affront to somebody
бы́вший – former
бундесве́р – the armed forces of West Germany
бюдже́т – budget

В

валово́й национа́льный проду́кт (ВНП) – gross national product (GNP)
валю́та – currency
валю́тный курс – rate of exchange
валю́тно-фина́нсовая поли́тика – monetary-fiscal policy
ввод во́йск – bringing in the troops
введе́ние нало́гов – introduction of taxes
вводи́ть/ввести́ войска́ – to bring in the troops
веду́щие стра́ны – leading countries
вертолётный отря́д – helicopter detachment
весо́мый – noticeable
Верхо́вный суд – Supreme Court
вести́ (no perf.) ого́нь по чему́-то – to fire at something
веде́ние – conducting
взаимопо́мощь – mutual assistance
взро́слые – adults
взя́тка – bribe
ви́дный де́ятель – prominent statesman
в ито́ге голосова́ния – as a result of ballot
ви́це-президе́нт – vice-president
включа́ть/включи́ть в пове́стку дня – to include in the agenda
власть – power
вла́сти – authorities
вложе́ние – investment
вне́шняя торго́вля – external trade
внешнеэкономи́ческая де́ятельность – external economic activity
вну́тренный долг – internal debt
во главе́ с кем-то – led by somebody
военнопле́нные – prisoners of war
вое́нно-промы́шленный ко́мплекс – military-industrial complex
вое́нный объе́кт – military installation

военные – the military *(adj.)*
военный óкруг – military district
военщина – the militarists
возглавля́ть/возгла́вить – to be the head of, to lead
возлага́ть/возложи́ть отве́тственность за что-то – to place responsibility for something on somebody
возраста́ть/возрасти́ – to grow
война́, во́йны – war
войска́ *(pl.)* – troops
волна́, во́лны – wave
воо́чию – with your own eyes
вооружённый си́лы – armed forces
восста́вшие – the rebels
восстана́вливать/восстанови́ть авторите́т – to restore authority
восста́ние – rebellion
вою́ющие сто́роны – fighting parties, sides
враг – enemy
вра́жеский – enemy *(adj.)*, hostile
в ра́мках програ́ммы СОИ – within the framework of the SDI program
всео́бщие вы́боры – general elections
в соотве́тствии с чем-то – in accordance with something
вступа́ть/вступи́ть во что-то – to become a member of something
вступа́ть/вступи́ть в строй – to become operational
в како́й-то ме́ре – to some degree
входи́ть/войти́ в си́лу – to come into effect
входи́ть/войти́ в употребле́ние – to go into use
в честь кого́-то – in honor of somebody
выбира́ть/вы́брать на срок в 4 го́да – to elect for a 4-year term
вы́бор – choice
вы́боры – elections
выводи́ть/вы́вести из соста́ва – to withdraw from the composition
выводи́ть/вы́вести из боево́го соста́ва – to take out of service
вы́годный – profitable
вы́садка – landing
высвобожда́ться/вы́свободиться – to be released
выска́зываться/вы́сказаться – to speak up
высо́кий гость – guest of honor
выступа́ть/вы́ступить с ре́чью – to make a speech
выполня́ть/вы́полнить – to fulfill, to complete
выра́внивание торго́вого бала́нса – leveling of trade balance
выража́ть/вы́разить – to express
выска́зывание – expression, opinion
выходи́ть/вы́йти на пе́рвое ме́сто – to come in first, to take first place
выходи́ть/вы́йти из употребле́ния – to become obsolete
вы́ход в отста́вку – resignation

Г

газопрово́д – gas pipeline
гара́нтия – guarantee
га́убица – howitzer
гварде́йская диви́зия – guards division
Генера́льная Ассамбле́я – the General Assembly
генера́льный секрета́рь – General Secretary
глава́, гла́вы – head, leader
глоба́льное ору́жие – global weapons
глубо́кий – deep
говори́льня – hoopla
годовщи́на – anniversary
го́лод – hunger, famine
го́лос, голоса́ – voice, vote,
голосова́ние – ballot, voting, election
го́нка вооруже́ний – arms race
госпо́дство – mastery, hegemony
госуда́рственный департа́мент – the State Department
    (госдепарта́мент)
госуда́рственный де́ятель – statesman
госуда́рственный долг – national debt
госуда́рственный секрета́рь – secretary of state
гото́виться/подгото́виться к чему́-то – to prepare for something
гото́вность – readiness, preparedness
гражда́нское населе́ние – civilian population
грози́ть – to threaten
группиро́вка – faction
гру́стный – sad
губерна́торские вы́боры – gubernatorial elections

Д

дава́ть/дать я́сно поня́ть – to make clear
дава́ться нелегко́ – to not come easily
далекоиду́щий – far-reaching
да́нные – data
движе́ние – movement
двусторо́нние свя́зи – bilateral relations
делова́я акти́вность – business activity
деловы́е круги́ – business circle
демократи́ческая па́ртия – the Democratic Party
демократи́ческие свобо́ды – democratic freedoms
депре́ссия – depression
де́йствующие си́лы – active forces
демокра́т – democrat
де́нежное обраще́ние – monetary circulation
дефици́т бюдже́та – budget deficit

дискримина́ция по при́нципу по́ла – sex discrimination
ди́спут – dispute
доба́вка – addition
добива́ться/доби́ться успе́ха – to achieve success
до́брая во́ля – good will
дове́рие – trust
доверя́ть кому́-то – to trust somebody
догово́р о чём-то – treaty on something
доказа́тельство – proof
доктри́на – doctrine
до́ктор истори́ческих нау́к – post-doctoral degree in history
долг – debt
долгосро́чный креди́т – long-term credit
должни́к – debtor
до́ля секу́нды – fraction of a second
дополни́тельные нало́ги – additional taxes
дополне́ния к конститу́ции – amendments to the constitution
дораба́тывать/дорабо́тать – to bring to complition
дохо́ды – income
драко́новская цензу́ра – draconian censorship
дух – spirit

Е

единогла́сие – unanimity
единогла́сный – unanimous
единоду́шно – unanimously
еди́нство – unity

Ж

жарго́н – jargon
жела́ние – desire
желе́зный за́навес – iron curtain
же́ртва – victim
жёсткое регули́рование – rigid managment
жило́е стро́ительство – residential construction
жи́зненный у́ровень – standard of living

З

забасто́вка – strike
заве́дующий отде́лом – department chairman
заверша́ть/заверши́ть – to complete
зави́симость – dependence
завоёвывать/завоева́ть – to conquer

зада́ние – assignment
задо́лженность – debt, indebtedness
закла́дывать/заложи́ть осно́ву – to lay a foundation
заключа́ть/заключи́ть – to conclude, to sign
зако́н – law, bill
законода́тельный – legislative
законопрое́кт – draft of a bill
зало́жник – hostage
замедле́ние – slowdown
замести́тель (*masc.*) – deputy, assistant
замора́живание расхо́дов – a freeze on expenditures
замора́живать/заморо́зить – to freeze
за недоста́тком чего́-то – for lack of something
запреща́ть/запрети́ть я́дерное ору́жие – to ban nuclear weapons
запа́с – reserve
за́работная пла́та (зарпла́та) – salary
зара́нее соста́вленные спи́ски – previously composed lists
заседа́ние – meeting
засекре́ченный – classified
за счёт чего́-то – 1) at the expense of something
                   2) through something
засто́й – stagnation
затра́чивать сре́дства на оборо́ну – to spend money for defense
затя́гивание спа́да – prolongation of recession
захва́тывать/захвати́ть зало́жников – to capture hostages
захва́т – seizure
защи́та – defense
заявля́ть/заяви́ть о чём-то – to announce something
земно́й шар – globe, earth
звёздные во́йны – Star Wars
земля́, зе́мли (*pl.*) – earth, the Earth
зерно́ – grain
здравоохране́ние – public health
зло – evil

И

игра́ть на чём-то – to play on something, to exploit something
идти́/пойти́ на по́льзу – to be beneficial
идти́/пойти́ на усту́пки кому́-то – to make concessions to somebody
идти́ сле́дом за кем-то – to follow somebody
избавля́ться/изба́виться от чего́-то – to get rid of something
избега́ть/избежа́ть чего́-то – to avoid something
избира́тель (*masc.*) – voter, constituent
избира́тельное пра́во – right to vote
избира́ть/избра́ть – to elect
избира́ть/избра́ть по спи́ску – to elect on the slate of
измене́ние – change

измéна – betrayal, treason
изъя́ть – to remove, to do away
иллюзóрность – illusion
имéть сомнéния в чём-то – to have doubts about something
импéрский – imperial
и́мпорт *(no pl.)* – import, imports
инакомы́слящий – a dissident
инсти́нкт – an instinct
интерьéр – interior
интесифика́ция – intensification
иска́ть – to search
исхóд – outcome
исключáть/исключи́ть из чегó-то – to exclude from something
искупáть тáнки в Ла-Мáнше – to wash tanks in the English Channel
искýсственный – artificial
исполни́тельный óрган – executive branch
испóльзовать – to use
испы́товать/испытáть – to test
испытáние – test *(noun)*
испы́танный – tested, reliable
исслéдования – research
исслéдовательский – research *(adj.)*
и́стинные намéрения – true intentions
исчислéние и́ндекса цен – pricing

К

каза́к – Cossack
кандидáт в президéнты – presidential candidate
кара́тельно-полицéйская опера́ция – police operation
кассéтный снаря́д – cluster shell
катю́ша – katusha (an artillery piece)
квартáл – quarter
квартáльный – quarterly
ключевáя систéма – key system
колхóзник – collective farmer
комендáнтский час – curfew
комменти́ровать/прокомменти́ровать – to comment on something
коммунисти́ческая пáртия – the Communist Party
коммуни́ст – communist
конгрéсс – congress
конкурéнт – rival
конкурентноспосóбность – ability to compete
компáния – company, firm
констати́ровать – to state the fact
констрýкти́вное сотрýдничество – constructive cooperation
контрóль над вооружéниями – arms control
кончáться/кóнчиться чем-то – to finish with something

ко́рпус морско́й пехо́ты – Marine Corps
ко́свенные нало́ги – indirect taxes
ко́смос – outer space
косми́ческий зо́нтик – space umbrella
кошелёк госуда́рства – government coffers *(pl.)*
краткосро́чный креди́т – short-term credit
креди́тные ста́вки – credit rate
кру́пный капита́л – large capital

Л

ла́герь, лагеря́ – camp
ла́зер – laser
ла́зерный луч – laser beam
лейбори́стская па́ртия – labor party
лейбори́ст – Laborite
лёгкая промы́шленность – light industry
лёд тро́нулся – the ice is broken
либера́л – liberal *(noun)*
либера́льные круги́ – liberal circles
ли́дер – leader
ликвиди́ровать – to liquidate
лиша́ть/лиши́ть чего́-то – to deprive of something
лише́ние – privation
ло́бби *(unchanged)* – lobby, interest group
лобби́ровать – to lobby
людски́е ресу́рсы – people's resources

М

максима́льная отда́ча – maximum result
манда́т – mandate
масшта́б – scale
    в масшта́бе чего́-то – on the scale of something
материа́льные сре́дства – material resources
мемора́ндум – memorandum
медици́нское обслу́живание – medical care
междунаро́дный – international
ме́ры по борьбе́ – measures against
ме́сто – 1) place 2) seat
ме́стное самоуправле́ние – local self-government
мечта́ – dream
микрокомпью́тер – microcomputer
милитариза́ция – militarization
милитари́ст – militarist
мини́стр иностра́нных дел –1) Secretary of State (U.S.) 2) foreign minister
мини́стр торго́вли –1) Secretary of Commerce 2) minister of commerce

мини́стр фина́нсов –1) Secretary of the Treasury (U.S.)   2) minister of finance
мини́стр энерге́тики – 1) Secretary of Energy   2) minister of energy
мину́вший год – last year
многовеково́й – many centuries old
многоцелева́я а́томная подво́дная ло́дка – multi-purpose nuclear-powered submarine
мобилиза́ция – mobilization
мости́ть доро́гу – to pave the road
моторизо́ванный – motorized
мо́щный – powerful
муниципа́льные вы́боры – municipal elections

Н

наблюда́тель ООН – UN observer
наблюде́ние за чем-то – to observe something
нагнета́ть обстано́вку – to worsen the situation
наде́жда на что-то – hope *(noun)* for something
наде́яться на что-то – to hope for something
надзо́р – supervision
надстро́йка – superstructure
назва́ние – name
назначе́ние на пост – appointment to the position
накану́не – on the eve
налёт – raid
нало́г на потребле́ние – tax on consumption of
нало́говое послабле́ние – tax leniency
намеча́ть/наме́тить – to plan
наноси́ть/нанести́ уда́р – to deliver a strike
напада́ть/напа́сть на кого́-то – to attack somebody
нападе́ние – attack
направля́ть/напра́вить – to direct something
напряжённость – tension
нара́щивание вооруже́ний – arms race
наро́д – people
наро́дное хозя́йство – people's economy
наруше́ние – violation
населе́ние – population
наси́лие – violence
наста́ивать/настоя́ть на чём-то – to insist on something
настоя́щая ситуа́ция – current situation
наступа́тельные возмо́жности – offensive capabilities
наступле́ние – offensive *(noun)*
нау́ка – science
нау́чный – scientific
нау́чные иссле́дования – research *(noun)*
находи́ть/найти́ – to find
находи́ться с визи́том – to be on a visit
находи́ться *(no perf.)* на вооруже́нии – to be in the arsenal

национа́льная безопа́сность – national security
невино́вность – innocence
негра́мотность – illiteracy
негра́мотные – the illiterate
негритя́нский – black (adj.)
недово́льство – discontent
недопусти́мо – unacceptably
недоста́ток – shortage
недосту́пный чему́-то – inaccessible
незави́симость – independence
неизбе́жный – inevitable
необрати́мый – irreversible
неофаши́ст – neofascist
неприсоедине́ние – nonalignment
несправедли́вость – injustice
нести́/понести́ пораже́ние – to suffer defeat
нести́/понести́ поте́ри – to suffer losses
нести́/понести́ уще́рб – to suffer damage
не́фть – oil
нефтяно́й – oil (adj.)
нейтро́нная бо́мба – neutron bomb
нехва́тка – shortage
ни́зкий – low
но́вое мышле́ние – new thinking
но́вый соста́в – new composition
носи́ть делово́й хара́ктер – to be businesslike
нужда́ться (no perf.) в подде́ржке – to need support
нужда́ющиеся – the needy
ны́нешний – current

О

обанкро́титься – to go bankrupt
обеспече́ние – guarantee
обеспе́чивать/обеспе́чить – to provide
обеща́ние – promise
облада́ть чем-то – to possess something
областны́е вы́боры – 1) local elections   2) oblast elections
обме́н мне́ниями – exchange of opinions
оборо́на (no pl.) – defense
оборони́тельная доста́точность – defense sufficiency
оборони́тельный хара́ктер – defensive character
обору́дование – equipment
обостря́ться/обостри́ться – to deteriorate
образо́вывать/образова́ть –1) to form   2) to educate
образова́ние   1) formation   2) education
обра́тная реа́кция – adverse reaction
обраща́ться/обрати́ться к чему́-то – to address something

обслу́живание – service
обстано́вка – situation
обсужда́ть/обсуди́ть – to discuss
обще́ственный де́ятель – public figure
обще́ственность – public
О́бщий ры́нок – the Common Market
обы́скивать/обыска́ть – to search
о́быск – a search
обы́чные вооруже́ния – conventional weapons
объедине́ние – group
объясня́ть/объясни́ть – to explain
обяза́тельство – obligation
ограниче́ние – limitation
оде́рживать/одержа́ть верх – to be the winner
оде́рживать/одержа́ть побе́ду над чем-то – to win the a over something
однозна́чный – simple
односторо́нний хара́ктер – unilateral character
ожида́ть – to expect
оздоровля́ть/оздорови́ть – to bring recovery
оздоровле́ние – recovery
ока́зываться/оказа́ться – to prove to be
ока́зывать/оказа́ть по́мощь – to render assistance
ока́зывать/оказа́ть влия́ние на кого́-то – to influence somebody
о́круг, округа́ – district
опа́сность – danger
операти́вно-манёвренная гру́ппа – operational-maneuver group
опережа́ть/опереди́ть в чём-то – to be ahead in something
определя́ть/определи́ть – to define
о́птика – optics
о́птико-электро́нный – fiber-electronic (adj.)
опуска́ть/опусти́ть – to lower
о́рганы вла́сти – organs of power
о́рганы ме́стного управле́ния organs of local government
о́рдер на о́быск – search warrant
ору́жие (no pl.) – weapons
ОСВ (ограниче́ние стратеги́ческих вооруже́ний) – SALT (limitation of strategic
    weapons)
освобожда́ть/освободи́ть – to free, to liberate
осмо́тр войск – troop review
оснаща́ть/оснасти́ть –   1)to support   2)to supply
оставля́ть/оста́вить – to leave behind
остана́вливать/останови́ть – to stop something
осужда́ть/осуди́ть – to condemn
осуществи́мость – feasibility
осуществля́ть/осуществи́ть реше́ния – to implement decisions
отбыва́ть/отбы́ть – to depart
отверга́ть/отве́ргнуть – to reject, to turn down
отве́тственный де́ятель – high-standing official
отве́тственность за что-то – responsibility for something

отвлече́ние сил на что-то – diversion of forces into something
отводи́ть/отвести́ ва́жное ме́сто чему́-то – to give an important place to something
отделе́ние от чего́-то – secession from something
отложи́ть/откла́дывать – to postpone
отзыва́ть/отозва́ть – to recall
отка́зывать/отказа́ть в чём-то – to deny something
открещиваться/открести́ться от чего-то – to separate oneself from something
отлича́ться от чего́-то – to differ from something-
отменя́ть/отмени́ть – to cancel
отме́на – cancellation
отноше́ние – attitude
отноше́ния (no sing.) – relations
отправля́ть/отпра́вить – to send, to dispatch
отпра́вка – a dispatch
отража́ть/отрази́ть – to reflect
о́трасль – branch
отстава́ть/отста́ть от кого́-то – to lag behind somebody
отставно́й – retired
отста́лость – backwardness
отстраня́ть/отстрани́ть – to remove
отступле́ние – retreat
отря́д – detachment, unit
отстава́ть/ отста́ть от чего́-то – to lag behind something
отчётность – accountability
отчи́тываться/отчита́ться – to give an account
офице́р запа́са – reserve officer
официа́льное лицо́, ли́ца – an official
охва́тывать/охвати́ть – to embrace
оцепля́ть/оцепи́ть – to cordon off
очаро́ванный чем-то – enchanted with something
очередно́й круг бесе́д – regular round of talks
ошиба́ться/ошиби́ться в чём-то – to be mistaken about something

П

паде́ние – fall, drop
падчерица – stepdaughter
пала́та представи́телей – House of Representatives
пала́та о́бщин – House of Commons
партиза́н – guerrilla, partisan
партнёры из-за океа́на – partners from across the ocean
патрули́ровать – to patrol
перви́чные вы́боры – primaries
первонача́льный – initial
перебро́ска – (air)lift
перева́л – crossing
переворо́т – coup, overthrow

переговóры (*no sing.*) – negotiations
передáча технолóгии – transfer of technology
переживáть/пережúть – 1) to experience, 2) to live through
перемéна – change
перестрóйка – perestroika
переходúть к чемý-то – to resort to something
перехóд к чемý-то – transition to something
печáть – press
пехóта – infantry
питьевáя водá – drinkable water
пищевóй – food (*adj.*)
планúровать – to plan
платúть/заплатúть за что-то – to pay for something
побéда – victory
побеждáть/победúть – to win
поберéжье – coastline, seashore
побывáть – to visit
повáльные óбыски – mass searches
повéстка дня – agenda
подчинúть – to subjugate
погúбшие – those killed
погрóм – pogrom
подавлять/подавúть – to suppress
подвóдная лóдка – submarine
подготóвка к чемý-то – preparation for something
поддéржка – support
поддéрживать/поддержáть – to support
подкреплять/подкрепúть – to make stronger
подлóдка – submarine
пóдлинная незавúсимость – genuine independence
поднимáть/поднять – to lift
подóбным óбразом – in a similar fashion
подозревáть в чём-то (*no perf*) – to suspect of something
подпúсывать/подписáть – to sign
подрóсток – teenager
подрывáть/подорвáть – to undermine
подрывнáя дéятельность – subversive activity
пóдступ к чемý-то – approach to something
подчиняться/подчинúться чемý-то – to subjugate oneself to something; to defer
to something
пожúзненное заключéние – life imprisonment
пóиск – search
показáтель (*masc.*) – index, indicator
показнóй – for show, ostentatious
покóнчить с чем-то – to be done with something
покýпка – purchase
полагáться/положúться на что-то – to rely on something
полагáться (*impers*) – to be due (to)
политúтеский дéятель – politician

поли́тик – politician
полнове́сные плоды́ – sound results
полномо́чие – authority, right
помо́щник – assistant
поощре́ние – encouragement
попада́ть/попа́сть в зави́симость – to become dependent
попада́ть/попа́сть в плен – to be taken prisoner
попада́ть/попа́сть в чёрный спи́сок – to be blacklisted
попра́ние норм – flagrant violation of norms
пораже́ние – defeat
поража́ть/порази́ть – 1) to defeat, 2) to amaze
после́дний но́мер – latest issue (of journal)
после́дствия – cosequences
поступле́ние нало́гов – tax revenues
посо́л, послы́ – ambassador
посо́льство – embassy
поста́вка – supply
поступи́ться/поступа́ться чем-то – to forgo something
поте́ри (pl.) – (human) losses
поте́ря – loss
потреби́тельская корзи́нка – consumer goods basket
поучи́тельный – instructive
поэта́пный – by stages
пра́во, права́ pl – right
права́ челове́ка – human rights
пра́вильность – correctness
правово́е госуда́рство – legal state
пра́вый режи́м – right-wing regime
пра́вящая па́ртия – ruling party
пра́порщик – warrant officer
предава́ть/преда́ть гла́сности – to make public
преде́лы – limits, border
предвы́борная кампа́ния – election campaign
предвори́тельный – preliminary
предоставля́ть/предоста́вить по́мощь – to give assistance
предотвраще́ние – prevention
предприя́тие – enterprise
председа́тель (masc.) – chairman
предсказа́ние – prediction
представи́тель (masc.) – representative
предстоя́ть (imprs.) кому-то – to be faced with something
предпринима́тельство – enterpreneurship
предпринима́ть/предприня́ть попы́тку – to undertake an attempt
предрассу́док – prejudice
предстоя́щий – forthcoming
представля́ть собо́й – to represent (by itself)
предше́ствовать чему́-то – to precede something
предыду́щий – previous
президе́нт – president

Президиум Верхо́вного Сове́та – Presidium of the Supreme Soviet
прекраща́ть/прекрати́ть – to cease
прекраще́ние огня́ – cease-fire
премье́р-мини́стр – prime-minister
прибыва́ть/прибы́ть с официа́льным визи́том – to come on an official visit
приве́тствовать – to welcome
привыка́ть/привы́кнуть к чему́-то – to get used to something
приводи́ть/привести́ да́нные – to cite the data
приводи́ть/привести́ к чему́-то – to result in something
приглаше́ние – invitation
    по приглаше́нию – by the invitation
при́знаки появи́лись – signs appeared
при́зрак – ghost
прила́вки – shelves in the store
при́городы – suburbs
приезжа́ющие – those arriving (people)
прие́м – reception
при́зван,а,о,ы – entitled, called forth to do something
призыва́ть/призва́ть к чему́-то – to call for something
присоедине́ние к чему́-то – addition to something
приспоса́бливаться/приспосо́биться к чему́-то – to get adjusted to something
приходи́ть с о́быском – to come to search
принима́ть/приня́ть – receive, accept
принима́ть/приня́ть реше́ние – to make a decision
принима́ть/приня́ть уча́стие в выбора́х – to participate in elections
приро́дные ресу́рсы – natural resources
приро́ст – growth
пробива́ть/проби́ть брешь в чрезме́рной секре́тности – to begin to reduce
                                    excessive secrecy
пробива́ться/проби́ться во что-то – to make it somewhere
пробива́ться/проби́ться к чему́-то – to get to something
пробле́ма – problem
прова́л – collapse, gap
прова́ливать/провали́ть – to fail something
провинциа́льный – provincial
проводи́ть/провести́ – to conduct
проводи́ть/провести́ в жизнь – to implement
проводи́ть/провести́ свои́х кандида́тов – to bring in one's own candidates
прогно́з – prognosis
прода́жа – sale, sales
продово́льствие – food-stuffs, provisions
прое́кт зако́на – draft of a bill
производи́тельность труда́ – labor productivity
произво́дство – production
произво́л – tyranny
произноси́ть ре́чи – to make speeches
промы́шленность – industry
проникнове́ние – infiltration
пропа́вшие без вести – missing in action

проти́вник – opponent
противостоя́ние – standoff
противота́нковый – anti-tank *(adj.)*
противоре́чить – to contradict
противораке́тный – anti-missile
противоре́чить чему́-то – to contradict something
противоре́чие – contradiction
противостоя́ть чему́-то – to resist something
профсою́з – trade union
проявля́ть/прояви́ть – to manifest something
проявле́ние – manifestation
прямы́е нало́ги – direct taxes
пуга́ть/напуга́ть – to scare
путь *(masc.)* – path
пу́шка – cannon, artillery piece
пшени́ца – wheat

Р

рабо́тать на что-то – to work for something
рабо́чая си́ла – labor
рабо́чие – workers
рабо́тник нау́ки – someone engaged in the area of science
равнове́сие – balance
равнопра́вие – equality
ра́вный – equal
развива́ть/разви́ть – to develop
развора́чивать/разверну́ть войска́ – to deploy troops
разгора́ться/разгоре́ться – to flare up
разли́чный – different, various
разногла́сия *(pl.)* из-за ры́нков – differences over markets
разоблача́ть/разоблачи́ть себя́ как что-то – to expose oneself as
разочарова́ние в чём-то – disappointment
разраба́тывать/разрабо́тать – to develop something
разреше́ние конфли́кта – solution of a conflict
разря́дка междунаро́дной напряжённости – relaxation of international tension, detente
раке́та сре́дней да́льности – medium-range missile
раке́тная систе́ма за́лпового огня́ – Multiple Launcher Rocket System (MLRS)
раке́тная устано́вка – missile installation
раке́та – missile
ра́неный – a wounded man
ра́ньше наме́ченного сро́ка – ahead of time
ра́са – race
раси́стский – racist
ра́совый – racial
распоряди́тельный о́рган – managerial organ (body)
рассма́тривать/рассмотре́ть – to consider, to examine something

расстано́вка сил – balance of power
расстоя́ние – distance
расстре́л – execution by a firing squad
расти́/вы́расти – to grow
расшире́ние торго́вли – expansion of trade
расхо́ды на оборо́ну – expenditures for defense
расформиро́вывать/ расформирова́ть – to liquidate
ратифици́ровать догово́р – to ratify a treaty
реа́кция на что-то – reaction to something
регули́рование – regulating
ре́зкий – sharp, abrupt
резолю́ция – resolution
рейгано́мика – Reaganomics
режи́м фаши́стского то́лка – regime of fascist type
режи́м наибо́льшего благоприя́тствования – most favored nation status
репре́ссия – repression
республика́нец – a Republican
республика́нское большинство́ – Republican majority
республика́нское меньшинство́ – Republican minority
региона́льный – regional
регули́рование эконо́мики – regulation of economy
речь идёт о... – the topic is...
реши́мость – determination
риско́ванный – risky
ро́бот – robot
робототе́хника – robotics
рожда́емость – birth rate
рост цен – rise in prices
рыво́к – leap, jump
ры́нок, ры́нки – market
рыча́г, рычаги́ – lever
ряд договорённостей – number of treaties

С

самолёт – airplane
самохо́дный – self-propelled
са́нкции против чего́-то – sanctions against something
сбаланси́рованный бюдже́т – balanced budget
сверхпла́новый – extra, above what is planned
сверхсовреме́нная те́хника – high-technology
сверше́ние – deed, accomplishment
свиде́тельствовать о чём-то – to testify to something
свобо́да сло́ва – freedom of speech
свобо́да со́вести – freedom of conscience
сво́дка – forecast
свора́чивание – curtailment
сде́лка – deal

сдвиг – move, progress

Североатлантический союз (НАТО) – the North Atlantic Treaty Organization, the NATO

секретарь райкома – secretary of the regional party committee

секретный – secret

сельское хозяйство – agriculture

сельскохозяйственный – agricultural

серьёзность намерений – seriousness of intentions

силы передового базирования – forward-based forces

силы специального назначения – special forces

система управления – guidance system

ситуация – situation

скачок – leap, surge

следовать чему-то – to follow (observe) something

слияние – merger

сломить волю – to break the will

служащие – white-collar

служить чему-то – to serve something

смертная казнь – death penalty

смертоносный – deadly

смертность – mortality

снижение – decline

собираться/собраться – 1) to get together   2) to convene

собственный корреспондент – accredited correspondent

совершать/совершить нападение – to make an attack

Совет безопасности – Security Council

Совет Министров – Council of Ministers

современник – contemporary

согласие – consent

согласованное решение – balanced decision

соглашение – agreement

создание – creation

сокращение стратегических вооружений – reduction of strategic weapons

сомнение – doubt

сомневаться в чём-то (*no perf.*) – to have doubts about something

сопротивляться чему-то – to resist something

составная часть – component part

состояться – to take place

сотрудничество – cooperation

сообщество – community

сосуществование – coexistence

сохранять/сохранить – to maintain

социалистический – socialist

социалист – socialist

социал-демократическая партия – the Social-Democratic party

социал-демократ – social-democrat

социал-христианская партия – the Social-Christian party

социальное обеспечение – social welfare

сочувствовать чему-то – to sympathize with something

сою́зник – ally
спад – recession
специа́льный корреспонде́нт – special correspondent
спи́сывать/списа́ть обору́дование – to retire equipment
спи́сок – list
спосо́бность – ability, capability
спосо́бный – able, capable
спосо́бствовать чему́-то – to contribute to something
сре́дство прове́рки – means of verification
срок – term
ста́вить/поста́вить на коле́ни – to put on one's knees
ста́вить/поста́вить на ноги – to put on one's feet
ста́вленник – protege
станкостро́ительный – machine-tool building
сто́имость (fem.) – cost
    сто́имостью... – which costs...
сторо́нник – supporter
страда́ние – suffering
стра́ны-чле́ны – member-countries
стратеги́ческая оборо́нная инициати́ва (СОИ) – Strategic Defense Initiative (SDI)
стратеги́чески ва́жный – strategically important
стреля́ть по толпе́ – to shoot into a crowd
стреми́ться к чему́-то – to seek something
стро́ительный – construction (adj.)
стро́ительство – construction
суд, суды́ – court, trial
судья́, су́дьи – judge
счита́ть чем-то (no perf.) – to consider to be something
сугу́бо – particularly
судьба́ – fate
с учётом чего-то – taking something into consideration
сырьё (no pl.) – raw materials

Т

та́йное голосова́ние – secret ballot, secret voting
такти́ческие вооруже́ния – tactical weapons
тво́рческий труд – creative work
танк – tank
темп – speed, rate
тень наде́жды – shadow of hope
тео́рия относи́тельности – theory of relativity
терра́кт – act of terror
территориа́льный – territorial
теря́ть/потеря́ть большинство́ – to lose majority
те́хника – technology
техни́ческий – technical
техноло́гия – technology, method of production

технологи́ческий – technological
това́ры пе́рвой необходи́мости – first necessity goods
това́ры широ́кого потребле́ния – consumer goods
толпа́ – crowd
торгова́ть чем-то – to trade with somebody
торго́вля чем-то – trade with somebody
торго́вый – trade (adj.)
то́чка зре́ния – point of view
трансли́ровать – to broadcast
трансля́ция – broadcast (noun)
тре́бование – demand
тре́ния (pl.) – frictions
трудова́я па́ртия – the Labor party
тру́дность – difficulty
трудоспосо́бный – able-bodied
трудя́щиеся – working people
тяжёлая промы́шленность – heavy industry

У

убежда́ть/убеди́ть в чём-то – to convince of something
убеди́тельный – convincing
уби́тые – those killed
увели́чивать/увели́чить – to increase
увольня́ть/уво́лить – to retire somebody
у́голь (masc.) – coal
угро́за – threat
удава́ться/уда́сться – to succeed
уда́рное косми́ческое ору́жие – space strike weapons
уда́рно-тра́нспортный самолёт – assault-transport plane
уделя́ть/удели́ть внима́ние чему́-то – to pay attention to something
указа́ния све́рху – directions from above
укрепля́ть/укрепи́ть – to strengthen
улучше́ние – improvement
уничтожа́ть/уничто́жить – to destroy, to annihilate
управле́ние ко́рпуса – command of the corps
управля́ть чем-то с расстоя́ния – control something from a distance
упроче́ние ми́ра – strengthening of peace
ура́н – uranium
урегули́рование – settlement
у́ровень (masc.) – standard, level
ускоря́ть/уско́рить – to speed up
успе́х – success
установле́ние – establishment
устано́вленный поря́док – established order
устаре́вший – outmoded
усто́йчивый – stable (adj.)
устра́ивать/устро́ить – to arrange

устранять/устранить в корне – to eliminate completely, to root out
утаивать/утаить – to hide something
учёный – scientist
учётные ставки – interest rates
ущерб – damage

Ф

фабрика Гознака – the Mint
финансы (*no sing.*) – finance
финансовый год – fiscal year
фирма – firm
фотографировать – to take pictures
фундаментальные исследования – fundamental research

Х

хватать/хватить (*impers.*) чего-то – to have sufficient amount of something
химическое оружие – chemical weapons
хозрасчёт – self-accounting
хозяйство – economy

Ц

цель – goal, target
цитировать – to cite, to quote

Ч

человечество – mankind
численность – number
член КПСС – member of the CPSU
член-корреспондент – Associate-Member
чрезвычайная встреча – extraordinary meeting
чрезвычайные силы – emergency forces, peace-keeping forces
чрезмерный – excessive
чувство локтя – team spirit

Ш

шар – sphere
шаткость – precariousness
шпионаж – espionage
штаб – staff, headquaters

штра́фовать/оштрафова́ть за что-то - to fine for something

Э

эконо́мика - economy, economics
экономи́ческий - economic
эконо́мия - saving
эконо́мный - economical, sparing
э́кспорт - export, exports
экпорти́ровать - to export
э́кстренная встре́ча - emergency meeting
эмба́рго на что-то - embargo on something
эми́ссия - issuing of money
энергети́ческий кри́зис - energy crisis

Я

я́дерное ору́жие - nuclear weapons
я́кобы - allegedly